Coloniality of Power in Postcolonial Africa

Coloniality of Power in Postcolonial Africa

Myths of Decolonization

Sabelo J. Ndlovu-Gatsheni

CODESRIA

Council for the Development of Social Science Research in Africa
DAKAR

© CODESRIA 2013
Council for the Development of Social Science Research in Africa
Avenue Cheikh Anta Diop, Angle Canal IV
BP 3304 Dakar, CP 18524, Senegal
Website: www.codesria.org
ISBN: 978-2-86978-578-6

Typesetting: Alpha Ousmane Dia
Cover Design: Ibrahima Fofana

Distributed in Africa by CODESRIA
Distributed elsewhere by African Books Collective, Oxford, UK
Website: www.africanbookscollective.com

The Council for the Development of Social Science Research in Africa (CODESRIA) is an independent organisation whose principal objectives are to facilitate research, promote research-based publishing and create multiple forums geared towards the exchange of views and information among African researchers. All these are aimed at reducing the fragmentation of research in the continent through the creation of thematic research networks that cut across linguistic and regional boundaries.

CODESRIA publishes *Africa Development*, the longest standing Africa based social science journal; *Afrika Zamani*, a journal of history; the *African Sociological Review*; the *African Journal of International Affairs*; *Africa Review of Books* and the *Journal of Higher Education in Africa*. The Council also co-publishes the *Africa Media Review*; *Identity, Culture and Politics: An Afro-Asian Dialogue*; *The African Anthropologist* and the *Afro-Arab Selections for Social Sciences*. The results of its research and other activities are also disseminated through its Working Paper Series, Green Book Series, Monograph Series, Book Series, Policy Briefs and the CODESRIA Bulletin. Select CODESRIA publications are also accessible online at www.codesria.org.

CODESRIA would like to express its gratitude to the Swedish International Development Cooperation Agency (SIDA/SAREC), the International Development Research Centre (IDRC), the Ford Foundation, the MacArthur Foundation, the Carnegie Corporation, the Norwegian Agency for Development Cooperation (NORAD), the Danish Agency for International Development (DANIDA), the French Ministry of Cooperation, the United Nations Development Programme (UNDP), the Netherlands Ministry of Foreign Affairs, the Rockefeller Foundation, FINIDA, the Canadian International Development Agency (CIDA), the Open Society Foundations (OSFs), TrustAfrica, UN/UNICEF, the African Capacity Building Foundation (ACBF) and the Government of Senegal for supporting its research, training and publication programmes.

Contents

Preface

This book has been written at a crucial time in global history in general and African history in particular. On the one hand, the history is dominated by a climate of interventionist global neoliberal imperialism which increasingly manifests its violent character through the military invasion of Iraq, bombardment of Libya, imposition of sanctions on Zimbabwe and military invasion of Afghanistan. Violent invasions of weaker countries by the United States of America (USA) and its North Atlantic Treaty Organization (NATO) partners, are often justified as humanitarian interventions to introduce democracy and human rights, dethrone dictators, eradicate terrorism and restore order within those states characterized by United States as outposts of tyranny and part of 'the axis of evil'. But the military interventions, rhetorically premised on the noble 'right to protect', seem to be selective and guided by the West's permanent strategic interests rather than genuine global humanitarian concerns.

On the other hand, there was the unexpected outbreak of popular uprisings in North Africa that have resulted in the collapse of dictatorial regimes in Tunisia and Egypt, and the aerial bombardment of Libya by NATO-led forces in support of an onslaught by disparate opposition groups that culminated in the overthrow of Colonel Muammar Gaddafi's 42-year iron rule and his death. These new developments in global history have provoked animated debates with some scholars like David Harvey (2003, 2007) and Ellen Meiksin Wood (2003) raising issues of the spectre of 'new imperialism' that is involving new players from East and South-East Asia. Some left-leaning scholars have concluded that we are living in a new world of 'universal capitalism in which capitalist imperatives are universal instruments of capitalist domination'. They see this development as a very recent phenomenon (Wood 2003: 127).

At another level, the popular uprisings that have rocked the North African region, spreading to the Middle-East and provoking panic responses among dictators in Sub-Saharan Africa, are interpreted as part of an indictment on Francis Fukuyama's (1993) end of history thesis and an indicator of ordinary people's agency to continue the project of making history as well as revolutions. But the military intervention by NATO in Libya is raising the danger of the mantra of humanitarian intervention being used as a fig-leaf covering the nakedness of violent global neoliberal imperialism that is quick to fish in troubled waters of those countries that are endowed with strategic resources such as oil, gas and diamonds. At the same time, the popular uprisings which are also referred to as 'facebook revolution' are being celebrated as the dawn of 'second independence' involving the people directly fighting to translate the myths of decolonization and illusions of freedom that resulted from the attainment of juridical freedom into popular freedom, including restructuring of colonially crafted postcolonial states into what Nzongola-Ntalaja (1987:75) termed 'a people's state' dedicated to serve popular interests and demands. This people's state is a result of a 'people's revolution' (Nzongola-Ntalaja 1987: 75).

Another global development worth noting is the financial crisis that has rocked the Northern industrialized countries since 2008 with ripple effects spilling over to other parts of the world, particularly those peripheral economies that are closely linked to the West. This recent capitalist crisis has provoked renewed debates on the viability of the modern capitalist system with scholars like Slavoj Zizek (2009b) vigorously arguing for a return to socialism as part of human salvation. Latin Americanists like Walter D. Mignolo (2007), Arturo Escobar (2007), Ramon Grosfoguel (2007), Anibal Quijano (2007) and others have for some time intensified their push for alternative knowledge as part of their revolt against the oppressive character of the racially-organized, hegemonic, patriarchal and capitalist world order alongside Euro-American epistemological fundamentalism that denies the existence of knowledge from the non-Western parts of the world.

Yet, at another level, African scholars and Africanists such as Ngugi wa Thiong'o (1986), Chinweizu (1987), Basil Davidson (1992), Crawford Young (1994), Tukumbi Lumumba-Kasongo (1994), Claude Ake (2000), Pita Ogaba Agbese and George Klay Kieh Jr. (2007), Mueni wa Muiu and Guy Martin (2009) and others, have also been frustrated by the continued use of imported Euro-American ideas and institutions in Africa. They have unanimously called for the reconstitution and reconstruction of African postcolonial states on the basis of African history, African knowledge and

African positive values if these states are to be considered legitimate and to serve their African constituency fully. They are responding vigorously to one of the long standing and difficult questions in any analysis of the national question in postcolonial Africa – a question that has revolved around which relevant socio-historical entity the African nation-state should be anchored on among three equally problematic alternatives, namely: the pre-colonial ethnic nation whose construction and full realization was disrupted by colonialism; the colonially-crafted territorial nation born out of the contradictions of the colonial situation; or the imagined pan-African nation that was envisaged by Kwame Nkrumah (Nzongola-Ntalaja 1987: 48).

What all these debates (some old and others new) reveal is that in the realm of ideas and knowledge production there is increasing concern over finding the correct choice of language and concepts that have the potential to capture well the complexities and the spirit of the current human age dominated by uncertainty without compromising on the analytical principles (Fine 2006: 135). This development is taking place within a context where there is gradual return of the relevance of historical materialism and the dual retreat of postcolonial and postmodernist theoretical interventions on the nature of the realities of current racially-organized, hegemonic, patriarchal and capitalist world order, which is trying to hide its exploitative and oppressive nature behind the post-Cold War normative concepts of liberal democracy, human rights and good governance.

These recent developments around the globe have ignited a new interest in history in general and the politics of empire in particular. As a historian, my thinking is informed by the view that the present and the future cannot be fully understood without a clear knowledge of the past. Also, I place much confidence in the intellectual value of taking a long historical view in order to see into the present and the future. I am interested in understanding the multifaceted manifestations of the present-day colonial matrix of power that is wrecking havoc on postcolonial Africa, compromising, diluting and truncating trajectories of liberation struggles, preventing economic development and unleashing epistemic violence. I fully subscribe to Mudimbe's Foucualdian ideas of 'history as both a discourse of knowledge and a discourse of power' (Mudimbe 1988: 188).

Nevertheless, this book does not fall within the purview of pervasive consultancy-type scholarship that is dominant in African universities where research is conceived in prescriptive terms rather than as diagnosis of issues. I am against the pervasive culture of consultancy that is threatening to destroy serious academic research within African universities. Consultancy cultures have even blinded some policy makers to the extent that they question the value of social sciences and humanities market-driven, parastatalized and commercialized institutions of higher education. Hence, this book should not be approached simplistically as an 'answer-book' on particular African problems. The book is informed by the idea of research as diagnosis and formulation of a problem (Mamdani 2011).

The orization or conceptualization of issues is not considered an anathema as this approach helps in thinking through complex African socio-economic and political realities. I am also revolting against the tendency to reduce African intellectuals and academics into mere 'hunters and gatherers' of raw data and 'native informants' who collect and provide empirical data that is then processed in the West into theories and concepts that are consumed in Africa (Mamdani 2011). I see great value in theorizing about the African predicament as a form of production of knowledge by African intellectuals and academics for use by Africans in Africa. Theory, to me, is a light that assists in avoiding ill-focused, positivistic, shallow and prescriptive narratives divorced from complex historical, discursive and epistemological terrains that reproduce political and economic crises and problems that bedevil Africans today.

Therefore, this book seeks to understand the role of colonialism of power (a global neo-colonial hegemonic model of power that articulates race and labour, as well as space and people in accordance with the needs of capital and to the benefit of white European people) in shaping the complex history of the African postcolonial present. It is a 'present' which is 'absent' because what exists is not what Africans aspired for and struggled to achieve. Africans and other peoples of the Global South who experienced 'darker' manifestations of modernity which included such processes as the slave trade, mercantilism, imperialism, colonialism and apartheid, aspired for a new humanity in which species of the human race would coexist as equal and free beings. African nationalism and decolonization were thus ranged against all the dark aspects of modernity, including underdevelopment and epistemic violence. But what emerged from the decolonization process was not a new world dominated by new humanist values of freedom, equality, social justice and ethical coexistence. African people found themselves engulfed by a 'postcolonial neocolonized world' characterized by myths of decolonization and illusions of freedom.

The term 'postcolonial neocolonized world' best captures the difficulties and unlikelihood of a fully decolonized African world that is free from the snares of the colonial matrix of power and the dictates of the rapacious global power. The current configuration of the world is symbolized by the figure of America at the apex and that of Africa at the bottom of the racialized and capitalist hierarchies, of a world order. Such dark aspects of European modernity as the slave trade, mercantilism, imperialism, colonialism and apartheid bequeathed to Africa a convoluted situation within which the 'postcolonial' became paradoxically entangled with the 'neocolonial', to the extent that the two cannot be intellectually approached as mutually exclusive states of being.

In short, the term 'postcolonial neocolonized world' captures a normalized abnormality whereby issues of African identity formation, nation-building and state-construction, knowledge production, economic development and democratization remained unfinished projects mainly because of their entrapment within colonial matrices of modern global power. African leaders are also entrapped within a disciplining colonial matrix of power and those who try to deviate and question the commandment from the powerful Euro-American world are subjected to severe punishments and in extreme cases even assassinations. Therefore, within the context of a 'postcolonial neocolonized world' such issues as identity formation, nationalism, decolonization, nation-building, liberal democracy, epistemology and economic development form a single part of a complex discursive formation whose genealogy is traceable to the underside of modernity and so cannot be treated separately if a clear and broader picture of the African postcolonial present is to be understood. As such, the book is basically concerned with the invisible entanglement and entrapment of the African continent within the complex colonial matrices of power in which full African decolonization remains a myth and African freedom is reduced to an illusion.

The second important theme explored in this book is that of a dominant Western power backed up by hegemonic Euro-American epistemologies which resulted not only in the colonization of African imagination and displacement of African knowledges, but continues to take a leading role in shaping what constitute progressive global values and imposing these on the African people. The book delineates the core foundations of a new colonialism of power rooted in the social classification of the world population by race as a mental construct that informed the making of Africa according to the dictates and imperatives of Eurocentrism. What is also subjected to systematic analysis is the evolving idea of Africa and the difficult question of colonization of African imaginations which is proving very hard to decolonize; epistemological issues relating to the confinement of African knowledges to the barbarian margins of society and out of global intellectual and academic space; and how a combination of these developments has affected the African condition including issues of Africanism, liberation, economic and social development as well as ideology and consciousness.

In theoretical and conceptual terms, the book draws insights from Latin American theorists who have been active in reading and interpreting modernity from the margins and borders, and revealing in the process how the ex-colonies of the world experienced the darker aspects of modernity. Through their Latin American Modernity/Colonialism Research Programme, Latin American theorists such as Arturo Escobar, Walter D. Mignolo, Nelson Maldonado Torres, Anibal Quijano and Ramon Grosfoguel, have been able to re-interpret modernity since the conquest and control of the Atlantic in 1492. Such concepts as colonialism of power, of being and of knowledge have been very useful in unpacking the current position of Africa within the global matrices of power. This approach has enabled this book to venture into a comparative study linking Latin American colonial experiences and anti-colonial struggles to the African situation, despite the fact that the two spaces were not colonized at the same time.

African scholars such as Claude Ake, Paul Tiyambe Zeleza, Ali Mazrui, Fantu Cheru, Valentin Mudimbe, Mueni wa Muiu, Achille Mbembe, Mahmood Mamdani and many others, as well as Africanists like Terence Ranger, Crawford Young and others, have dealt with some of the issues discussed in this book and I, therefore, build on where they left off by bringing insights from the perspective of Latin Americanists to reflect on the African condition from a colonialism with its emphasis on the importance of a new locus of enunciation of modernity. Concerned African scholars like Mueni wa Muiu, Pita Ogaba Agbese, George Klay Kieh, Jr, George B. N. Ayittey, Tukumbi Lumumba-Kasongo and others, emphasise the need for a new paradigm of the African state predicated on what Mueni wa Muiu and Guy Martin (2009) termed 'Fundi wa Afrika' theory. The theory locates the roots of the postcolonial African predicament on Africa's relationship with the Western countries and emphasizes reconstruction of the African postcolonial state by re-connecting it with the positive values from indigenous African political systems.

These African scholars emphasize the need for systematic analysis of the creation and evolution of the African state from the pre-colonial indigenous roots right to the present; explaining how internal and external events and actors shaped the African state and its leadership; and prescription of what the ideal state and its leadership, as determined by Africans themselves, should be. Indeed, it is necessary to reconstitute the African state since the founding fathers of postcolonial Africa did not engage in radical transformation of the state but were content with inheriting the colonially-designed structures that did not serve African needs and demands very well. Hence, Muiu and Guy's (2009: 3) adoption of an interdisciplinary and long-term historical perspective as well as their definition of 'indigenous Africa' as referring to 'Africa from the ninth century BCE (before the Christian era) to AD 1500 (the onset of the trans-Atlantic slave trade)' is well-taken as an innovative contribution to global and African knowledge based on a period that is not often included in the curriculum on African history. They are also correct in saying that the period from AD1500 onwards is a story on colonial encounters that resulted in fragmentation, distortion and displacement of African value systems, worldviews, cultures and political systems.

But it is precisely because of the adverse and long-term impact of the post-1500 era, its meaning and implications for the African postcolonial present that it becomes necessary to try and understand the complex discursive, historical and epistemological interventions that created the present-day racialized, hegemonic, patriarchal and capitalist world order within which Africa occupies a subaltern position. In other words, the book reinforces 'Fundi wa Afrika' approach through systematic unpacking of the dark underside of modernity and how it resulted in subjugation of Africa without necessarily reducing Africans to a mute and passive subaltern group that could not speak and fight for itself. Colonial modernity was not a mere footnote in African history as it radically created a world informed by imperatives of capital and needs of white Westerners.

This thinking links well with the main Latin American perspective which emphasizes analyzing modernity from colonized and subaltern standpoint to reveal its enduring negative impact on the ex-colonized world. Furthermore, the Latin American perspective has already made impressive advances in unpacking complex epistemological and discursive issues that are very relevant for understanding the postcolonialism in Africa the last part of the world to fight and defeat direct colonialism. If the legacy of colonialism is still strongly felt in Latin America where political independence was achieved much earlier, then its impact on Africa would be much worse because the decolonization process only began in the late 1950s and early 1960s. The decolonization of Africa also coincided with the ascendance of two superpowers, American and Soviet Union (now Commonwealth of Independent States) on the world stage, taking over the space opened by the strategic withdrawal of older world powers, including Britain, France, Germany, Spain, Italy and Portugal. As is well known, the arms race between America and the Soviet Union fuelled the Cold War which generated considerable heat and unease in Africa continent.

Having said all this, it must also be emphasized that an ambitious book such as this could not have been written without the help of some scholars who were kind enough to read the manuscript and to provide me some research material that I could not have accessed from my South African base. Also, the three anonymous reviewers who read the manuscript identified some gaps which I gratefully filled.

Professor Ramon Grosfoguel of the University of California (Berkeley) not only encouraged me to forge ahead with the project, but also generously sent me useful literature on coloniality as articulated from the Latin American perspective, including his own writings that enabled me to sharpen the conceptual/theoretical framework of this book. Professor Valentin Yves Mudimbe of Duke University also read the manuscript and provided very comprehensive and useful comments that helped me to strengthen and consolidate the central arguments and structural organization of the book. This resulted in its division into three broad parts with Part One dealing with the thematics of colonial matrices of power; Part Two with the discursive and historical constructions of Africa and African identities in the shadow of modernity; and, Part Three with case studies of South Africa and Zimbabwe and the conclusions.

Emeritus Professor Terence Ranger of Oxford University quickly read through the manuscript and encouraged me a great deal. I am also grateful to Dr Wendy Willems of the University of the Witwatersrand for alerting me to the special issue of *Cultural Studies* (March/May 2007) immediately it was published. Reading the articles in this special issue deepened my understanding of the coloniality and decolonial thinking as articulated from Latin America perspective. Kudzai Matereke, a doctoral student at the University of New South Wales in Australia, read three draft chapters of this book and provided very useful comments.

Tendayi Sithole, Eric Nyembezi Makoni, Pearl Nontyatyambo Dastile, Sebeka 'Eddie' Plaatjie and Morgan Ndlovu (who are all grappling with their individual master's and doctoral studies) and I have been busy recruiting into the decoloniality perspective, were an enriching community of friends and a reliable source of encouragement throughout the writing of this book.

So too did Professor Sam Moyo, the former President of CODESRIA, help by linking me with the publications section of his organization. Moyo also provided useful comments on the chapter on Zimbabwe and made available his recent articles on the agrarian issues in Zimbabwe. It certainly has been a pleasure working with academic colleagues at the CODESRIA Publications Department from the time the manuscript landed on their table, through the organization of external peer review process, revision and final publication.

Finally, I wish to extend my thanks to my son, Vulindlela Kings Zwelithini, whose love sustains me in all my endeavours, and other members of my extended family -- particularly my young sisters Sifiso and Sibonokuhle -- who have never failed to be a source of strength and encouragement.

Sabelo J. Ndlovu-Gatsheni
Pretoria, South Africa

Part I

Colonial Matrix of Power

1

Introduction
A Neocolonized Africa

One of the most powerful myths of the twentieth century was the notion that the elimination of colonial administrations amounted to the decolonization of the world. This led to the myth of a 'postcolonial' world. The heterogeneous and multiple global structures put in place over a period of 450 years did not evaporate with the juridical-political decolonization of the periphery over the past 50 years. We continue to live under the same 'colonial power matrix.' With juridical-political decolonization we moved from a period of 'global colonialism' to the current period of 'global coloniality.'

(Ramon Grosfoguel 2007: 219)

This book deals with the predicament of Africans in a 'postcolonial neocolonized world' that was created by the negative processes of Western modernity as it spread across the world. The term 'postcolonial neocolonized world' is used to capture the structural, systemic, cultural, discursive, and epistemological pattern of domination and exploitation that has engulfed Africans since the Conquest (with a capital 'C' to signify it as a multifaceted process rather than an event and to underline its foundational influence on the domination of modern African history by global (i.e., Western) history. Spivak (1990: 166) used the term 'postcolonial neocolonized world' to describe the problematic terrain in which the ex-colonies operated with the Western world that occupied the apex of global power hierarchy while the developing world languished at the subaltern bottom. Since that time, the colonies have found it hard to climb on ladder of global power hierarchy and have thus remained at the bottom where norms and rules are routinely handed down to them from the metropolitan capitals of the industrial North. The term 'postcolonial neocolonized world' thus captures an entangled situation where the African and the Western world meet under highly racialized, hegemonic, hierarchical and unequal terms.

While the term 'postcolonial neocolonial world' might sound convoluted, it best captures a complex situation of truncated African liberation project that gave birth to a problematic and fragile African nation-building process. It encapsulates an African state of 'becoming' that never materialized. The envisaged new African postcolonial world and a new African humanity that were expected to be borne by the decolonization struggle were soon captured and engulfed by strong neocolonial imperatives that shaped the African liberatory process into emancipatory reformism. Therefore, at the centre of the 'postcolonial neocolonized world' are the delicate issues of African liberation and freedom as well as African development and knowledge production which were never fully realized beyond some emancipatory pretensions. The main weakness of emancipatory projects is that they do not question the core logic of Western modernity that globalized Euro-American views of the world and that constructed a racialized, hierarchical, hegemonic, patriarchal and capitalist global social system. Part one of this book discusses the colonial matrices of power including how Euro-American hegemonic knowledge banished alternative epistemologies from Africa and other parts of the Global South to the barbarian margins of society and out of the global intellectual space. It also articulates and elaborates on the core differences between emancipation and liberation as utopiane registers of freedom and explains why decolonization became a terrain of myths of independence and illusions of freedom.

Within Africa, the envisaged 'postcolonial' dispensation was submerged and engulfed by the 'neocolonial' world. Eventually the aspired for African 'postcolonial' world and the existing 'neocolonial' world have been panel-beaten into a cul-de-sac, better described as the 'postcolonial neocolonized world' by invisible colonial matrices of power underpinning the current unequal world social order. The 'postcolonial' and the 'neocolonial' as states of being were forced into an uneasy and abnormal coexistence where they had to interact tendentiously, with the latter policing and preventing the former from fully emerging and disengaging from debilitating colonial matrix of power.

This book, therefore, returns to one of the foundational moments in the development of modern African history whose implications for the postcolonial African present and future are far-reaching. Most African scholars have largely studied and articulated this monumental but negative process from a restrictive political economy perspective where it is commonly reduced to a problem of economic underdevelopment and inequalities.

While analyses of the economic predicament of Africa are important, they focus on only one key trap that disabled the birth of a brave postcolonial African world after 1945. What this book demonstrates is that the global neocolonial snares, otherwise known as colonial matrix of power were a complete package with social, economic, cultural, ideological, aesthetic and epistemological contours that combined to reduce, silence, dominate, oppress, exploit and overshadow the non-Western world. Throughout the book an attempt is made to read and interpret modernity from the perspective of the Global South in general, and Africa in particular, and to produce knowledge on Africa from a decolonized perspective.

One of the strategies that have sustained the hegemony of the Euro-American-constructed world order is its ability to make African intellectuals and academics socially located in Africa and on the oppressed side to think and speak epistemically and linguistically like the Euro-American intellectuals and academics on the dominant side. This trap has made it very difficult for African intellectuals and academics to sustain a robust and critical perspective of Euro-American hegemonic knowledge and the asymmetrical power relations it enables. In this book the hidden Euro-American epistemological locus is unmasked with a view to reveal how Euro-American colonial expansion and domination was able to construct a 'hierarchy of superior and inferior knowledge and, thus, of superior and inferior people around the world' (Grosfoguel 2007: 214). What African intellectuals and academics must do is to strive to shift the location from which the hegemonic paradigms are enunciated and in the process read and interpret African history from a critical African and Global South perspective.

Already such African scholars as Muiu and Martin (2009) have initiated a new reading of African history and African postcolonial present from what they termed 'Fundi wa Africa' (close English equivalents of the Kiswahili word 'fundi' would be 'tailor', 'builder', 'mechanic' or 'repairer'). Their intervention takes the form of a new paradigm of the African state informed by the simple principle that the 'core of the state is the people who reside within its boundaries' whom it must serve (Muiu and Martin 2009: 191). What these scholars have done is to try and unearth the values that underpinned what they term the 'indigenous Africa' that existed from ninth century BCE (before the Christian era) to AD 1500 (the onset of the trans-Atlantic slave trade).

Muiu and Martin (2009) trace the history and cultural unity of Africa from as far back as Egypt and Kush in the ninth century BCE without necessarily falling into romanticization of African history as glorious and dominated by pristine village and state democracies. Far from it. Rather, they reveal diversity of political systems, social stratification, economic inequalities and a variety of African religious beliefs and languages. In short, the 'Fundi wa Africa' theory is indeed one of the emerging knowledge systems poised to contest Euro-American hegemonic knowledge, which has consistently denied the existence of an orderly and progressive Africa prior to the colonial Conquest.

The locus of enunciation of African history from the 'Fundi wa Africa' perspective is clearly African, interdisciplinary and historical. It is also clear on the fact that the Westphalian template of the state that was imposed on Africa by colonial modernity and carried over into the postcolonial African present does not work well for Africans. Hence the need to reconstitution of the postcolonial state with a view to grounding it within positive African values, embedding it within African society and imbuing it with indigenous institutions. This approach is indeed laudable and this book brings another angle to complement these constructivist paradigms on the African state.

My entry point is clear. On top of recovering 'indigenous' institutions, values and systems, there is further need to understand the history of colonial conquest from AD 1500 to the present moment because it is the era that covers the dark aspects of modernity, including such reprehensible practices as exploitative mercantilism, slave trade, imperialism, colonialism, apartheid and neocolonialism wrecked havoc on indigenous histories, institutions, values and systems, creating the fundamental problems of the neocolonial Africa we live in today. It was during this period that the ideas of race and racism were unleashed on Africa and used to construct and 'organize the world's population into a hierarchical order of superior and inferior people that becomes an organizing principle of the international division of labour and of the global patriarchal system' (Grosfoguel 2007: 217).

In my opinion, before we can even begin to suggest reconstitution of the postcolonial state on the basis of indigenous African values, institutions and systems that have been unearthed by Muiu and Martin (2009), we need a thorough knowledge of the operations of the present-day colonial matrix of power that made it impossible for decolonization to be carried to its logical conclusion of creating a new Africa imbued with new humanism and inhabited by truly free and liberated African people. It is not enough to argue that the founding fathers of African postcolonial states did not restructure inherited colonial states to make them accountable to the African people. The difficult question is how feasible was this option within a postcolonial neocolonized world?

There is need for new intellectual and academic interventions that transcend the twentieth century mythology of a decolonized African world. The decolonization standpoint obscured the continuities between the colonial past and current global colonial, racial, patriarchal and hegemonic hierarchies and, in the process, contributed towards continuities of 'invisibility of "coloniality" today' (Grosfoguel 2007: 220). These observations led me to revisit whole issues about empire, new imperialism and coloniality with a view to elaborating on the neocolonization of Africa world. But my approach does not in any way foreclose possibilities of radical alternatives to colonial modernity as well as initiatives to de-Europeanize modernity of its alleged Greek genealogy through studies that explain such earlier African civilizations and cultures as those of Carthage, Egypt and Kush dated to the ninth century BCE. For Africa, therefore, the terrible and long-lasting consequences of colonial modernity unfolded from the onset and process of colonial conquest.

Therefore, to gain a deeper and complete understanding of the neocolonization of Africa, this book draws conceptual and theoretical tools from the critical coloniality perspective. This is a perspective articulated by radical Latin American scholars operating under the Modernity/Coloniality Research Programme that seeks to construct a 'de-colonial thinking' that refracted and transcended the present problematic 'postcolonial neocolonized world' underpinned by Western epistemologies of domination and exploitation. As defined by the Anibal Quijano:

> Coloniality is one of the specific and constitutive elements of global model of capitalist power. It is based on the imposition of a racial/ethnic classification of the global population as the cornerstone of that model of power, and it operates on every level, in every arena and dimension (both material and subjective) of everyday social existence, and does so on a societal scale (Quijano 2000: 342).

The book focuses on three main concepts of coloniality: coloniality of power; coloniality of knowledge; and coloniality of being. These are useful analytical tools enabling a deeper understanding of the roots of African predicaments and dilemmas, be they political, social, ideological, economic or epistemological. Briefly stated, coloniality of power confronts and speaks directly to the four constitutive elements of Western domination and exploitation of the non-Western world. The first being control of African economies, including land expropriations, and exploitation of labour and natural resources. The second aspect was the usurpation and control of African kingly and chiefly authority and power by colonizers. This process entailed the reduction of defeated African chiefs into lowest-ranking colonial officials responsible for supervision of Africans as providers of cheap labour and taxpayers. The third lever is control of gender and sexuality together with influencing the structuring of African families and forms of education. The final contour is control of subjectivity and knowledge, including imposition of Western epistemology and shaping the formative processes of development of black subjectivity.

Coloniality of power articulates continuities of colonial mentalities, psychologies and worldviews into the so-called 'postcolonial era' and highlights the social hierarchical relationships of exploitation and domination between Westerners and Africans that has its roots in centuries of European colonial expansion but currently continuing through cultural, social and political power relations (Quijano 2007; Grosfoguel 2007).

On the other hand, coloniality of knowledge addresses the epistemological questions of how colonial modernity interfered with African modes of knowing, social meaning-making, imagining, seeing and knowledge production, and their replacement with Eurocentric epistemologies that assumed the character of objective, scientific, neutral, universal and only truthful knowledges (Escobar 2007). Since the time of the European Renaissance and Enlightenment, Westerners worked tirelessly to make their knowledge the only truthful and universal knowledge and ceaselessly spread it through Christianity and other means across the world, in the process appropriating and displacing existing African knowledges. Western knowledge and imperial power worked together to inscribe coloniality across the African continent and other parts of the non-Western world. That way, Western domination and Eurocentrism assumed universality (Quijano 2000).

Coloniality of being is another useful analytical tool that helps to analyse the realities of dehumanization and depersonalization of colonized Africans into *damnes* (the condemned people and the wretched of the earth) (Fanon 1968a; Maldonado-Torres 2007). Under colonialism, colonized Africans endured hellish life experiences informed by existing racialized hierarchies of power that prevented any humane coexistence between the black colonized Africans and white colonizers. The world of the colonized became a domain of violence, war, rape, diseases, death and mourning as they were denied full humanity and reduced to non-beings who subsisted and lived within the underworld of coloniality (Mignolo 2007; Quijano 2007; Grosfoguel 2007; Maldonado-Torres 2007; Escobar 2007).

Life in the informal settlements (shacks) of South Africa provides a good example of a hellish life as an underworld of coloniality of being where human beings live in unearthed shacks without protection from lightning. There are no toilets and no sources of clean water. Violence is endemic. Poverty has become an identity itself. Social peace and human security is perpetually absent. The South Africa experience is discussed in detail in chapters five and six of this book.

Samir Amin, the Egyptian political economist, is one of those African scholars who have consistently engaged with the problems of neocolonialism, imperialism, globalization and neoliberalism from a world systems perspective (Amin 1989, 1991, 1997, 1998, 2000). Amin is well-known for his 'delinking thesis' among his other various important intellectual interventions and contributions to the agenda of Third World liberation. As a political economist his ideas have an economic slant. He is also a strong believer in socialism as a universal alternative to capitalism. In presenting delinking as a pre-requisite and transitional strategy to socialism. Amin articulated four propositions in justifying delinking:

> First, the necessity of delinking is the logical political outcome of the unequal character of the development of capitalism [...] Unequal development, in this sense, is the origin of essential social, political and ideological evolutions [...] Second, delinking is a necessary condition of any socialist advance, in the North and in the South. This proposition is, in our view, essential for a reading of Marxism that genuinely takes into account the unequal character of capitalist development. Third, the potential advances that become available through delinking will not 'guarantee' certainty of further evolution towards a pre-defined 'socialism.' Socialism is a future that must be built. And fourthly, the option for delinking must be discussed in political terms. This proposition derives from a reading according to which economic constraints are absolute only for those who accept the commodity alienation intrinsic to capitalism, and turn it into an historical system of eternal validity (Amin 1990: xiv).

The delinking Amin has in mind is a careful and strategic one that takes the form of a transition during which underdeveloped countries would adopt new market strategies and values that are different from those of the developed nations. He also uses delinking to mean a consistent refusal to bow to the dominant logic of the world capitalist system (Amin 2006: 27). To Amin, therefore, delinking means 'the pursuit of a system of rational criteria for economic options founded on a law of value on a national basis with popular relevance, independent of such criteria of economic rationality as flow from the dominance of capitalist law of value operating on a world scale' (Amin 1990: 62). In short, delinking should involve placing less emphasis on comparative advantage, and playing more attention to the introduction of economic, social and political reforms in the interest of the underdeveloped countries.

The key weakness in the delinking thesis, however, is the belief that a major problem like economic underdevelopment can be solved through piecemeal national interventions. How can a global problem be solved through national or local solutions? Chapter Two of this book provides a detailed interrogation of the limits of some of the solutions dependency theorists offered to the African problems of economic development and political domination. It was Amin who identified 'five monopolies' used by the dominant Western world to keep the developing world in a subjugated position. These are the monopoly of technology, including military superiority of the dominant nations; monopoly over global finances; the monopoly of access to natural resources; monopoly over international communication and the media; and the monopoly of the military means of mass destruction (Amin 2000). If African and other developing nations were trapped in this exploitative and dominating monopolies, how then could delinking premised on individual nations be a solution?

At another level, Amin (2009) meticulously dealt with the problem of Eurocentrism as a core component of the present world. He defined 'Eurocentrism' as a world view fabricated by the domination of Western capitalism that claimed that European cultures reflected the unique and progressive manifestation of the metaphysical order of history. To Amin, Eurocentrism is nothing but an ideological distortion of reality, an incredible mythology as well as a historical and moral travesty based on appropriation of Greek rationality and Christianity to create, legitimize and justify the exploitative capitalist social order together with the conquest of the non-Western world (Amin 2009: 160-175). In this way, Amin was engaging in a worthwhile deconstruction of the making of a dominant Western world which today masquerades as a divinely-ordained scheme of the world. Amin has revealed that 'Europe' is nothing but a culturalist construction that masquerades as universal (Amin 2009: 165).

Two warnings were flagged in Amin's analysis of Eurocentrism relating to how non-Europeans were reacting to it. The first is the common navel-gazing attempts at returning to the ancient cultural roots, a position that informed some Islamic religious and African nationalist fundamentalisms. To Amin, this is a reactionary, blind and unprofitable rejection of the scientific view of the world and the progress made so far. The second involves attempts to project socio-economic diversities and pluralism as the basis of difference. To Amin, this response is inappropriate because its provincialism invites inevitable and insoluble conflicts among nations (Amin 2009). He concluded his interrogation of Eurocentrism with a legitimate call for a 'Non-Eurocentric View of History and a Non-Eurocentric Social Theory'.

The key problem with Amin's suggested solutions to Eurocentrism is that they fall into the same Eurocentric emancipatory option that believes that in spite of its myriad of problems, capitalism reflected a certain universal rationality that must be accepted by the developing world. Emphasis on rationality is in itself a reflection of the extent of how interpellated by Western epistemologies some of Amin's articulations are. Therefore, his call for 'the socialist universalism' founded on non-European, universal and rational world order able to overcome the contradiction inherent in capitalist universalism, is informed by political economic thought that is itself not freed from Western epistemology.

Amin seems to be concerned about how to remove Eurocentrism from the modernist project. Which he believes to be tainted by European culturalism, thus preventing it from becoming a progressive universal project (Amin 2009: 17). What is however not clear in Amin's analysis is what constitute universal values. He calls for what he termed 'modernity critical of modernity' (Amin 2009: 17). It is also not clear whether this 'modernity critical of modernity' is a reformist agenda or a call for alternative modernity informed by African thinking and imagination of the world. But this critique of Amin's interventions is not meant to diminish his overall contribution to progressive thinking about how the developing world might free itself from the snares of global matrices of power, which are fully discussed in Chapter Two of this book. Amin remains one of the most consistent and unwavering critics of Western domination of Africa in particular and the developing world in general.

This book builds on the extensive literature on neocolonialism, Euro-centrism and globalization, focusing specifically on how the 'postcolonial neocolonized world' was created and how its structures and modes of power continue to impinge on African identity formations, nation-building projects, and politics of knowledge production; as well as how the poorest Africans have remained the worst victims of the racially-constructed world build by Western modernity..

Neocolonialism is studied not as the last stage of imperialism as Kwame Nkrumah (1965) would have us believe, but as the present global condition within which subsists the 'postcolonial African world' as a disciplined and shattered imagination of freedom. Neocolonialism today underpins global coloniality which currently flexes its muscles in the form of globalization through which Western particularistic ideas, values and traditions are being spread across the world as global norms of governance. Global coloniality refers to the continuities of colonial practices and imaginations across space and time on a global scale (Grosfoguel 2004:315-336). It helps our understanding of the global power imbalances between Africans and Europeans in and out of the continent.

When we think along these lines, it becomes clear that the 'postcolonial neocolonized world' is a domain of myths of decolonization and illusions of freedom and a terrain of unfinished nation-building, fragmented identities and failing economic development. At its centre is the reign of epistemological colonization. The 'postcolonial neocolonized world' lacks coherence, essence and life of its own. It is an arena of frustrated dreams and shattered visions. In short, it is a world that is overseen and controlled remotely by global coloniality through invisible colonial matrices of power. It is this depressing situation that forced the Marxist revolutionary Che Guevara (1965:10) to argues that. 'As long as imperialism exists it will, by definition, exert its domination over other countries. Today that domination is called neocolonialism.'

The implication of this is that the postcolonial African world exists only as that which is absent. It exists as an African idea of liberation and an aspiration for freedom. This is an idea for which some Africans have paid the ultimate price, while others were incarcerated for a long time, including Nelson Mandela who was jailed for 27 years. Despite the sacrifice of these people postcolonial Africa is still far from being truly freen; if anything, it has merely entered into another phase in the colonial continuum. Kwame Nkrumah was quite right in describing neocolonialism as the 'last stage of imperialism'. His further remark on the subject is equally instructive. According to him:

> In place of colonialism as that main instrument of imperialism we have today neo-colonialism. [...] Neo-colonialism, like colonialism, is an attempt to export the social conflicts of the capitalist countries. [...] The result of neo-colonialism is that foreign capital is used for the exploitation rather than for the development of the less developed parts of the world. Investment under neo-colonialism increases the gap between the rich and the poor countries rather than decreasing the gap between the rich and the poor countries of the world (Nkrumah 1965: 8).

In place of the imagined postcolonial world, there exists a 'postcolonial neocolonized world' as a problematic terrain of emptiness, illusions, myths and shadows of being free and decolonized. Within this 'postcolonial neocolonized world', African leaders have no power and freedom to decide on the course of any development of their countries without approval from Washington, London, Paris and other Western capitals.. Those who try to defy this logic of dependence are severely disciplined, if not eliminated. African scholarship has also becomehostage to Western epistemological hegemony installed by what is called 'Enlightenment'. All these problems are rooted in what Chabal and Daloz (1999) call 'a crisis of modernity'.'

It must be surprising to some that this book is focusing on the problems of neocolonialism some fifty years after the end of colonial empires. My quick response is that a postcolonial African world has not yet been fully realized and there is need to explain why this is the case and dispel some dangerous myths of decolonization and illusions of freedom that compelled and induced Africans to relax and postpone the liberation struggles before achievement of its set goals. The second response is given by the leading Nigerian historian, Toyin Falola, who had this to say:

> [...] how can one theory replace another so fast, how can scholarship resemble fashion and weather, changing so rapidly? Why should scholars of Africa follow and accept all fast-changing academic trends, if their conditions are either constant or changing for worse? Why should they keep replacing one mode of analysis with another if they are yet to overcome their own limitations, both practical and intellectual? They can do so in order to participate in the debate in a 'global academy,' but they must consider the consequences for Africa (Falola 2001: 20).

The twentieth century dream of decolonization was only partially accomplished. Africans continue to live in a neocolony dominated by the 'coloniality of power'. Grosfoguel (2007: 217) has defined 'coloniality of power' as an entanglement of multiple and heterogeneous global hierarchies and heterarchies of sexual, political, epistemic, economic, spiritual, linguistic and racial forms of domination and exploitation where the racial/ethnic hierarchy of the European/non-European divide transversally reconfigured all of the global power structures.

In simple terms, the concept of 'coloniality of power' is useful in capturing colonial experience and epistemologies even now that direct colonial adminis-trations have been rolled back. The coloniality of power that is addressed in this book manifests itself in the cultural, political, sexual, spiritual, epistemic and economic spheres. Grosfoguel (2007: 220) is correct in arguing that decolonization discourse has obscured the continuities between the colonial past and current global colonial/racial hierarchies and, therefore, contributed to the invisibility of coloniality today. Abiola Irele is in full agreement with this, arguing that the West has exerted so much pressure on the African experience to the extent that 'it is no exaggeration to say that all forms of modern African expression have been conditioned by it' (Irele 1991: 58)..

What Africans celebrated as independence was a myth taken for reality as invisible snares of coloniality of power were ignored, thereby denying the birth of a truly postcolonial African world. In other words, the authentic postcolonial era is still part of unfulfilled African aspirations. The postcolonial African world is an imagined space of freedom and identity reconstruction that is still being fought for. It forms a major part of African aspirations that emerged from the terrain of colonial encounters of the 15th century which Comaroff and Comaroff describe in the following terms:

> The colonial encounter also had the effect of reinforcing some features of indigenous lifeways, altering or effacing others, and leaving yet others unengaged. Along the way, too, new hybrids came into being: new aesthetic styles and material arrangements, new divisions of wealth and sense of identity, new notions of peoplehood, politics and history (Comaroffs 1997: 8-9).

The Comaroffs further argue that colonization was multifaceted from its beginning. It was as much a cultural as a political enterprise. It was as much about cartography and counting. It was as much about the practical logic of capitalism as about bodily regimes. It was also about the brute extraction of labour power 'as much as anything else about inscribing in the social world a new conception of space, new forms of personhood, and a new means of manufacturing the real' (Comaroffs 1997: 16-17).

A postcolonial African world was expected to be a terrain of African re-birth and socio-political recreation of African selfhood that had been affected by alienating forces of colonialism. A new African consciousness of being free from colonialism was expected to dominate and shape the postcolonial African world. A series of struggles were fought to achieve this objective. These struggles ranged from the primary resistance of the nineteenth century, through the pan-Africanist congresses that began in 1900, the Negritude movement of the 1930s, the anti-colonial liberation wars of the 1950s and 1960s, struggles for economic development of the 1970s and 1980s that were torpedoed by the Washington Consensus-inspired Structural Adjustment Programmes (SAPs) and civil society-spearheaded struggles for democracy of the 1990s right up to the revived pan-Africanist initiatives galvanized by the millennial African Renaissance.

The envisaged end product was supposed to be a new and brave African postcolonial world and a new humanity where African agency, dignity and identity have been restored after years of colonial and neocolonial domination. But this African dream has not yet materialized. The African postcolonial world remains an aspiration rather than a reality. Ashcroft (1997) has argued that the term 'postcolonial' was does not refer to 'after colonialism'. On the contrary, he posited that postcolonialism began when the colonizers arrived and did not vanish when the colonialists rolled back direct colonial administrations after 1945. To him, postcolonial analysis examined the full range of responses to colonialism. The term thus describes 'a society continuously responding in all its myriad ways to the experience of colonial contact' (Ashcroft 1997: 21). But in this book, the term 'postcolonial' African world is extended to also depict an imagined independent African future without colonialism that the decolonization process was expected to achieve but failed.

Therefore, what exists as the African postcolonial world is characterized by a lack of essence. The African crisis of essence had to do with the fact that instead of African revolutionaries taking full and effective charge of the birth of a fully liberated and confident African political baby, the decolonization process became overseen by the erstwhile colonial masters who were bent on building a neocolonial world rather than an African postcolonial world. For the 'Anglophone' world, Lancaster House became the political maternity ward for the delivery of truncated African re-birth with British and American powers overseeing the overall process and channelling it straight into a neocolonial direction. The situation was worse for the 'Francophone' countries on the continent where the former colonial power (France) was embraced as an innocent father figure and decolonization was interpreted in simplistic terms of 'democratization' under the tutelage of France. Leopold Sedar Senghor, the founding father of Senegal, expressed the pathetic view of decolonization of the Francophone countries when he said:

> In Africa, when children have grown up they leave their parents' hut, and build a hut of their own by its side. Believe me; we don't want to leave the French compound. We have grown up in it and it is good to be alive in it. We simply want to build our own huts (Senghor 1957:13).

French neocolonialism operated under what became known as *Francafrique* or *Francophonie*, concepts that captured a false decolonization where the colonial power (France) continued to dominate the French West African countries (Whiteman 1997). Some African leaders like Senghor, Felix Houphouet-Boigny of Cote d'Ivoire, Omar Bongo of Gabon, Gnassigbe Eyadema of

Togo, Denis Sassou-Ngesso of the Republic of Congo, Idris Deby of Chad and Hamani Diori of Niger celebrated this neocolonialism as a sign of continuation of good relations between France and Africa. Consequently, what was expected to be postcolonial states and nations became mere small huts within the bigger neocolonial houses that managed the economic affairs and influenced the political trajectory of the continent!

This compels a new book that captures the reality of the African postcolonial world as a terrain of truncated visions and frustrated aspirations. The book provides a new critical interpretation of African history and politics predicated on a discursive reading of dominant narratives of the trajectories of the making of the African continent and African identities. The coloniality perspective is employed in unpacking the politics lying behind the idea of Africa in general and the construction of African identities in particular. This approach to African history and politics takes full account of the role of power and its epistemology in constructions of identities and institutions as well as inscription of particular forms of knowing and knowledge on Africa. In this new reading of African history and politics, the African postcolonial world is discussed as existing but absent. What exists is the 'postcolonial neocolonial world' which Africans continue to contest as they struggle for freedom and strive to reconstruct their identities.

The coloniality perspective privileges the subaltern side of colonial difference as it critiques and challenges hegemonic European paradigms that have assumed 'a universalistic, neutral, objective point of view' (Grosfoguel 2007: 213). The concept of coloniality is different from colonialism as it refers to the longstanding patterns of power that emerged from colonialism and continue to define culture, labour, intersubjective relations and knowledge production, long after the end of direct colonialism. It is that continuing dominating phenomenon that survived colonialism. It is hidden in discourses, books, cultures, common sense, academic performances, and even self-images of Africans (Maldonado-Torres 2007: 243). Africans have breathed and lived coloniality since their colonial encounters and it continues to shape their everyday life today.

Coloniality emerged as the darker side of Western modernity that unfolded in terms of racial classification of human population as new identities were created such as European, white, Indian, black, African, Negro, mestizo and others. At the centre of this classification was the birth of Eurocentrism as an identity forming process that proceeded through binaries and dichotomies of inferior-superior, irrational-rational, primitive-civilized, and traditional-modern (Quijano 2000: 348). These binaries enabled a shift from the Cartesian notion of cogito ego sum (I think, therefore I am) to the imperial motto of ego *coquiro/ego conquistus* (I conquer, therefore I am) that legitimized all sorts of colonial conquests and violence against those considered non-Western people (Maldonado-Torres 2007: 245).

The ideological life-spring of colonial conquest and colonial violence was the questioning of the very humanity of colonized people. It was this questioning of the humanity of the colonized people that authorized slavery and other forms of abuse, repression, exploitation and domination of Africans in particular and other ex-colonized people in general. Within this imperialist scheme, colonized and racialized subjects were considered dispensable beings of very questionable humanity. To crown it all, a Western conception of human history emerged which ran from state of nature to Europe as the centre of world civilization, creator and exporter of modernity (Mignolo 1995; Quijano 2000). One of the core logics of coloniality and the colonizer's model of the non-Western world is the notion of emptiness which Blaut aptly expressed in the following words:

> This proposition of emptiness makes a series of claims, each layered upon the others: (i) A non-European region is empty or nearly empty of people (hence settlement by Europeans does not displace any native peoples). (ii) The region is empty of settled population: the inhabitants are mobile, nomadic, wanderers (hence European settlement violates no political sovereignty, since wanderers make no claim to territory). (iii) The cultures of this region do not possess any understanding of private property—that is, the region is empty of property rights and claims (hence colonial occupiers can freely give land to settlers since no one owns it). The final layer, applied to all of the Outside sector, is an emptiness of intellectual creativity and spiritual values, sometimes described by Europeans as an absence of 'rationality' (Blaut 1993: 15).

South Africa is one country where white settlers once claimed that they did not dispossess the Africans of land since they found the land depopulated by the devastating black-on-black violence initiated and directed by King Shaka of the Zulu Kingdom. This view has, however, been countered by modern historians like Julian Cobbing (1988) who argued that the notion of Mfecane (traditionally dubbed Shakan wars of conquest) that caused depopulation of the interior regions of South Africa was an alibi for white invasion, conquest and occupation of African lands (see also Etherington 2001). A detailed case study of South African discourse in this regard is given in Chapter Six of this book. The chapter also details the dynamics of race politics, including mobilization of scientific racism to justify the exclusion of Africans/blacks from the nation and to re-identify them as uncivilized natives whose course of development could not be pitched at the same level with white trajectories of development. Blacks were only wanted within the racially fenced white space as providers of cheap labour to the white-owned farms, factories and mines.

At the centre of the imperial/colonial world in general, race classification and control of labour complimented each other, resulting in the colonized peoples being reduced to unpaid and unwaged labour forces with paid labour reserved for whites. The racial inferiority of Africans/blacks constructed by colonial modernity implied that they were not worth any wages. Quijano has observed that:

> Thus, in the control of labour and its resources and products, it is the capitalist enterprise; in the control of sex and its resources and products, the bourgeois family; in the control of authority and its resources and products, the nation-state; in the control of intersubjectivity, Eurocentrism (Quijano 2000: 545).

Coloniality of power is, therefore, one of the main levers of colonial modernity and has continued to sustain the notions of inferior-superior motif in the intersubjective relations of whites and blacks. The concept of coloniality of power speaks directly to the entanglement and entrapment of Africa and other ex-colonized parts of the world in the ever-present colonial matrix of power of the modern/colonial world (Mignolo 2007: 158). It is a global hegemonic model of power established since the colonial encounters that articulated race and labour, as well as space and peoples, according to the needs of capital and to the benefit of white European peoples. Thus, the neoliberal democracy that currently masquerades as a global salvation for the multitudes only hides coloniality of power that maintains the hierarchies of races created in the sixteenth and seventeenth centuries as Europe constructed itself as the centre of the world civilization and whites put themselves at the apex of the human development ladder while pushing Africa into a permanent subaltern position.

Ramon Grosfoguel (2007: 216) has distilled nine contours of coloniality of power that underpin the current world order. The first is the formation of a particular global class formation where various forms of labour (slavery, serfdom, wage labour to petty-commodity production and many others) were co-existing and being organized by capital as a source of production of surplus value through the selling of commodities for profit in the world market. The second contour was the international division of labour of the core and periphery, where in the periphery coercion and authoritarian forms predominated. The third contour was the creation of an inter-state system of politico-military organizations manned by European and American males and ready to discipline deviant states like Iraq and others (Grosfoguel 2007: 216).

The fourth contour was an elaborate global racial/ethnic hierarchy that privileges Western people over non-Western ones. The fifth strand is an equally elaborate global gender hierarchy that privileges males over females and Western patriarchy over other forms of gender relations (Spivak 1988). This strand is related to the next one of a sexual hierarchy that privileged heterosexuals over homosexuals and lesbians, invariably feeding into some politics of homophobic ideologies that are noticeable in countries like Zimbabwe, an ex-British colony that seems to adhere strongly to idea of heterosexuality as the norm. The seventh contour is that of privileging Christianity over all other non-Christian/non-Western spiritualities.

The eighth contour is an epistemic hegemony that privileges Western knowledge and cosmology over non-Western knowledge and cosmologies that is evident in universities across the world. The final strand is a linguistic hierarchy between Western languages and non-Western ones leading to the pushing of African languages to the barbarian margins of folklores (Grosfoguel 2007: 216-217). The concept of coloniality is very useful as it enables ex-colonized peoples to understand why the present racial/ethnic hierarchy of the capitalist world system continues to be constituted on a cultural criterion whose origins lie in colonial encounters and colonial relations. It enables historians to historicize and explain why some human beings were at the bottom of the ethnic/racial hierarchy while the Anglo-Saxons remained dominant at the top of the world. Quijano summarized the situation very well when he said:

> Racism and ethnicisation were initially produced in the Americas and then expanded to the rest of the colonial world as the foundation of the specific power relations between Europe and the populations of the rest of the world. After five hundred years, they still are the basic components of power relations across the world. Once colonialism became extinct as a formal political system, social power is still constituted on criteria originated in colonial relations. In other words, coloniality has not ceased to be the central character of today's social power [...] Since then, in the intersubjective relations and in the social practices of power, there emerged, on the one hand, the idea that non-Europeans have biological structure not only different from Europeans; but, above all, belonging to an 'inferior' level or type. On the other hand, the idea that cultural differences are associated to such biological inequalities [...] These ideas have configured a deep

and persistent cultural formation, a matrix of ideas, images, values, attitudes, and social practices, that do not cease to be implicated in relationships among people, even when colonial political relations have been eradicated (Quijano cited in Grosfoguel 2004: 326).

Coloniality of power is closely linked with coloniality of knowledge which is another important concept that is very useful in any understanding of the dilemmas of the 'postcolonial African neocolonized world'. Coloniality of knowledge directly addresses the crucial question of how Western modernity spread through displacing other cultures, subordinating others and colonizing the imagination of the colonized peoples. This took the form of repression of existing African beliefs, ideas, images, symbols and forms of knowledge that were found to be repugnant to global colonial domination (Quijano 2007: 169). The other strategy was to expropriate and siphon from the colonized their knowledge that was found useful to the global colonial agenda.

Having done this, Westerners then imposed their own forms of knowledge, which they mystified and placed far out of reach of the generality of the colonized population. They made it seductive and only accessible to a few colonized people who were expected to provide service to the colonial projects. The teaching of Western culture and knowledge was done for the purposes of reproduction of colonial domination (Quijano 2000: 541). The African continent has not managed to free itself from epistemological, cognitive and colonization of the mind and imagination, as detailed in Chapter Two of this book.

Another long-lasting impact of the underside of modernity in the non-Western world is what Maldonado-Torres termed coloniality of being which clearly encapsulates the lived experiences of colonized people during and after direct colonialism. It grapples with the question of effects of coloniality on the lived experience of the colonized and ex-colonized ordinary people. As noted by Nelson Maldonado-Torres (2007) imperialism and colonialism were underpinned by a racist/imperial Manichean misanthropic scepticism as a form of imperial/colonial attitude that questioned the very humanity of the colonized people and doubted whether they had souls.

This imperial/colonial attitude was a deliberate strategy that opened the door to all forms of abuse, including killing, enslaving and raping and use of various forms of violence that could not be inflicted on Western people. The colonized people experienced not only alienation but also depersonalization as they were stripped of humanity. Race played a central role to create what Frantz Fanon (1961) termed damne as a conquered being deprived of their humanity. Colonized people became the condemned of the earth. Maldonado-Torres (2007: 255) had this to say on the coloniality of being:

> Hellish existence in the colonial world carries with it both the racial and the gendered aspects of the naturalization of the no-ethics of war. *Indeed, coloniality of Being primarily refers to the normalization of the extraordinary events that take place in war.* While in war there is murder and rape, in the hell of the colonial world murder and rape become day to day occurrences and menaces. 'Killability' and 'repeability' are inscribed into the images of the colonial bodies. Lacking real authority, colonized men are permanently feminized (emphasis in the original source).

The key problem is that this colonial psyche reproduced itself in African nationalists as products of colonial rule and the authoritarian and violent streak has continued into the 'postcolonial neocolonized world' where, in countries like Zimbabwe, the dominant nationalist party (the Zimbabwe African National Union-Patriotic Front-ZANU-PF) that professes to have liberated Africans from settler colonialism has subjected Africans to the worst forms of violence and death. (A detailed case study of Zimbabwe is provided in Chapter seven of this book).

The other important point emerging from deployment of coloniality perspective towards understanding the 'postcolonial neocolonized world' is that of 'locus of enunciation'. This concept reveals that all writers, thinkers and speakers write, think and speak from a particular location in the power structures:

> Nobody escapes the class, sexual, gender, spiritual, linguistic, geographical, and racial hierarchies of the modern/colonial/capitalist/patriarchal world-system (Mignolo 2000: 54).

The fact is that all knowledges and worldviews are always situated. It is, therefore, important to analyse the 'locus of enunciation' of thinkers and writers on African issues if one is to gain a deeper understanding of the African world. The 'locus of enunciation' refers to 'the geo-political and body-political location of the subject that speaks' (Grosfoguel 2007: 213). What is challenging is that often thinkers and dominant Western paradigms tend to hide their locus of enunciation. A major crisis in the imagination of an African postcolonial world was that some of those socially located in the oppressed side of power relations did not openly think from a subordinate epistemic location.

Colonial interpellation and neocolonial imperatives forced some Africans that were socially located on the oppressed side of the colonial difference, to think and speak epistemically like those on the dominant positions. Others fell into epistemic populism that was never translated into concrete emancipatory projects. Writing about this African crisis Ngugi wa Thiong'o had this to say:

> Is an African renaissance possible when we keepers of memory have to work outside our own linguistic memory? And within the prison house of European linguistic memory? Often drawing from our own experiences and history to enrich the already very rich European memory? If we think of the intelligentsia as generals in the intellectual army of Africa including foot soldiers, can we expect this army to conquer when its generals are captured and held prisoner? And it is worse when they revel in their fate as captives (Ngugi wa Thiong'o 2009: 92).

Therefore, while not losing sight of the disempowering effects of colonial modernity that enabled such crippling processes as the slave trade, imperialism, colonialism, apartheid, neocolonialism and globalization on the African continent, the book is equally concerned about the problematics of African struggles aimed at transcending negative aspects of colonial modernity as well as attempts to domesticate the positive aspects of modernity if not launching a new form of African modernity that is liberating and empowering. The immanent logic of colonial modernity has deeply interpellated African imaginations of liberation and continues to shape African worldviews.

Pratt (1992) and Ahluwalia (2001) introduced the notions of 'contact zones' and 'African inflections' which help in gaining a deeper understating of the making of the 'postcolonial neocolonized world' and how Africans have consistently responded to its challenges and discursive constraints. The making of the African postcolonial world emerged within complex contact zones imposed on the world by accidents as well as a combination of deliberate imperial/colonial interventions unleashed by western modernity.

Pratt's concept of 'contact zones' covers the process of how people who were geographically and historically remote from each other came into contact with one another through such processes as navigation, migration, the slave trade, mercantilism, imperialism, colonialism and evangelism resulting in some measure of peaceful co-existence, conquest, coercion and violence as well as blending and conflict. At the centre of contact zones exists 'radically asymmetrical relations of power' (Pratt 1992: 7). The African postcolonial world has remained hostage to these radically asymmetrical power relations that developed during the colonial encounters of the fifteenth century.

There is no doubt that what exist as the African postcolonial world reflects the paradoxes and contradictions of the past. The reality was captured by the Comaroffs who argued that:

[...] how many features of the present have emerged out of the paradoxes and contradictions of the past; out of the tensions, endemic to the colonial out-reach, between 'universal truths' and 'parochial cultures,' between a society founded on individual rights and one characterized by racial (dis)enfranchisement, between the world of the free citizen and that of the colonial subject. These tensions suffused the encounter between Africans and Europeans, animating histories that eluded easy control by their dramatis personae, histories carved out of the dialectics of exchange, appropriation, accommodation, struggle (Comaroffs 1997: xv).

Africans have been struggling since then to extricate themselves from the complex and sometimes invisible snares of colonial matrix of power bequeathed them by colonial modernity. Colonial modernity is not reducible to the events of colonialism and the post-Berlin Conference scramble and partition of Africa. It is read discursively as a broad worldview that was underpinned by strong epistemological interventions that culminated in the colonization and transformation of African consciousness. The broader meaning and implication of colonial modernity for Africa was well captured by Mudimbe (1988: 2) as 'the domination of physical space, the reformation of natives' minds, and the integration of local economic histories into Western perspective.'

This book, however, does not reduce all present-day African problems to what Mudimbe (1988: 6) termed the 'colonializing structure.' Africans themselves have also exercised their agency not only to resist colonial modernity but to create new forms of oppression and exploitation of one another. Ahluwalia's (2001) concept of 'African inflections' is important in that it provides a critical lens of reading how African societies have constructed and reconstructed themselves through engagement with western and colonial modernity. In this book the overarching theme is that of how Africans have confronted legacies of colonialism and present-day snares of colonial modernity while trying to define and shape a postcolonial future.

What is often ignored in existing accounts of the making of the African postcolonial world together with its problems of fragmented identities is that colonial modernity delayed the processes of state-building and nation-building up until the 1960s for West, East and Central Africa and until the 1980s and 1990s for Zimbabwe, Namibia and South Africa. It was not until the end of the Second World War in 1945 that the decolonization project was embraced globally as human progress and Africans were accepted as a people who deserved national self-determination. Consequently, the decolonization of Africa launched into the international political landscape a coterie of the youngest, weakest, poor and artificial states that had to masquerade as nations soon after birth (Clapham 1996).

Jackson (1990) described these young and fragile African postcolonial states as 'quasi-states'. These were states which were readily recognized as sovereign and independent units by other states within the post-1945 normative terms of the international system, while in reality they did not meet the demands of 'empirical statehood' (Jackson 1990). The criteria for 'empirical statehood' entailed the capacity to exercise effective power within their own territories and the ability to defend themselves against external attack. Christopher Clapham (1996: 15) argued that postcolonial African states enjoyed negative sovereignty ascribed to them by other states rather than positive sovereignty rooted inside and manifested in effective internal control and popular acceptability.

At the centre of African struggles to define and shape a postcolonial future, the challenges of nation-building and identity formation loom large. Nation-building continues to be contentious work-in-progress alongside the pan-African politics of forging continental unity. The celebrated anti-colonial nationalisms of the 1960s failed to create stable postcolonial nation-states. Ethnicity and regionalism have remained strong forces reverberating beneath weak and fragile African nationalisms.

The current African postcolonial world suffers terribly from weak nationalisms that camouflage ethnicity and regionalism even when they may be serving as state ideologies. The result has been manifest in state weakness and even state failure that has created theatres of conflict, war and violence. Weak and fragile nationalisms were rooted in poor and skewed social base of imaginations of the nation that had to carefully navigate and synthesize complex precolonial histories into usable past, contested myths of foundations of the nation that hardly agreed to hang together, unresolved definition of authentic subjects of the nation, unclear criteria of belonging and citizenship, contested and undefined sources of political legitimacy as well as rules of political succession to political office.

But at another level, African leaders have since the beginning of the new millennium been busy with building pan-African institutions as part of the resolution of past problems. These initiatives have witnessed the transformation of the Organization of African Unity (OAU) into the African Union (AU), the establishment of the Pan-African Parliament (PAP), the adoption of the New Partnership for African Development (NEPAD), the construction and adoption of the innovative African Peer Review Mechanism (APRM) and many other AU institutions such as the African Standby Force that is meant to deal with the problems of conflict and security on the continent.

Kwame Nkrumah's long deferred dream of a United States of Africa gained new resonance, this time galvanized by the philosophy of African Renaissance. At the launch of African Renaissance Institute on 11 October 1999, the then president of South Africa, Thabo Mbeki, proclaimed that the 21st century was to be 'Africa's Century' (Mbeki 1999). The AU was expected to concretize this African dream. Hence Kay Mathews argument that the establishment of the AU in July 2002 was the most important development in the trajectory of the African future (Mathews 2008: 25). The AU's *2004 to 2007 Strategic Framework of the African Union Commission* spelt out the AU vision as 'Africa integrated, prosperous and peaceful, an Africa driven by its own citizens, a dynamic force in the global arena' (African Union Commission 2004: 7).

However, beneath these noble initiatives and millennial optimism, conflicts continue to haunt the African continent with devastating impact on economic development, human security and social peace. Such areas as the Democratic Republic of Congo (DRC), Ivory Coast (Cote d'Ivoire), Northern Uganda, Chad, Sudan, Somalia, Kenya and Zimbabwe have become flies inside the pan-African ointment spoiling everything and becoming speed traps tied to the wheels of pan-Africanism. South Africa, whose post-apartheid leaders Nelson Mandela and Thabo Mbeki articulated the philosophies of 'ubuntu' (African humanism) and the African Renaissance, was engulfed in embarrassing xenophobic violence in May 2008 that shocked the continent. Can we read these conflicts positively as signs of the violent death of the old order bequeathed on the continent by colonial modernity?

It is not easy to say whether the continent is experiencing a Gramscian interregnum characterized by the traumatic but slow death of the old order bequeathed on it by colonial modernity as a darker side of Western modernity on the one hand, and a violent re-birth characterized by washing away of the old order with the blood of martyrs, on the other. Only time will tell. This book, which grapples with the complex question of the current trajectory and future direction of the African continent, however, cannot ignore the complex questions of discursive formation of African identities and the conflict-laden nation-building processes together with issues of power and epistemology that are at the core of the African predicament. These issues are posed and interrogated over a long time, from the time of the cartographic construction of the continent itself to the present.

But Fantu Cheru has already warned us about flaws of Thabo Mbeki's version of African Renaissance. He noted that it was merely an 'expression of desire, need and hope rather than a plan for the future.' He also lamented 'the absence of any coherent, continent-wide agenda or framework for change' (Cheru 2002: xii). The key crisis in Mbeki's vision of African Renaissance is that it is 'in line with the much-discredited neoliberal project of the 'Washington Consensus' than what the idea actually implies' (Cheru 2002: xii-xiii).

As a way forward for Africa, Cheru suggested that African leaders must understand globalization as an irreversible process that needed to be navigated carefully. He dismissed radical counter-hegemonic strategies to global neo-liberalism as 'unthinkable in the near future' (Cheru 2002: xiii). What African leaders must work towards is to try and appropriate and 'manage globalization to their own levels, without heavy-handed intervention by the institutions of the world system' (Cheru 2002: xiii). Cheru suggested the following as the future-oriented strategy for Africa: '*a guided embrace of globalization with a commitment to resist* through pre-emptive national or regional development strategies and economic policy coordination' (emphasis is in the original source) (Cheru 2002: xv).

While Cheru's strategy is attractive to a pan-African audience, its implementation is impossible within a continent that is still deeply ensnared by colonial matrix of power. Chapters 3 and 4 of this book explore in detail the invisible snares of colonial matrix of power that make it very difficult for the African people to enjoy self-determination over economic and political development of their continent. But the trajectory and future of the African continent has continued to pre-occupy academics and intellectuals, including Ali A. Mazrui who:

> The ancestors of Africa are angry. For those who believe in the power of ancestors, the proof of their anger is all around us. For those who do not believe in ancestors, the proof of their anger is given another name [...] But what is the proof of the curse of the ancestors? Things are not working in Africa. From Dakar to Dar es Salaam, from Marrakesh to Maputo, institutions are decaying, structures are rusting away. It is as if the ancestors had pronounced the curse of cultural sabotage (Mazrui 1986: 11).

In a recent preface entitled 'Black Berlin and the Curse of Fragmentation: From Bismarck to Barack' in Adekeye Adebajo's book *The Curse of Berlin: Africa after the Cold War*, Mazrui reiterated his deep concern about making sense of the current developments taking place within the African continent. This time around he exposed his anguish through a series of rhetorical questions:

> Are we facing birth-pangs or death-pangs in the present crisis of boundaries of identity? Are we witnessing the real bloody forces of decolonization—as the

colonial structures within arbitrary borders are decaying or collapsing? Is the post-Berlin colonial slate being washed clean with the blood of victims, villains and martyrs? Are the refugees victims of a dying order, or are they traumatized witnesses to an epoch-making rebirth? [...] Is this blood from the womb of history giving painful birth to a new order? (Mazrui 2010: xxii).

Not only Mazrui was concerned about understanding the trajectories of the African continent. Terence Ranger, one of the fathers of African nationalist historiography, and Olufemi Vaughan, also added their voices to the debate:

At its beginning African states were indicted before the bar of 'world opinion,' first by humanitarians and missionaries and then conquerors and colonizers. Halfway through the process, colonial states were indicted before the bar of an enlarged world opinion by nationalists and humanitarians and, increasingly, by missionaries. Today it is African states once again who find themselves on trial for rapacity and authoritarianism. The indictments are brought by humanitarians, church leaders, and the sort of young Africans who would once have been nationalists and are now democrats [...] whatever else this irony tells us, it abundantly reveals that the problem of legitimacy has been central to the state in late nineteenth and twentieth-century Africa (Ranger and Vaughan 1993:1).

Indeed, the question of legitimacy continues to generate conflicts in postcolonial Africa and these are taking the form of what is often termed election-related violence or post-election violence that rocked Kenya, Zimbabwe and Ivory Coast recently. It seems the post-Cold War global neo-liberal values that privileged elections as a source of legitimacy were locking horns with resilient and intolerant one-party mentalities and psychologies that dominated the African ideological landscape in the 1960s and 1970s. Election time has often become a terrible period of violence rather than a peaceful opportunity for the electorate to choose their preferred candidates for political office.

The interpretation of election time in war terms has been clearly manifested by the experience of Zimbabweans where violence has been part of electioneering process since the country became an independent state in 1980. In Zimbabwe, liberation war credentials rather than elections were viewed by the ruling Zimbabwe African Union-Patriotic Front (ZANU-PF) as the main source of political legitimacy (Ndlovu-Gatsheni 2009; Ndlovu-Gatsheni & Muzondidya 2011). Chapter Seven of this book provides a detailed analysis of the Zimbabwean crisis as rooted in the formulation of the idea of Zimbabwe in the 1960s.

Achille Mbembe, a leading African postcolonial theorist, has also offered his own interpretation of the trajectory of postcolonial Africa. He says:

African social formations are not necessarily converging towards a single point, trend or cycle. They harbour the possibility of a variety of trajectories neither convergent nor divergent but interlocked, paradoxically. More philosophically, it may be supposed that the present as experience of a time is precisely that moment when different forms of absence become mixed together: absence of those presences that are no longer so and that one remembers (the past), and absence of those others that are yet to come and are anticipated (the future) (Mbembe 2001: 16).

To Mbembe, postcolonial Africa which he termed the 'postcolony' is manifesting a complex sedimentation of the past, present and the future in one moment of time, creating what he termed an entanglement. What Mbembe (2001: 14) termed the postcolony enclosed 'multiple durees made up of discontinuities, reversals, inertias, and swings that overlay one another, interpenetrate one another; an entanglement'. The concept of entanglement was further deployed by Sarah Nuttall to unpack and understand the trajectory of post-apartheid South Africa, one of the case studies explored in this book:

Entanglement offers [...] a rubric in terms of which we can begin to meet the challenge of the 'after apartheid.' It is a means by which to draw into our analyses those sites in which what was once thought of as separate—identities, spaces, histories—come together or find points of intersection in unexpected ways. It is an idea which signals largely unexplored terrains of mutuality, wrought from a common, though often coercive and confrontational, experience. It enables a complex temporality of past, present and future; one which points away from a time of resistance towards a more ambivalent moment in which the time of potential, both latent and actively surfacing in South Africa, exists in complex tandem with new kinds of closure and opposition. It also signals a move away from an apartheid optic and temporal lens towards one which reifies neither the past nor the exceptionality of South African life (Nuttall 2009:11).

Chapter six of this book deals directly with the genealogy of the idea of South Africa tracing it from its emergence within the context of destruction of the precolonial African order and the inscription of colonialism. Nuttall's intervention becomes very relevant as it speaks of the 'need for a utopian horizon'. In short, the significance of Nuttall's deployment of concept of entanglement lies in her bold pre-occupation with a future-oriented politics. One of the key challenges in Africa is how to enable African people move forward beyond colonial mindset and the neurosis of victimhood inflicted on Africans by a combination of exploitative and demeaning processes of the slave trade, imperialism, colonialism and apartheid.

Recently, a leading pan-African scholar, Mahmood Mamdani, also reflected on how the trajectories of the African continent were imagined by African intellectuals since the 1970s from the comfort of the University of Dar es Salaam, that once vibrant centre of pan-Africanist and nationalist thinking. This is how he put it:

> There were times when we were sure ourselves: we knew what we were up against, and we knew where we were going. We were against monarchy, against dictatorship, against neo-colonialism, against imperialism. And we were for socialism, sometimes for democracy, but always for socialism. Socialism had become a language in which we spoke to one another. For some, it was a badge; for others, it was a brand name. We were the first generation of post-independence African intellectuals. We thought in historical terms. We knew that history was moving, more or less like a train, heading to a known destination, and none of us had any doubt that we were on that train. We were certain that the future would be better than the past, much better. If there would be violence, it would be revolutionary, the violence of the poor against the rich, the oppressor against the oppressed. Good revolutionary violence would do away with bad counter-revolutionary violence (Mamdani 2010:48).

Here Mamdani was being nostalgic, reflecting on a time when Africans were enveloped by the euphoria of independence and were clear on the trajectory they were following and their ultimate destination. Two destinations lay ahead --socialism and pan-African unity. But Africans have not yet achieved or reached this destination. The train was derailed by a combination of selfish and visionless leaders as well as by external forces of neocolonialism that did not want to see confident Africans taking charge of their political, economic and social destiny, away from the world constructed by exploitative colonial modernity. Gilbert Khadiagala lent credence to this argument when he said:

> There is yet another instructive paradox in this regard: leaders that have ideas with some coherence and force of action have seldom survived, while those with neither credible philosophic standing nor kingly dispositions have had more staying power (Khadiagala 2010: 376).

This situation was further complicated by the fact that, since 1945, Africa became a proxy theatre in the Cold War that pitted the Western capitalist world led by the United States of America against the communist world led by the then Union of Soviet Socialist Republics (now Commonwealth of Independent States). Within that period some cruel and visionless leaders such as Idi Amin Dada in Uganda and Mobutu Seseko in Zaire were parachuted into power just as Mozambique and Angola plunged into civil war soon after gaining independence in 1975. Also, military coups rocked East and West Africa while Visionary leaders like Kwame Nkrumah, Patrice Lumumba and Thomas Sankara became victims of coups and assassinations. The short golden age was over in no time. Mamdani summed up his reflection on this crisis in the following words:

> Two decades later, we found ourselves in a world for which we were least prepared. Not only was it a world drenched in blood, but the battle lines were hardly inspiring. There was little revolutionary about the violence around us: instead of the poor rising up against the rich, we could see the poor pitted against poor, and rich against rich. This was hardly the final struggle promised in the International—*la lute finale*—beyond which would lie the rosy dawn of socialism. It seemed more like the fires of hell. The most fitting metaphor for that quagmire was the Rwanda genocide of 1994 (Mamdani 2010: 48).

Optimistic pan-Africanists were not only shocked by the Rwandan genocide of 1994 but also by the xenophobic violence that engulfed South Africa in May 2008. Added to these disappointing events was the fall of Kenya from being the centre of stability within a volatile Eastern Africa and the Horn into violence in 2007/8. In Southern Africa, Zimbabwe's rapid degeneration into unprecedented crisis did not help matters. Taken together, these events disturbed the optimism that greeted the third millennium.

Some new appraisals of the trajectory of the African continent had to be made. Mamdani argued that the post-apartheid and post-genocide Rwanda had the impact of changing intellectual prognoses—'we realized that history is not a story with predestination' and that 'History is not just a train set out on a fixed journey' (Mamdani 2010: 48). It is clear that the current generation of Africans need to do more work to imagine different futures. One of Mamdani's core messages to the students of Addis Ababa University was:

> [T]oday more than ever, we need the capacity to imagine different futures. In 1973, in Dar and in Addis, we thought of ourselves as being in transition to an already known destination, first it was a transition to socialism; after the fall of Soviet Union, the convention was to think of a transition to democracy; after 9/11, it became a transition to modernity. [...] Experience has taught us that there is no given destination. The destination is negotiable. Keep in mind that the journey you will embark on has no fixed destination. Where you will go will depend on you and those around you. The better you understand the nature of forces defining your choices, the more you will be able to gather in your own hands possibilities of forging the future. I wish you the best in the journey ahead (Mamdani 2010: 49).

This message has a deep meaning for the African continent as a whole. Is there any destination for Africa beyond the neoliberal democracy mantra largely imposed from the West? How is Africa negotiating its destiny within a global village? Has Africa reached the TINA (There Is No Alternative) mode? Is the destiny of Africa separable from global human emancipatory struggle in general?

This book responds to these complex questions in a variety of ways. It transverses the complex terrain dominated by what Gramsci (1971) described as pessimism of the intellect and optimism of the will. He argued that, 'It is necessary to direct one's attention violently towards the present as it is, if one wishes to transform it' (Gramsci 1971: 175). As elaborated by Hume (2010), pessimism of the intellect does not mean the intellectual enterprise of always looking for the worst-case scenarios. It means approaching world issues as they are; refusal to accept anything at face value; questioning existing narratives; and transcending fantasies. Pessimism of the intellect also questions existing Afro-pessimism and doom-mongering scares that humanity is on the verge of climatic destruction.

Throughout this book, pessimism of intellect is counterbalanced with optimism of the will. Optimism of the will means a secular belief in the human ability and capacity to meet the new challenges of history, overcoming them and creating new forms of society and humanism. In short, this book is not a treatise in lost faith in human ability to make history even under circumstances not of their own choosing. The book speaks consistently to historical realities, human ingenuity, human inventiveness, human agency and ceaseless human struggles to recreate the world.

Scope and organization of the book

This book is organized into three parts. Part I deals with what I call the Colonial Matrix of Power; while Part II covers the discursive constructions. Part III focuses essentially on case Studies and broadly interrogates the postcolonial and liberation predicament; the crisis of dependence (cultural and economic) in relation to ideological explanations; and interpretive conflicts concerning Eurocentrism, decolonization, and politics of integration. The book also discusses three main African problems, namely: the grammar of decolonization, including the question of what is and who is an African; the operationaly mode of coloniality that sustains Western global dominance; and explanations of the entanglement of the 'postcolonial' and 'neocolonial' in present-day Africa. The book also provides deep reflections on the realities of the postcolonial oppressive state and postcolonial realities; African structural contradictions and the problem of epistemology. It is clear from the book how African identity has remained hostage to a modernist grammar and how current autochthonous discourses have their deep roots in African colonial experience traceable to the time of the colonial encounters. Throughout the book, an attempt is made to explain the recurrent logic of violence from a historical perspective.

This book is further divided into eight chapters. The first introduces the politics of the making of the African postcolonial world predicated on concepts of coloniality of power, coloniality of knowledge and coloniality of being. It also provides an overview of key imaginations of the trajectory of Africa spawned by both the independence euphoria of the 1960s and the crisis of the 1970s. Finally it explains how the process of decolonization plunged into neocolonialism world producing a 'postcolonial African neocolonial world' rather than an African postcolonial world inhabited by liberated Africans capable of determining their own destiny.

The second chapter deals with how the African continent and its people have remained ensnared in the invisible but strong colonial matrices of power that descended on the continent since the spread of Western modernity into other parts of the world carried on the backs of explorers, missionaries and colonialists. Despite the celebration of decolonization as a milestone in African history of liberation, Africa has not managed to free itself from epistemological colonization inscribed on the continent and its people by mission and secular schools, religious denominations, and other institutions that carried western cultural imperialism.

The central argument of Chapter 2 is that what exist today as schools, colleges and universities continue to be 'Western-oriented institutions' located within the African continent producing Westernized graduates who are alienated from the African society and its African values. The chapter engages with the important problem of epistemologies of alterity that continue to shape the African trajectory in Western terms and in the process reducing postcolonial Africa into a world of myths of decolonization and illusions of freedom. The result of all this has been ideological confusion informed by cognitive colonization within the continent with some Africans dreaming in both African and European languages, others imbibing lock, stock and barrel the neo-liberal thought as salvation for Africa and others degenerating to nativism and essentialness of African identities into very narrow ones that breed various phobias.

The third chapter re-evaluates the often celebrated decolonization process and reveals the myths and illusions of freedom obscured by the idea of decolonization. Its entry point into unmasking the limits of decolonization is through disentangling the ideas of liberation from those of emancipation as these concepts mean different things if critically examined. It proceeds to analyse how decolonization bequeathed on Africa juridical freedom, that is, freedom for the African state that was enjoyed by those who occupied the positions of the departing white political and economic elites and posits that this juridical freedom did not translate into freedom for the ordinary African people.

The central argument in Chapter 3 is that while those elites who ascended to state power at the time of physical departure of colonial masters celebrated their achievement of freedom and access to wealth as African freedom, the ordinary African citizens had to wage new struggles to either free themselves from the chains of the postcolonial state that became a leviathan or fight to democratize it so as to serve their interests too. The struggle for popular sovereignty is still ongoing in postcolonial Africa, this time ranged against African political elites who have embarked on primitive accumulation of wealth, just like the colonizers, while silencing the citizens. The chapter also captures the complex daily politics of citizens as they struggle to exit, disengage, migrate and evade the postcolonial state that became a new source of oppression and exploitation of citizens. The popular uprisings that rocked the North African region beginning with Tunisia and spreading to Egypt, Libya and others is a testimony of how juridical freedom is being translated by the ordinary people into popular freedom.

The fourth chapter engages the question of the discursive formation of African identities. It begins with interrogation of the construction and development of the idea of Africa beginning with its cartographic origins and the politics of social classification of the world population along racial lines by Europeans using the social Darwinist philosophies and scientific racism of the late nineteenth and early twentieth centuries. Its key argument is that the Africa is not only a social and political construction but also a victim of imposed identities and this reality has made African political trajectories to continue to progress into a ceaseless direction of struggling to negotiate themselves above externally imposed singularities as part of resisting the realities of being 'fenced in' by particular identity markers which they have not chosen for themselves.

The fourth chapter also interrogates the major identity-forming processes such as the slave trade, imperialism, colonialism, pan-Africanism, and nationalism which have combined to form the discursive terrain within which

African identities were constructed across history and space. The chapter ends by grappling with the complex question of who is an African, and provides various historically informed definitions of Africanism -- some generous and inclusionary, and others restrictive and exclusionary.

The fifth chapter addresses the question of the logic of violence in Africa and locates its roots within colonial modernity and its reproduction of African subjectivities where race was not only used to condemn black people into *damnes* (the condemned beings) but also to deny their very humanity. The chapter deploys the concepts of coloniality of being and the racist/imperial Manichean misanthropic scepticism about African humanity as lenses to examine the logic of violence and other abuses that were not allowed in Europe. The case studies of the Herero people of Namibia who became victims of German colonial genocide; the Congolese under King Leopold II where violence was the mode of governance; and South Africa where neo-apartheid situation recreated systemic violence that is manifest in the black townships and informal settlements are used to amplify and qualify arguments advanced in this chapter. The other major concern of the chapter is to explain how colonial violence reproduced itself on the psyche of African nationalists to become a major feature of postcolonial governance.

The sixth chapter provides a detailed case study of the genesis and development of the idea of South Africa from the nineteenth century to the present. This case study is important as it reveals the interplay of imperial, colonial and versions of nationalisms that combined to create a unique African national identity called South African at the end of the twentieth century. The chapter interrogates such identity-forming processes as Anglicization and Afrikaner republican nationalism that culminated in the institutionalization of apartheid. It proceeds to examine African nationalism as another layer in the genealogy of the idea of South Africa.

One of the arguments of Chapter 6 is that African nationalism in its various forms that included radical Africanism of 'Africa for Africans' represented by the Pan-African Congress (PAC), the moderate imagination of a multi-racial nation represented by the African National Congress (ANC), Afro-Marxist workers imaginations of South African nation as a socialist republic represented by the South African Communist Party (SACP), the ethno-cultural imagination of the nation represented by Inkatha Freedom Party (IFP) as well as the decolonization of the mind project represented by the Black Consciousness Movement (BCM), benefitted from being able to consistently reflect on the limits of previous imaginations of the nation and synthesizing these into new ones that culminated in the creation of the current rainbow nation of South Africa in 1994. The chapter ends by reflecting on the current nation-building challenges particularly the efforts at transcending race as an organizing as well as divisive forces in South African society that is striving to re-build itself on principles of non-racial and civic belonging.

The seventh chapter continues the subject of imagination of the nation with a specific focus on the genealogies of the idea of Zimbabwe, another intriguing case study that has attracted international media coverage because of the current socio-economic and political crisis which continues to puzzle policy makers and analysts. This chapter traces the roots of the crisis from politics of the imagination of Zimbabwe in the 1960s where it began from a fallacy that Zimbabwe has primordial roots in the great and noble pre-historic civilization of Great Zimbabwe. The chapter analyse how the liberation struggle itself as a discursive terrain within which the idea of Zimbabwe was being translated from an imaginary phenomenon into reality was not only characterized by retribalization and regional ethnic divisions but also hijacked at the Lancaster House Conference by the British and Americans to produce a neocolonial state of Zimbabwe.

Chapter 7, therefore, begins with the politics of naming of the imagined nation in the 1960s that were imbricated in contesting colonial modernity that denied Africans any respectable past, right through its problematic constructions during the liberation struggle and its formal adoption of the name Zimbabwe as a national identity in 1980. It points to the chequered history of the formation of the idea of Zimbabwe, particularly how it was compromised by forces of ethnicity, regionalism, racism, and neocolonialism resulting in the creation of a deeply tribalized neocolonial state in 1980 and an openly racist state in 2000 as the nationalist leadership struggled to complete the decolonization project, accommodate oppositional forces, and navigate racial and ethnic fault lines.

What has distinguished the Zimbabwe case study from others is not only the crippling politics of violence that has been used to invite different ethnicities and races into a partisanly-imagined nation with little space for pluralism and diversity, but also the fact that it has since 2000 become a direct theatre to stage colonial matrix of power, namely, the disciplining of a small peripheral state for trying to challenge Western hegemony through redistributing land that was owned by the white farming community ('the children of the empire') with roots in Rhodesian settler colonialism. Up till today, the idea of Zimbabwe remains a highly contested one with questions of belonging and citizenship being mediated by race, ethnicity and access to material resources and continuing to generate political and communal conflicts some thirty years after the end of direct colonialism.

The last chapter looks into the future of Africa through contextualizing the continent's ideological, political and economic challenges, predicaments and dilemmas within the global context where disillusionment with radical politics reigns and where uncertainty is rife about the future trajectory of humanity in general, beyond the current neoliberal meta-narratives. The chapter introduces the concept of phenomenology of uncertainty and utopian registers deployed by Africans and other human beings elsewhere to imagine the future. Utopian registers of civil society and public sphere are interpreted as part of African aspirational politics emerging from the phenomenology of uncertainty.

As part of concluding remarks, the last chapter also revisits African nationalism with a view to revealing its weak social base that made it fail to create stable nations and to prosper as an emancipatory and liberatory force. The chapter further discusses the limits of neo-liberal democracy as an emancipatory project provides glimpses of the future political direction of Africa.

2

In the Snare of Colonial Matrix of Power

Introduction

> The repression fell, above all, over the modes of knowing, of producing knowledge, of producing perspectives, images and systems of images, symbols, modes of signification, over the resources, patterns, and instruments of formalised and objectivised expression, intellectual or visual. It was followed by the imposition of the use of the rulers' own patterns of expression, and of their beliefs and images with reference to the supernatural. [...] The colonisers also imposed a mystified image of their own patterns of producing knowledge and meaning. At first, they placed these patterns far out of reach of the dominated. Later, they taught them in a partial and selective way, in order to co-opt some of the dominated into their own power institutions. Then European culture was made seductive: it gave access to power. After all, beyond repression, the main instrument of all power is its seduction. [...] European culture became a universal cultural model. The imaginary in the non-European cultures could hardly exist today and, above all, reproduce itself outside of these relations.
>
> (Anibal Quijano 2007: 169)

Africa is still entangled and trapped within the snares of the colonial matrix of power. Quijano (2007: 168-178) identified the key contours of the colonial matrix of power as consisting of four interrelated domains: control of economy; control of authority, control of gender and sexuality; and, control of subjectivity and knowledge. This chapter deals with the impact of this colonial order on the African continent and the African minds since the onset of colonial encounters. Frantz Fanon correctly noted that colonialism was never simply contented with imposing of its grammar and logic upon the 'present and the future of a dominated country'. Colonialism was also not simply satisfied with merely holding the colonized people in its grip and emptying 'the native's brain of all form and content'. Rather, 'By a kind of perverse logic, it turns to the past of the oppressed people, and distorts it, disfigures and destroys it' (Fanon 1961: 67).

It is therefore important to track the mechanics and manifestations of the inscription of hegemonic Western forms of knowledge and coloniality of power and to unpack how colonial modernity succeeded in pushing African forms of knowledge into the barbarian margins; and by that fact depriving African people of initiative and agency to take control of their destinies. The chapter focuses on the processes of universalizing Western particularism through epistemological colonization (colonization of the mind) that de-centred pre-existing African knowledge systems. It posits that the worst form of colonization of a people is that which created epistemological mimicry and intellectual dependency. As Quijano (2007: 169) observes,, this 'colonization of the imagination of the dominated' remains the worst form as it dealt with and shaped people's consciousness and identity. Our concern here is the manifestation of 'coloniality' rather than 'colonialism'. Nelson Maldonado-Torres has differentiated coloniality and colonialism in this way:

> Coloniality is different from colonialism. Colonialism denotes a political and eco-nomic relation in which the sovereignty of a nation or a people rests on the power of another nation, which makes such nation an empire. Coloniality, instead, refers to long-standing patterns of power that emerged as a result of colonialism, but that define culture, labour, intersubjective relations, and knowledge production well beyond the strict limits of colonial administrations. Thus coloniality survives colo-nialism. It is maintained alive in books, in the criteria for academic performance, in cultural patterns, in common sense, in the self-image of people, in aspirations of self, and so many other aspects of our modern experience. In a way, as modern subjects we breathe coloniality all the time and everyday (Maldonad-Torres 2007: 243).

Toyin Falola (2001: 262) also emphasized this same point by admitting that the impact of the West 'is even more direct'. What began as colonial encounters in the fifteenth century produced both historical and intellectual realities mediated by inferior-superior relations.

> As a historical reality, Africa was integrated into an international system on terms defined by the West. African intellectuals cannot escape the reality of this integra-tion. Neither can they escape the fact that the ideology that drives scholarship is controlled by the West nor that what African scholars have done is primarily to respond. For instance, nationalist historiography was a response; so was cultural nationalism before it, and both faced the challenge of countering negative Euro-centric ideas about Africa (Falola 2001: 262).

Mapping the key contours of colonial matrix of power

The colonial encounters of the fifteenth century set in motion a new constitution of the world order as Western modernity exported its darker aspects to the non-Western world. The initial peaceful colonial encounters were soon followed by direct political, social and cultural domination that engulfed the African continent mediated principally by force of arms and evangelism that mollified and softened African imagination and consciousness while stealing their souls and destroying their sense of being. A lot has already been written about colonization of Africa and how Africans resisted being dominated and there is no need to venture into that terrain here. What needs to be further analysed though is how colonialism has continued to wreck havoc on the mind of the ex-colonized after the end of direct colonialism. One of the enduring legacies of colonialism was its ability to universalize Western particularism. Ernesto Laclau captures this point quite well:

> The crucial issue here is that there was no intellectual means of distinguishing between European particularism and the universal functions that it was supposed to incarnate, given that European universalism had constructed its identity precisely through the cancellation of the logic of incarnation and, as a result, through the universalisation of its own particularism. So, European imperialist expansion had to be presented in terms of a universal civilizing function, modernisation and so forth. The resistances of other cultures were, as a result, presented not as struggles between particular identities and cultures, but as part of an all-embracing and epochal struggle between universality and particularisms—the notion of people without history expressing precisely their incapacity to represent the universal (Laclau, 1996: 24).

What began as violent colonization was accompanied by various epistemological interventions, some religious and others secular. Therefore, any systematic mapping of the making of the colonial world and inscription of the colonial modernity in Africa is basically a study of the history of global power construction whose structure and framework continues to shape social and political relations across the globe. Quijano (2007: 168-9) has correctly noted that:

> [...] it is very clear that the large majority of the exploited, the dominated, the discriminated against, are precisely the members of the 'races,' 'ethnies,' or 'nations' into which the colonized populations, were categorised in the formative process of that world power, from the conquest of America and onward.

One of the terrible consequences of the colonialism was to destroy the full gamut of alternative modernities together with alternative imaginations of the world that were not necessarily influenced and unleashed by Protestantism, European Renaissance, Enlightenment and Industrial Revolution.

Independent African contribution to the shaping of global cultural order was denied by colonialism. Instead, human history in general became hostage to the Western worldview and ultimately, what we know as Europe, America, Latin America, Asia, Oceania, Caribbean and Africa became largely social and political creations of Europeans. Global history became conceived as a continuum running from:

> [...] the primitive to the civilised; from the traditional to the modern; from the savage to the rational; from pro-capitalism to capitalism [...] And Europe thought of itself as the mirror of the future of all the other societies and cultures; as the advanced form of the history of the entire species. What does not cease to surprise, however, is that Europe succeeded in imposing that 'mirage' upon the practical totality of the cultures that it colonised; and, much more, that this chimera is still so attractive to so many (Quijano 2007: 196).

Europe and America have appropriated human ideas of progress, civilization and developmentalism as exclusive virtues of Western modernity that had to be exported to other parts of the world.

Idea of progress and developmentalism

The idea of progress rooted in Enlightenment became a gift that Europe had power to export to the non-Western World. This idea became lodged within the notion of the civilizing mission and its justification of violent colonial conquest of the non-Western world in general, and Africa in particular -- which was christened as pacification of barbarous tribes and taming of savages. The idea of progress asserted the possibility of a conscious rational reform of society based on virtues of science and other secular knowledges. Within Europe the idea of progress treated each individual as a free-centred-subject with rational control over his or her destiny. European nation-states were considered sovereign and free to control their progressive development and shape their destinies rationally. The non-Western world, on the other hand, was said to lack rationality; and progress and this lack was used to justify imperialism and colonialism. The African historian, Paul Tiyambe Zeleza, had this to say about colonial developmentalism:

> As an ideology of colonial and neo-colonial modernity, developmentalism was born during the Great Depression and bred into a hegemonic discourse in the immediate aftermath of the Second World War. The seeds were sown with the 1929 British Colonial and Welfare Act. They turned into sturdy developmentalist weeds under the Colonial Development and Welfare Act of 1945. It was in co-lonial Africa that most of these seeds and weeds were nurtured. It was there that

the term development lost its naturalistic innocence and acquired the conceited meaning of economic growth modelled on the West (Zeleza 1997: 218).

Beyond its colonial roots, developmentalism, just like the idea of progress; is a child of Enlightenment and modernity. Grosfoguel (2000: 348-349) argued that: 'Developmentalism is linked to liberal ideology and to the idea of progress. [...] Developmentalism became a global ideology of the capitalist world-economy'. At the same time, developmentalism became another lever of justifying Western intervention and interference in the internal affairs of Africa. Within Eurocentric thinking, development and modernization were conflated into one thing. The lack of Western modernization was therefore equated with the lack of development. But it was after the Second World War that the term 'underdevelopment' was used by President Harry Truman of the United States of America in his speech of 1949 to describe the non-Western part of the world. Critical scholars like Wolfgang Sachs (1992) described the representation of the non-Western world as another form of 'Othering' of Africa as a humanitarian case that deserved Western intervention.

The idea of development of non-Western countries became subject to various debates since its emergence alongside colonial modernity. One problem was that as an idea that originated with Eurocentrism, it implied that development of any kind could only take place within the parameters of the capitalist world system that manifested its ugly face within the non-Western world in terms of the slave trade, imperialism and colonialism. The idea of development assumed hegemonic tendencies whereby it denied other imaginations of progress and development not rooted in Enlightenment and Western modernity. There was no tolerance for precolonial notions of development that did not resemble those of the Western world. In short, anything that did not resemble what the Western world knew was dismissed as not yet developed or dismissed outright as a relic of barbarism.

In the 1970s, such critical scholars as Andre Gunder Frank (1976), Samir Amin (1974), and Walter Rodney (1973) were concerned with explaining the problems of underdevelopment that were manifest within the formerly colonised parts of the world. Their intellectual interventions grappled with the impact of the colonial matrix of power on development within peripheral societies. They interrogated the dialectics of the centre-periphery relations that were created by colonial modernity and located the roots of underdevelopment in this exploitative relationship within which the ex-colonial powers continued to reap economic benefits from the former colonial world to develop their nations at the expense of the ex-colonized peoples.

These scholars revealed that such processes as mercantilism, the slave trade, imperialism, colonialism, neocolonialism and globalization had the enduring effect of creating development in the North while generating underdevelopment in the South. There is no doubt that colonialism created dependency of the ex-colonized societies on finished products manufactured by ex-colonial powers. African consumption patterns, tastes and values were drastically shaped by colonial modernity to resemble those of the West.

While dependency scholars were criticised for privileging external structural factors in their explanation of underdevelopment of Africa at the expense of internal ones, but there is no denying that they correctly unearthed a particular and important economic dimension of the colonial matrix of power that continued to wreck havoc on Africa and other formerly colonized parts of the world. It is also becoming clear that any analysis of the fundamental contradiction of the capital-labour question in Africa cannot be fully understood without a clear understanding of the principal contradiction of the centre-periphery problem created by imperialism, colonialism and capitalism.

I, therefore, do not see the value of criticizing the dependency theory for being pessimistic on the future development prospects of Africa. For instance, Leys' (1996) criticism of dependency theory for not being clear on the definition of 'development'; for being unclear on the question of oppression and exploitation of the masses in underdeveloped countries; for being economistic and too broad; for treating imperialism as an 'extra'; for being vague on its central unit of analysis; and, for not explaining why more capital was not invested and accumulated in the Third World, is not convincing and does not succeed in disqualifying the contribution of dependency theory to the understanding of the African and Third world predicaments as emanating from its links with the world capitalist system. To expect a single theory to answer all these questions is in fact to be unrealistic. Theories are not answer-books but attempts to explain problems from various perspectives.

Leys also ignores the fact that interventions of dependency theorists of various schools of thought competed from start to finish with the imperial-inspired modernization paradigm well represented by Walt W. Rostow (1960:2) and his stages of modernization. Modernization theory interpreted the processes of economic and social development as a natural phenomenon that followed evolutionary path from traditional society to capitalist development. Modernization thinking was deeply Eurocentric and it put the Northern nations at the apex of the economic development ladder and Africa at the lowest level. Within the modernization discourse, Africa was in the traditional stage of development and its path of development was to follow the steps that were taken by European and American nations. Historical peculiarities and particularities that explained the condition of the African continent were ignored.

The key crisis in the modernization paradigm was its assumption of a 'universalistic, neutral, objective point of view' that was informed by hiding the locale (locus of enunciation) of its analysis (Grosfoguel 2007: 213). Within the modernization paradigm in its many guises and variants, Africa's problem was that it was not yet like Europe. Development was assumed to be a linear process with clearly identifiable stages. Within mainstream discourses of development, modernization continues to influence thinking while hiding dangers of colonial matrices of power. There is need to unveil the 'naked emperor' hidden within discourses of development has been assuming new names and vocabularies of deception since the end of the Second World War. Cornwell (2010) has engaged in a fruitful exercise of deconstructing the development discourse with a view to unveiling what is hidden behind 'buzzwords' and 'fuzzwords'. Cornwell (2010: 16) correctly noted that 'reflections on the language of development evoke bigger questions about the world-making projects that they define and describe'.

On the other hand dependency scholars blamed the global South's relative underdevelopment and problems on such broad processes as mercantilism, imperialism and colonialism. They also alerted the world on how Africa and Africans were frog-marched as they fought, kicked and screamed into the evolving capitalist world system, without being allowed to make any choices of their own. The world economic accumulation system a core target of critical analysis unmasked the colonial matrix of power in the process. This dependency theorists' locus of enunciation of development was the South where economic progress was problematic. Unless one looks at the problem of the African continent from the right location in the spectrum of global power relations, Africans will continue to be blamed for the crisis in which they find themselves.

While dependency scholarship managed to bring forth some new ideas explaining the African condition from a radical perspective that was very critical of Western modernity and the power relations it introduced into Africa, it also blundered on many accounts. In the first place, the thinking was trapped in the Western modernist-developmentalist ideology which made the boundaries of its interventions limited epistemologically. At least Grosfoguel's

(2000: 361) criticism of the epistemological poverty of dependency theory is well taken. He noted that:

> Dependency questions were trapped in the problematic of modernity. [...] Dependency assumed the modernist idea that progress was possible through a rational organization of society, where each nation-state could achieve an autonomous national development through the conscious, sovereign, and free control of their destiny.

Dependency thought also reproduced the myths and illusions that even within the periphery, autonomous development and rational economic organization could be achieved under the control of the nation-state. Remember Kwame Nkrumah's dictum of 'seek ye the political kingdom and all will be added on it'. Dependency theorists tended to minimize the fundamental reality that all so-called postcolonial African nation-states were not free from structures of the capitalist world system. Delinking rooted in revolutionary processes taking place within individual states is a myth. Grosfoguel (2000: 362) described this myth by saying, 'Therefore, a global problem cannot have a national solution.' The solution must also be pitched at the global level spearheaded by transnational radical social movements of the people of the South such as the World Social Forum.

But the works of dependency scholars like Fernando Henrique Cardoso and Enzo Faletto contributed new concepts to the development discourse some of which still make a lot of sense as analytical categories today. These include 'dependency' that referred to the conditions of being remotely controlled and dominated from a particular centre; 'periphery' that referred to the subordinated role underdeveloped economies played in the international markets; and 'underdevelopment' that referred to a situation of economic poverty created by capitalist operations outside Europe (Cardoso 1979). While the coining of these terms went hand-in-hand with the myth of dependent nation-states being able to develop sustainable economic systems without having an autonomous control over the decision-making process, they extended frontiers of knowledge in the field of development studies.

The other useful terms and typologies produced by dependency thinkers include: 'autonomous-developed centres' as a reference to Western nations; 'dependent-developed peripheral centres' as a reference to countries like Brazil and Argentina in the 1970s; 'autonomous-underdeveloped non-peripheral states' that included Cuba and China; 'dependent-underdeveloped peripheral states' that included the entire African states and others in Latin America and other ex-colonized parts of the world. If used with care these typologies are not really useless. All countries of the postcolonial neocolonized world suffer from various forms of dependent-development (Cardoso 1979).

But how do we explain the ability of countries like Botswana, Mauritius and South Africa that are doing far much better economically than the rest of Africa on the development index? Are they free from the chains of dependent-development or are they shining examples of possibilities of dependent-development? Grosfoguel (2000: 371) provided part of the answer when he argued that: 'The capitalist world-system gains credibility by developing a few successful semi-peripheral cases. These are civilizational and cultural strategies to gain consent and to demonstrate the "superiority" of the "West".' The West does this by favouring a few countries in the non-Western world to showcase as success stories while in the process reproducing its hegemony through the developmentalist ideology. Such showcases often received disproportionately large sums of foreign aid and flexible terms to pay their debts. Outside Africa, examples of showcases included Taiwan and South Korea. This argument, however, must not be used to deny the ingenuity of some non-Western states that enabled them to forge ahead economically even within the debilitating effects of the colonial matrix of power.

In the 1980s, new researchers emerged who sought to explain the African condition through postcolonial theoretical interventions of different types, ranging from post-structuralism, postmodernism and postcolonialism. While some of the theoretical interventions of postcolonial theorists have extended the frontiers of knowledge on the African condition and deepened our understanding of the postcolonial world, the main problem is that the focus on hybridities, negotiations, blending, syncretism, mimicry, and borderlands end up overshadowing the deeply negative and violent structural rather than agential processes that were unleashed by the spreading of European modernity through mercantilism, imperialism, colonialism, neo-colonialism and neo-liberalism. These processes were never peaceful to the extent of inscribing themselves on the African continent through sharing of cultures and negotiation of discursive spaces (Chakrabarty 1992; Bhabha 1994; Appiah 1992; Spivak 1990; Mbembe 2001; Mbembe 2002).

At another level, the 'posts' (post-structuralism, postmodernism and postcolonialism) were accused of depicting Western modernity's spread from its centre in Europe via mercantilism, imperialism and colonialism as mainly mediated by the blending of cultures leading to the emergence of hybridities and for minimizing the negative impact of these processes that led Africa to occupy a subaltern position within world history and the world capitalist accumulation system (Zeleza 2003; Zeleza 2007; Parry 1995). Paul Zeleza noted that:

However, the posts emerged, or were named as discursive systems, in northern institutional locations. The production and promotion of the posts in the 1970s and 1980s as Northern intellectual fads gave them a distinctly Western accent, if not grammar, that did not resonate well with the intellectual and ideological languages of the South, even though, as is true of postcolonial theory, some of the leading theorists hailed from the South and were only translocated in the North (Zeleza 2003: 1).

What is made poignant here is the locus of enunciation of the African experience. As articulated by Grosfoguel (2007) the key problem is that even those socially located in the oppressed and exploited side of global power and colonial difference, end up thinking epistemically like those on dominant side of global power relations. This is considered to be one of the key weaknesses of the 'posts'. Zeleza (2006b: 89-129) has engaged with what he termed the 'troubled encounter between postcolonialism and African history' rooted in ideological and ethical imperatives as well as 'apparent intellectual and epistemic incongruities'. Zeleza (2006b: 89) is one of the strongest advocates and defenders of 'nationalist humanism in the African imaginary' and the 'historic agendas of African historiography'.

Zeleza provided a series of criticism of the 'posts'. His first critique is that the 'posts' emerged in the Anglo-American academy in the mid-1980s in the wake of the rise of post-structuralism and postmodernism. Their roots were not African. Key postcolonial theorists like Homi Bhabha and others were said to be located in the citadels of capitalism where they were beneficiaries rather than victims of the capitalist exploitative system. As such their post-colonialism was seen as aimed at avoiding making deep sense of the African crisis that originated in structures of global capitalism. Zeleza's argument is supported by Ahmad (1992) who categorized the 'posts' as part of imperialism's ideological armoury to weaken and decentre African struggles for liberation, democracy and socialism. Ahmad accused the 'posts' of 'having mystified the ways in which totalising structures persist in the midst of apparent disintegration and fluidity' (Ahmad 1992: 315).

Zeleza is of the idea that the 'posts' have abandoned categories of nation and class through mischievous celebration of hybridity and borderlands and in the process encouraging 'the sanitization and depiction of imperialism and colonialism as shared cultures, negotiated discursive spaces' (Zeleza 2006b: 124; Dirk 2000). One of Zeleza's key interventions is that:

> The multiplication of identities, memories, and resistances surely must not be used to forget that larger contexts, the hierarchies of power between the coloniser and the colonised, Europe and Africa, the unequal impact of empire had and left behind for

the metropoles and the colonies, the fact that imperial power was upheld by physical force not simply ideas and images, that it was underpinned by material structures not simply ideological constructs, by political economy not simply by discursive economy. The erasures of revolution, nation, class, history, and reality turn the 'posts', even if they may have started as critiques, into legitimating ideologies of contemporary global configurations of power and production (Zeleza 2006b: 124).

Zeleza (2006b: 125) is worried that postcolonialism's fixation on colonialism might result in the re-inscription of 'Eurocentrism back on the pedestal' despite the years of efforts by African historians to install African nationalist historiography in its place since the 1960s. His concern is to 'recentre African history by deepening and globalising it in its temporary scope and spatial scale, taking seriously the place of Africa in world history' (Zeleza 2006b: 128). My position on this is that the 'posts' and political economy must be forced to speak to each other, complement each other and reinforce each other's intervention if the African condition is to be clearly understood.

Pal Ahluwalia, is an ardent defender of postcolonial theory is critical of scholars who casually link postcolonial theory with post-structuralism and post-modernism. He says:

> Such a reading denigrates the authenticity of post-colonial theory and renders it subservient and theoretically vulnerable to charges levelled at post-structuralism and postmodernism (Ahluwalia 2001: 1).

Ahluwalia argues for differentiation between postcolonialism and other 'posts'. To him, postcolonialism's core pre-occupation is 'about understanding the dilemmas of modernization and the manner in which African states negotiate their way through complexities that have grown out of the colonial experience' (Ahluwalia 2001: 1). According to him, postcolonialism is a counter-discourse which seeks to disrupt the cultural hegemony of the modern West with all its imperial structures of feeling and knowledge. On the other hand, postmodernism is primarily a counter-discourse against modernism (Ahluwalia 2001: 6). In short, postcolonialism as a theory recognizes that colonialism is an ongoing process and is not antagonistic to nationalist historiographies and pan-Africanism.

The tragedy of the African continent and its people is that of forced 'dependency' and reduction of Africans to 'copycats' of other people. Africans were bundled, entangled, woven, and entrapped into the colonial matrix of global power that is tilted in favour of the Northern industrialized nations economically and politically. This entanglement is underpinned by what Mignolo (2007: 159) correctly termed 'tyranny of abstract universals'. The dependency I am talking about is an epistemological one that is at the base of all African economic, political and social problems. It is a result of imperial and colonial processes of silencing, decentring, and relegating of African epistemologies to barbarian margins.

This tragedy stands as an indictment on Western modernity, particularly the way it forced itself violently on the African continent and on the African people's lives. It is well captured by Hubert Vilakazi in these words:

> The peculiar situation here is that knowledge of the principles and patterns of African civilisation remained with ordinary, uncertified men and women, especially of those in rural areas. The tragedy of African civilisation is that Western-educated Africans became lost and irrelevant as intellectuals who could develop African civilisation further. Historically, intellectuals of any civilisation are the voices of that civilisation to the rest of the world; they are the instruments of the development of the higher culture of that civilisation. The tragedy of Africa, after conquest by the West, is that her intellectuals, by and large, absconded and abdicated their role as developers, minstrels and trumpeters of African civilisation. African civilisation then stagnated; what remained alive in the minds of languages of the overwhelming majority of Africans remained undeveloped. Uncertified Africans are denied respect and opportunities for development; they could not sing out, articulate and develop the unique patterns of African civilisation (Vilakazi 1999: 203).

What is celebrated in some circles today as universalism or global or 'common interests' were not arrived at through peaceful means of cultural negotiations, mutual borrowings or gradual cross-cultural blending as some postcolonial theorists want us to believe. Conquest, violence and exploitation dominated the relations between Africa and that part of the world today calling itself the 'civilized world' or the 'free world'. If there is indeed a 'free world' then there is an 'un-free world' and Africa is part of the latter.

In the first place, Africans and their continent are 'un-free' because they were drawn into the evolving world capitalist system fighting, crying and kicking from the time of the slave trade to the present global age (Ndlovu-Gatsheni 2007: 160-189). In the second place, Africa is 'un-free' because its power to determine its economic, political and social destiny is circumscribed by global power dynamics and unequal world economic order that unfolded from the slave trade, through imperialism, colonialism, neocolonialism up to the current global information age that radiates from the western metropolitan centres.

While the dawn of Western modernity bequeathed on the West new technologies that gave it the political, economic and military power to dominate the world, this same process unleashed havoc on the African continent such as imperial capitalism, slavery, colonialism, apartheid, neo-colonialism and neoliberalism. However hard some apologists of colonialism try to say the exploitative processes of slavery, imperialism, and colonialism were behind us as Africans, the truth remains that since the dawn of modernity, the African continent has never gained freedom to take control of its economic, political and social destiny.

Taken together, these processes have all been negative on Africa—the negative impact far outweighed their incidental and accidental positive impacts. It was within these processes that 'epistemological dependency' was created. Within this set of things, the West eventually emerged as representing the 'haves' in terms of democracy in abundance to export to other parts of the globe; civilization in abundance to embark on 'civilizing mission' in Africa, progressive religion in abundance to export Christianity to Africa, and economic development in abundance to lecture Africans on efficient management of economies, ethics in abundance to lecture Africans on corruption. On the other hand, Africa emerged as representing the 'have nots' and this is well put by Grosfoguel (2007: 214):

> We went from the sixteenth century characterisation of 'people without writing' to eighteenth and nineteenth century characterisation of 'people without history,' to the twentieth century characterisation of 'people without development' and more recently, to the early twenty-first century of 'people without democracy.'

This was the discourse of construction of epistemological dependency within which Africans were marked by lack and deficiencies whereas the West was said to be progressing very well from the 'rights of people', in the sixteenth century to the eighteenth century 'rights of man' and to late twentieth century 'human rights' (Grosfoguel 2007: 214). Quijano provides a comprehensive and useful genealogical unfolding of epistemological colonization of the dominated peoples:

> In the beginning colonialism was a product of a systematic repression, not only of specific beliefs, ideas, images, symbols or knowledge that were not useful to global colonial domination, while at the same time the colonisers were expropriating from the colonised their knowledge, especially in mining, agriculture, engineering, as well as their products and work (Quijano 2007: 169).

The implications were dangerous and have endured to this day. The colonizers became the originators of progressive knowledge (science) and Africans became producers of fatalistic superstitions and mythologies (Wiredu 1980). Western ideation systems mystified themselves and were pitched far above the reach of the dominated Africans except for very few individuals that were trained to assist with colonial administration. The Western way of life and culture was made seductive as the only gate-way to power, dignity and full humanism. It was transformed into a 'civilization standard'. Western culture assumed universality, becoming a standard bearer of development. Quijano (2007: 169) rightly noted that, 'The imaginary in the non-European cultures could hardly exist today and, above all, reproduce itself outside of these relations.' In short, the Africa that exists today is the creation of Western hegemonic thought that subordinated everything in Africa as they pushed Europe and North America into the top level end of the civilization and development ladder.

Coloniality and the limits of decolonization

The path to decolonization was rough. It passed through reverses and compromises and was sabotaged by those within and external to it. It was, therefore, never taken to its logical conclusion. And because of the miscarriage of decolonization, Africa has never been afforded any space to recapture the power to decide the course of its destiny. Whenever Africans tried to capture and put the destiny of their nations into their own hands, the powerful forces of the colonial matrix of power were quicker to interrupt, de-centre and discipline the initiatives. Nothing was ever subjected to as much disciplining as African nationalism and pan-Africanism. Their true champions suffered isolation, sanctions, assassinations and coups (see Chapter 1).

Mental colonization is the hardest part to decolonize and the worst form of colonialism. It stole the African souls, invaded their consciousness, destroyed and distorted their imagination of the future. This crisis was well captured by Zeleza (2006: 124) when he posited that: 'Foreclosed are the possibilities of visioning a world beyond the present, imagining alternatives to capitalist modernity.' It was so terrible that even those Africans who initiated the political decolonization of the continent were the worst affected by mental colonialism. All of the founding fathers of postcolonial Africa were graduates from colonial schools and Western universities.

No wonder then that what they fought for was initially simply part of their desire to be included within the colonial state. It was only after they were not accepted that they then mobilized workers and peasants to fight against the colonial state. But they never lost the terrible tendency of standing astride the African world they were taught and socialized to hate, and the European world they were seduced to aspire to and to like. The founding fathers of African nations had deeply bifurcated consciousness that made them dream in both European and African languages. This analysis is very important because it reveals the epistemological roots of the limits of decolonization. According Ramon Grosfoguel:

> One of the most powerful myths of the twentieth century was the notion that the elimination of colonial administrations amounted to decolonisation of the world. This led to the myth of a 'postcolonial' world. The heterogeneous and multiple global structures put in place over a period of 450 years did not evaporate with the juridical-political decolonisation of the periphery over the past 50 years. We continue to live under the same 'colonial power matrix.' With juridical-political decolonisation, we moved from a period of 'global colonialism' to the current period of 'global coloniality.' Although 'colonial administrations' have been almost entirely eradicated and the majority of the periphery is politically organised into independent states, non-European people are still living under crude European/ Euro-American exploitation and domination (Grosfoguel 2007: 219).

The crucial point here is to emphasize the distinction between 'colonialism' and 'coloniality.' Grosfoguel further makes this distinction clearer:

> Coloniality allows us to understand the continuity of colonial forms of domination after the end of colonial administrations, produced by colonial cultures and structures in the modern/colonial capitalist/patriarchal world-system. 'Coloniality of power' refers to a crucial structuring process in the modern/colonial world-system that articulates peripheral locations in the international labour division with the global racial/ethnic hierarchy and Third World migrants' inscription in the racial/ethnic hierarchy of metropolitan global cities. In this sense, there is a periphery outside and inside the core zones and there is a core inside and outside the peripheral regions (Grosfoguel 2007: 219-220).

What Grosfoguel is saying is what is generally referred to as 'neo-colonialism' in Africa. He uses a more fitting term 'global coloniality' that is currently imposed through and maintained via the International Monetary Fund (IMF) and the World Bank conditionalities and trade regimes. It is high time Africans woke up from the mythology about decolonization of the continent because, as Grosfoguel says, this mythology only obscures the terrible continuities between the colonial past and current global colonial/racial hierarchies (Grosfoguel 2007: 220). Believing in the mythology of decolonization contributes to the hiding and 'invisibility' of coloniality today. As long as coloniality continues, then independence of Africa is just an illusion.

In an article entitled 'A Battle for Global Values', the former British Prime Minister Tony Blair urged the Western and American powers to intensify the globalization of their values systems and traditions as global norms. To him, Euro-American/Anglo-Saxon values represented humanity's progress throughout the ages. In his justification of the 'war against terror' and occupation of Iraq, Blair stated that these values were fought for and defended over time. The key task of the 'civilised' world, according to him, was to demonstrate that Euro-American values were not. 'Western, still less American or Anglo-Saxon, but values in the common ownership of humanity, universal values that should be the right of the global citizen' (Blair 2007: 3-4).

Knowledge production has continued to reinforce Western hegemony over the African continent; and the schools, colleges and universities continue to contribute towards universalization of Western values. There is need for an African epistemological rebellion entailing putting the African experience at the centre of intellectualism and the African taking a leading role in the production of situated and relevant knowledge.

Towards African epistemological freedom

Knowledge production in Africa is deeply ensnared within the colonial matrix of power and reproduces Western ideational domination on the African continent. What is needed in Africa is a decolonization of knowledge consisting of a double movement of consistently deconstructing and fracturing Euro-American 'geo-political location of theology, secular philosophy and scientific reason' while at the same time 'simultaneously affirming the modes and principles of knowledge that have been denied by the rhetoric of Christianisation, civilisation, progress, development, market democracy' (Mignolo 2007: 463). Zeleza (2003: 97) emphasized the need for African universities and African intellectuals to overcome dependence, to Africanize global scholarship and global African scholarship, to produce knowledge that address and explain the problems and possibilities facing the peoples, economies, societies and cultures of Africa.

But the key to African success in decolonizing knowledge is dependent on successfully fighting for political and economic autonomy. Power and knowledge, as Michel Foucault made clear, are inextricably intertwined. Foucault elaborated on the genealogical birth of human and social sciences as part of Western culture, emphasizing that the epistemological field 'traversed by the human sciences was not laid down in advance' as there was 'no philosophy, no political or moral option, no empirical science of any kind, no observation of the human body, no analysis of sensation, imagination, or the passions' ever encountered in the seventeenth century (Foucault 1972: 344). According to him, the historical emergence of each one of the human sciences was occasioned by a problem and necessity as well as the new norms imposed by industrial society upon individuals (Foucault 1972: 344-345). In the same manner, African academics and intellectuals must engage in the production of knowledge that addresses the current African problems created by colonial modernity.

At the centre of colonial modernity that introduced Western epistemology to the African continent were three key variables: knowledge, racism and capital. Mignolo (2007: 477-478) says:

> As a matter of fact, the modern/colonial world cannot be conceived except as simultaneously capitalist. The logic of coloniality is, indeed, the implementation of capitalist appropriation of land, exploitation of labour and accumulation of wealth in fewer and fewer hands. [...] The control of knowledge in Western Christendom belonged to Western Christian men, which meant the world would be conceived only from the perspective of Western Christian Men (emphasis in the original source).

Imperial knowledge was deployed to repress colonized subjectivities and the process proceeded from there to construct structures of knowledge informed by experiences of African humiliation and marginalization. Consequently, African people have continued to be major consumers of ideas generated in the West and tested on the African soil and on African minds. This reality has forced some African scholars to call for a liberatory Afrocentric epistemology as a remedy to the hegemonic Western epistemology. According to Archie Mafeje:

> Afrocentrism is nothing more than a legitimate demand that African scholars study their society from inside and cease to be purveyors of an alienated intellectual discourse [...] when Africans speak for themselves and about themselves, the world will hear the authentic voice, and will be forced to come to terms with it in the long-run [...]. If we are adequately Afrocentric the international implications will not be lost on others (Mafeje 2000: 66-67).

What the African struggle for a decolonized knowledge involved is not only engagement with fundamentalist socio-economic and political processes like imperialism but also with paradigms, theories, perspectives and methodologies that 'inferorize, misrepresent, and oversimplify African experiences, conditions, and realities' (Zeleza 2003: 97). Contributing to the debate on the decolonization of the African mind through de-westernization of the social sciences, Claude Ake said:

> Every prognostication indicates that Western social science continues to play a major role in keeping us subordinate and underdeveloped; it continues to inhibit our understanding of the problems of our world, to feed us noxious values and false hopes, to make us pursue policies which undermine our competitive strength

and guarantee our permanent underdevelopment and dependence. It is becoming increasingly clear that we cannot overcome our underdevelopment and dependence unless we try to understand the imperialist character of Western social science and to exorcise the attitudes of mind which it inculcates (Ake 1979: ii).

This means that the African struggle for decolonization had to extend to the realm of ideas where colonialism remained hanging and dominant like a nightmare on the minds of Africans long after direct colonial administration was defeated. While some African intellectuals have begun the struggle to challenge and question the legitimacy, truths and relevance of knowledge emanating from the West for Africa together with its grammar of alterity and thematics of neutral, objective, universal, monolithic, timeless and abstract knowledge, there is no substantial change on the ground (Mlambo 2006; Obi 2001).

At the centre of the African search for self-knowing are six core concerns which are about complete African self-rule, self-regeneration, self-understanding, self-definition, self-knowing, and self-articulation of African issues after centuries of domination and de-oracization/silencing. Unlike Achille Mbembe (2002a, 2002b), who dismisses these legitimate African concerns as nativism and Afro-radicalism, these aspirations form a core part of quests for freedom, development and identity, in a world still dominated by Western particularistic worldviews that have been universalized and globalized.

In an essay on the 125th Anniversary of the Berlin Conference, the Ghanaian novelist Ayi Kweyi Armah used the term 'Berlin consensus' to describe a process rather than an event through which Europeans configured African space and time in ways beneficial to themselves. He used the term 'Berlin consensus' metaphorically to refer to one of the nerve centres of 'coloniality of power'—that global hegemonic model of power in place since the partition and conquest of Africa that articulated race and labour, space and peoples, according to the needs of capital and to the benefit of European peoples. The process has postdated direct colonial administration. Armah prefers to characterize the Berlin consensus as a process of 'dismemberment of Africa'. He likened the Berlin Conference of 1884-85 to the 'butchering of a huge elephant for sharing among jubilant hunter kin' (Armah 2010: 5).

Within this scheme of things, the Bible and Christianity played a central role in the inscription of Western epistemology, giving it a moral touch and divine dimension. Biblical teaching tempered with African spiritualities wrecked havoc on the development of African consciousness and identity.

In the words of Ngugi wa Thiong'o (2005), Christianity became a grand re-naming ritual in Africa, with those Africans who converted to it being given European names as part of violating and destroying their being and reconstructing it in European terms.

At the present moment, Africans are torn apart between resignation to the Berlin consensus including the neoliberal call for Africans to board the globalization train as quickly as possible if they are to develop to the levels of the Westerners, and the struggle to embrace the African Renaissance that seeks to re-assert the primacy of African ideas as key weapons in the struggle to reverse the imperatives of the Berlin consensus and replace it with the African consensus. The construction of the African consensus has been a long, painstaking and complex pedigree that began with anti-slavery slave revolts, primary resistance, initiatives such as Ethiopianism, Garveyism, Negritude, Pan-Africanism right through to the post-1945 decolonization struggles. The construction of the African consensus has taken the form of 're-membering Africa' after centuries of 'dismembering' imperatives of the Berlin consensus (Ngugi 2010).

As defined by Ngugi wa Thiong'o (2010) the process and struggle for 're-membering Africa' took various forms of imagination, visions, and deliberate initiatives dating back to the Egyptian stories of Osiris that spoke directly to the African quest for 'wholeness'. Some of the well-known 're-membering visions' included the grandest religio-secular eschatologies aimed at reconnecting the dismembered continent. African struggles aimed at scrapping the Berlin consensus are still being waged at different intellectual, cultural, ideological and political levels.

The key challenge is that the ghost of Berlin obstinately persists in resurrecting every time Africans bury it. It has managed to hide behind global structures and institutions of governance and among languages and discourses such as liberal democracy, cosmopolitanism, multiculturalism and globalization. It has managed to perch itself on the wings of universalism as well. It has also managed to hide behind paradigms and epistemologies that assume truthful, universalistic, neutral, objective point of view.

As noted by Zeleza (2003: 97), African intellectuals, as a professional formation, have complex histories that need deep reflection and systematic research. What can be said for now is that there are many African producers of knowledge that have mounted pressure on Western epistemologies through mimicry, counter-factualization of dominant discourses and other means. These include what Toyin Falola (2001: 3) termed the 'traditional intellectuals/ traditional elites' that comprised priests, kings, chiefs, magicians, praise poets, and merchants. These people produced mainly oral knowledge that drove precolonial African societies and it is their knowledge that was pushed into the barbarian margins under colonial modernity. The next set of knowledge producers consisted of Christianized ex-slaves and 'creoles' of Sierra Leone and Liberia that had imbibed Western thought and experienced the Western life style from the traumatic experiences of bondage. These early African knowledge producers drove inspiration from revival of Christian teaching and the rising liberal humanitarianism that swept across Europe and America (July 1968). The key crisis here was that these early African intellectuals operated within the colonial episteme.

The third group of African intellectuals consisted of early educated African elites consisting of evangelists, bishops, reverends, doctors and teachers. Examples included Tiyo Soga in South Africa and the leading cultural nationalist Edward Wilmot Blyden. Their ranks increased due to the production of 'evolues/assimilados/mulattoes' by the French colonial system of assimilation. They were dominant mainly in the four communes of St Louis, Goree, Rufisque and Dakar (July 1968: 155-176). The well known representative of this group was Blaise Diane who believed in the redemptive potential of French colonial system of assimilation and dreamt of the extension of French citizenship to the whole of French West Africa.

The fourth group consisted of 'intellectual activists/intellectual revolutionaries' that included Frantz Fanon, Aime Cesaire, Patrice Lumumba, Agostihno Neto, Eduardo Mondlane, Albert Luthuli, Obafemi Awolowo, Nnamdi Azikiwe, Jomo Kenyatta, Tom Mboya, Leopold Sedar Senghor, Julius Nyerere, Kwame Nkrumah, Amilcar Cabral, Joshua Nkomo, Robert Mugabe, Sekou Toure and many others. These 'intellectuals' were united by their adherence to African nationalism and Pan-Africanism.

They produced and instrumentalized knowledge to fight against imperialism and colonialism. These worked side-by-side with 'scholar-activists' like Cheikh Anta Diop, Walter Rodney, Wole Soyinka, Chinua Achebe, Ali Mazrui, Bernard Magubane, Kwesi Wiredu, and many others. A later cohort of scholars belonging to the first or second generation of African scholars includes Paul Tiyambe Zeleza, Thandika Mkandawire, Claude Ake, Issa G. Shivji, Sam Moyo, Ibbo Mandaza, Brian Raftopoulos, Achille Mbembe, Fantu Cheru, Ngwabi Bhebe, Adebayo Olukoshi, Mahmood Mamdani, Dani Nabudere, Archibald Mafeje, Paulin Hountodji, Herbert Vilakazi and many others who were also concerned about colonialism, underdevelopment, social and economic justice as well as democracy. It was from among this group that some intellectuals and academics began to lose faith in the emancipatory and liberatory potential of the postcolonial state due to its entrapment in neocolonialism and corruption.

What distinguished African intellectuals and academics was that they never produced knowledge just for mere intellectual enjoyment and mere professional vocation. The activist aspect was embedded through and through (Arowosegbe 2008). Modern African intellectuals have always operated as theorists, empiricists, ideologists, and activists simultaneously. Even intellectual-cum-politicians like Leopold Senghor, Kwame Nkrumah, Jomo Kenyatta, Julius Nyerere, Kenneth Kaunda and others became 'philosopher-kings' and formulated various discourses of liberation such as Negritude, Consciencism, African Socialism, African Humanism and so on as they struggled to counter the imperatives of the Berlin consensus and its epistemological outreach on the African continent.

What is disturbing though is that even after African intellectuals have produced numerous books and journal articles speaking directly on pertinent issues of freedom, development and democracy, their work has not fully succeeded in reaching the same heights as that of Western theorists such as Plato, Machiavelli, Michael Foucault, Antonio Gramsci, Max Weber, Karl Marx and others. African intellectual productions have not yet assumed dominance in local and global knowledge in the way that Marx, Derrida, Foucault and others' ideas are doing currently. This reality perhaps vindicates Pieter Boele van Hensbroek's argument that:

> The history of African political ideas is a neglected field of study. [...] The study of African intellectual creations, in particular political thought, however, remains quite marginal. No comprehensive history of Europe or the United States, for instance, would fail to discuss the ideas of Locke, Montesquieu, Jefferson, Dewey, or Marx, but when it comes to Africa apparently one can do almost without African intellectuals. [...] Within Africanist scholarship the African intellectual remains an anomaly (Hensbroek 1999: 1).

This means that the African academies and universities have remained a conduit of inculcation of Western knowledge, values, ways of knowing and worldviews that are often taught as universal values and scientific knowledge. The African continent is still stuck with the problem of 'the place that Western thought occupies in non-Western discursive formations' (Diawara 1990: 79). Mudimbe called for reformulation of this discourse in these words:

> We Africans must invest in the sciences, beginning with the human and social sciences. We must reanalyze the claims of these sciences for our own benefit;

evaluate the risks they contain, and their discursive spaces. We must reanalyze for our benefit the contingent supports and the areas of enunciation in order to know what new meaning and what road to propose for our quest so that our discourse can justify us as singular beings engaged in a history that is itself special (cited in Diawara 1990: 87-88).

Such traumatic experiences as the slave trade, colonialism and apartheid influenced the way Africans imagined freedom and shaped the content of African intellectual interventions. Africa is a continent that suffered and experienced multiple levels of subjugations and denigrations that affected its identity formation and ways of knowing. Its traumatic experiences date back to the Punic Wars of 264-146 BC which pitted 'African Carthage against European Rome' (Mbeki 2010).

This was followed by other violent-laden processes and events such as mercantilism, slave trade, imperialism, colonialism, apartheid and neocolonialism. These historical processes influenced and shaped the character of intellectual interventions and epistemological development across the 'three generations' of African intellectuals identified by Mkandawire (1995). Thuynsma 19998) has explained why issues such as freedom, development and democracy have pre-occupied the African intellectual minds and African struggles for epistemological freedom. He words:

> Africanists have never been able to afford scholarship for its luxury. In whate-ver field, we have worked with an unwritten command to tell our people about our people. We have had to work our way out from under a number of histori-cal boulders rolled over us by foreign interests (emphasis in the original source) (Thuynsma 1998: 185).

Once one understood the core factors that drove African intellectual interventions, it is not surprising that some of their works sounded deeply polemical if not aggressive. Toyin Falola explains why:

> Reading the works of Africans or listening to their lectures, you may form an im-pression that they are polemical or defensive, bitter or apologetic. Yes, you are ri-ght! However, you need to know the reason for this. Scholarship in Africa has been conditioned to respond to a reality and epistemology created for it by outsiders, a confrontation with imperialism, the power of capitalism, and the knowledge that others have constructed for Africa. The African intelligentsia does not write in a vacuum but in world saturated with others' statements, usually negative about its members and their continent. Even when this intelligentsia seeks the means to intrude itself into the modern world, modernity has been defined for it and presented to it in a fragmented manner (Falola 2001: 17).

For Africans, the themes of freedom, development, and identity permeate the greater part of their imagination, visions, trajectories, and eschatologies. This is so, precisely because, of experiences of slavery, colonialism, and apartheid that underpinned underdevelopment and impoverishment of the continent. Amartya Sen (1999): defined 'development as freedom.' To him, attainment of freedom is the primary end and principal means of development. To Sen, 'Development consists of the removal of various types of unfreedom that leave people with little choice and little opportunity of exercising their reasoned agency' (Sen 1999: xii).

For Africa, the problem is that since the expansion of Western modernity into the continent, via the slave trade, mercantilism, imperialism and colonialism, 'reasoned agency' became truncated and the search to capture it is still ongoing. African intellectuals together with some African leaders have consistently sought for various ways through which a formerly colonized continent and its people could regain lost confidence, dignity, and control of destiny. This intellectual intervention is taking place against bedrock of lost African epistemological freedom. The key challenge is how to break from the snares of the global colonial matrix of power that consistently subordinated African voices and cries for freedom.

The other challenge for the African struggle for epistemological freedom is that most of the leading African intellectuals that are expected to spearhead this struggle were produced in Europe and America. Most of the leading African intellectuals of today have stationed themselves either in Europe or in America. This means that African intellectualism and knowledge production is deeply situated within Western epistemology, orientation and pedigree.

Inevitably, African ideas are not free from Western ideas. The key conundrum has been how to turn and influence an African intellectual community that has for years been taught and trained along Western lines to rebel against the Western episteme and at minimum work towards domestication and deployment of Western ideas to serve African purposes and, at maximum, construct a new African episteme informed by realities of the subjugated peoples of Africa.

Chakrabarty (2000) argued in favour of the appropriation and adaptation of Western thought to help solve non-Western problems. He acknowledged that colonialists preached a humanism that they denied in practice in Africa and that Western secular and theological vision 'have historically provided a strong foundation on which to erect – both in Europe and outside – critiques of socially unjust practices' (Chakrabarty 2000: 4). Chakrabarty further proposes appropriation of Western epistemologies and thoughts rather than rejection. This he calls 'decentering' and 'provincialising' Europe and European thought (2000: 16). Indeed, what is being fought for is not a total rejection of Euro-American knowledge but a democratization of this hegemonic knowledge so that it recognizes other knowledges from the ex-colonized world as equally important and relevant.

At another level, Africans have been disillusioned by the failure of decolonization project to culminate in decolonization of the mind as advocated by Steve Bantu Biko's Black Consciousness Movement and Ngugi wa Thiong'o in *Decolonizing the Mind* (1986). Even such strong believers in the redemptive and progressive aspects of African nationalism such as Issa Shivji (2009) had to ask the key question: 'where is Uhuru? (Where is freedom?), reflecting their disillusionment with both the first phase of political liberation that failed to achieve decolonization of African minds and economic empowerment of ex-colonized peoples.

The struggle to decolonize knowledge and minds of ex-colonized peoples has also been fought by black Diaspora scholars like Molefi Asante who came up with what they have termed 'Afrocentric thought' or 'Afrocentricity' (Asante 1988; Asante 1987; Gray 2001). Afrocentricity is defined as 'the belief in the centrality of Africans in post-modern history' and a 'critical perspective placing African ideals at the center of any analysis that involves African culture or behavior' (Asante 1988: 6). The bottom line in this epistemological initiative is how to transcend Eurocentrism embedded in conventional thinking and pedagogy. Asante and others whose intellectual interventions have been informed by Afrocentric thought have indeed succeeded in reading and interpreting the human story from an African perspective and to mainstream African agency in the making of global history.

Within the continent such scholars as Dani Nabudere have been vocal on issues of epistemological decolonization that transcended Eurocentrism. Nabudere, in particular, has emphasized that all sources of knowledge were valid within their historical, cultural and social context. He uses the term 'Afrikology' to refer to an Africa-focused epistemology that fully takes into account African history, culture, and context. Such an epistemology is envisaged to put African experience and problems at its centre. Nabudere argued that:

> The construction of the science of Afrikology therefore directly flows from the need for Africans to redefine their world, which can enable them to advance their self-understanding and the world around them based on their cosmologies.

> [...] Afrikology must proceed from the proposition that is a true philosophy of knowledge and wisdom based on African cosmologies because it is *Afri-* in that it is inspired by ideas originally produced from the Cradle of Humankind located in Africa. *It is not Afrikology* because it is African but it is *Afri-* because it emanates from the source of the Universal system of knowledge in Africa (emphasis is in the original source) (Nabudere 2011: 17-18).

Broadly speaking, all these initiatives are a response to the logic of the Berlin consensus that has continued to dominate in the realm of epistemology. But some scholars like Mbembe (2002a: 239-273, 2002b: 621-641) and Kwame Anthony Appiah (1993, 2006) who strongly believe in the therapeutic potential of globalization and cosmopolitanism for Africans do not see any redemptive potential in Afrocentric approaches. Such thinking is labelled 'nativism' that strives on essentialization African identity and 'narcissism of minor difference'.

Owing to the pervasive use of race as a construct that underpinned Western's imagination and construction of the world, African deconstructions of Euro-American hegemonic epistemology cannot ignore the complex issue of identity. Santos (2007) has emphasized that modern Western thinking was informed by 'an abyssal' thought which consisted of 'a system of visible and invisible distinctions, the invisible ones being the foundation of visible ones'. What Santos was referring to was how the Western metropolitan side 'visibilized' itself through 'invisibilizing' the non-Western world into a zone of incomprehensible beings. This division of the world of Europeans from the world of non-Europeans was meant to popularize the ideas of 'impossibility of co-presence of the two sides of the line' as well as colonial domination. The zone of Europeans was governed according to ethics, social regulation and imperatives of social emancipation; whereas the African zone was to be governed through appropriation and violence as ethics did not apply (Santos 2007).

No wonder then that one of the enduring legacies of the Berlin consensus is that of fragmenting African identities into contending tribes and ethnicities. The introduction of colonialism and the creation of colonial states were predicated on preventing of African identities from developing and coalescing towards larger national identities. Consequently, there was the issue of who is an African in a postcolonial world where such other identities as Indian, Afrikaner, English and many minority identities also compete for Africanity. Current debates on African freedom and development have to deal with the increasing importance of identity politics and the concomitant issues of shifting and contested belonging and citizenship. What links the politics of knowledge production with politics if identity is that the white race arrogated all progressive ideas as production of Western civilization and denied any existence of progressive ideas emanating from African civilization. In short, the colonial drive that pushed African knowledges into the barbarian margins of society happened in tandem with denial and alienation of African identity.

The real challenge has been how to ensure ethical conditions of human peaceful coexistence that takes into account the politics of recognition and difference. This politics of recognition is linked with new questions of social justice, ownership of resources and reclamation of subdued African knowledges to make them part of the drivers of the postcolonial African world. It is also linked to the question of who is the authentic subject of the colonially-crafted postcolonial nation-states. Since the end of the Cold War, new issues have arisen linked to the central question of identity. These have taken the form of new politics of nativism, xenophobia, and autochthony that cannot be ignored in any book dealing with ideational issues of freedom, development and democracy in Africa (Geshiere 2009; Comaroffs 2009; Ndlovu-Gatsheni 2009; Ndlovu-Gatsheni 2010).

Cornwall (2009: 471) wrote about how 'words make the world' and for Africa it is Western words and knowledge that continue to take the leading role in influencing the making of the world. The realm of ideas is one area where the Berlin consensus continues to strive and reshape the African world. The situation is worsened by the fact that schools, colleges and universities in Africa have failed to shake off the colonial character of being Western transplants propagating Western and American ideas (Muzvidziwa 2005: 79).

It is within African institutions of learning that the African agenda continues to be lost. These institutions have failed to privilege indigenous knowledge that was pushed to the margins by colonialism and that continues to languish in the margins as a result of the presence of the colonial power matrix. African values and aspirations have remained outside the school, college and university curriculum. These institutions continue to produce 'mimic' men and women. They also led Victor Muzvidziwa to conclude that:

> African universities continue to lag behind as far as rooting their curricula and pedagogy in African settings. Universities in Africa in many ways continue the project designed to uproot Africans from their origins. The greatest battle yet to be won is that of the mind. While the African University is rooted within the African postcolony, it still falls far short of identifying with indegenes and local communities (Muzvidziwa 2005: 88).

African scholars like their continent, their economies and cultures, are still caught up in the snares of the colonial power matrix (Mkandawire 1995;

Vilakazi 2001). Received Western epistemological imports have continued to wreck havoc on the minds of young Africans in schools, colleges and universities. This must not come as a surprise to those whose analysis is informed by de-coloniality thought and who are aware of the continued presence of the colonial power matrix as a guardian of western epistemology.

Conclusions

Unless Africans take a serious leap forward from what Santos termed 'learned ignorance' emanating from the realities of coloniality and understand the operations of the modern racialized, hegemonic, patriarchal and capitalist global world that was created by Western modernity, they may continue to celebrate illusions of decolonization and myths of freedom. The reality of Africa today is that it is deeply ensnared within the strong but invisible colonial matrix of power that does not allow Africans to take control and charge of their social, economic and political destinies. A postcolonial African world is not yet born. This chapter therefore has tracked and unpacked the broader contours of the colonial matrix of power and how it continues to suffocate African initiatives of development and freedom.

What is emphasized in this chapter, therefore, is that the worse form of colonization that has continued to wreck havoc on the continent is the epistemological one (colonization of imagination and the mind) that is hidden in institutions and discourses that govern the modern globe. African universities have not managed to produce knowledge for African freedom and empowerment because they are largely operating as Western institutions located on the continent. African intellectuals continue to operate within the episteme constructed by the West. They have not managed to successfully counter epistemologies of alterity that continue to subordinate and subjugate everything African, if not totally ignoring it. Western ideas have assumed the character of universal values that are said to contribute towards maintenance and stabilization of the existing global order. It is not yet time for Africans to celebrate anything as the struggle for epistemological freedom still needs to be waged on all fronts if a postcolonial African world is to be realized.

3

Myths of Decolonization and Illusions of Freedom

Introduction

> In a Habermasian type of scenario, liberation would be subservient to emancipa-
> tion; and, decolonization, likewise, would still be covered over and managed by
> the emancipating rhetoric of modernity, either liberal or Marxist. In other words,
> if 'emancipation' is the image used by honest liberals and honest Marxists from
> the internal and historical perspectives of Europe or the US, then looking at the
> world history from outside of those locations […] means coming to terms with
> the fact that there is a still further need for 'liberation/de-coloniality' from the
> people and institutions raising the flag of 'emancipation.' Thus, in this precise
> sense, emancipation cannot be the guiding light for liberation/de-coloniality but
> the other way round: liberation/de-coloniality includes and re-maps the 'rational
> concept of emancipation.' In this complexity, we need a relentless critical exercise
> of awareness of the moments when the guiding principle at work is liberation/de-
> coloniality and when, on the other hand, the irrational myth directs social actors
> in their projects for political, economic and spiritual (epistemic, philosophical,
> religious) decolonization.
>
> Walter D. Mignolo

The momentous people's uprisings rocking the North African region since
January 2011, culminating in the collapse of the oppressive regimes of Zine el
Abidine Ben Ali of Tunisia and Hosni Mubarak of Egypt in quick succession
as well as the collapse of Colonel Muamar Gaddafi's forty-two years of iron
rule in Libya, and his death in the process, have put to rest notions of an
'end of history and the last man' that was popularized by Francis Fukuyama

at the end of the Cold War. The popular uprisings by the masses indicated beyond doubt the continuing ability of the ordinary people to make history. Massiah (2011:2) identified one of the key lessons from the uprisings that rocked the Maghreb region as the opening to the possibility of a new phase of decolonization and depicted this new phase as relating to the 'passage from the independence of states to self-determination of the people'. These uprisings which no social scientist or journalist was able to predict and forecast compel us to revisit the African past and rethink the limits of the decolonization process that culminated in the achievement of juridical freedom by African colonies from the late 1950s onwards.

The process of decolonization which Zeleza (2003: vi) calls the 'proudest moment' of African nationalism, is believed to have marked the triumphalism of black liberatory nationalism over white exploitative and oppressive colonialism. Being liberated and/or emancipated were subsumed under the rubric of decolonization to mean a single state of being. The day each of the African colonies achieved political independence is celebrated annually as 'independence day' throughout the African continent save perhaps for Ethiopia that was never colonized. But even Ethiopia celebrates its triumphalism over Italian invasion at the famous battle of Adowa in 1896. There is no doubt that decolonization occupies a nerve centre of pride in African historiography and nationalist humanism. Those who actively participated and led the struggles for decolonization became heroes of the African nationalist revolution and founders of the postcolonial African states.

This chapter re-evaluates the decolonization process in order to understand its grammar and eventually unpack it as a process that was never completed and, therefore, continues to obscure and hide the disempowering colonial matrix of power that prevented the re-birth of Africa as a confident and brave postcolonial world. Decolonization is better understood as a terrain of illusions of liberation and myths of freedom. This intervention is in no way meant to down play the sacrifices some Africans made in the name of decolonization. It is common knowledge that Nelson Mandela spent twenty-seven years in prison while many others like Eduardo Mondlane of Mozambique, Amilcar Cabral of Guinea-Bissau, Chris Hani and Solomon Mahlangu of South Africa, Jason Ziyaphapha Moyo and Herbert Chitepo of Zimbabwe all lost their lives. The analysis is meant to expose the ideational traps constructed by colonial modernity that diluted the liberatory ethos of decolonization and channelled it towards emancipation that did not question the alienating logic of modernity itself but called for reforms within the same system.

Moreover, the chapter articulates three core arguments. The first is that, for one to gain a deeper meaning of decolonization and its limits one needs to unpack its grammar. By its 'grammar' I mean its genealogy, ethical and ideological aspects as well as its political assumptions and implications. In unpacking the core essence of decolonization I engage with two utopic registers of liberation and emancipation that are subsumed under decolonization discourses. I disentangle liberation from emancipation as I reveal the myths and illusions of freedom bequeathed Africa by decolonization. The second is that decolonization largely manifested itself in the form of juridical freedom albeit of a complicated nature that was mistakenly conflated with popular freedom for the ex-colonized peoples. This argument is explicated by analysing the problematic character of the African postcolonial state that emerged from colonial rule rather than from African society and operated through coercion rather than consent to impose its will on the African people.

The final argument is that existing studies of decolonization have been blinded by nationalist celebratory politics to the extent of ignoring the ordinary citizens' new struggles aimed at liberating themselves from the domination, exploitation and repression of the postcolonial state. Therefore the chapter provides details of strategies the ordinary citizens use to liberate themselves from the postcolonial, neocolonized African state and which continues even today by taking the form of popular uprisings in North Africa with potential ripple effect on sub-Saharan Africa.

Disentangling 'emancipation' from 'liberation' in the decolonization discourse

Some critics would probably think simplistically that disentangling 'emancipation' from liberation is an exercise in futility. Those who might think so are totally mistaken because without clearly disentangling both terms, failure it would be difficult to realize that the active forces of the colonial matrix unleashed by colonial modernity always fought to dilute liberation struggles into emancipatory struggles that ended up celebrating the achievement of democracy instead of freedom. The post-1994 South African situation speaks volumes about how the liberation movement was disciplined into an emancipatory force that finally celebrated the achievement of liberal democracy instead of decolonization and freedom. This means the day was won by liberals rather than nationalists. The other example is that of slaves who were emancipated rather than liberated to the extent that they continued to languish at the bottom of the racial-hierarchy of societies like the United States of America and engage in further civil rights struggles to change their oppression and domination.

So there is, indeed, a real danger in African studies accepting that the utopic registers of emancipation and liberation can be used interchangeably to mean freedom. Emancipation and liberation are related utopic registers but they do not mean the same thing and their genealogies are different. In his studies of philosophies of liberation, Dussel (1995, 2000) makes it clear that emancipation belongs to the discourse of the European Enlightenment and is today a common term used in liberal and Marxist discourses. Dussel's argument is reinforced by that of Walter D. Mignolo who argues that:

> The concept of emancipation belongs to the universe of discourse framed by the philosophical and historical concepts of modernity, which becomes apparent if we look at the particular intersection of Theo-and Ego-politics that later, in the eighteenth century, gave rise to the idea of emancipation—the Reformation. In terms of philosophical modernity, the Reformation was a crucial break-through for the emergence of critical self-reflexivity and it is easy to see how—and why—the concept of emancipation emerged from the 'transition' to 'freedom of subjectivity' and 'critical self-reflexivity' from lack thereof that began with the Reformation. The individual freedom sought to some degree within the Church by Luther became more and more autonomous through secularization until its detachment in Descartes dictum, 'I think, therefore I am,' in Kant's transcendental subject and in Hegel's freedom of subjectivity and critical self-reflexivity (Mignolo 2007: 467).

Emancipation was used in the eighteenth century to refer to three historical events, namely the Glorious Revolution of 1668 in England, the independence of the colonists in America from the British colonial empire (American Revolution of 1776) and the French Revolution of 1789 (Mignolo 2007: 455). In these three events emancipation was with reference to the bourgeois revolutions that did not fight against the edifice of modernity but for reformism and class ascendancy within the same capitalist system.

Emancipation is always informed by the reformist spirit rather than total change. It is more of a strategy used by oppressive systems to deal with opposition by opening up new concessions while gaining a new lease of life. As Mignolo (2007: 445) argues, emancipation 'proposes and presupposes changes within the system that doesn't question the logic of coloniality'. The most dangerous assumption in this thinking is that freedom for the non-Western world had 'to be planned, dictated, and executed from Europe or the US itself only' (Mignolo 2007: 457). This thinking led to such ideas of decolonization as mere transfer of power from white colonialists to black nationalists.

It is also ideas of emancipation that underpin present-day Western powers' use of military power and violence as part of their crusade to introduce liberal democracy and human rights on non-Western parts of the world. The example of the invasion of Iraq is an indication of this mentality. Such military adventures, which were justified on the basis of emancipation were seen reality as a continuation of the spread of Western modernity by force to engulf the non-Western world, especially the Islamic world that is seen as resisting some aspects of cultural imperialism, including embracing Christianity. Even Marxism was informed by the spirit of emancipation; hence it did not question the logic of Western modernity and its colonial mission but simply emphasized the emancipation of the working class instead of the bourgeoisie. Today, part of the dominant Western discourse is about emancipation of the multitudes (Hardt and Negri 2000).

Understood from this perspective, emancipation is different from liberation notwithstandingthat they are two sides of the same coin of modernity/coloniality. The genealogy of liberation is in resisting the imposition of Western modernity and revolting against the darker and negative aspects of Western modernity such as the slave trade, imperialism, colonialism, apartheid and neocolonialism. In Africa, the genealogy of liberation discourse is traceable to slave revolts and primary resistance, and in the Diaspora to the 1781 Tupac Amaru Uprising in Peru and the 1804 Haitian Revolution. The resisters who participated in these struggles did not fight for internal reform within Western modernity and its logic of imperialism and colonialism. The revolutions in Peru and Haiti challenged and questioned the whole edifice of Western modernity and its concomitant logic of slavery, imperialism and colonialism. The clarion call was for independence not reform of the system as emancipatory demands tended to do. Liberation is the expression of aspirations of the oppressed non-Western people who desired to de-link with the oppressive colonial empires. Its grammar had a double meaning: political-economic independence and epistemological freedom.

Ideally, African liberation was expected to destroy the colonial state and culminate in the creation a new dispensation of freedom, equality and justice. Mignolo (2007: 454), in his differentiation of emancipation from liberation, posed some crucial questions: Who needs emancipation? Who needs liberation? Who benefits from emancipation? Who benefits from liberation? Who are the agents and the intended targets of emancipating or liberatory projects? What subjectivities are activated in these projects? Does the distinction even matter when emancipation has a universal ring that seems to cover the interests of all oppressed people in the world? It is clear from this chapter that emancipation is a watered-down variant of liberation in the sense that it does not take into account the hierarchies of oppression and exploitation introduced by Western modernity across the world mediated by race. Emancipation was a strategy of the white bourgeoisie that questioned only the excesses of the logic of imperialism and colonialism such as the slave trade and apartheid, for instance.

Those who wanted liberation were the colonized people who desired a re-birth as free citizens and new, liberated beings. But the decolonization project in Africa was permeated by both imperatives of emancipation and liberation coexisting uneasily and tendentiously. The agenda of decolonization was hijacked by the 'native bourgeoisie' and channelled towards emancipation. The 'native bourgeoisie', despite its black colour, was a creation of colonial modernity and had imbibed colonial languages and embraced Western cultures; as such it aspired to occupy the positions monopolized by the white colonial bourgeoisie. Its agenda was limited to replacing the colonial white bourgeoisie (Fanon 1961: 87).

The emancipatory strand in the decolonization project was easily embraced by the 'native bourgeoisie' that was not really opposed to colonial modernity but wanted to be accommodated within the system. On this point Peter Ekeh argued that:

> In many ways, the drama of colonization is the history of the clash between Euro-pean colonisers and African bourgeois class. Although native to Africa, the African bourgeois class depends on colonialism for its legitimacy. It accepts the principles implicit in colonialism but rejects the foreign personnel that rule Africa. It claims to be competent enough to rule, but has no traditional legitimacy. In order to replace the colonisers and rule its own people, it has invented a number of inte-rest-begotten theories to justify that rule (Ekeh 1975: 96).

Reverend Ndabaningi Sithole, a leading Zimbabwean nationalist and historian of nationalism, celebrated how colonial modernity eradicated tribalism in Africa and proclaimed that the African political trajectory was moving from tribalism to nationalism and to modernity (Sithole 1968: 98). What Sithole and his bourgeois class were fighting for was not very different from what the British bourgeoisie wanted during the Glorious Revolution of 1668. The difference was only that colonial modernity had added the race element to the African situation as a variable in bourgeois power struggles.

The black native bourgeoisie that spearheaded the decolonization project stirred it in the direction of emancipation rather than liberation. As long as decolonization was conceived in emancipatory terms, its failure to fulfil Fanon's expectations of total, complete and instantaneous substitution of the colonial species and colonial subject with another liberated and confident

African species and the birth of 'new men, new language and new humanity' were inevitable. Fanon emphasized that, 'The production of the new men is solely a result of their act of obtaining their freedom' (Fanon 1961: 1968a). Decolonization did not result in complete reversal of the order of society whereby, 'The last shall be first and the first shall be last' and the 'native goes from "animal" to "human"' (Fanon 1968a: 102).

At another level, Grosfoguel (2007: 219) argued that decolonization must not be articulated in terms of conquering power over the juridical political boundaries of a state akin to the old national liberation and socialist strategies of taking power. Such approaches ignored global coloniality which operates without a direct colonial administration. This means that decolonization that was simply aimed at the elimination of colonial administrations amounted to a myth, a 'postcolonial world', because from direct colonialism African states fell directly into neocolonialism.

In the 1960s and 1970s, revolutionary African cadres like Amilcar Cabral (1969: 75) became worried about the 'ideological deficiency' of the decolonization movements. Cabral urged the existing African liberation movements to pay particular attention to the form of society they wanted to construct at the end of colonial rule. He clearly understood that the attainment of political independence was not the same thing as national liberation. He was concerned about the failure of African nationalist leaders to distinguish between genuine national liberation and neocolonialism (Cabral 1969: 89).

Cabral was not alone in this endeavour to rescue the liberatory ethos of decolonization that was being confused with emancipation. Kwame Nkrumah was also very vocal about the dangers of neocolonialism being taken for African freedom. He was very concerned about the vulnerability of postcolonial African societies to the 'extended tentacles of the Wall Street octopus' (Nkrumah 1965). Nkrumah visualized postcolonial Africa as trapped within the snares of 'neocolonialism' which he called the 'last stage of imperialism' (Nkrumah 1965). He was indeed very correct.

Slavoj Zizek even derided the logic of decolonization in these words:

> One is tempted to say that the will to gain political independence from the colo-
> nizer in the guise of a new independent nation-state is the ultimate proof that the
> colonized ethnic group is thoroughly integrated into the ideological universe of
> the colonizer (Zizek 2000: 255).

This critical analysis of the myths of decolonization and its illusions of freedom takes us to the higher order question of what constitute decolonial resistance and liberation for the African people. In simple terms, African resistance to colonial modernity had to exceed the terms and constraints imposed on Africa by Western modernity. Such resistance was expected to create decolonization as a double operation that involved the liberation of both the colonizer and the colonized. The end product was to be 'de-coloniality' which Mignolo defined thus:

> De-coloniality, then, means working towards a vision of human life that is not dependent upon or structured by the forced imposition of one ideal society over those that differ, which is what modernity/coloniality does and, hence, where decolonization of the mind should begin. The struggle is for changing the terms in addition to the content of the conversation (Mignolo 2007: 459).

At the time of writing this book, the majority of those who led the nationalist inspired decolonization process had already displayed signs of capitulation to the dominant world constructed by Western and colonial modernities. Replacement of white colonial administrators at the state level was celebrated as independence and as freedom in countries like Zimbabwe and South Africa. In Zimbabwe they celebrate 'independence day' every April and in South Africa they have celebrated 'freedom day' since 1995. In both countries, the African political elite proclaimed the policy of reconciliation, which Ibbo Mandaza correctly characterized as:

> The mourn of the weak, even when pronounced from positions of apparent moral superiority over oppressors and exploiters of yesterday. The reconciliation exercise, therefore, serves largely a political function, facilitating the necessary compromise between the rulers of yesterday and the inheritors of state power, within the context of incomplete decolonization (Mandaza 1999: 79).

Mandaza also emphasized that what is generally celebrated as the postcolonial state 'has no life of its own, it has no essence; it is a state modeled on the (European) bourgeois state but without a national bourgeoisie that would otherwise provide it an anchor and even a semblance of independence' (Mandaza 1998: 3). All this analysis underscores the fact that a postcolonial world was never born; rather what decolonization facilitated was a postcolonial neocolonized world.

At the abstract level one can still begin to identify some of myths of decolonization. For instance, the idea of politically sovereign and economically independent postcolonial states ignored the crucial reality of entrapment of these states within the snares of the global colonial matrix of power that denies African leaders policy space to chart any autonomous economic or political trajectory. To argue that colonial situations ceased to exist after the demise of colonial administrations some fifty years ago also constitutes a myth of a decolonized postcolonial African world. Grosfoguel (2004: 320-321) added credence to this argument:

> For the last 50 years, states that had been colonies, following the dominant Euro-centric liberal discourses [...] constructed ideologies of 'national identity,' 'national development,' and 'national sovereignty' that produced an illusion of 'independence,' 'development,' and 'progress.' Yet their economic and political systems were shaped by their subordinate position in a capitalist world system organised around a hierarchical international division of labour [...] These multiple hierarchies (including the racial/ethnic hierarchy), together with the predominance of Eurocentric cultures [...], constitute a global coloniality' between Europeans/ Euro-Americans and non-Europeans. Thus, 'coloniality' is entangled with, but is not reducible to, the international division of labour. The 'colonial' axis between European/Euro-Americans and non-Europeans is inscribed not only in relations of exploitation (between capital and labour) and domination (between Europeans and non-Europeans), but also in the production of subjectivities.

Another myth of decolonization is that of conflating the attainment of juridical freedom with the achievement of popular freedom by the African citizens. The post-apartheid poverty that the black majority experienced in South African is a clear testimony of the dangers of degeneration of liberation movements into emancipatory formations concerned with simple politics of the right to vote and removal of discriminatory legislation from statute books without embarking on systematic and radical restructuring of the apartheid state. Those who fought for the liberation of South Africa from the vicious apartheid colonialism found themselves celebrating not freedom and independence but democracy. Today, one of the most defended things in South Africa is the national constitution mainly by those who benefited from apartheid simply because the celebrated South African constitution officially adopted in 1996 protects the ill-gotten wealth concentrated in the hands of white bourgeoisie and a few black elites. The constitution of South Africa does not facilitate and enable radical redistribution of resources such as land and mines. Ironically, predominantly black the African National Congress (ANC) who fought against apartheid oppression and brought about the new constitution, are now closely watched as a threat to the same constitution by the right-wing and white dominated political formation known as the Democratic Alliance (DA). South Africa is a typical example of a society where myths of decolonization and illusions of freedom are manifesting themselves in broad daylight in a most detestable form.

Myths of decolonization and problems of juridical freedom

A body of critical literature by such scholars as Tukumbi Lumumba-Kasongo (1994), Claude Ake (2000), Pita Ogaba Agbese and George Klay Kieh, Jr (2007), Mueni wa Muiu (2009) and others have focused attention on the problems emanating from the character and structure of the postcolonial African state, in the process exposing some of the core myths of decolonization and illusions of freedom. Ake emphasized how the postcolonial state was shaped by colonial legacy into an all-powerful and arbitrary political formation that set it on collision course with the citizens.

The triumphant African nationalist leadership continued the colonial legacy of turning against democracy. This was so because the achievement of political independence only changed the composition of the managers of the state but not the character of the state, which remained much as it was in the colonial era. Consequently, the postcolonial state emerged as an apparatus of violence; its embedding within society was very shallow, its rootedness in social forces remained extremely narrow and this made it to rely for compliance on coercion rather than consent (Ake 2000: 35-37). Ake's central argument and observations were also echoed by Lumumba-Kasongo (1994: 58) who depicted the postcolonial African state as 'an institution of domination par excellence.'

In his interrogation of the idea and meaning of freedom in Africa, Foltz (2002) came up with a four-dimensional thesis on the trajectories of the African struggles for freedom. These are: freedom for the African state, freedom from the African state, freedom within the African state, and freedom through the African state system. Used in conjunction with the existing rich literature on the problems of the African postcolonial state, Foltz's intervention provides an ideal entry point for critical interrogation of the core myths of decolonization; how ordinary citizens have responded to postcolonial state's alienating practices, oppression and exploitation; and the pathways taken by ordinary citizens and excluded elites in search of popular freedom.

Scholars like Young (1994) and Mamdani (1996) have studied closely the colonial state which formed the template for the postcolonial state. They noted that the colonial state lacked three essential attributes found in other modern states, namely, sovereignty, nationalism and external autonomy; and crisis emanated from the fact that the colonial state was imposed by force of arms on the African society. At the initial construction level, the colonial state did not even pretend to serve the interests of the colonized African people in terms of provision of services. Coercion became the DNA of the postcolonial state.

As Muiu and Martin (2009: 54) have argued, the colonial state was 'essentially a foreign construct that could not possibly take root on African soil'. It even destroyed existing African indigenous civil society that had taken the form of age-grades and other forms. The postcolonial state was merely a de-racialized colonial state that was never structurally changed to enable it to suit African demands and aspirations. Thus the myths of decolonization and illusions of freedom become very clear if one closely analyses the politics around the transfer of political office from white colonial administrators to black administrators.

In the Francophone Africa, except Guinea, the postcolonial states were born with diminished sovereignty which still remained with France. They had no control over foreign, economic, monetary and defence matters (Mueni wa Muiu and Martin 2009: 56). In the Anglophone Africa, Chinweizu (1975: 167) noted that the African nationalists had to sign agreements to uphold some negotiated neocolonial compromises including safeguarding properties accumulated by white colonialists such as land and mines even before entering new offices. Independence constitutions were written for the African leaders by the departing colonial masters. Muiu and Martin (2009: 56) argued that Duncan Sandys who became Britain's Secretary of State for Commonwealth Relations in 1960, was a notorious expert in persuading African leaders to sign independence constitutions which did not favour the aspirations of the black majority through keeping the participants talking until they signed out of sheer exhaustion. They concluded that:

> Thus decolonization was just a façade barely disguising the continuation of colonization by other means and leading to the mere 'flag' (or juridical) independence of utterly impotent and powerless quasi-states lacking the substance of sovereignty (Muiu and Martin 2009: 56).

Myths of decolonization and illusions of freedom had the negative impact of silencing the ordinary citizens through giving them a false hope that through hard work they would harvest the concrete fruits of freedom that were denied by colonialism. The postcolonial state itself was not free because multinational corporations and the ex-colonized still controlled the economy in league with metropolitan governments that ran African affairs by remote control and through African elites. The difficult question to answer is whether it was really possible for African leaders to pursue an independent political, ideological and economic path without provoking reaction from the ex-colonial powers?

This question is pertinent because Muiu and Martin (2009) and other scholars who argue for the reconstitution and reconstruction of African postcolonial states on the basis of indigenous knowledges and institutions, seem to imply that African founding fathers of postcolonial states had a choice not to ignore indigenous institutions and to alter the states to meet the priorities and needs of the African people. At the same time, they point to the case of such leaders as Patrice Lumumba, Modibo Keita, Thomas Sankara, Mirien N'Gouabi, Samora Machel and Laurent-Desire Kabila who lost their lives while trying to radically transform the African states to serve the interests of their citizens.

What we see here is a cul-de-sac within which the African leaders operated; a path policed by colonial matrices of power that included CIA operatives, sponsored coup plotters, assassins and all sorts of dirty tricks ranged against those African leaders who tried to transcend the coloniality of power and translate myths of decolonization and illusions of freedom into real African freedom. Even Kwame Nkrumah fell victim to the snares of these forces and was toppled in 1966.

This cul-de-sac meant that the African leaders had to tread carefully including choosing to suppress African people's aspirations and demands than provoke the anger of the Euro-American political league that was capable of disciplining those who deviated from the given script on governance and state management. Instead of delivering services to the people, African leaders engaged in deluding their own people by pretending to be in charge and inviting the hungry and angry population to partake of annual celebrations of flag independence that did not change their well-being.

Having inherited the colonial state together with its repressive apparatus, African leaders presided over a leviathan that was active in suffocating alternative popular struggles for freedom. The first group of people to react against the postcolonial state was the excluded elite who found themselves at the mercy of those who controlled the state. According to Ake (2000: 37), the excluded elite fought for incorporation, manifesting a situation where 'Africa is in constant turmoil from struggles between people who must secure power and those who must access it by incorporation'. It was often the excluded elite that resorted to mobilization of ethnicity to build a political constituency to use in bargaining for power. On the other hand, were ordinary masses of peasants and workers who struggled for economic incorporation and this demand propelled them to seek what became known as 'second independence' not from colonial masters but from the indigenous elite (Ake 2000: 47).

Generally speaking, the ordinary citizen's struggles for freedom took various forms involving disengagement from the state; agitating for internal democratization of the state; supporting opposition parties; trying to take control of the state; outright emigration; mocking the state; trying to influence state policy from within, agitating for secession, and other subtle and softer forms of resistance and engagement such as conviviality and use of music, jokes, comic strips and satire to reveal the vulgarity, debauchery and buffoonery of those in control of state power.

In the face of internal opposition, the postcolonial state evolved various survival techniques. Mbembe' (1992; 2001) focused on the ideological production of power within the postcolonial neocolonized African world and how this configuration of political power impinged on the development of relations between the state governors and the governed (state-society relations). But scholars like Mikael Karlstrom have criticized Mbembe for overestimating the ideological power of the postcolonial state and for 'unjustifiably' creating a pessimistic portrayal of state-society relations in postcolonial Africa 'as terminally mired in inherently dysfunctional political dispositions and practices' (Karlstrom 2003: 57). While Mbembe drew his examples from Cameroon and Togo, Karlstrom studied the rural communities of southern Uganda from a Bakhtinian perspective and discovered 'reciprocity and ritualized "dialogism" between state and society' (Karlstrom 2003:57).

Karlstrom spent energy demonstrating that 'the disabling paradoxes of postcolonial politics identified by Mbembe do not arise out of any inherent pathology of the African political imagination, but rather out of the postcolonial state's tendency to deploy local models and practices of the public sphere in ways that evacuate them of much of their legitimating content' (Karlstrom 2003: 57-8). While Karlstrom tries to create a positive image of the postcolonial neocolonized world as characterized by harmonious state-society relations based on particular case study of Uganda, there is overwhelming counter-evidence that reveal what Mbembe has uncovered.

The fact was that the postcolonial state was not well embedded in society meant that state-citizen relations were not stable and political elites and ordinary citizens were constantly engaged in struggles since those who did not control the state remained closed out of economic benefits of decolonization. As such the general thesis that postcolonial state-society relations have not been characterized by deep and horizontal comradeships running across interactions of ruling elites and the governed is very plausible. Tensions rather than 'ritualized dialogics' remained a common factor in state-society relations across postcolonial Africa, with minimum achievement of consent in only exceptional cases and on very brief occasions particularly during the first decade of independence dominated by false hopes and euphoria.

A combination of Foltz's four-dimensional thesis of trajectories of ordinary citizens' struggles for freedom and Mbembe's studies of thematics and aesthetics of power constructions in postcolonial Africa reveals an intricate disjuncture between forces of juridical freedom and those of popular freedom that have a bearing on further understanding the myths of decolonization, illusions of freedom and vicissitudes of society-state relations since the end of direct colonial rule in Africa.

What revealed the myths of decolonization and illusions of freedom was the lack of legitimacy of the African postcolonial state. Ali Mazrui offered a ground-breaking explanation for this legitimacy crisis:

> In situations where the leaders are identified too readily as people who have arisen from the ranks, it is easier for those who remain in the ranks to become envious of the privileges enjoyed by their former peers. Long-established elites are sometimes forgiven luxurious living more easily by 'lower classes' than newly successful members of the privileged classes. Those who have been rich for generations have consolidated their social distance and made it appear natural if not deserved. But the newly opulent are more easily accused of 'giving themselves airs'—and are more easily resented as a result. Resentment arises not from a defined social distance but, on the contrary, from the persistent residual social nearness between these newly opulent and the power fold from whom they spring. The Africa of the first generation of independence was an Africa bedeviled by precisely this close interpenetration between the elite and the masses (Mazrui 1988: 476).

Mazrui's intervention is very important as it challenges the common intellectual wisdom which generally explained tensions between the governed and the governors (state and citizens) in terms of widening distance between the ruling elites and the ordinary citizens. To Mazrui, the issue of postcolonial legitimacy crisis must not be sought in 'social distance' but in 'social nearness' that breeds envy among the ordinary members of society and other elites excluded from corridors of power.

In African studies there is a large corpus of literature which emphasized that despite its ambiguities African nationalism was a positive force which sought to achieve decolonization, nation-building, development, democracy, and regional integration (Mkandawire 1997: 71-107). What is ignored is the reality that once liberated from colonial rule, the postcolonial state went on to deny African citizens freedom within its boundaries on a massive scale, in the process denting the whole agenda of decolonization from a freedom perspective. Celebrated nationalist discourses of nation-building and development of the 1960s became justifications for denial of freedom for citizens as well as authoritarianism. This is confirmed by Ake who emphasized the pervasive presence of the postcolonial state in all walks of African people's lives, making it a phenomenon to be loathed, courted, and even avoided (Ake 1993: 17-25).

Praise-texts that emerged during the independence euphoria of the 1960s were less critical of denials of freedom to citizens by the postcolonial state. The freedom for the African state was celebrated as freedom for the ordinary people. Those people who questioned whether decolonization bequeathed freedom on the ordinary citizens were quickly branded as traitors and enemies of the postcolonial state. They were either forced to flee to exile or were detained, if not liquidated completely. The earliest targets were excluded elites who were trying to create opposition political formations and critical intellectuals who were easily branded as counter-revolutionaries as though decolonization was ever a revolutionary enterprise in the first place.

What has dominated and pre-occupied the minds of those who assumed state power at the end of direct colonial administration was coaxing ordinary citizens to celebrate with them what is termed 'Independence Days' each year as the time when freedom was attained. Whose freedom was it that is being celebrated, one may ask? In his studies of how postcolonial power was institutionalized, performed and displayed in his native country Cameroon and Togo, Mbembe revealed how ordinary citizens were forced to celebrate the 'taste for lecherous living' enjoyed by those in control of the postcolonial state and how elites constructed and deployed a particular official discourse that served to maintain the fiction of an African postcolonial society of happy citizens devoid of conflict (Mbembe 1992: 6).

Mbembe (1992: 3-37) introduced the concept of the 'postcolony' which is useful in capturing the mindset of a particular calibre of leadership and a particular configuration of power and unique mode of postcolonial governance (Mbembe 2001). According to him:

> To be sure, the postcolony is chaotically pluralistic, yet it has nonetheless an internal coherence. [...] The postcolony is characterized by a distinctive style of political improvisation, by a tendency to excess and a lack of proportion as well as by distinctive ways in which identities are multiplied, transformed and put into circulation. [...] In this sense, the postcolony is a particularly revealing, (and rather dramatic) stage on which are played out the wider problems of subjection and its corollary, discipline (Mbembe 1992: 3).

The postcolony is dominated by tensions between the state and citizens, and the governors and the governed. These tensions were deeply rooted and traceable to the practices and politics of postcolonial power routine, institutionalization, and broadcasting within a terrain dominated by colonial matrices of power. As the postcolonial state and those who manage it try to institutionalize their power, they invariably provoke reaction from those over whom they governed. Mbembe (1992: 4) described the complex postcolonial state-citizen relationship as 'illicit cohabitation, a relationship made fraught by the very fact of the commandment and its "subjects" having to share the same living space'.

What has not received adequate scholarly attention in this scheme of things is how 'subjects'/ordinary citizens fought and resisted being captured, dominated, exploited and being used to indulge in officially imposed postcolonial order that did not benefit them. Worby (1998: 337-354) argued that postcolonial African leaders rarely enjoyed undisputed power, meaning that their hold on power has always been tenuous and contested. This forced them to opt for and try to depend on the performance of quotidian ceremonies underpinned by extravagant dramaturgical and improvisational content, aimed at fostering popular collusion and eliciting citizen consent.

Because the postcolonial neocolonized state lacked strong essence – which forced it to operate through coercion rather than consent -- such Western institutions as the World Bank and International Monetary Fund called for 'limited state' and dominance of market forces as a solution to problems of governance and development bedevilling Africa. The postcolonial state became a condemned institution that not only threatened people's freedom but distorted operations of laws of demand and supply. On this situation, Mkandawire argued that:

> For Africa the 1980s and 1990s were a period of wanton destruction of institu-
> tions and untrammeled experimentation with half-baked institution ideas. The
> result was 'unconstructive destruction' in its most institutionally debilitating form.
> The view by BWIs of African institutions was a jaundiced one borrowing eclec-
> tically from both the rational choice and new Weberian view of the state. From
> either point of view the message was African institutions should be circumvented
> or simply destroyed often because they were guilty by association (Mkandawire
> 2003: 10).

The World Bank and IMF recommended the burial of the 'age of intervention' by the African state of the 1960s and 1970s that was blamed for economic and political crises. The postcolonial state was derided as 'a giant theft machine' captured by corrupt and renting-seeking leadership (Mkandawire 2003). But the current economic and political thinking is that the postcolonial state is not only the creator of the desperately needed institutions but also an indispensable engine rather than an enemy of development and freedom if well democratized and made accountable to the people. It is within this context that the notions of using the postcolonial state as an institution that can facilitate the attainment of freedom for the people re-emerged.

This is informed by the metamorphosis of economic thinking from 'getting prices right', through 'getting institutions right' to the current thinking of 'getting everything right' (Mkandawire 2003: 25). In short, the current efforts are focused on building strong institutions, not dismantling the state. Dangers remain though that the state still continues to be captured by certain interest groups that deny others freedom as is the case in Zimbabwe where a nationalist-military oligarchy is keeping the whole nation hostage while looting such resources as land and minerals under the guise of indigenization of the economy (Hammar et al 2003; Ndlovu-Gatsheni 2009).

The question of freedom has always been a central aspiration of the colonized peoples, and decolonization was supposed and expected to bring it to the ordinary people. Freedom in general is linked to the development of human consciousness and was articulated in various languages, metaphors and idioms. As a concept, freedom is often used interchangeably with such other broader ideas in political and social theory, as liberty, development, liberation, emancipation, democracy and even revolution. Robert H. Taylor argues that:

> Freedom is an idea which was not merely discovered once and then spread around the world like a new commodity. Rather, freedom and its institutions emerge and re-emerge out of concrete circumstances of individuals' lives in history. The story of freedom knows no cultural barriers and continues to unfold in unexpected ways (Taylor 2002: 7).

The challenge in studies of freedom is how to define it as it covers a wide spectrum of human aspirations and visions subsumed under both emancipation and liberation. It is a loaded concept. Any attempt to coin a generic meaning of freedom is a futile exercise as it means different things to different people across space and time. R. W. Davis chose to define freedom from a Western modernist, liberal and emancipatory perspective:

> We use freedom in the traditional and restricted sense of civil and political liberty—freedom of religion, freedom of speech and assembly, freedom of the individual from arbitrary and capricious authority over persons or property, freedom to produce and to exchange goods and services, and freedom to take part in the political process that shapes people's destiny (Davis 2002: vii).

But in Africa, freedom can be easily understood in its relationship to those processes that denied it. This is why Crawford Young has argued that for Africa, freedom is generally understood in relation to 'its negative other'. This is how he put it:

> The ultimate sources of unfreedom, in much of the reflection upon it, are exter-
> nal to Africa: the Atlantic slave trade; colonial subjugation; great-power imperial
> pretensions, globalizing capitalism (Young 2002: 9).

African notions of freedom emerged from the sites of struggle against oppression and exploitation. The sites of struggles for freedom ranged widely from those of one person resisting domination of another person, and one society resisting the domination of another. Karl Marx, for instance, was concerned with oppression and exploitation of one class by another.

Freedom, therefore, is articulated in various forms such as the Marxian class struggles, liberation wars such as the anti-colonial wars, as well as feminist struggles against patriarchal forms of domination and exploitation of women by men. But to gain a deeper understanding of the vicissitudes and tensions within politics of juridical freedom and popular freedom, it is important to briefly analyse the nature and character of post-1945 normative order within which the postcolonial state was born and under which ex-colonized peoples graduated from being subjects into citizens (Mamdani 1996).

The end of the Second World War in 1945 witnessed the birth of a transformed global normative international order. The right of self-government and self-determination was inscribed in the United Nations Charter. By 1948, a Universal Declaration of Human Rights was adopted that codified human rights as another major ingredient of the post-1945 global normative dispensation. For Africa, the post-1945 period witnessed intensified struggles for decolonization.

Decolonization gained a further boost from the fact that the post-1945 international system became dominated not by major colonial powers like Britain and France but by new superpowers, the United States of America and the Soviet UnionEven though these post-war superpowers became engrossed in a complex Cold War rivalry, both of them 'by different logics favoured the dissolution of the colonial order' (Foltz 2002: 28). During this period, African freedom was simplistically defined in relation to colonial rule. The conception of freedom was articulated by Kwame Nkrumah (1962: 175) who said: 'When I talk of freedom and independence for Africa, I mean that the vast African majority should be accepted as forming the basis of government in Africa.' This point is further amplified by Crawford Young who wrote that:

> 'Freedom' as the transcendental political goal, with the rise of anti-colonial natio-
> nalism, thus had as primary referent alien rule. Colonial subjects, in this doctrine
> of protest, achieve standing and rights only collectively as members of a commu-
> nity defined by territorial geopolitics of the colonial partition. [...] The compelling
> need both for solidarity in anti-colonial challenge and for consolidating the unity
> of the new state gave a collective cast to the idea of freedom (Young 2002: 31).

What is often missed in studies of decolonization with the exception of the
work of Frantz Fanon is that the departure of direct colonial rule resulted in
the birth of an undemocratic postcolonial neocolonized states that inherited
repressive structures and oppressive institutions created by colonial rule. This
is a point well captured by Frederick Cooper who argued that:

> African states were successors in a double sense. First, they were built on a set of
> institutions--bureaucracies, militaries, post offices, and (initially) legislatures--set
> up by colonial regimes, as well as on a principle of state sovereignty sanctified
> by a community of already existing states. [...] Second, African states took up
> a particular, and more recent, form of state project of colonialism: development
> (Cooper.2002: 156).

This means that colonialism deeply interpellated African nationalism and the
postcolonial state could not escape the snares of colonial matrices of power.
Young captured this point is well by Young when he stated that:

> African nationalists, at the time, sought no other formula; even as they fought
> colonial power, their own education and socialization had schooled them to hold
> the institutions of the imperial occupant in high regard as exemplary models of
> freedom (Young 2002: 29).

Just like colonial administrators, African leaders embarked on state consolidation
that privileged the freedom of a clique of people and their clients and patrons
rather than expansion of frontiers of freedom for the citizens. A state-centric
concept of freedom emerged that ran counter to popular discourses of
freedom. Mbembe argued that the postcolonial state soon considered 'itself
simultaneously as indistinguishable from society and as the upholder of the
law and the keeper of the truth. The state was embodied in a single person: the
President' (Mbembe 1992: 5). Cascading from this mentality was a complicated
relationship between the state and citizens. Liisa Laakso and Adebayo Olukoshi
have an apt description of this development:

> At independence, most African governments set themselves the task of under-
> taking a vigorous process of nation-building with the aim of welding their mul-
> ti-ethnic, multi-lingual, multi-cultural, and multi-religious countries into 'one

nation'. A central element of this official project of nation-building was the assumption that only the state could constitute it. The nation-building project was, therefore, state-driven from the outset, often relying on a top-down approach that carried far-reaching centralizing implications. In time, the unity project increasingly took on the form of a unitary project which sometimes rested on a narrow ethnic base around which a system of patronage networks was then built linking other groups and their elites. Another element of the nation-building project was the assumption that the diversity of ethnic identities was inherently negative and obstructive and that it was a requirement of successful nation-building that the different identities be eradicated, submerged under or subordinated to the identity of the group(s) that dominated state power (Laakso and Olukoshi 1996: 13).

This conception of freedom by the African elites in charge of the postcolonial state marked the beginning of the crisis of the postcolonial nation-state project. One after another, the postcolonial states 'abandoned the multi-party political framework on the basis of which freedom from direct colonial was attained and adopted single party rule or slid into military rule' (Laakso and Olukoshi 1996: 13-14). Once this process was on course; the state increasingly became predatory and unrepresentative. A majority struggled to free themselves from predatory postcolonial states. Victor Azarya and Naomi Chazan argued that this struggle involved a shift from an 'engagement paradigm' to a 'disengagement paradigm' as the state failed to afford ordinary people material welfare and freedom (Azarya and Chazan 1998: 110-111).

Given the cataclysmic changes of the 1990s, described by Larry Diamond as the 'second wind of change', provoked by the collapse of the Soviet Union, implosion of communist regimes of eastern and central Europe and the fall of the Berlin Wall did not succeed in facilitating the gaining of sovereignty by the ordinary people (Diamond 1998: 263-271). This argument is amply demonstrated by recent political developments that took place in Kenya and Zimbabwe between 2007 and 2008 where political elites continued to display extreme lack of respect for citizens' lives, disdain for ordinary people's choices in elections, and proclivities to use violence to re-assert freedom for the governing elites as opposed to the freedom for the people (Ranger 2008). During a campaign for the March 2008 elections, President Mugabe of Zimbabwe had the audacity to tell the electorate:

> You can vote for them [MDC], but that would be a wasted vote. I am telling you. You would just be cheating yourself. There is no way we can allow them to rule this country. Never, ever! We have a job to do, to protect our heritage. The MDC will not rule this country. It will never happen. We will never allow it (Quoted in Solidarity Peace Trust 2008).

This extreme disdain for the sovereignty of the citizens prompted a leading Zimbabwean opposition leader and academic Welshman Ncube to argue that:

> If all political players were to accept that it is the sovereign right of the people to freely elect a government of their choice no matter how we may disagree with their judgment. Even if we fiercely believe that it is wrong judgment we must accept it as their sovereign choice. If the political parties were to embrace that principle that the will of the people is sovereign [...] in my view that is the problem that faces the country at the moment—the refusal by the major political players that people can make a judgment, which is different from theirs. For as long as there is unwillingness to accept the judgment of the people we will have this crisis where the major political players seek to manipulate the will of the people (Financial Gazette, 22 November 2008).

Both in Kenya and Zimbabwe, citizens have found themselves hostage to the elites in charge of the postcolonial state. For both countries, it became clear how difficult it was to remove from power those elites that had entrenched themselves within the postcolonial state structures. Elections proved to be inadequate as a means used by the ordinary people to reclaim their sovereign power to choose their leaders. In Kenya, the December 2007 elections resulted in the worst form of violence ever experienced since the Mau Mau period; and in Zimbabwe, the post-29 March 2008 harmonized parliamentary, council and presidential elections were greeted with extreme forms of violence that targeted ordinary citizens (Prunier 2008; Masunungure 2009; Ndlovu-Gatsheni 2009). These examples help to show that juridical freedom cannot be conflated with popular freedom.

Struggles to translate juridical freedom into popular freedom

Since the end of colonization the struggle for freedom has taken complex forms. As noted by Foltz (2002: 40): 'Often, these relations have pitted freedom--or freedom of manoeuvre--for the political elite against the freedom and human rights of the ordinary citizens.' What is beyond doubt is that freedom of the African state entailed among other things admitting it to membership in the international society of sovereign states. The immediate struggle by the elite in charge of the young postcolonial states was to consolidate 'freedom of the state' into 'freedom for the state' (Foltz 2002: 40). This thinking developed within a terrain of emergence of African states as unique 'quasi-states'. Robert H. Jackson defined 'quasi-states' as new polities which were recognized as sovereign and independent units by other states within the international system, but which could not meet the demands of 'empirical' statehood (Jackson 1990).

Empirical statehood is measured by the state's capacity to exercise effective power within its boundaries and ability to defend itself from external attack (Clapham 1996: 15). The crisis of the postcolonial African state was well captured by Christopher Clapham who said: 'African independence launched into international politics a group of the world's poorest, weakest and most artificial states' (Clapham 1996: 15). These realities forced the African leadership to search for 'freedom for the African state' (Foltz 2002: 40). This took various forms including nationalization of the economy making it the domain of elite plunder and introduction of authoritarian one-party-state regimes and other forms of regime security rather than human security.

The postcolonial state assumed the character of the proverbial goat that grazed where it was tethered—preying upon the people, capturing, dominating, exploiting, and squeezing the local citizenry. Examples include Ghana and Guinea under Kwame Nkrumah and Sekou Toure (see Azarya and Chazan 1998: 115). These two West African states were practicing socialism that was used to justify extreme forms of centralization and politicization of every aspect of society.

Youth movements, trade unions, women's movements and other voluntary associations became integrated within the ruling parties. At the end of it all: 'Every citizen had to be a party member, and every village, neighbourhood, factory, and office had its party committee' (Azarya and Chazan 1998: 115). The underlying logic was to bring larger and larger segments of the population into the state domain of surveillance, repression, domination and exploitation.

No doubt the search for the freedom to African states in reality became the search for the freedom of those who were in control of the postcolonial neo-colonized state and their select clients and cronies. Sooner than later, it became apparent that the immediate benefit of decolonization accrued to the political elites in charge of the state rather than ordinary citizens. The postcolonial state soon became a symbol of repression, oppression and deprivation rather than a facilitator and guarantor of ordinary people's freedom. Those who felt excluded from the state responded by seeking 'freedom from the African state' (Foltz 2002: 41). This happened when the postcolonial state had undergone a cycle of deliberate circumscription of opposition, closure of the democratic space, squandering of political legitimacy, and increasing failure to deliver public services.

Seeking freedom from the state

The failure by the postcolonial state to deliver material benefits and freedom to the ordinary people resulted in a problematic relationship between the state and the citizens. Those in control of the state became the only full citizens together with their clients and cronies. The majority of the ordinary people became subjects once more after the end of colonial rule (Mamdani 1996). Instead of governing, the elites in charge of the state became rulers in the crudest sense of the term whereby their words became law and they reduced citizens not only to subjects but also to powerless sycophants and hungry praise-singers (Mazrui 1967).

Azarya and Chazan identified four common mechanisms employed by ordinary people to disengage from the state. These are 'suffer-manage syndrome', 'escaping', 'creation of systems parallel to those of the state', and 'self-enclosure' (Azarya and Chazan 1998: 110-135). One can add secession and attempts to seize the state itself as other forms employed by the dominated to attain freedom. The 'suffer-manage syndrome' involved constant adjustment to a deteriorating state performance. It encompasses a coterie of activities of learning to manage life and survive during moments of depravity and crisis. The activities ranged widely from altering diets and adjusting consumption habits to accord with existing meagre food supplies; urban dwellers cultivating vegetable gardens for home consumption and conversion of home craft into cottage industries (Azarya and Chazan 1998: 115-116).

These survival and suffer-management strategies were recently manifest in Zimbabwe where the economy experienced a free-fall from 2000 to 2008 (Vambe 2008). Those groups and individuals that failed to extricate themselves physically from the domain of the malfunctioning state resorted to 'suffer-management' as a mode of survival. Suffer-management is a form of coping with crisis and cannot be seriously considered as amounting to a form of freedom or a form of disengagement from the state. The advocates of active citizenship often blame those people who 'resort to suffer-management 'suffer-management' as passive citizens open to victimization by the state.

But when all avenues of exiting from the predatory state become closed, some citizens rely on resilience and constant adjustment to endure diminishing circumstances (Azarya and Chazan 1998: 117). In Zimbabwe, those responsible for causing deterioration of the economy through corruption and implementation of ill-conceived policies like the fast-track land reform programme, turned around and advised the suffering citizens to persevere in the midst of extreme scarcity of basic commodities. The common 'official jingle' that became banal on Zimbabwean television and radio was a song 'Rambamakashinga' (remain resolute and persevere).

The other common route is that of escaping from the malfunctioning or oppressive state physically. This takes the form of emigration. This option is commonly utilized by those who are better educated such as teachers, nurses, doctors, and academics. This group is usually followed by unskilled and semi-skilled groups who also experienced unbearable consequences of socio-economic and political crises. Political activists opposed to those in control of the state form another layer of those who emigrate.

During the crisis years under Kwame Nkrumah, 10 per cent of Ghana's population exited the country while about half of the Guinean population moved to live in countries such as Senegal, Ivory Coast, Sierra Leone, Liberia, Gambia and Mali. Ghanaians were mainly trooping to oil-rich Nigeria (Azarya and Chazan 1998: 115). In the southern African region, too, Zimbabweans have responded to the unprecedented economic and political crisis in their country through emigration. About 3 million Zimbabweans are estimated to be living in South Africa and another 2 million in the United Kingdom and other parts of the world (Sisulu et al 2007: 552-573). Escaping or migrating to another country is one of the oldest strategies that have been employed by Africans to escape political persecution, economic depravity and other forms of oppression.

The main constraint to this form of disengagement is the existence of modern boundaries that are often manned by state functionaries that require such documentation as passports and visas that are issued by the same state they are disengaging from. While in exile and in the Diaspora, some groups organize themselves into various political movements, campaigning for democracy such as the Campaign for Democracy in Ghana that was headed by Boakye Djan in the 1970s. Zimbabweans in exile and in the Diaspora have also formed various quasi-political groups including Mthwakazi People's Congress (MPC) calling for secession of Matabeleland from Zimbabwe as well as numerous welfare associations (Ndlovu-Gatsheni 2008: 167-199).

Secession is another of the routes to freedom that some frustrated constituencies and groups tired of oppression, domination and expression have attempted. It was the most radical form of claiming political freedom. The idea was to disengage from the state and attain recognition as a new sovereign state. The most commonly cited examples are those of Biafra in Nigeria and Katanga in Congo in the 1960s. Other stirrings of secessionist struggles occurred in Senegal (Casamance), Ethiopia (Eritrea) and Sudan (Southern Sudan). For sometime Eritrea remained the only example of successful secession until recently when Southern Sudan succeeded in breaking away from Arab dominated Northern Sudan..

Foltz (2002: 48) has explained why secessionist movements were few and had limited success in Africa. According to him, Secession 'ran strictly against the African state system's norms of preserving territorial integrity and the inherited colonial boundaries'. This norm was underwritten by the Organization of African Unity (OAU) which institutionalized the principles of inviolability of existing colonially-crafted borders in its Charter. The consequences of this decision by the founding fathers of postcolonial states was that minority groups that were often segregated from employment, excluded from benefitting from the national wealth and whose history, culture and languages were deliberately sidelined, had to endure bondage of boundaries.

The other option that was available to politically motivated military elites was to try and seize state power. This took the form of rebellion and military coups. The earliest examples included that of the Chadian rebellion of 1965. This was followed by other examples that culminated in civil wars in Uganda (1981-1986), Angola (1975-2002); Ethiopia (1974-94); Rwanda (1990-1994); and Mozambique (1980-1993) (Foltz 2002: 48). For several decades in countries like Ghana and Nigeria, military coups became the means of changing government and military strong-men succeeded each other via the barrel of the gun (Austen and Luckham 1975). Monopoly of force rather than elections and other softer forms of political bargaining became a raw material for political power.

The other option available to those excluded from power and its elaborate clientilist and patronage networks was to create alternative if not parallel systems to those of the state as an outlet for human needs that the state failed to fulfil. Examples include informal markets (black markets), smuggling, corruption and the use of alternative methods of justice. The logic behind these alternatives is that they override official channels and skirt the state's laws (Azarya and Chazan 1998: 123).

This form of disengagement involves attempts at beating the state systems and laws. In Zimbabwe, the late 1990s and early 2000, witnessed the mushrooming of flea markets that were not fully regulated by the state. There was also proliferation of informal street money-markets where hard currencies were sold and bought. But as the state became more and more desperate with the national banks running short of money, it had to act through a military style 'Operation Murambatsvina' (Operation Clean-Up) (Vambe 2008). It involved the demolition of structures and displacement of over 70,000 people as the state reacted against overriding cynicism towards official structures and widespread non-compliance with its laws (Tibaijuka 2005).

Azarya and Chazan have also noted that other forms of disengagement from the state have taken the form of conversion to new Pentecostal religious sects and magical cults where the ordinary people seek new spiritual redemption and material security (Azarya and Chazan 1998: 127). John and Jean Comaroff have drawn our attention to the proliferation of 'occult economies' involving ritual killings, use of magic, witchcraft and zombie conjuring in South Africa. They see these developments as an integral element of a thriving alternative modernity (Comaroffs 2000: 310-312). One of the most striving new religious movements in South Africa is the Universal Church of the Kingdom of God whose roots are traceable to Brazil. It has skilfully deployed the protestant ethic and combined it with enterprise and urbanity to link spiritual and material world issues that appeal to the poor.

Within the Universal Church, prayers are deployed in such a way that they speak directly to mundane issues of depression, lack of employment and financial problems (Comaroff 1996: 297-301). Because of this, the Universal Church and other Pentecostal religious movements have become an alternative space where people concentrate their search for material and spiritual deliverance. This is happening alongside with the proliferation of popular cultures with anti-establishment overtones, drawing on both traditional and Western sources. These forms of popular protest take the 'soft' forms of underground press, song, dance, poetry, theatre and literature. Ayi Kwei Armah's widely read novel The Beautiful Ones Are Not Yet Born, was part of protest literature (Armah 1971).

Mbembe (1992: 8) has identified ways by which ordinary citizens used their laughter to 'kidnap power and force it, as if by accident, to examine its own vulgarity'. For Zimbabwe, those in the Diaspora have evolved other forms of doing the same thing by setting up private radio stations and online newspapers. Examples include the British-based SWRADIO Africa and American-based Voice of America's Studio 7 staffed with exiled journalists and DJs. The most popular online newspaper is Newzimbabwe.com that consistently carries uncensored writings very critical of the state and its leadership.

Disengagement also took the form of 'self-enclosure' (Azarya and Chazan 1998: 128). This involved attempts to insulate oneself from the state, thereby gaining protection from its uncertainties. For example, the white minority groups in Zimbabwe have been using this strategy from as far back as 1987 when the twenty seats reserved for them were scrapped from the voter's roll. They withdrew from national politics and took refuge in their farms, business premises and gated communities located in the expensive suburbs (Muzondidya 2010: 5-38). They only came back to the public political domain when their land ownership was threatened through the Fast-Track Land Reform Programme whose modus operandi was compulsory acquisition of white-owned farms for resettlement of the black people. Only then did they become visible in large numbers in support of the opposition Movement for Democratic Change (MDC).

'Self-enclosure' also took the form of withdrawal: some urban dwellers withdrew to the rural enclaves; medical doctors withdrew from government contracts to establish their own firms; and other professionals loosened their ties with the state as a means of self-protection (Azarya and Chazan 1998: 130). Goran Hyden has argued that even peasants also participated in the evasive 'self-enclosure' technique, particularly those he described as 'uncaptured' ones who opted for a return to an ancestral 'economy of affection' (Hyden 1980).

Seeking to democratize the postcolonial state

Some African people still believe that they can attain freedom through fighting from within the boundaries of the oppressive state. The main method has been to deploy post-Cold War global normative values of democracy, human rights, and good governance to contest the basis of state authoritarianism. This strategy became very popular in the 1990s following the collapse of the Soviet Union and implosion of the communist regimes in Eastern Europe.

A convergence of local and global voices called for democracy as the pre-condition for any economic and military support for African postcolonial regimes. This began in 1990 with the French president, Francois Mitterrand, telling the Franco-Africa Summit attended by numerous heads of state from Francophone Africa that French economic and military assistance would be given to those regimes that were committed to progress towards democracy (Marchesin 1995: 5-24).

Since that time, France has scaled-down on its practise of giving military support to autocratic African leaders, the first casualty being Hissein Habre of Chad who was toppled violently from power while and the French stood aloof because he refused to follow the new path of democratization. The global financial institutions -- notably the World Bank, the International Monetary Fund and even the African Development Bank -- joined the voices of those fighting for democracy and made financial aid conditional on progress towards good governance (World Bank 1995). Foltz concluded that: 'Taken together, these external factors, interacting with domestic pressures, opened a political space in which Africans seeking political freedom could manoeuvre' (Foltz 2002: 53).

The 1990s also witnessed the mobilization and organization of Africans into civil society organizations (CSOs) ranging widely from churches, trade unions, women's movements, student movements, to ethnic-based pressure groups. As the Comaroffs:

> [...]Civil Society has served as a remarkably potent battle cry across the world. During inhospitable times, it reanimates the optimistic spirit of modernity, providing scholars, public figures, poets, and ordinary people alike a language with which to talk about democracy, moral community, justice, and populist politics; with which, furthermore, to breathe life back into, 'society,' declared dead almost twenty years ago by powerful magi of Second Coming [...] (Comaroffs 2000: 331).

African-based CSOs worked closely with Western non-governmental organizations (NGOs) and aid agencies to campaign for freedom. In Francophone Africa, the embers of freedom culminated in what became known as 'the National Conference' phenomenon that began in Benin as a convergence zone of those groups fighting for an end to authoritarianism practised by the one-party regimes (Robinson 1994: 575-610).

Indeed, a few one-party authoritarian regimes that had come to power in the 1960s crumbled under the weight of a combination of civil society and opposition forces' resistance to oppression and exploitation. Ready examples include Mathieu Kerekou of Benin, Mengistu Haile Mariam of Ethiopia, Kenneth Kaunda of Zambia, and Kamuzu Banda of Malawi. These regime changes were celebrated by Samuel P. Huntington as the 'third wave' of 'democratization in the late twentieth century' (Huntington 1991).

Despite the chequered history of the freedom struggles of the 1990s, with some proving to be false starts and others hijacked by incumbent dictators thirsty for relevance and re-birth, they formed a strong background for the current push for transparency, accountability, predictability, good corporate management and good political governance. By 2000, a new continental and global consensus had emerged on the complementarities of democracy and development.

The development of authoritarianism of the 1960s and 1970s was replaced by a strong belief in democratic development of the 1990s and 2000s (Sen 2000). Those fighting for freedom were no longer calling for the death of the state but for its restructuring to serve the interests of the people rather than that of the elites. Issues of corruption, kleptocracy and nepotism were identified as obstacles that needed to be removed if the African state was to serve the interests of the ordinary people. Some of the most corrupt and kleptocratic states like that of Mobutu Sese Seko of Zaire (now Democratic Republic of the Congo) could no longer rest until Mobutu himself was forced to leave the country to die in shame in exile. These realities led Young to conclude that:

> The democratic era of the 1990s, in spite of its disappointments and limitations, situated ideas of freedom in a multiplicity of sites, opened many new debates, and revived older ones on making freedom authentic by rooting it in an indigenous heritage (Young 2002: 37).

The new millennium witnessed the continuing struggles of ordinary people for widened frontiers of freedom consonant with the millenarian mood of hope for new life. The voices range from those of women and girls still pushing the remaining frontiers of patriarchy into the dustbin of history; youths claiming their space as a new generation; ethnic groups flexing their muscles for recognition and calling for decentralized forms of governance; and religious congregations creating a niche for their flock. What is common among these voices is the clarion call for democracy that would free them from the control of the centre and how to make the centre serve the ordinary people.

Seeking to reconfigure the postcolonial state into an engine of development

Since 2000 increasing voices have been calling stridently for new African states that would serve the ordinary people and promote popular freedom. In some literature, this type of state is described as a democratic developmental state. It is a state that is capable of working to fulfil the democratic and developmental aspirations of the majority of the people within its borders.

The envisaged democratic developmental state is to be defined by its institutional characteristics. The first key feature is that of embedding in African society, that is, a state that has formed strong and broad-based alliances with society and ensures effective and active participation of citizens in decision-making. The second is that of building autonomous institutions free from control by capricious and venal cliques bent of fulfilling personal selfish agendas. Such a state is expected to be totally freed from the trappings of autocracy of the 1960s and 1980s (Mkandawire 2001: 289-314).

Foltz attributed this change in thinking about the state to the impact of normative and historical transformation in the larger external environment. He identified two factors responsible for this normative shift: reduced global and continental tolerance for those leaders who seized power through coups and other violent means, and the questioning of the non-interference in national affairs norm (Foltz 2002: 58). The other contributory factor was the coming to power of a 'new generation of African leaders' that included

Thabo Mbeki of South Africa, Yoweri Museveni of Uganda, Paul Kagame of Rwanda, Meles Zenawi of Ethiopia, Isaias Afewerki of Eritrea and Olusegun Obasanjo of Nigeria, who were less authoritarian and less dogmatic unlike the founding fathers of the postcolonial states of the 1960s and the military leaders of the 1970s (Ottaway 1998).

While the 'new generation of African leaders' degenerated into authoritarianism of varying degrees, they remained better than those who presided over one-party and military dictatorships of the 1960s and 1970s. They were committed to the reconstruction of the African state in the direction of the fulfilment of popular demands for economic development and democracy. In combination or as individuals, they engaged and toyed with bigger plans for Africa such as the New Partnership for African Development (NEPAD), Pan-African Parliament (PAP), and the African Peer Review Mechanism (APRM). These pan-African institutions were meant to create a new momentum for Africa characterized by economic development and democratization (Murithi 2005). As Timothy Murithi puts it:

> With the creation of the African Union, African governments and their societies are expressing the desire, as yet unfulfilled, to address the unjust practices of the past which led to the social and economic marginalization of members of their societies. In so doing it is also an expression that Africa wants to play a constructive role in international relations as an equal partner and that the first step towards achieving this is to put its own house in order (Murithi 2005: 166).

The decision to build pan-African institutions as part of the plan to concretiz African aspirations for economic development and democracy is happening in conjunction with the return of the state as the legitimate driver of development and democratization. The Nigerian scholar, Eghosa Osaghae, noted that it has dawned on many researchers that the state remains the sole anchor for citizenship. It has also been realized that the state is the only institution that can carry and drive the distribution of resources (Osaghae 2010). The continuing struggle is over the nature and the type of state that will not be a menace to the people but a facilitator of economic development and provider of freedom and security.

Conclusion

Decolonization cannot just be celebrated uncritically. Such praise-oriented approaches towards decolonization have obscured the myths and illusions of freedom and tend to ignore the poor and problematic ethical, ideological, and political foundations of this project. Decolonization remained hostage to Western notions of emancipation that did not seriously question the ontological and epistemic essence of colonial modernity from the snares of which it tried to free Africans. Throughout the unfolding of decolonization, the radical liberatory aspects were compromised by the privileging of emancipatory-reformist ideas that did not predict the neo-colonial traps.

On top of unpacking decolonization in general, this chapter also analyzed the complexities of African struggles for freedom transcending those studies that conflated juridical freedom (freedom for the state) with popular freedom (freedom for the people). It has given empirical flesh, expanded and further problematized the pathways followed and pursued by ordinary people in search of freedom beyond Foltz's four-dimensional thesis.

Combining Foltz's thesis and Mbembe's work on dialectics, dynamics and entanglement of the interests of those who command and those expected to obey those commands within the postcolony, the chapter has discussed the complexities of postcolonial constructions of power and hegemony and how ordinary people have ceaselessly satirized, mocked, deflected, contested it; and even exited from the harsh domains of the postcolonial state at its most predatory moments.

The chapter unearthed multiple pathways to freedom pursued by ordinary citizens that transcended the conventional binary categories of domination and resistance, power and passivity, and autonomy and subjection that have shaped conventional wisdom. In the process, such issues as the crisis of legitimacy of the postcolonial state and the supposed redemptive aspects of the decolonization process are cast in new light that expands frontiers of knowledge on constructions of power within the postcolony, struggles for citizenship and popular sovereignty.

Part II

Discursive Constructions

4

Discursive Construction of
the African People

You have all heard of African personality; of African democracy; of the African way to socialism, of negritude, and so on. They are all props we have fashioned at different times to help us get on our feet again. Once we are up we shall not need any of them anymore. But for the moment it is in the nature of things that we may need to counter racism with what Jean-Paul Satre has called an anti-racist racism, to announce not just that we are good as the next man but that we are better.

Chinua Achebe

Introduction

The major African discourses on identity construction have acknowledged, and perhaps been hostage to, a modernist grammar and logic of alterity. Those discourses, informed by the aspirations of African liberation from colonial domination in particular, have always made efforts to seek an alternative foundational alterity and to articulate a transcendental subject that would constitute a radical alternative to the equally homogenized non-African Other. Of course, Of course, this is not the best way to approach the complex subject of identity formation and construction. The best approach is to begin from the acknowledgement of the openness, partiality, historicity, contingency, heterogeneity and (re)construction of all human identities.

This chapter use s a combination of historical and discursive approach to explain   the politics behind the making of the African postcolonial world and the construction of African identities. It deals specifically with what Ernesto Laclau (2005: 65) termed 'constructing the "people"'.

The chapter focuses is on the construction of the 'African people' as a political and social force as well as a product of the coloniality of power of racial classification of human population mediated by inferior-superior, irrational-rational, primitive-civilized and traditional-modern dichotomies imposed by Western and colonial modernity. While Laclau's work emphasizes the centrality of populism as a way of constructing the political realities as the 'royal road' towards understanding 'something about the ontological constitution of the political', there is also a need to factor in the concrete historical realities that played a central role in the making of the 'African people'. Therefore, theory and historical analysis are twinned throughout this chapter to enlighten the complex debates on the idea of Africa and the discursive construction of the 'African people'.

The discursive construction of the 'African people' is a continuing process. This is so because there is no consensus on what Africa means and who is an African. What has been said remains partial, provisional and open to debate. Even those like Cheikh Anta Diop who worked hard to define what Africa was and sought to capture its meaning in African terms could not contain the slippery nature of the idea of Africa together with its mirage character that made it to always melt away into the domains of representation, cartography, profiling and race (Diop 1974). The making of Africa and its people involved the work of explorers, cartographers, missionaries, travellers, colonial anthropologists, colonialists, African kings and chiefs, ordinary Africans as makers of history, historians, imperialists, pan-Africanists and African nationalists and others too numerous to mention.

My entry point into the construction of Africa and African identities is the complex states of being and becoming mediated through and through by spatial, agential, structural, historical and contingent variables. While African nationalist historians, in the their demolition of the imperial historiography that denied African people any credible history, worked hard to construct Africa as a coherent entity with a singular trajectory of civilization, their successes was only partial. Africa and African identities still continue to be the subject of contestation in social and political theory as well as in practical political discourses of nationalism and pan-Africanism.

No doubt the formation of African identities has been characterized by crises and conflicts. Deeply lodged within the discursive formation of African identities were complex historical processes and activities ranging from the politics of naming, physical cartography, religious demarcations, physical boundaries, cultural mapping, and linguistic classifications to ideological gerrymandering. Cooper (2002: 11) captured the complexity of the idea of Africa by describing it as 'many Africas'. He added that: 'At any one moment, Africa appears as a mixture of diverse languages and diverse cultures; indeed, linguistically, it is the most varied continent on earth.' Two questions immediately emerge: How then did the idea of Africa as a home of a people called Africans emerge? Do Africans exist as a collectivity pursuing common political and cultural objectives? Cooper noted, quite rightly in my view, that: 'It is only by looking over time that "Africa" begins to appear' (Cooper 2002:11).

Already Mudimbe (1988) has revealed that the idea of Africa was born out of multiple layers of inventions and constructions that commenced with explorations, so-called 'voyages of discovery', missionary activities and colonial processes. What emerged were equally complex African identities that were not underpinned by any semblance of common cultures and languages. This means that extrapolations of 'African' culture, identity in the singular or plural remained quite slippery as the notions tended to swing unsteadily between the poles of essentialism and contingency (Zeleza 2006: 13). The discursive formation of African identities was permeated by complex externally-generated discourses about the continent as well as internally-generated paradigms and politics through which the idea of Africa has been 'constructed and consumed, and sometimes celebrated and condemned' (Zeleza 2006:14).

One of the core challenges rocking the construction of African postcolonial nations is the refusal of existing heterogeneous identities to converge toward a single trajectory despite the untiring efforts of pan-Africanists who since 1900 regularly hosted pan-African conferences during which the idea of Africa was channelled towards a pan-African direction encompassing the various Diasporas. The latest manifestation of this refusal by African identities to coalesce into broader and friendly pan-African ones was demonstrated by the metamorphoses and mutations of African nationalism from civic principles founded on the slogan of 'diverse people unite' into narrow, autochthonous, nativist and xenophobic forms that breed violence rather than deep horizontal pan-African comradeship envisioned by the pan-Africanists (Ndlovu-Gatsheni 2010).

The present challenge for pan-Africanists and nationalists is how to deal with the phenomenon of degeneration of plural and civic forms of nationalism into nativism, xenophobia, and even genocides that have become manifest since the decolonization period and become even more virulent since the end of the Cold War. These issues need serious and careful consideration at this juncture when African leaders were busy toying with and implementing the mega project of establishing the United States of Africa. This is taking place within a terrain dominated by various forms of destabilizing and fragmenting bigotry, prejudices and phobias occurring within Africa itself and elsewhere.

The making of the African continent itself as both an idea and cartographic reality cannot be understood outside a clear understanding of such identity-forming processes as Orientalism, Occidentalism, the slave trade, imperialism, colonialism, apartheid, and ideologies such as pan-Africanism, Garveyism, Negritude, African Personality, Black Consciousness Movement right up to African Renaissance thought. These are some of the major discourses, that established the world of thought in which African people conceived their identities (Mudimbe 1988). The encounters between Europe and Africa, often dated to the fifteenth century, inaugurated the active imagination, naming and profiling of Africa in the West. To make meaning of what the explorers and missionaries encountered in a new environment, they had to mobilize their existing western knowledge and then re-inscribed the new geographical spaces and inhabitants in European discourse (Ahluwalia 2001: 20). Mbembe noted that:

> It is now widely acknowledged that Africa as an idea, a concept, has historically served, and continues to serve, as a polemical argument for the West's desperate desire to assert its difference from the rest of the world. In several respects, Africa still constitutes one of the metaphors through which the West represents the origin of its own norms, develops a self-image, and integrates this image into the set of signifiers asserting what it supposes to be its identity (Mbembe 2001: 2).

But the most simplistic approach that needs to be avoided at all costs is to consider Africans as a mere datum or census rather than as a collectivity organized in pursuit of a common political and cultural end due to existing diversities. Such a positivist-empirical approach tends to gloss over the fact that the complex question of identity-making itself is a political process mediated through and through by imperatives of inclusion and exclusion. Since the time of colonial encounters Africans have ceaselessly engaged in various political projects within which they continued to struggle to define themselves in political and cultural terms. The best way to approach the idea of Africa and African identities is as political projects mediated by identifiable but complex historical and political processes.

At another level, it is important to disabuse the old Marxist thinking which tended to dismiss ethnic, religious and racial identities as false consciousness and opiums of the unsophisticated minds that were soon to be replaced by market-generated class identities as the realities of the end of the Cold War in 1989 indicated that identities were a powerful force able to change the course of the world. For instance, the force of identities resulted in the implosion of the Soviet Union and the crumbling of pan-Slavism alongside socialism as unifying ideologies. Eastern and central Europe were not spared of the aggressive return of identity politics resulting in Yugoslavia falling into contending ethnic pieces and Czechoslovakia breaking into two ethnic pieces.

The marauding ghost of identity did not spare Africa with its fragile nation-states. For example, Somalia collapsed into contending clans rooted in precolonial history and the efforts to re-build Somalia into a single nation once more have proven very difficult and costly. Cote d'Ivoire experienced a war of 'who is who' as autochthonous discourses occupied the political centre-stage. In Zimbabwe, President Robert Mugabe proclaimed a *Third Chimurenga* that not only repudiated the policy of reconciliation but also enabled violent 're-conquest of settler colonialism' through forcible reclamation of land from whites to create a 'Zimbabwe for Zimbabweans' only (Ndlovu-Gatsheni 2010).

While this chapter is not dealing with the theme of African conflicts directly, it is clear that the subject of identity formation and its politics conjures up images of identity-based outbursts mediated by racial, ethnic, class, gender, regional and generational divisions. The slave trade, imperialism, colonialism, apartheid, African nationalism and pan-Africanism were all permeated by identity considerations of one form or another. During the slave trade, black races were victims of white races who used their labour to create wealth in the Americas and Europe. Imperialism and colonialism saw white races scrambling and partitioning the African continent among European powers galvanized by the Berlin Conference of 1884-1885. Colonialism was a racial affair through and through, with white races ruling over black ones.

This means that even unequal socio-economic and political privileges that continue to mark-out white and black races within the African continent were built using racial profiling and discrimination. Asymmetric inter-group economic power relations in a country like South Africa were largely a creation of apartheid racial discourses. No wonder then that social identities feature at the centre and across precolonial, colonial and postcolonial African terrain as a tool open to mobilization or rallying the different groups around their socio-economic and political grievances. Colonialists and African nationalists have a fair share in the manipulation of social differences for their hegemonic projects.

Zeleza (2008) has linked African conflicts to the complex discursive constructions and conjunctures of Africa's political economies, social identities, and cultural ecologies as configured out of specific local, national, and regional historical experiences and patterns of insertion into and engagement with an ever-changing world system. On the other hand, as Dorman, Hammet and Nugent (2007:4) noted, 'It is arguably in the nature of nationalism to distinguish insiders from outsiders.' The politics of 'Othering' and creation of strangers generated the Rwandan genocide and fuels other conflicts across the continent as African identities continue to be defined and redefined for various purposes. These examples vindicate the argument that the development of the idea of Africa as it unfolded across various historical epochs ceaselessly generated conflicts and new crises.

Even within the decolonization projects that were meant to create independent nations and sovereign states in Africa, lay some autochthonous and nativist forces existing as hidden script that propped up parochial rather than broader pan-African identities. For instance, Parry (2004: 40) revealed that whenever intellectual considerations of the narratives of decolonization were taken, 'rhetorics in which nativism in one form or another are evident' was noticeable. But whenever these forces of nativism and xenophobia were noticed, scholars were quick to pull out the disciplining theoretical whip to dismiss these as catalogues of epistemological errors, mannish dissent and anti-racist racism. No one was bold enough to carefully interrogate of such articulations as reflecting the problematic politics that were inherent in the development of the idea of Africa itself and the construction of African identities.

Inevitably Africa is a continent that is ceaselessly seeking to negotiate itself above the Eurocentric egoisms of singularities that continue to inform conventional and often insensitive notions of identities imposed on it and its people by external agents, such as the 'dark continent' for instance. Nyamnjoh (2001: 25) noted that Africans continued to refuse to be defined by particular identity markers imposed on them from elsewhere, choosing instead to draw from the competing and different influences in their lives as individuals and communities. This is in line with the nature of identity as a relational concept that is always permeated through and through by imperatives of power and resistance, subjection and citizenship, action and reaction as well as naming and controlling.

The idea of Africa emerged within a complex terrain of naming, conquering and controlling of weaker parts of the world by powerful ones. African politics of identity construction is permeated by complex desires for freedom and self-reconstitution after centuries of domination of the African continent and its people by the powerful nations of the North. Even identity politics that dominated and haunted the post-Cold War world were partly informed by popular struggles for material redistribution and justice, autonomy and desires for existential integrity and security in a context of collapsing and failing states and weakening regimes.

It is not surprising that as some African postcolonial states became weaker and others collapsed including Somalia, Liberia, Sierra Leone and the Democratic of Congo (DRC), identity politics became the dominant mode of mobilization, further fragmenting the already weak states and inflaming more conflicts. Contemporary postcolonial politics is dominated by such negative phenomena as xenophobia in South Africa, nativism in Ivory Coast and Zimbabwe, 'ethnic cleansing' in the DRC and the Sudan, and genocide in Rwanda. The idea of Africa and African identity is constantly reproduced within these conflict situations.

Mbembe (2006: 144) identified the dominant elements of current intellectual thinking on Africa as dominated by rethinking histories of freedom and modernities; the nature of liberal democratic order mediated by complex politics of shifting and contested citizenship and identity; how to ensure ethical conditions of human peaceful coexistence that is sensitive to politics of recognition and inclusion across the globe; and the questions of social justice in an unjust global economic, social, and political order. Politically explosive identities and the associated politics of difference, alterity, as well as resurgent discourses of nativism, xenophobia, and autochthony, continue to impinge on definitions of belonging, citizenship and broader politics of being African. But let us begin with how Europeans constructed global identities in general before focusing specifically on the making of African identities in particular.

The social construction of global human identities and spatialization of the world

Present-day continents and their current reduction into homes of various named identities is a product of operations of coloniality of power rooted in Western modernity. The foundational myths of social classification of human population were rooted in Darwinian social evolutionism and dualism within which Eurocentrism and racial ethnocentrism emerged. In this scheme of things, those people who ended up being called Europeans deployed the benefits of Western modernity to appropriate the course of human history and defined it as proceeding from state of nature as the point of departure and culminating in Western civilization (Quijano 2000: 551).

In this appropriated course of history, the Western world became the centre of the world. In the first place, Iberians conquered, named and colonized America that was dominated by different peoples such as the Aztecs, Mayas, Chimus, Aymaras, Incas, and Chibchas. Through colonization and naming, these people re-emerged with a single identity called Indians. In the second place, those peoples who were enslaved and were taken out of their homes bearing various ethnic names such as Ashanti and others were renamed as Negroes or blacks to distinguish them from Indians and Europeans (Quijano 2000: 551-552). In the third place, Western modernity and its coloniality created the African continent and Africans. During the same time of creating the Western identity of being white, Europeans and Americans emerged as superior beings compared to others. This is how Quijano summarized the processes:

> The first resultant from the history of colonial power had, in terms of colonial per-
> ception, two decisive implications. The first is obvious: peoples were dispossessed
> of their own and singular historical identities. The second is perhaps less obvious:
> their new racial identity, colonial and negative, involved the plundering of their
> places in the history of the cultural production of humanity. From then on, there
> were inferior races, capable only of producing inferior cultures. The new identity
> also involved their relocation in the historical time constituted with America first
> and with Europe later: from then on they were the past. [...] At the other hand,
> America was the first modern and global geocultural identity. Europe was the
> second and was constituted as a consequence of America, not the inverse. The
> constitution of Europe as a new historic entity/identity was made possible, in the
> first place, through the free labour of American Indians, blacks, and mestizos [...]
> It was on this foundation that a region was configured as the site of control of the
> Atlantic routes, which became in turn, and for this very reason, the decisive routes
> of world market. [...] So Europe and America mutually produced themselves as
> the historical and the first two new geocultural identities of the modern world
> (Quijano 2000: 522).

Three discursive processes were at play that created Eurocentrism, namely, the articulation of human differences into dualisms of capital/pre-capital, Europe/ non-Europe, civilized/ primitive, modern underpinned by a linear conception of human history from state of nature to European society/traditional; the naturalization of the cultural differences between human groups by means of their codification with the idea of race; and the distorted-temporal relocation of all those differences by relocating non-Europeans in the past (Quijano 2000: 552-553). All these are core elements of the coloniality of power introduced in Chapter One. Nelson Maldonado-Torres has ascribed what he calls the myth of continents as artificial creations of Western modernity. This is how he put it:

> In this sense it is possible to say that the 'myth of continents' is part of a larger racial myth in modernity formed in relation to imperial enterprises, in which continents denote not only space but also a well ordered hierarchy of customs, habits and potentials that are said to inhere in the people who live in them. Spaces thus become gendered and coloured, just as the forms of rationality, tastes, and capabilities of the peoples who occupy them (Maldonado-Torres 2006: 3).

What is clear is that the spatial, topological and cartographic set-up of the world today is nothing but a product of European coloniality of power (Lewis and Wigen 1997) as a continent, Africa emerged from this imperial scheme of things and African identities continued to be reconstructed since that time into barbarians, primitives, natives, blacks, Negroes, Bantu, Africans and other typologies across history and space.

The making of African identities

It is clear from the above analysis that the discursive formation of Africa is complex and has a chequered history. The name 'Africa' is an external label. Its roots are traceable to the Roman times where it was used with specific reference to North Africa before it was extended to the whole continent at the end of the first century before the current era. Zeleza (2006: 15) noted that the cartographic application was both gradual and contradictory as the idea of Africa became divorced from its original North African coding to be used with specific reference to Sub-Saharan Africa. Gayatri Spivak had this to say:

> *Africa*, a Roman name for what the Greeks called 'Libya,' itself perhaps a latini-zation of the name of the Berber tribe Aourigha (perhaps pronounced 'Afarika'), is a metonym that points to a greater indeterminacy: the mysteriousness of the space upon which we are born. *Africa* is only a time-bound naming; like all proper names it is a mark with an arbitrary connection to its referent, a catachresis. The earth as temporary dwelling has no foundational name (Spivak 1991: 170).

Inventions and ideas are always open to manipulation, re-constructions, representation and historical engineering. The idea of Africa has not been immune to these dialectics (Mudimbe 1988, 1994).

The processes of 'invention' and 'construction' of Africa left the definition of an African open to contestation and appropriation just like all other identities. Such processes as the slave trade, imperialism, and colonialism not only further complicated the picture but also actively played a role in the making of African identities. African nationalism and pan-Africanism that emerged as anti-theses to imperialism and colonialism did not succeed in settling the question of who was an African. No wonder then that the question of who an African is has come to engage the attention not only scholars but also politicians in postcolonial Africa.

The safest way to define Africa is as a reality as well as a construct 'whose boundaries—geographical, historical, cultural, epistemological and representational—have shifted according to the prevailing conceptions and configurations of global racial identities and power, and African nationalism, including, Pan-Africanism' (Zeleza 2006: 15). Among key historical processes that contributed to the current identity complexion of Africa is the slave trade. Neocosmos (2008) argued that the slave trade was perhaps one of the greatest forced migrations in history that had, and continues to have, profound effects on the development of the African continent's identity complexion and meaning of Africanness. The slave trade not only led to the formation of an African Diaspora in the Americas and Caribbean but also to the formation of whole states composed of Africans transposed to other parts of the world such as Haiti and Jamaica.

The formation of African Diasporas led to the popularization of the name Africa and the increasing racialization of African identity (Zeleza 2006: 15). With this reality, the definition of an African became even more complex. Jean-Francois Bayart (2000) wrote about miscegenation (racial mixing (miscegenation) that unfolded in tandem with the unfolding of trans-Atlantic commerce leading to the production of assimilado (mixed race) elites on the Angolan and Mozambican region as one of the legacies of the slave trade.

External definition of Africa is not only attributed to white people. Rather the slave trade contributed to the creation of a large black Diaspora and these enslaved people began to think of themselves as Africans. The term 'African' was used interchangeably with the name 'Ethiopian' that was used mainly by those black people who had converted to Christianity. As Cooper (2002: 12) argued, the term Ethiopian 'evoked Biblical histories of King Solomon and the Queen of Sheba. "Ethiopia" or "Africa" marked their place in a universal history.' He also added that: 'The point is that "Africa" emerged as a Diaspora asserted its place in the world' (Cooper 2002: 12).

At another level, a combination of mercantilism, imperialism, colonialism and other processes introduced whites, Indians and foreign Diasporas such as Lebanese as well as other people into the African continent from as far back as before the fifteenth century. Colonialism introduced race as a major factor in the definition of belonging and citizenship in Africa. Mamdani (1996) argued that colonialism produced colonial states that were bifurcated into citizens and subjects. What emerged out of the encounters between indigenous Africans and the colonizing whites was a complicated citizenship in which the white settlers tried to exclude the natives from full belonging. Mamdani (2001a) described this problem as 'the settler-native' question that has continued to haunt countries like South Africa and Zimbabwe that contained large populations of white settlers. He further argued that:

> In the context of a former settler colony, a single citizenship for settlers and na-tives can only be the result of an overall metamorphosis whereby erstwhile colo-nizers and colonized are politically reborn as equal members of a single political community. The word reconciliation cannot capture this metamorphosis...This is about establishing, for the first time, a political order based on consent and not conquest. It is about establishing a political community of equal and consenting citizens (Mamdani 2001a: 66).

Mamdani's intervention addressed three key questions in African studies. The first is the structure of political power inherited from the colonial state that did not facilitate easy construction of a genuinely postcolonial African nation-state. The second is the place of local African ethnic powers rooted in precolonial histories but also invented by colonialism within the postcolonial state that continued to function as a source of identity fragmentation. The third is how African postcolonial states failed to transcend ethnic differences that sat uneasily with notions of civic conceptions of belonging and citizenship. But Mamdani's main point is that the 'native question' pre-occupied and determined the form of rule which shaped colonial experience and that postcolonial African governments are finding it hard to transcend this tradition (Mamdani 1996).

This pre-occupation with the 'native question' made the African state different from the European nation-state. Indirect rule as a key colonial system of administration impinged on identity formation to the extent that the postcolonial state had the task of de-racializing civil society, de-tribalizing native authority and developing the economy in the context of unequal international relations (Mamdani 1996: 287). But Pal Ahluwalia (2001: 104-5) criticized Mamdani for constructing a new set of binaries of the citizen and subject while he set out to demystify others. This criticism, however, does not diminish the force of Mamdani's argument on the pertinent issues of identity construction and power articulation in Africa.

Mamdani's analysis of colonial forms of governance and how they impinged on African identities is amplified by other scholars like Cooper (2002) who engaged the issue of re-tribalization of Africa as colonialists abandoned the rhetoric of 'civilizing mission'. On the other hand, African nationalism as a deeply interpellated phenomenon had no capacity to solve the 'settler-native' question. Rather it turned the scale upside down, putting the 'native' where the settler was and struggling to pull the settler down to where the native was. Kuan- Hsing Chen (1998: 14) captured the explanation for this limit of nationalism well by arguing that:

> Shaped by the immanent logic of colonialism, Third World nationalism could not escape from reproducing racial and ethnic discrimination; a price to be paid by the colonizer as well as the colonized selves.

While colonial officials initially presented colonialism as a civilizing mission aimed at remaking Africans in the image of Europeans, Cooper (2002: 18) argues that by the 1920s colonial governments had realized the cost of such ventures and the limits of colonial power to govern directly using white personnel. Colonial polices shifted from the rhetoric of 'civilizing' Africans into attempts to invent African tradition. As Cooper (2002: 18) explains it, the aim was to 'conserve African societies in a colonizer's image of sanitized tradition, slowly and selectively being led towards evolution, while the empire profited from peasants' crop production or the output of mines and settler farms'. It was during this period that the idea of Africans as tribes that were static and enveloped in tradition gained importance. Those Africans that had imbibed Christianity and received western education became identified as troublesome 'detribalized natives' who were lost from their roots and traditions.

Another important contour in the debates on the identity of Africa and Africans is one that tries to reduce African identity to the 'phenotype'. As Neocosmos argued , in the attempts to define Africa at such institutions as the World Bank and even at the United Nations, there is the tendency to see North Africa more as part of the Middle East rather than Africa. In this case, Africa is defined as 'Black Sub-Saharan Africa' that is largely inhabited by Bantu-speaking peoples (Neocosmos 2008: 7). The other colonially-produced layer of identity in Africa is that which stressed the division of Africans into Francophone and Anglophone identities.

To Mbembe, African identities were a product of the combination of the 'the elsewhere' and 'the here' (Eurozine www.eurozine.com). This is so because even before the age of colonialism, Africa was already open to external influences that further complicated its identity complexion. Bayart (2000: 217) has successfully challenged the Hegelian idea of an African continent that is 'cut off from all contacts with the rest of the world [...] removed from the light of self-conscious history and wrapped in the dark mantle of the night'. Bayart argued that if the history of Africa is understood from the perspective of *longue durées*, the continent was never isolated from the rest of the world particularly Europe, Asia and the Americas.

This was evidenced by the antiquity of Christianity in Ethiopia, the spread of Islam on the coasts, the establishment of Austronesia colonies in Madagascar, regular trade with China, India, the Persian Gulf and the Mediterranean. Due to these connections, the eastern and southern parts of Africa were integrated for centuries into the pre-modern economic systems of the so-called the Orient. According to Bayart (2000: 218) even the Sahara Desert was never an 'ocean of sand and desolation' that demarcated and enclosed Sub-Saharan Africa from external influences.

A combination of all the processes outlined above reinforces Kwame Appiah's (1992) argument that Africa is not a primordial fixture but an invented reality. But while it is true that Africans were not made of the same cultural clay, they have experienced some common historical processes that largely justify their claim of a common identity. But the contingency of African identities should not be used to deny that we today have an identity called African. There is abundant evidence that numerous peoples and societies have carved out a place of their own across the African continent and in the process created their own 'little Africas, each laying their bricks across the huge and intricate cartographic, cognitive, and cultural construct, known as "Africa"' (Zeleza (2006: 18).

The flows of commodities, capital, ideas, and people have coalesced to create an African identity. Even the tragedies that have befallen the continent, including conflicts and underdevelopment, have indirectly provoked a consciousness of being African. In short, even negative interpretations of Africa that created a picture of Africa as 'possessing things and attributes' never 'properly part of human nature', contribute to the consciousness of being African (Mbembe 2001: 1). Then positive works of pan-Africanists informed by discourses of African Renaissance and the languages unity used at meetings at the African Union and Pan-African Parliament consistently build the idea of a pan-African identity.

African nationalism and the making of Africans

African nationalism was the laboratory within which African identities were created. The process of creating a common African identity had to contend with the historical realities on the ground of trying to homogenize ethnic, racial and religious differences. Indeed, due to the complex historical processes dating as far back as the 'voyages of discovery', the slave trade and beyond which coalesced to produce what we now call Africa and African identities, these became nothing but 'states of being and of becoming' (Zeleza 2006: 19). Like all identities, being African became open to claims by various peoples residing in and outside the continent.

Chipkin (2007: 2) argued that Africans across the continent 'emerged primarily in and through the process of nationalist resistance to colonialism'. This is indeed a logical argument since nationalism was and is basically a process of making people-as-nation and nation-as-state (nation-building and state-building) through homogenization of differences (Ndlovu-Gatsheni 2009a). African nationalism was, therefore, a grand project and a process of making African citizens out of colonial subjects. But earlier processes such as mercantilism, imperialism, colonialism and pan-Africanism also contributed to the making of African identities of particular kinds.

But born out of a continent whose identity has remained hard to define, African nationalism was never a straightforward human affair. Its progenitor—Pan Africanism was never a singular phenomenon. Pan-Africanism fell into six versions reflective of the complexities of historical experiences of the African people. These versions were Trans-Atlantic, Black Atlantic, continental, sub-Saharan, Pan-Arab, and Global. Zeleza (2003) summarized the core imaginations in each of the six Pan-Africanisms as follows: proponents of trans-Atlantic version imagined a pan-African world stretching from the continent right into the Diaspora in the Americas; the Black Atlantic version pre-occupied itself with African Diaspora community in the Americas and Europe excluding continental Africans; the continental version was primarily focused on the unification of continental Africa; sub-Saharan and Pan-Arab versions restricted themselves to the peoples of the continent north and south of the Sahara, with Pan-Arabism extending into western Asia and the Middle-East. The global version sought to reclaim African peoples dispersed to all corners of the world into one identity.

But it was continental Pan-Africanism that became popular in Africa at the end of the Second World War. Its main achievement was the formation of the Organization of African Unity (OAU) in 1963. Continental Pan-Africanism accepted the cartographic realities imposed by the Berlin Conference of 1884-1885 that resulted in the partition of Africa into various colonial states and protectorates. But again there was no consensus among African leaders on how to proceed concretely to create a union of African states. The leaders were pitched into two broad camps, namely, the Casablanca and the Monrovia groups. Led by Ghana under the charismatic Kwame Nkrumah, the Casablanca block wanted immediate formation of the United States of Africa. The Monrovia group led by Nigeria, opted for the gradualist approach towards integration of the African continent into a single government (Adejumobi and Olukoshi 2008: 3-19).

African nationalism had an ambiguous relationship with Pan-Africanism. Sometimes it reinforced it and at other times subverted it due to issues of sovereignty. This also shows that African nationalism was a very complicated socio-political phenomenon on its own. It was mediated by complex antinomies of black liberation thought and propelled and also constrained by ideological conundrums (Ndlovu-Gatsheni 2008: 53-86). It was fuelled by a complex combination of ambiguous local struggles, diverse micro- and macro-histories and sociologies. Emerging within a colonial environment, it was already deeply interpellated by the immanent logic of colonialism including its racist and ethnic undertones, but was not completely disconnected from the fading precolonial past, myths, spiritualities and memories.

African nationalism was also shaped from 'above', meaning its enunciations remained open to continental and global ideologies, as they were seen to fit and advance local agendas. It is within this context that nationalism incorporated such external and Diaspora ideologies as Garveyism, Negritude, Marxism, Ethiopianism, Christianity, Pan-Africanism, Leninism, Maoism, Republicanism and liberalism—mixing these with indigenous resources of entitlement to land for instance (Ndlovu-Gatsheni 2009b).

In short, African nationalism was basically a particular form of imagination of freedom. Decolonization was a popular term to define this imagined freedom. Five fundamental questions pre-occupied African nationalists as potential and actual nation-and state-builders: (i) How to forge national consciousness out of a multiplicity of racial and ethnic groups enclosed within the colonial state boundaries; (ii) How to fashion a suitable model of governance relevant to societies emerging from colonialism; (iii) What models of economic development were relevant for promotion of rapid economic growth to extricate postcolonial societies from underdevelopment; (iv) What role was the independent African postcolonial state to play in the economy and society; (v) How might the new African political leaders promote popular democracy and mass justice that was denied by colonialism.

No African leader had clear answers to these complex questions. All nationalists embarked on trial and error backed by various grand theories of re-making the African identity. One of the projects of cultural and identity reconstruction was known as Negritude. Negritude first developed among African and Caribbean artist-intellectuals and emerged in Paris in the early 1930s (Wilder 2009: 101-140). It was a complex reaction to the racism and alienation that was cloaked under the French colonial policy of assimilation. Its objective was to reverse the representations ascribed to the Africans, turning those negative identities into positive images. Leopold Sedar Senghor explained it this way:

> In what circumstances did Aime Cesaire and I launch the word negritude between 1933 and 1935? At that time, along with several other black students we were plunged into a panic-stricken despair. The horizon was blocked. No reform was in sight and the colonizers were justifying our political and economic dependence by the theory of the *tabula rasa*...In order to establish an effective revolution, our revolution, we had first to divest ourselves of our borrowed attire—that of assimilation— and assert our being; that is to say our negritude (cited in Ahluwalia 2003: 32).

Indeed, such African initiatives in identity-making such as Pan-Africanism, Negritude, Consciencism, *Ubuntu* (African Humanism), and African Personality up to African Renaissance cannot make sense outside the broader African search for self-definition and identity reconstruction.

At least five imaginations of community, citizenship, belonging and coexistence are discernible from the history of freedom and modernity in Africa. Zeleza (2006: 14) identified these as: the nativist, the liberal, the popular democratic, the theocratic, and the transnational prescriptive models. The nativist imagination of African freedom has elicited widespread condemnation for being backward-looking, navel-gazing and founded on false metaphysics of difference and alterity (Mbembe 2002: 629). It is feared as the crucible of reverse racism and the nursery for xenophobia and even genocide. At the centre of the debates is the long-standing question of who is an African which sounds very clear but is very hard to answer in countries like South Africa where white races like Afrikaners were also claiming African identity, to the extent that during the heydays of apartheid, Afrikaners had managed to claim nativity and indigeneity. Yet they denied black people the collective term Africans and pushed them into Bantustans where they were identified in ethnic/tribal terms.

Who then is an African?

The question of who an African is still needs to be confronted head-on even within the midst of complex politics of xenophobia and nativism currently operational in Africa and undermining pan-African efforts. Ali Mazrui (2009) classifies Africans into two categories: '*Africans of the blood*' and '*Africans of the soil*' (emphasis in the original source). He went further to say:

> Africans of the blood are defined by racial and genealogical terms. They are iden-
> tified with the black race. Africans of the soil, on the other hand, are defined in
> geographical terms. They are identified with the African continent in nationality
> and ancestral location (Mazrui 2009: xi).

Among Africans of the soil, Mazrui included the light complexioned Libyans, Egyptians and Tunisians whose genealogical roots are traceable to somewhere else. Also, Diaspora Africans located in such places as Jamaica, Haiti, Brazil, the Caribbean and the United States of America, are defined by Mazrui as Africans of the soil but not of the blood. Whites located in Africa like Afri-kaners and such other racial minorities as Arabs (Afrabians) to use Mazrui's term, Lebanese, Helens, Indians and others were African of the soil too (Ma-zrui 2009: xi-xv). The intervention by Mazrui is one way of dealing with the question of who an African is. He concluded that: 'Africans of the soil and Africans of the blood were converging into newer and more comprehensive identities' (Mazrui 2009: xv). The strength of Mazrui's intervention on this controversial and sensitive issue is that he adopts a non-xenophobic but histo-rical definition of African-ness.

But there are other classificatory and definitional schemes that have been deployed to isolate one as an African, namely; racial, geographical/territorial, and consciousness/commitment to Africa (Adibe 2009: 16). The racial definition is found wanting in that it does not cater for those who were not black just as it wrongly assumed that all black people were Africans. The geographical-territorial definition simplistically categorizes all those born in the continent of Africa as Africans irrespective of their colour and other external and consciousness attributes. Its key weakness is that it excluded those Africans living in the Diaspora who define themselves as Africans.

The definition of African-ness through the consciousness of being African is one that was used by former president of South Africa, Thabo Mbeki, in his famous 'I am an African' speech of 1996. It is a pragmatic and politically loaded one. But its weakness is that it is too fluid to the extent of embracing 'anyone expressing any sort of interest in African affairs' (Adibe 2009: 22). Kwesi Kwaa Prah is also very critical of the definition of the African as anyone and anybody 'committed to Africa'. He sees it as a South African version of the definition of 'African-ness' that is specific to the context of a former apartheid society (Prah 2009: 57-60. His conclusion is that:

It is important to remember that, the African identity (like all identities) is not a closed phenomenon cast in stone. It is a changing condition with evolving terms and conditions of reference. What remains the touchstone in this evolutionary process is that, the emerging understanding of Africanness must be emancipatory for Africans and the rest of humanity (Prah 2009: 60).

One attempt to describe Africanness in plural terms is offered by Eno and Eno (2009: 63) who tried to synthesize the complex discourses of African identity by coming up with six different typologies of Africanness. These are:

- *Africanness of accident of geography*; This refers to people who happene to find themselves in Africa without wish to be there; they are individuals who find themselves living in the continent by virtue of circumstances beyond their control.

- *Africanness by birth*; This refers to Someone who is born in Africa regardless of his/her race or ethnic group, or even political ideology or cultural doctrine.

- *Africanness by settlership*; This refers to citizenship conferred on settlers by the colonial regimes. Usually, the settlers first arrived as prospectors, then the colonial governments expropriated land for them from the African indigenes. Unlike others who came to Africa to see what prospects lay in the virgin continent, these settlers and decided to make Africa their home even after independence, and either continue to exploit African land and manpower or sell 'their' land and property to other Africans before venturing into other activities.

- *Africanness by culture or acculturation;* This refers to someone who may not be an African by ethnicity but who has lived in the continent long enough to have adopted the way of life, culture and tradition of the average African.

- *Africanness by ideology*: Someone who may or may not be an African by ethnicity background, but whose shares African thought, values, ideology and other sentiments and has the intuitive desire to be part of the African world.

- *Africanness by pretension or circumstantial Africanness*, this group comprises individuals or societies who use African identity as and when it suits them for their specific purposes; in other words, they are circumstantial Africans. Members of this group are not pleased to be identified with Negritud or blackness; they do not share, values, ideology, culture, ethnicity or any other quality except the sheer 'the accident' of existing on the continent.

While these typologies are open to further debate, they leave us with a clear message that African identity is complex, multi-layered and open to different interpretations. Both the idea of Africa and African identities are best understood as states of being and becoming that are better studied as open-ended and as developing. What is disturbing however is the tendency of this identity politics to degenerate into various phobias that run counter to the broader pan-African philosophy of unity.

Autochthonous discourses and Afro-phobias

The question of who is an African pre-occupied early African thinkers such as Edward Blyden who coined the term 'African personality' in the 1880s and who believed that Africans would forge modern, liberated and confident personalities to reclaim their rightful place in the world once they emerged from the uneasy mixture of traditional, Western and Islamic values and traditions, (Bly- den 1967). Since then the question has continued to pre-occupy the minds of academics and politicians. This is indicated by the emergence of new literature on social identities such as Ivor Chipkin (2007); Ndlovu-Gatsheni (2009); John and Jean Comaroff (2009), Peter Geshiere (2009), Jideofor Adibe (2009) and many others that are focused on the theme of African iden- tities and their latest articulations in narrow terms.

This new literature explores a range of intriguing, and absurd phenomena within the broad history of African identity that is refusing to easily succumb to modernization and the current global discourses of globalization, cosmopo- litanism and neoliberalism. What emerges poignantly is that humanity in ge- neral and Africans in particular, are caught up in deepening frictions between the universal and the local, with more and more people asserting their iden- tities in local, autochthonous, nativist and even xenophobic ways. Ngugi wa Thiong'o describes the situation rather well. His words:

> The pan-Africanism that envisaged the idea of wholeness was gradually cut down to the size of a continent, then a nation, a region, an ethnos, a clan, and even a village in some instances. [...] But pan-Africanism has not outlived its mission. Seen as an economic, political, cultural, and psychological re-membering vision, it should continue to guide remembering practices (Ngugi wa Thiong'o 2009: 61).

Mamdani (2001b; 2009) has again taken the lead in making sense of identity-based forms of violence including genocides in Rwanda and Darfur. In his examination of the factors that contributed to the outbreak of genocide in Rwanda in 1994, he tracked how colonialism drilled into the natives and settlers Tutsi and Hutu identities by emphasizing their differences and even going as far as to concretize them by issuing identity cards along this identity/ethnic fault lines. According to Mamdani, the Belgian colonialists turned Hutu and Tutsi into racial identities, with the Hutu reconstructed as indigenous and the Tutsi as aliens. They also created a segregated school system that amplified the reconstructed Hutu-Tutsi racial distinctions. They went further to exclude the Hutu from priesthood and local government and, in the process, built a historic grievance among the excluded and marginalized communities (Mamdani 2001b).

The consequences of the colonial-crafted, racialized citizenship caused animosity not only between the colonialists and the Hutu-Tutsi, but also between the Hutu and Tutsi. Hutu nationalism became opposed to both colonialism and Tutsi domination, culminating in the revolution of 1959 where the majority Hutu overthrew the Tutsi monarchy and sent thousands of Tutsi into exile. This reinforced the perception of Tutsi as aliens. When the Tutsi tried to come back in 1990 through military invasion, a can of worms broke open as the Hutu mobilized to eliminate the Tutsi 'race'. The overall result was a deadly genocide that left the world puzzled. Mamdani also located the violence in Darfur within colonial history:

> We shall see that the violence in Darfur was driven by two issues: one local, the other national. The local grievance focused on land and had a double background; its deep background was a colonial legacy of parcelling Darfur between tribes, with some given homelands and others not; its immediate background was a four-decades-long process of drought and desertification that exacerbated the conflict between tribes with land and those without. The national context was a rebellion that brought the state into an ongoing civil (tribal) war (Mamdani 2009: 4).

The degeneration of African identities into contending and violent factions within a single state continues to be a big challenge today. Frantz Fanon (1968) predicted that the decolonization project predicated on an impoverished African nationalism that was permeated by what he termed 'pitfalls of national consciousness' was going to fail to facilitate a re-birth of African humanity free from the event of colonialism and its racial bigotry. To Fanon, such phenomena as nativism and xenophobia were an inevitable product of pitfalls of national consciousness reflective of native bourgeois intellectual laziness. The lazy native bourgeoisie eventually spearheaded the liberation struggle. The consequences were what Fanon termed 'repetition without difference'. This repetition without difference unfolds from nationalism to ultra-nationalism, to chauvinism and then to racism and xenophobia (Fanon 1968). This metamorphosis and mutation of African nationalism is a departure from the civic and pluralist imaginations of the African national project founded on the earlier nationalist slogan of 'diverse people unite'.

But as nationalism assumed the new form of postcolonial state ideology, the terms of citizenship changed as chauvinism and racism were mobilized by the triumphant African bourgeoisie towards formulation of 'bourgeoisie nationalism' as opposed to 'popular-democratic nationalism' (Neocosmos 2006). Postcolonial nativism and xenophobia began with the 'native bourgeoisie' violently attacking colonial personalities as constituting an insult to 'our dignity as a nation'. These attacks would be justified as part of furthering the cause of decolonization, Africanization and nationalization processes. While the 'native bourgeoisie' attacked the 'white bourgeoisie', the workers would start a 'fight against non-national Africans'. Fanon concluded that:

> From nationalism we have passed to ultra-nationalism, to chauvinism, and finally to racism. These foreigners are called on to leave; their shops are burned, their street stalls are wrecked, and in fact the government [...] commands them to go, thus giving their nationals satisfaction (Fanon 1968: 122).

The Zimbabwean 'nativist revolution' known as the Third Chimurenga falls neatly within the Fanonian explanation. It witnessed the government supporting and assisting war veterans and peasants to invade white-owned commercial farms at the beginning of 2000. The 'native bourgeoisie' in ZANU-PF declared that 'Zimbabwe is for Zimbabweans' and that as 'sons and daughters of the soil', they were entitled to land and mines of Zimbabwe (Ndlovu-Gatsheni 2007; 2009). The same logic lay behind Idi Amin's expulsion of the Asians in Uganda in 1972 that was justified on the ground of a combination of fulfilling mass justice that was denied by colonialism and on the basis of indignity.

Xenophobic violence that broke out in South Africa in May 2008 is explained by Neocosmos (2006) as another example of degeneration of nationalism into nativism and xenophobia, albeit with some contextual variations. Neocosmos' interpretation of xenophobia is informed by Fanonian thought. To him, nativism and xenophobia were founded on a politics of nationalism predicated on and stressing indignity as the central imperative of citizenship. Neocosmos defined xenophobia as a political discourse and practise lodged within particular ideologies and consciousness that has arisen in post-apartheid South Africa permeated by a politics of fear prevalent in both state and society. It has three contours: a state discourse of xenophobia; a discourse of South African exceptionalism; and a conception of citizenship founded exclusively on indignity (Neocosmos 2008: 587).

The roots of xenophobia in South Africa lay in official national discourse of a democratic country with a robust economy that was being invaded by illegal immigrants who were criminals, who constituted a threat to national stability, and who put pressure on social services and made the government to fail to deal effectively with unemployment and housing shortage (Neocosmos 2008). The second strand of argument emphasizes the role of the discourse of South African exceptionalism, i.e., an industrialized, democratic and economically performing nation that was not part of the African continent invaded by poor people from Africa. The third string of argument explains how indignity has come to be used as the only way to define citizenship and claim entitlement to resources, jobs and other services. Birth place and phenotype thus become factors in defining citizenship (Neocosmos 2008).

Neocosmos is also very critical of the liberalism-based human rights discourse that produced passive citizenship and continuously reinforced notions of victimhood among the black constituencies as well as a sense of primal entitlements to resources. He sees xenophobia as also rooted in 'agency-less' people who competed to appeal to the state. His conclusion is that:

> Xenophobia and the authoritarianism of which it is but an example, are a product of liberalism, liberal democracy and Human Rights Discourse. It is not an irrational aberration brought from outside the liberal realm [...] rather it is made possible/enabled by liberalism itself [...] The problem is that an emancipatory politics has disappeared from post-apartheid society in favour of appeals to the state (Neocosmos 2006: 133).

What must be said is that African nationalism was itself a terrain of retribalization of identities and this compromised its ability to create stable postcolonial national identities. Secondly, nationalism suffered greatly from interpellation by the immanent logic of colonialism and apartheid, making it reproduce racism and ethnicity (Ndlovu-Gatsheni 2009a). For South Africa, Neocosmos (2006) argued that apartheid colonialism created what he described as 'foreign natives' and 'native foreigners' through such projects as the creation of Bantustans. Bantustan mentality, for instance, explains the failure by some South Africans to know that people of Shangani and Venda origins were part of South Africa.

Mbembe (2002) provided a philosophically informed explanation of nativism and xenophobia. In the first place, he saw nativism as nothing but a politics of lamentation of loss of African purity, a form of culturalism pre-occupied with the question of identity and authenticity, inspired by 'a so-called revolutionary politics which seek to break away from imperialism and dependence' (Mbembe 2002: 629). Nativism was a twin sister of Afro-radicalism—and both were 'discourses of self' and 'projects of self-regeneration, self-knowledge, and self-rule'.' Mbembe wrote that:

> A more significant development has been an emerging junction between the old anti-imperialist thematics—'revolution,' 'anticolonialism'—and the nativist theses. Fragments of these imaginaries are now combining to oppose globalization, to relaunch the metaphysics of difference, to reenchant tradition, and to revive the utopian vision of an Africanity that is coterminous with blackness (Mbembe 2002: 263-264).

These discourses constituted a crucible within which the argument of autochthony was born with its perception that 'each spatio-racial formation has its own culture, its own historicity, its own way of being, and its own relationship with the future and with the past' (Mbembe 2002: 264).

A more recent study of xenophobia in South Africa that is propelled through the ideology of *Makwerekwere* (see Matsinhe 2011) reveals more clearly what is at stake. Matsinhe saw Africa as suffering from 'fear of itself' that is 'exemplified by the loathing of black foreign nationals in south Africa.' His key question is framed in terms of: 'How did victims of apartheid become victimizers with such violent gushing of ire almost exclusively against Africans?' (Matsinhe 2011: 295-296). His explanation based on empirical research done in South Africa is that xenophobia in South Africa, is located within complex dynamics of colonial group relations constructed by apartheid that built a collective Afrophobic self-contempt among Africans as a result of painful 'socio-emotional imprints of apartheid power asymmetries that produced a colonised self among blacks' (Matsinhe 2011: 299). He concludes thus:

> In the context of South African history the violent aversion towards African foreign nationals in South Africa can best be described as Afrophobia. The ideology of Makwerekwere seeks to make visible the invisible object of fear in order to eliminate it. The roots of this ideology "must be sought in the psychological realm of ego-weak characters who construct their identity by denigrating others [...] [in need of] scapegoats to externalize what cannot be sublimated.' The ideology of Makwerekwere externalizes internal repression (Matsinhe 2011: 310).

On the other hand, Dunn (2009: 115) dismissed autochthonous politics as functioning as a trope, without any substance of its own, within the process of constituting political identities, which revolved round questions of citizenship and the concept of citizenship as the bearer of rights. But the ghost of xenophobia continues to haunt many postcolonial societies such as Ivory Coast where the Ivorian crisis that began in September 2002 with its Ivoirian ultra nationalism at its centre. There was some amalgamation of anticolonial and autochthonous discourses in Ivory Coast with those peddling autochthonous politics not only expressing anti-foreign elements but also railing against the presence of French forces as a reminder of continuation of colonial tutelage (Marshal-Fratani 2007: 31). Richard Banegas (2006: 1) argued that since September 2002, 'Cote d'Ivoire has been floundering in a poisonous morass of identity politics.

On the other hand, Zimbabwe's *Third Chimurenga* (third liberation war for black/native economic empowerment) was also punctuated by some xenophobic politics, anti-colonial trope and pan-African rhetoric, making it very hard to classify as a form of nationalism (Ndlovu-Gatsheni 2009a; 2009b). Like the Young Patriots in Cote d'Ivoire who christened their struggles as the second national liberation, the *Third Chimurenga* was articulated as 'conquest of conquest' whereby African sovereignty was prevailing over white settler colonialism ushering in new economic independence. But the *Third Chimurenga* had some positive aspects, the most important of which was its distributive agenda that witnessed land that was monopolized by white settlers being given back to the African people who were dispossessed of their land by settler colonialism (Moyo and Yeros 2007). (The case study of Zimbabwe is discussed further of chapter seven of this book). At its centre were rival patriotisms competing over redefinition of the contours of political community as well as the content and modes of citizenship. Banegas (2006: 2) correctly described the violence that accompanied the autochthonous struggle in Cote d' Ivoire as 'a war of identification, with deep historical roots.'

Cote d'Ivoire has since 1960 exercised a much compromised sovereignty as France maintained suzerainty over its ex-colony, including placing a permanent French garrison in Abidjan. This colonial presence provoked 'Operation Dignity' that resisted continued French presence. The second strand was the anti-foreign nationals who were not purely Ivoirians and had come to the country as migrants to work on plantations. Thus Cote d'Ivoire provides yet another case study of degeneration of plural and civic nationalism into nativism and xenophobia. For Zimbabwe, the nationalism that had emerged in the 1960s, proclaiming civic and liberal ideals founded on 'one man, one vote' and projecting the policy of reconciliation in the early 1980s, quickly degenerated into Afro-radicalism, nativism and xenophobia at the beginning of 2000 (Ndlovu-Gatsheni 2009a).

Conclusion

What is clear from this chapter is that the idea of Africa and the issue of African identities can be safely approached as part and parcel of complex and dynamic historical process mediated by equally complex spatial, agential, structural and contingent factors that have continuously changed since the fifteen[th] century. This chapter, however, managed to track historically the complex processes that combined and coalesced in the formation of what is today termed Africa and African identity. The way the African continent emerged as an idea as well as a reality impinged on the complexion of African identity.

Pan-Africanism and nationalism, as the two major laboratories within which African identity was constructed, became dominated by various experiments—some inspired by Liberalism, Africanism, Christianity, Marxism, Republicanism, Nativism and even precolonial African religion and communalistic ideologies. What exist as African identity or identities are products of complex histories of domination, resistance, complicity, creolization, and mimicry—all mediated by various vectors of identity such as race, ethnicity, gender, class, region and generation.

The process of unifying Africans into a common community to pursue common ideological, economic and political ends has been ceaseless. What is disturbing is that the pluralistic and civic nationalist traditions of the 1950s and 1960s had been increasingly degenerating into nativism, xenophobia and, in extreme cases, into genocides. The roots of these negative aspects are traceable to the ontology of nationalism itself as an identity phenomenon seeking to create a 'nationalist' state as a successor to the colonial state. The colonial state on which the postcolonial one is based was deeply racist and xenophobic. African nationalism, in principle, sought to represent what was considered authentic national subjects and it inevitably proceeded through exclusion of those considered outsiders. It is in the centre of complex economic, social and political histories of the making of Africa a continent and Africans a people that the roots of nativism, xenophobia and other phobias are to be found.

Throughout the nationalist struggle there was no agreement among nationalists as to who constituted the subject and object of liberation. The subjects of liberation were vaguely and variously defined as Africans, the oppressed, peasants or workers. The issue of nativity was central in the debates on inclusion and exclusion, though some nationalist organizations like the African National Congress (ANC) evolved an all-encompassing definition of citizenship based on the slogan 'South Africa belongs to all who live in it'. But its splinter group, the Pan-Africanist Congress (PAC) vehemently opposed this fluid definition of belonging, preferring the Garveyist slogan of 'Africa for Africans' (Ndlovu-Gatsheni 2009c).

What has worsened the degeneration of African nationalism into nativism and xenophobia is the globalization process that provokes uncertainties. Deepening poverty and diminishing resources have heightened struggles over resources and also increased reliance of the poor on the state. The liberal ideology of rights has not helped to prevent the flourishing of autochthonous, nativist and xenophobic politics of entitlement. Unless Africans re-launch African national projects that are not antagonistic to pan-Africanism and that form the basis for a United States of Africa, the phobias will remain to haunt the continent.

5

Coloniality of Being and the Phenomenon of Violence

Is there not something suspicious, indeed symptomatic, about this focus on subjective violence—that violence which is enacted by social agents, evil individuals,
disciplined repressive apparatuses, fanatical crowds? Doesn't it desperately try to
distract our attention from true locus of trouble, by obliterating from view other
forms of violence and thus actively participating in them?

Slavoj Zizek (2009: 9).

Introduction

In the preface to *Law and Disorder in the Postcolony* (2006), Jean and John
Comaroff addressed the paradox of the ubiquity of violence in the postcolonies
in general. Their entry point to the debate on violence was predicated on whether
postcolonies were 'haunted more by unregulated violence, un/civil warfare, and
random terror than are other twenty-first-century nation-states'? Their response
was that, 'Yes, postcolonies are especially, excessively, distinctively violent and
disorderly. Yes, they are sinking ever further into a mire of conflict, coercion
and chaos. Yes, this does seem to be a chronic, not temporary, state of being'
(Comaroffs 2006: vii). The Comaroffs' explanation for this state of being is that
the postcolonies were located within a world order dominated by new modes
of governance, new sorts of empires and new species of wealth where poverty
and race were criminalized (Comaroffs 2006: 1-42). This is indeed part of the
answer; but there is need for further interrogation of the roots of violence which
has cost many lives, disrupted social life, retarded economic development, and
fragmented nation-states in postcolonial Africa.

This chapter discusses the all-pervading atmosphere of violence in Africa which has seriously affected African people's lives across precolonial, colonial, and postcolonial historical epochs. While violence has manifested itself in everyday African life in the form of wars of conquest, inter and intra-community raiding, terrorism, criminality, rape, torture, maiming, and killing, to mention a few, its logic remains hard to understand beyond naming and condemning. Precolonial violence involved people of the same colour who were not permanently demarcated by what Santos (2007: 45-89) termed Western 'abyssal thinking' that underpinned colonial violence that was premised on 'impossibility of the copresence' between white colonizers and black colonized peoples. During the pre-colonial era, African socio-political formations and ecologies of knowledge did not develop along what Maldonado-Torres (2007: 240-270) termed the 'racist/imperial Manichean misanthropic skepticism' whose essence was not only to doubt the very humanity of non-Western people but also to project them as 'racialized and sexualized subjects' open to all sorts of violence including enslaving, rape and genocide.

Precolonial African socio-political formations had room for full incorporation and successful assimilation of defeated communities into the host society. But under colonial modernity that was shot through with a racial order of identities, whites could not be accommodated into the African societies they despised and sought to transform and black people could not be accommodated into colonial white society that was fenced in by racism. The socio-political formation that was created by colonial modernity took the form of what Mamdani (2006) termed a bifurcated colonial state formation of citizens and subjects. In this set-up of intersubjective relations, the colonizers used violence to keep the colonized in a subordinated position, forcing them endure all forms of exploitation and abuses.

This chapter examines the concept of the coloniality of being as advanced by Maldonado Torres, in combination with Fanon's notion of the *damnes*, and Slavoj Zizek's ideas of subjective, objective and symbolic violence, as important conceptual tools to explore the logic of violence in African history from the time of colonial encounters to the present. The chapter locates the logic of violence in coloniality and its reproduction of African subjectivities where race was used not only to 'condemn' black people into *damnes* but to also deny their very humanity so as to justify such forms of violence as slavery, colonial conquest, dispossession, imprisonment, rape, shooting and killing. African nationalism as a deeply interpellated phenomenon reproduced colonial violence and authoritarianism, bequeathing it on postcolonial Africa as a mode of governance. While the key concern of this chapter is to explain the logic of violence, its central arguments are empirically proven through the case studies of the Herero people who became victims of German colonial genocide; Congo under King Leopold II where violence was the mode of governance; and South Africa where neo-apartheid situation recreated black townships and informal settlements as crouching villages of violence, civil tension and social strife.

Zizek (2009) has categorized violence into three forms. first he noted he common intellectual concentration on interrogation of visible 'subjective' violence perpetrated by identifiable agents with its obvious signals such as criminality, terror, civil unrest, war and international conflict. This, according to him, 'is just the most visible portion of a triumvirate that also includes two objective kinds of violence'; and for this violence to be understood, there is need 'to perceive the contours of the background which generates such outburst' (Zizek 2009: 1). Behind subjective violence there is an 'objective' kind of violence which falls into two forms. The first is 'symbolic' violence embodied in language and its speech forms. Its locale is the relation of domination and is reproduced in human speech forms. The second is 'systemic' violence located within economic and political systems and exists like the dark matter of physics but is the motive force of 'what otherwise seem to be "irrational" explosions of subjective violence' (Zizek 2009: 2).

Besides contributing to the categorization of violence, Zizek also suggested 'six sideways glances' as the ideal approach for studying violence rather than a direct glance. The six sideways glances help in transcending 'the overpowering horror of violent acts and empathy with the victims' which 'inexorably function as a lure which prevents us from thinking' (Zizek 2009: 3). He elaborated further that 'a dispassionate conceptual development of the typology of violence must by definition ignore its traumatic impact' (Zizek 2009: 3). The challenge facing researchers trying to understand the logic of violence is the possibility of maintaining a 'cold critical analysis' that is not disturbed by the horrors and moral outrage. Ideally, researchers of violence are constantly advised to maintain a 'distance' from the moralities of violence. This is not easy to maintain in the face of horrors of violence but still the subject of violence is so important that it cannot be abandoned as a field of study because of the emotions it provokes.

However, the key concern of this chapter is about the logic of violence that is pervasive in Africa rather than on methodologies of studying violence.

The psychoanalytical and philosophical work of Frantz Fanon and Nelson Maldonado-Torres who articulated the concept of coloniality of being is useful in understanding the logic of violence within colonized and ex-colonized zones of Africa. Fanon and Maldonado-Torres situated the logic of violence within coloniality. This chapter therefore proceeds by way of defining the concepts of coloniality and coloniality since they are central to understanding of violence in Africa.

Coloniality and the creation of a racialized/ethnicized adversarial world

Coloniality is an analytical concept developed by radical Latin American scholars such as Quijano, Mignolo, Escobar, Grosfoguel and others whose main concern was to develop a new understanding of modernity from the perspective of colonial difference and the side of the ex-colonized people who experienced its dark side (Escobar 2007: 179-210). Coloniality is rooted in colonialism but is different from colonialism. Colonialism is an encapsulation of political and economic relations in which the sovereignty of a nation or a people rests on the power of another nation which then proceeds to set up direct colonial administration over these people.

Coloniality, on the other hand, is a reference to long-standing patterns of power that emerged as a result of colonialism and continues to define culture, labour, intersubjective relations and knowledge production, well beyond the strict limits of colonial administrations. As defined by the Quijano, coloniality is one of the specific and constitutive elements of global model of capitalist power that is based on a racial/ethnic classification of the global population as the cornerstone of that model of power. It is rooted in Western modernity and colonial encounters. Today, coloniality operates on every level, in every arena and dimension of everyday human social existence (Quijano 2000: 342).

Coloniality lies at the centre of the modern/colonial world of yesterday and today where Europe and America are at the apex of global power hierarchy and Africa is at the bottom. It unfolded in terms of what became known as 'the voyages of discovery' that culminated in colonial encounters between Europe and Africa and invoked the ideas of mapping of the world. Western modernity is the source and motive force of expansion of European particularism into universalism. Imperialism and colonialism became the main vehicles in this expansion of European influence that were underpinned by violence through and through.

At the social level, coloniality was underpinned by 'a conception of humanity according to which the global population was differentiated into inferior and superior, irrational and rational, primitive and civilized, traditional and modern' (Quijano 2000: 343). Coloniality was and is shot through by Eurocentrism as a power matrix that encompassed the consistent drive to control labour and its product; nature and its productive resources; gender, its products and the reproduction of the human species; subjectivity, its material and intersubjective products as well as knowledge; and authority and its instruments of coercion, persuasion and violence which was to ensure the reproduction of the Euro-American-centric dominant power relations over Africa and the rest of the world (Quijano 2000: 344).

Coloniality is rooted in a particular socio-historical setting that included the discursive formation of racialized subjectivities that were linked to specific cartographic social formations known as continents. As Maldonado-Torres (2007: 243) argues, coloniality has survived colonialism and is kept alive in old and current books, in the criteria for academic performance, in cultural patterns, in common sense, in the image of peoples and in aspirations and perceptions of self. Human beings, as modern subjects, live and breathe coloniality all the time and every day.

At the centre of coloniality was and is race which formed the foundation of the codification and institutionalization of differences between conquerors (white races) and the conquered (black races). The conquerors assumed a superiority complex and assigned inferiority to the conquered and colonized peoples. This process happened in tandem with the institution and constitution of a new colonial structure of labour control and its resources that authorized the exploitative relations of slavery, serfdom, forced labour and other forms that were mediated by violence.

Santos (2007: 45) described Western thinking that underpinned colonial modernity as 'an abyssal thinking' consisting of 'visible and invisible distinctions, the invisible ones being the foundation of the visible ones'. He said further that Western 'abyssal thinking' was at the root of the making of the colonial zones as the 'other side of the line' radically different from the metropolitan zones as 'this side of the line'. The colonial zones which included most of what today is described as ex-colonized parts of the world (Latin America, the Caribbean, Asia, and Africa) were constructed and represented as a realm of incomprehensible way of being. According to him::

> What most fundamentally characterizes abyssal thinking is thus the impossibility of the copresence of the two sides of the line. To the extent that it prevails, this side of the line only prevails by exhausting the field of relevant reality, beyond it, there is only nonexistence, invisibility, nondialectical absence (Santos 2007: 45-46).

The metropolitan zones were represented as progressing through 'social regulation and social emancipation' whereas the colonial zones were caught up within the web of 'appropriation/violence' (Santos 2007: 46). Lawlessness and violence ruled the colonial zones as confirmed by Fanon who experienced colonialism in his native country of Martinique and in Algeria which that became his second home. He said:

> The colonial world is a world cut into two. The dividing line, the frontiers are shown by barracks and police stations. In the colonies it is the policemen and the soldiers who are the official, instituted go-betweens, the spokesmen of the settler and his rule of oppression. [...] In the colonial countries, on the contrary, the policemen and the soldier, by their immediate presence and their direct action maintain contact with the native and advise him by means of rifle-butts and napalm not to budge. It is obvious here that the agents of government speak the language of pure force. The intermediary does not lighten the oppression, nor seek to hide the domination; he shows them up and puts them into practice with the clear conscience of an upholder of the peace; yet he is the bringer of violence into the home and into the mind of the native (Fanon 1968a: 29).

While truce, peace, and friendship applied to social life in metropolitan societies; within the colonial zones the law of the strongest, violence and plunder reigned supreme. What assumptions, values, and ideas informed coloniality of radical divisions between the metropolitan and colonial zones? The creation of new identities of European, white, coloured, Indian, black, native, Negro and others was an important foundational component. Linking these new identities that emerged within coloniality was a type of social classification that was vertical rather than horizontal, depicting and reflecting superior-inferior assumptions that were developed as Western modernity expanded out of Europe into other parts of the world. The social hierarchy of new identities was not only informed by race but also by degrees of humanity attributed to the constructed identities. As Maldonado-Torres (2007: 244)) puts it:

> The 'lighter' one's skin is, the closer to full humanity one is, and vice versa. As the conquerors took on the role of mapping the world they kept reproducing this vision of things. The whole world was practically seen in the light of this logic. This is the beginning of 'global coloniality'.

Deployments of theories of scientific racism in the late nineteenth century were informed by well-established racial attitudes of the colonizers with regard to the degrees of humanity across the colonized-colonizer interactions. Philosophically, under coloniality, the principle of the Cartesian doubt codified in the famous statement cogito ergo sum (I think, therefore I am' underwent a quick metamorphosis to 'ergo conquiro'/'ergo conquistus' (I conquer, therefore, I am). The 'right of conquest' became an important legitimating value that authorized all sorts of violence deployed against the colonized.

The notion of colonized peoples as barbarians and savages was popularized as colonizers sought various means to justify their domination, exploitation, repression and other abuses of Africans. Maldonado-Torres (2007: 245) argues that the ideology of barbarity of the colonized was sustained by 'a radical questioning or permanent suspicion regarding the humanity of the self in question'. He termed this imperial attitude, the 'racist/imperial Manichean misanthropic skepticism' that sustained the superiority of the imperial white being (Maldonado-Torres 2007: 245). It was used to justify the inferiority of the black being under colonialism and is today hidden within structures of global coloniality where Westerners have remained at the top of racial hierarchies rooted in colonial modernity.

The racist/imperial Manichean misanthropic skepticism questioned the very humanity of colonized peoples as a deliberate strategy to justify all sorts of imperial and colonial interventions on the life and world of the colonized including enslaving them. What racist/imperial Manichean misanthropic skepticism authorized was the dangerous idea of colonial and racial subjects as usable and dispensable beings who had no souls, This further informed the popular imperial/colonial maxim that says, 'Beyond the equator there are no sins' (Santos 2007: 49-50). This meant that in dealing with non-Western/non-European/Black peoples located on the other side of the equator, ethics, law and other social sanctions that regulated life in Europe and other Western parts of the world had to be suspended for the law of nature including violence, became legitimate in encounters with those whose humanity was doubted.

At another level, the introduction of Western religion in Africa was also based on the imperial assumption that the black people had no religion. Such people were considered subhuman and unworthy of respect. The ideas of race, religion and empire reinforced one another. When adventurers like Christopher Columbus and colonizers emphasized that the people they encountered outside the Western world (Latin America, Caribbean, Asia, and Africa) had no religion, they were justifying a particular form of violence rooted in the notion of colonized people as empty beings lacking subjectivity and available for indoctrination with Christianity. To categorize the colonized people as subjects without religion was part of the strategy to excise them from the commonwealth of humanity (Maldonado-Torres n.d.).

In the Western cognitive map of the non-Western world and its people, such a people that did not have a religion did not deserve any form of respect and rights; hence brutal imperial wars were waged against Indians, Africans and such others. Genocide, scorched-earth policies, mutilation of bodies, and rape were legitimate part of the 'pacification of the barbarous tribes'. For instance, severed heads of African kings and chiefs were taken to Europe as trophies. Human beings like Sarah Baartman of the San-Khoi Khoi people of South Africa were captured and taken to Europe to be subjected to the most demeaning experiences of scientific experiments informed by racism. The predicament of the colonized was summed up by Maldonado-Torres in these words:

> Misanthropic skepticism posits its targets as racialized and sexualized subjects. Once vanquished, they are said to be inherently servants and their bodies come to form part of an economy of sexual abuse, exploitation, and control. The ethics of the *ego conquiro* ceased to be only a special code of behaviour for periods of war and becomes [...] a standard of conduct that reflects the way things are—a way of things whose naturalization reaches its climax with the use of natural science to validate racism in the nineteenth century [...] Thus, the treatment of vanquished peoples in conditions of war is perceived as legitimate long after war is over (Maldonado-Torres 2007: 248).

Santos (2007: 51) amplified the debate further by arguing that violence manifested itself in various ways, including the realm of knowledge, where indigenous black guides were forcibly used to reveal African secrets and pathways on African rivers. Other mechanisms of violence used include direct pillaging of indigenous knowledge of biodiversity; prohibition of use of native languages in public spaces; forcible adoption of Christian names; and destruction of ceremonial sites. The violence also extended to slave trade and forced labour; instrumental use of customary law and authority under the indirect rule; pillage of natural resources, massive displacement of populations, and wars (Santos 2007: 51-52).

Coloniality of being and practises of violence

The concept of coloniality of being locates the roots of violence against Africans and other colonized people within the expansion of Western modernity. It qualifies Casparus Barleus' colonial dictum of 'beyond the equator there are no sins' by making the lives of colonized hellish. Coloniality of being captures the central question of the effects of coloniality on lived experiences of the colonized people that were mediated by the master-slave and colonizer-colonized dialectic where violence was naturalized and routinized as a key feature of colonial government.

The anarchic and traumatic moment of the constitution of the colonizer and the colonized subjectivities within the colonial encounters symbolized by the meeting of Europeans and Africans led to the birth of what Fanon termed 'existentialia' of the 'subject' of the coloniality of being. Fanon in his critique of Hegel's ideas on ontology, Frantz Fanon did not only contribute towards an alternative depiction of the master-slave dialectic but, as Maldonado-Torres (2007: 242) argues, he also advanced a rethinking of ontology in the light of coloniality and the search for decolonization in his acclaimed book *Black Skins*, White Masks (1968).

The concept of coloniality of being is important as it captures not only the depersonalization of black people under colonialism but the constitution of Africans as racialized subjects with next to no value placed on their lives. In the space of the colonized, death was 'no extra-ordinary affair' but 'a constitutive feature of the reality of colonized and racialized subjects' (Maldonado 2007: 251). At the centre of coloniality of being is 'blackness' as a defining feature of what Fanon (1968b: 110-119) referred to as the damne (the condemned of the earth). Coloniality of being is meant to capture the hell that descended on the colonized lives and became naturalized and routinized as the African mode of being. This hellish life is well described by Maldonado-Torres in this way:

> Hellish existence in the colonial world carries with it both the racial and the gendered aspects of the naturalization of the non-ethics of war. *Indeed, coloniality of Being primarily refers to the normalization of the extraordinary events that take place in war*. While in war there is murder and rape, in the hell of the colonial world murder and rape become day to day occurrences and menaces. 'Killability' and 'rapeability' are inscribed into images of the colonial bodies. Lacking real authority, colonized men are permanently feminized. [...] Blackness in a colonial anti-black world is part of a larger context of meaning in which the non-ethics of war gradually becomes a constitutive part of an alleged normal world (emphasis is in the original source) (Maldonado-Torres 2007: 255).

One of the characteristics of the colonized person was is disappearance of their humanity under the shadow of dehumanization. Coloniality of being can be summarized as a state of human exception from the order of normal being as represented by the colonizer. It refers to 'the violation of the meaning of human alterity to the point where the alter-ego becomes a sub-alter' (Maldonado-Torres 2007:257). The daily life of the colonized 'approximated very closely with situations of war'. It is a humanity that is denied (Maldonado 2007: 257). Fanon described black subjectivity that emerged from the world of coloniality of being as damne, arguing that this subject has non-ontological resistance in the eyes of the dominant group. The damne are said to co-exist with death as their whole live are perpetually lived in 'the company of death' (Maldonado 2007: 257). It is a dark side of being characterized by neglect, denial of humanity and betrayals by other human beings.

Colonial modernity was accompanied by the proletarianization of Africans who were dispossessed and then forcibly pressed into serving as cheap labour for white-owned farms, industries and mines, thus entering another hell in the cities. The cities and urban centres were racially fragmented into two racial realms, feeding Fanon with the material to provide an informative comparison between the lives of natives and settlers within the urban colonial society

> The settler's town is a strongly-built town, all made of stone and steel. It is a brightly-lit town; the streets are covered with asphalt, and the garbage-cans swallow all the leavings, unseen, unknown and hardly thought about. The settler's feet are never visible, except perhaps in the sea; but there you're never close enough to see them. His feet are protected by strong shoes although the streets of his town are clean and even, with no holes or stones. The settler's town is well-fed town, an easy-going town; its belly is always full of good things. The settler's town is a town of white people, of foreigners (Fanon Ibid).

On the other side, is the town of the colonized people, which Fanon portrayed thus:

> The town belonging to the colonized people [...] is a place of ill fame, peopled by men of evil repute. They are born there, it matters little where or how; they die there; it matters not where, nor how. It is a world without spaciousness; men live there on top of each other, and their huts are built one on top of the other. The native town is a hungry town, starved of bread, of meat, of shoes, of coal, of light. The native town is a crouching village, a town on its knees, a town wallowing in the mire (Fanon 1968a: 30).

A few examples will help explain how violence has its roots deep in colonial encounters and colonial modernity as well as how violence migrated from the colonial period into the postcolonial neo-colonized present.

Racist Manichean Misanthropic Scepticism in practice: German-Herero War, 1904-1907.

The causes and courses of the German-Herero War of 1904-1907 are well known and cannot detain us here as many scholars such as Drechsler (1980), Bridgman (1981), Gewald (1999), and many others have dealt with these issues. At the same time, it is beyond dispute that the Germans committed genocide; hence the German government's apology of 2004 (Anderson

2005: 1155-1189). My concern here, however, is to demonstrate how the German-Herero War of 1904-1907 constitutes an example of how the 'racist/ imperial Manichean misanthropic scepticism' was practised by Germans on the African soil. It demonstrates how the ethics that governed the conduct of war in Europe were suspended in the way the Germans dealt with the Herero people of Namibia. Even German national laws governing war were suspended alongside international laws.

The ill-treatment of the Herero people is here taken as a macrocosm of how colonial powers dealt with non-Western and colonized peoples in violation of such standing declarations as the 1890 Anti-Slavery Conference that took place in Brussels, Belgium, as well as treaty of friendship and protection of 1885 signed between Germany and the Herero people (Anderson 2005: 1158). Thise 'war of annihilation' that was supported by many Germans as a legitimate response of the colonial power against the Herero who were resisting colonial ill-treatment, could only take place outside Europe and the Western world because of deep-rooted racism that underpinned colonialism and imperialism. For instance, the German Colonial League's Executive Committee released a pamphlet calling for a brutal, swift and harsh response to the Herero uprising and this is how they racially profiled the Herero people and justified their annihilation:

> Anyone familiar with the life of Africans and other less civilized non-white peoples knows that one can assert themselves only by maintaining the supremacy of their race. [...] The swifter and harsher the reprisals taken against rebels, the better the chances of restoring authority (cited in Anderson 2005: 1160).

The appointment of a rabid racist Lieutenant-General Lothar von Trotha by the German Emperor Kaiser Wilhelm II as the commander-in-chief of the German forces in Namibia was a clear indicator of the imperial intention to finish off the Herero people. Lieutenant-General von Trotha was an experienced and tested racist who was well-known for his brutal suppression of African resisters in East Africa where the Wahehe Uprising had broken out in 1896. He had also participated in the brutal suppression of the Boxer Uprising of 1901 in China (Drechsler 1980: 151). It was Lieutenant-General von Trotha that issued the infamous 'annihilation order' on 2 October 1904:

> The Herero people will have to leave the country. Otherwise, I shall force them to do so by means of guns [...] Every Herero, whether found armed or unarmed [...] will be shot. I shall not accept any more women and children. I shall drive them back to their people—otherwise I shall order shots to be fired at them. These are my words to the Herero people (cited in Drechsler 1980: 156-157).

In a follow-up report to the chief of the German Army General Staff of 4 October 1904, Lieutenant-General von Trotha clearly expressed his intention to exterminate the Herero people:

> The crucial question for me is how to bring the war against the Herero to a close [...] As I see it, the nation must be destroyed as such [...] I ordered the warriors to be court-martialled and hanged and all women and children who sought shelter here to be driven back into the sandveld [the Kalahari Desert] [...] To accept women and children who are for the most part sick, poses a grave risk to the force, and to feed them is out of the question. For this reason, I deem it wiser for the entire nation to perish [...] This uprising is and remains the beginning of a racial struggle (Excerpt from a Report from Lieutenant-General von Trotha to the Army Chief of Staff, 4 October 1904 cited in Drechsler 1980: 160-161).

The extermination order was enthusiastically carried out beginning with the hanging of Herero people who had been sentenced to death. They were publicly hanged where other Herero prisoners that included women and children were forced to come and watch (Anderson 2005: 1162). Lieutenant-General von Trotha even wrote a letter to Governor Leutwein on 27 October 1904 declaring that: 'The Herero nation must vanish from the face of the earth' (cited in Anderson 2005: 1162). The extermination of the Herero involved public hangings, random killing of any Herero found by the German army; and pushing others to the Omahenge Desert to die of hunger and thirst. Those who were not directly killed were taken into concentration camps where they were exposed to severe forced labour that led to death. Others became guinea-pigs for medical experiments. In total the Germans are said to have killed 65,000 Herero people out of a population of 80,000 (Drechsler 1980: 214; Anderson 2005: 1166).

Those members of the German nation who expressed opposition to the extermination of the Herero people were concerned about other issues rather than the humanity of the Herero. Their reasons ranged from economic reasons as African cheap labour was wanted for the colonial enterprise; saving the face of Christianity that was founded on humanistic principles; impact of extermination on the status of Germany as a civilized nation; and impossibility of the succeeding in the use of extermination as a war strategy (Drechsler 1980: 163-164). No wonder then that the German Emperor, Kaiser Wilhelm II, reluctantly rescinded the extermination order after the genocide had already been committed.

The treatment of the Herero by the Germans was a typical result of the practic of racist/imperial Manichean misanthropic skepticism founded on doubting the very humanity of black people in general. It did not take place in Namibia alone but wherever all the wars of conquest were fought and in all colonial responses to African uprisings. What varied were the scales of killing. The Herero people were even denied the option of surrendering. This is how far colonial violence could go vis-à-vis black people.

Violence as a colonial mode of governance: King Leopold II and the Congo Free State

The way King Leopold II of Belgium turned the Congo into his personal 'massive labour colony' where 'the distinction between the law of persons and the law of things, of both humans and nonhumans' permeated his style of governance is another case of how violence was routinized in colonial Africa (Santos 2007: 52). To Leopold II, the colonized Congolese people were nothing but providers of cheap labour. The Congo Free State was a special type of colony owned by a single person, the King of Belgium. It was created in 1885 soon after the Berlin Conference that authorized the scramble and partition of Africa among European powers.

King Leopold's ventures into the Congo were from start to finish a catalogue of chicanery, violence and genocide. In the first place, his company, called Association Internationale Africaine (AIA), disguised its imperial and colonial ambitions and intentions under scientific and philanthropic designs. For instance, he justified his colonial interventions in these words:

> Our only program, I am anxious to repeat, is the work of moral and material regeneration, and we must do this among a population whose degeneration in its inherited conditions it is difficult to measure. The many horrors and atrocities which disgraced humanity give way little by little before our intervention (cited in Religious Tolerance Organization, n.d.).

To acquire Congo, King Leopold II hired Henry Morton Stanley, a famous explorer who deceived African chiefs into signing away their land and power under the guise of treaties of friendship with a people who doubted their humanity in the first place. King Leopold II's takeover of Congo territory set in motion a brutal colonial regime unleashed on a polity of over 30 million people, turning them into a the property of a single individual driven by a profit motive and unrestrainedby any moral and ethical values besides those of making economic profits by any means necessary.

King Leopold's policies included introduction of the colonial idea of terres vacantes (the concept of vacant/empty lands). This was a common strategy to justify land expropriation. His next step was to demarcate Congolese territory into two zones. The first was the *Free Trade Zone* that was to be the domain of Europeans. It was a domain of free entrepreneurial enterprises, private ownership of land, and freedom to buy 10-15 year monopoly leases on anything of value, including ivory and rubber. The second zone was the Domaine Prive (the exclusive private property of the state and this state was embodied in the person of King Leopold II). It made up almost two-thirds of the Congo. There was no designated place reserved for indigenous African people of Congo; instead, they were regrouped into ethnicized rural labour camps for easy mobilization and labour recruitment under the supervision of defeated and terrified native authorities serving colonial interests (Emerson 1979; Pakenham 1991; Hochschild 1998; Ewans 2003; Olson 2008).

Black Congolese people were expected to provide set quotas of rubber and ivory to state officials. They laboured to produce food for the state. They worked under conditions of forced labour and slavery. A notorious armed force known as *Force Publique* (FP) enforced the rubber quotas. The FP was armed with modern weapons and a bull whip made of hippopotamus hide. Black Congolese who failed to meet their rubber quotas had their hands cut; some were tortured and others killed. The brutality unleashed on this population could only happen to beings that were considered sub-humanity as it involved cutting of heads and hanging of bodies on the village palisades. The FP carried severed hands to the white officials as evidence that they were enforcing the law on those who failed to provide the needed rubber and ivory (Olson 2008). King Leopold's violent soldier-merchants killed over 10 million Congolese during his personal rule over the Congo Free State (Hochschild 1998). The violence also involved the kidnapping of women and children to force men to come out to work in rubber plantations, raping of women and burning of entire villages in what came to be known as 'scorched earth tactics'.

The current violence bedevilling the Democratic Republic of Congo (DRC) has its roots in the violent reign of King Leopold. It was this same man who warlords that thrived by terrorizing the people. Moore (2001: 130-135) has fond a linkage between the reigns of what he called 'King Leopold' and 'King Kabila'. Similarly, Mamdani (2011) has traced the present-day violence in the eastern part of the DRC to the time of dictatorship of King Leopold II who created homelands as ethnicized labour colonies supervised by 'native/ black' authorities. The re-organization of the indigenous population into rigid ethnic homelands enabled easy colonial organization for recruitment of cheap and forced labour. This colonial arrangement inaugurated rigid ethnic identities and sensibilities as recruitment for mines, plantations, civil service, and army became based on tribal identity. For instance, in the diamond-rich Katanga region which experienced labour migration, ethnic identities became fragmented into Lunda who were considered indigenous, and the Luba who were again subdivided into indigenous and non-indigenous. The Luba who had migrated from neighbouring Kasai, were divided into 'Luba-Katanga' (those who had moved to Katanga prior to colonialism and were considered as indigenous) and 'Luba-Kasai' (classified as non-indigenous) (Mamdani 2011).

A colonial policy of ethnic 'regrouping' also took place in other parts of DRC such as Ituri and Kivu. Here the predominantly pastoral Hema were separated from Lendu populations, forcing each into its own homeland known as territoire supervised by a native tribal authority known as *chefferie* (Mamdani 2011). The long-term impact of this ethnic regrouping was predictable: First, when Congolese nationalism emerged, it did so as a deeply ethnicized political force. Second, the question of who was indigenous to particular areas led to the present-day question of citizenship that is generating violence in the eastern part of the DRC bordering Uganda, Rwanda and Burundi. The existence of 'Banyarwanda' and 'Banyamulenge' consisting of Hutu, Tutsi and Batwa has heightened the citizenship struggles and violence (Mamdani 2011).

Since the time of Leopold II, those who succeeded him including Patrice Lumumba, Mobutu Sese Seko, Laurent Kabila and Joseph Kabila have not managed to deal effectively with the questions of indignity and citizenship in the DRC. Colonialism invented indigene versus non-indigene dichotomies that have continued to breed intra-and inter-communal violence in the DRC. Some of the central state interventions politicized citizenship rather than solving the contestations rooted in bifurcation of Congolese into races of the cities and tribes of the countryside. Furthermore, the fluid migrant labour system added new layers of identities. Nzongola-Ntalaja (2002) blamed Patrice Lumumba for making the first major political blunder in trying to solve the Katangese secession through taking sides with one ethnic group in a struggle involving so-called 'indigenes' and 'non-indigenes'. Lumumba deployed the national army that went on the commit atrocities on one ethnic group, thus exacerbating the problem rather than solving it.

There were other complicated resolutions of the indigene versus non-indigene problems in the DRC, such as Mobutu's Citizenship Decree of 1972 that was prompted by increasing numbers of Hutu migrants running away from massacres in Burundi. The decree extended citizenship to all those who arrived in the DRC in 1959-1960. It provoked immediate protests from

Kivu residents who feared increasing numbers of Rwandese and Burundians (Mamdani 2011). The citizenship problem was further complicated by the Nationality Law of 1981 that restricted citizenship to people who could demonstrate an ancestral connection with Congo at the time of the Berlin Conference of 1885 (Mamdani 2011). In short, the violence that is currently haunting the DRC is intermingled with the question of citizenship whose roots are traceable to the time of Leopold II.

Identity politics created warlords who claim to be representing particular regions and particular ethnic groups such as the Mayi-Mayi that claim the status of indigenous people and the Banyamulenge that are excluded as non-indigenous. What is clear is that the DRC is paying a heavy prize in terms of inter-and intra-communal violence that has its deep roots in colonial regrouping schemes that created rigid and antagonistic ethnicities. This reality has led some analysts to doubt whether the DRC really exists as a nation.

Neo-apartheid and systemic violence in South Africa

South Africa can be best described as a 'contact zone' that is a space in which peoples of different races and ethnicities who were geographically and historically separated came into contact with each other and established ongoing relations mediated by conditions of coercion and inequalities that provoke intractable conflicts and violence (Pratt 1992: 6). At the centre of South Africa are racialized-ethnicities and ethnicized races that have all been struggling to be South African. What being South African means remains a form of 'state of becoming' and is the subject of contestations together with the concomitant question of who is a South African that is complicated by rival populisms and claims and counter-claims to nativity and indigeneity.

Blacks, Whites, Indians, Coloureds, Chinese and other racial groups have gone through several historical epochs and contacts but full assimilation into a singular and stable national identity is still in the making and is not following a smooth path that the traditional sociological assimilation school of thought projected based on metropolitan European migration models (Gordon 1964). We cannot, for instance, say that all South African groups were currently passing through several stages in the process of assimilation into the host African society. A claim to nativity and indigeneity by any single ethnic or racial group has the potential to render others stateless. No wonder, whites have often contested the claims of blacks to nativity despite the fact that they were the ones who called the African people 'natives' to distinguish them from whites and to exclude them from the wealth of the nation and conserve them into a reserve army to provide cheap labour (see Chapter Six for more historical exposition of the South Africa situation).

What makes South Africa unique in Africa is that its social complexion is very complex indeed. South Africa's social structure resembles that of an empire permeated by a violent colonial experience and where and strong racial/ethnic hierarchy persists. There is no space for migrant incorporation and assimilation into white society as white colonial subjects of the empire (English and Afrikaners) assumed nativity and, in the process, excluded the indigenous black people from the nation -- creating what Neocosmos (2006) termed 'native foreigners' and 'foreign natives'. It is a country characterized by layers and layers of competing and complex identities.

The first layer consists of various black ethnic groups that experienced colonial conquest, colonization and apartheid domination. Examples include the Zulu, Xhosa, Ndebele, San, Khoi Khoi, Suthu and other identities. The second layer consisted of 'colonial-racial subjects' who came to South Africa as part of a long imperial/colonial history, and examples include the English, Afrikaners, Indians, Malay and Chinese. Following the thinking of Grosfoguel (2008: 608) these groups can be termed 'colonial/racial subjects of empire'. They emerged within a highly racialized empire with discourses constructed in relation to these subjects as they interacted with indigenous black peoples.

In South Africa, the white colonial-racial subjects of the empire succeeded in assuming power and dominating indigenous black people and other non-white subjects of the empire like Indians and the Coloureds. The indigenous black African people occupied the bottom of the racial/ethnic hierarchy while in metropolitan empires like Britain, the indigenous whites are at the top and the colonial-racial subjects are at the bottom. The other development is that it became impossible for white colonial-racial subjects of the empire to be absorbed by the indigenous black African majority that they despised and dominated. Rather, the indigenous black majority races found themselves struggling to be incorporated into the white dominant state and well provisioned white society. It became very difficult for assimilation to take place. But only white immigrants from Europe were easily assimilated ahead of indigenous black people into the white-constructed state and society.

The other layer was that of black immigrants from within the African continent who, when they arrived in South Africa, had to join the ranks of black indigenous people languishing at the bottom of the racial hierarchy. New forms of racialization and ethnicization processes developed such as the 'Nigerianization' of West Africans and 'Zimbabweanization' of others.

Indigenous black South Africans struggled to racialize each other with those Africans who were phenotypically darker than others suffering 'Nigerianization'. Those who experienced 'Zimbabweanization' were subjected to crude language tests. At the bottom of racial hierarchy created by the coloniality of power were black indigenous South Africans and black immigrants who had to compete over scarce resources. This situation has generated to what is commonly termed xenophobic violence (Ndlovu-Gatsheni 2009).

What has escaped critical analysis is the fact that South Africa has never been decolonized and deracialized. In 1910, it gained what can be correctly be termed 'colonial independence' (independence without decolonization); hence the black indigenous people remained dominated and exploited. In 1994, South Africa gained liberal democracy without decolonization. Again the indigenous black population found itself still languishing at the bottom of racial/ethnic hierarchy. Even politicians within the African National Congress (ANC) did not talk about 'independence day' but about 'freedom day'. Whose freedom it was remains a key question. A few black people were able to take advantage of favourable state policies such as Black Economic Empowerment (BEE) and Affirmative Action (AA) to climb up the social and economic ladder into the middle stratum/middle class status. Examples include Cyril Ramaphosa, Patrice Motsepe, Irvin Khoza and others called the 'black diamonds'. These people were used by dominant white groups as showcases to counter accusations of racial discrimination and to hide continuations of racial discrimination.

The reality that continues to generate violence is the enduring old colonial/ racial order during established several centuries of successive colonial and apartheid administrations. South Africa is currently in the 'neo-apartheid' period not 'post-apartheid'. The key feature of the neo-apartheid era is the economic exclusion of the black majorities and the economic dominance of a white minority. Neo-apartheid is also characterized by featuring some black faces at the top of political hierarchy, including the presidency but without any meaningful social change for the majority of black people from whom the black political leaders emerged. Neo-apartheid also projects itself in the form of racialization of criminality in which the black face remains the symbol of criminality. Even poverty is racialized in a neo-apartheid situation (Grosfoguel 2008: 615).

Neo-apartheid also manifests itself through segregation of the excluded black poor through urban cartography which distinguished between the *damne* and the civilized zones. Santos (2007: 59) called this situation 'fascism of social apartheid'. The South African urban black poor have remained cocooned in black townships and *imikhukhu* (shacks) as zones of Hobbesian state of nature dominated by internal civil strife and violence. Santos concluded that:

> As social fascism coexists with liberal democracy, the state of exception coexists with constitutional normalcy, civil society coexists with the state of nature, and indirect rule coexists with rule of law (Santos 2007: 62).

This is the situation currently obtaining in South Africa, a country that has an acclaimed democratic constitution but has maintained its strong racial/ ethnic hierarchy constructed by colonialism and apartheid. The politics of compromise did not alter the existing status quo where in the white minority races were privileged by both colonialism and apartheid. Fanon depicted the compromises made between African nationalists and white oppressors as a strategy of avoiding a full-blown revolution through capturing the African leadership and turning the liberation movement to the right and thereby disarm the African people (Fanon 1963: 55).

Conclusion

One of the intriguing questions in the study of violence in Africa has been how to explain the continuation of colonial violence iwell into the postcolonial and post-apartheid periods. Why have African nationalists, some of whom were put in power by popular vote, fail to govern without resorting to violence as a form of governance. It is understandable that colonial governments were imposed on African societies by force of arms; hence they had to govern by violence. A coloniality perspective in general, and a coloniality of being in particular, provides some answers to this question of continuation of violence across colonial and postcolonial epochs.

Fanon has analysed how colonial violence influenced the colonized to be violent. In the first place, he noted that the abused and violated colonized people 'manifest this aggressiveness which has been deposited in his bones against his own people' (Fanon 1968a: 40). In the second place, he explained that the colonized people's confrontation with the 'colonial order of things' places them in 'a permanent state of tension' (Fanon 1963: 41). In the third place, Fanon argued that. 'The native is an oppressed person whose permanent dream is to become the persecutor' (Fanon 1968a: 41).

Fanon also argued that violence used in particular ways during the decolonization struggle 'does not magically disappear after the ceremony of trooping the national colours'. He explained the continuation of violence as informed by 'cut-throat competition between capitalism and socialism' (Fanon 1968a: 59). But now that socialism is dead and there is no 'cut-throat' ideological competition, how is the continuation of violence to be explained in postcolonial Africa? Friedrich Nietzsche (1990: 102) reiterated thesis rather aptly. According to him, 'He who fights with monsters should look to it that he himself does not become a monster. And when you gaze long into an abyss the abyss also gazes into you.' Fanon had this to say about continuation of violence after colonialism:

> The atmosphere of violence, after having coloured all the colonial phase, continues to dominate national life, for as we have already said, the Third World is not cut off from the rest. This is why the statesmen of under-developed countries keep up indefinitely the tone of aggressiveness and exasperation in their public speeches which in the normal way ought to have disappeared (Fanon 1968a: 60).

A typical example of the statesmen described here is President Robert Mugabe of Zimbabwe who consistently rails Western powers while simultaneously maintaining a very oppressive and violent regime at home (see Chapter Seven to this book). What is beyond doubt is that the colonial culture of violence formed a seedbed for future cultures of violence in the postcolonial era. The culture of violence simply reproduced itself in the psyche of African nationalist and liberation fronts because they needed the nationalist violence to eject the colonial violence oppressing them .

Those Africans who participated in the armed liberation struggles were taken on a course to 'gaze' into the colonial abyss of violence and in the course of fighting the colonial monsters, African liberation fighters underwent a process of becoming 'monsteris' too. It is no wonder that a leader like Mugabe, who actively participated and led the liberation struggle, often brags about his party's ability to unleash violence on its political opponents. Finally, the continuation of violence is one indicator of the continuation of coloniality after the end of colonialism.

Part III

Case Studies

6

The Idea of South Africa and Pan-South African Nationalism

If a crude and homely illustration may be allowed, the peoples of South Africa resemble the constituents of a plum-pudding when in the process of being mixed; the plums, the peel, the currants; the flour, the eggs, and the water are mingled together. Here plums may predominate, there the peel; one part may be slightly thinner than another, but it is useless to try to resort them; they have permeated each other's substance: they cannot be reseparated; to cut off a part would not be to resort them; it would be dividing a complex but homogenous substance into parts which would repeat its complexity. What then shall be said of the South African problem as a whole? Is it impossible for the South African peoples to attain to any form of unity, organization, and national life? Must we forever remain a vast, inchoate, invertebrate mass of humans, divided horizontally into layers of race, mutually antagonistic, and vertically severed by lines of political state division, which cut up our races without simplifying our problems, and which add to the bitterness of race conflict the irritation of political divisions? Is national life and organization unattainable by us? [...] We believe that no one can impartially study the condition of South Africa and feel that it is so. Impossible as it is that our isolated states should consolidate, and attain to a complete national life, there is a form of organic union which is possible to us. For there is a sense in which all South Africans are one [...] there is a subtle but a very real bond, which unites all South Africans, and differentiates us from all other people in the world. This bond is our mixture of races itself. It is this which divides South Africa from all other peoples in the world, and makes us one.

(Olive Cronwright Schreiner 1923: 60-61)

Introduction

South Africa has a long history of identity crisis and contested questions of belonging and citizenship. This crisis is captured in such literature as *There Are No South Africans* by G. H. Calpin (1941) and recently by Ivor Chipkin's *Do South Africans Exist* (2007). Calpin posited that, 'The worst of South Africa is that you never come across a South African' (Calpin 1941: 9). This means that one of the enduring themes and inconclusive questions in South African political and social history is that of the making of pan-South African nationalism to underpin the imagined nation. This argument is confirmed by three modern historians, Colin Bundy, Saul Dubow and Robert Ross. Bundy argued that:

> In the political catechism of the New South Africa, the primary enquiry remains the National Question. What is the post-apartheid nation? Who belongs or is excluded, and on what basis? How does a 'national identity gain its salience and power to transcend the particularities of ethnicity and race?' (Bundy 2007: 79)

Dubow urged historians to focus research on the making of the South African nation in these words:

> It is surely time [...] for historians to formulate detailed questions about how South Africa has been conceived and imagined, to analyze the different forms in which ideas about South Africa and South African societies have developed over time, and to trace the ways in which the South African 'problem' or predicament has been conceptualized. In order to do so, we should remember that the struggle *for* South Africa has long been, and continues to be, a struggle to *become* South African (Dubow 2007: 72).

Ross, on the other hand, observed that:

> [...] even if the essential unity of South Africa and the identity of South Africans are beyond dispute, there remains the question of what is, and what is not, South Africa. Who are, and who are not, South Africans (Ross 1999: 3).

All these arguments speak to the pertinent issue of who constitute the authentic subject of the post-apartheid nation. It is a new and old question as it pre-occupied the proponents of Anglicization, Afrikanerization and Africanization as discursive processes within which identities germinated and were reconstructed and contested. What further complicated the situation were the questions of indigeneity and nativity that have persistently existed as a hidden script across all imaginations of the nation within plural and multi-racial societies created by colonialism.

The metaphor of a 'rainbow' nation is an attempt to include various races and ethnicities into a single nation where there is a place and space for each and everyone. It is a clarion call and generous invitation of people of diverse cultures, languages, religions and races to unite under one nation. This is apparent in the country's coat of arms which carries the message: 'Diverse People Unite'. But South Africa is pushing the agenda of unity of diverse peoples at a time when other parts of the continent are experiencing narrowing conceptions of belonging and citizenship informed by what Geshiere (2009) termed 'the return of the local' with its 'perils of belonging' and what Comaroff and Comaroff (2009:1) termed 'Ethnicity, INC' (turning tribes into corporations) characterized by 'a lot of ethnic awareness, ethnic assertion, ethnic sentiment, ethno-talk; this despite the fact that it was supposed to wither away with the rise of modernity, with disenchantment, and with the incursion of the market.'

Theron and Swart (2009: 153) correctly noted that, 'Nowhere on the continent has this politics of identity been more prominent than in South Africa, during the pre- and post-apartheid eras.' South African leaders have not rested on their laurels and ignored the issue of identity and nation-building. A construction of a unique pan-South African nationalism that incorporates diverse ethnicities and races is ongoing and the challenging question is whether it will succeed in suturing and stabilizing this racialized and ethnicized society.

As far back as 1996, the then Deputy President of South Africa Thabo Mbeki attempted to define South Africanness as a historical rather than primordial fixture in his seminal 'I am an African' speech delivered to the National Assembly to mark the adoption of the Constitution of South Africa (Mbeki 1998). Mbeki unpacked various historical and genealogical processes that contributed to the construction of South Africanness as an African identity ranging from slavery to colonialism. His definition of an African clearly reflected his slant towards issues of commitment to the African cause of liberation as part of a process that created Africans.

Mbeki's definition also implied that being African was not an unconditional identity, rather it was imposed by history on people and was predicated on the form of consciousness that one exhibited towards the African cause and the sacrifices one made towards African redemption, liberation and freedom. What is missing in Mbeki's definition is who is a South African if understood outside the broader African identity that he eloquently espoused as flexible, generous and inclusive of people of different races and ethnicities. Mbeki's conception of Africanness was that of a hybrid identity; born out of coalescence of various historical processes over centuries that brought the San, Khoi Khoi, Nguni, Sotho-Tswana, British, Malayan, Indian, Chinese, Afrikaner and other groups together. Mbeki explicitly stated that:

> I owe my being to Khoi and the San [...] I am formed of migrants who left Europe to find a new home on our native land [...] In my veins courses the blood of the Malay slaves who came from the East. Their proud dignity informs my bearing, their culture a part of my essence [...] I am the grandchild of the warrior men and women that Hintsa and Sekhukhune led, the patriots that Cetswayo and Mphephu took to battle, the soldiers Moshoeshoe and Ngungunyane taught never to dishonor the cause of freedom [...] I am the grandchild who lays fresh flowers on the Boer graves at St Helena and the Bahamas [...] I come from those who were transported from India and China [...] Being part of all these people and in the knowledge that one dare contest that assertion, I shall claim that I am an African (Mbeki 1998: 31-36).

This was indeed a superb historical contextualization of the very complex and ambiguous nature of the South African identity and its diversities. But despite these efforts by Mbeki to define South African national identity as a historical product of the coalescence of historical events and processes, the question of who is an authentic South African often continue to surface, threatening the 'rainbow nation'. Race, nativity and indigeneity continue to complicate the debate. The connection between 'whiteness' and 'Africanness' continues to be doubted mainly by those who define Africanness in racial terms (Friedman 2009: 79-83). In Chapter Two in this book I provided details of levels, degrees and varieties of Africanness.

This chapter traces the historical development and genealogies of the idea South Africa together with the complex questions of belonging and citizenship over a longer time-span beginning with a precolonial background, slicing right through the imperial and colonial encounters of the nineteenth and early twentieth centuries, and up to the present constructions of the 'rainbow nation'. The key question here is how a plurality of identities develop, coalesce or condense around a popular imagination to create a singular national one? Does South Africa have a popular myth of foundation around which the nation can coalesce? The idea of South Africa is analysed as an encapsulation of the various initiatives and imaginations of the nation mediated by complex historical processes and human actions that often operated and unfolded tangentially and others that coalesced tendentiously, accidentally and directly to produce what we now call the South African 'rainbow nation'.

The central argument of this chapter is that the discursive formation of South African national identity is not only a product of the African nationalist struggle but something that has a long pedigree lodged within precolonial antecedents, imperial and colonial imperatives, 'Anglicization', 'Afrikanerization' and 'Africanization' as broad discursive identity processes. At the centre of these processes were differing definitions of who constituted the 'authentic' subject of the imagined South African nation. Throughout its development, the idea of South Africa was permeated by forces of inclusion and exclusion mediated by race, ethnicity, gender, and material accumulation considerations.

The idea of South Africa emerged as a figurative expression and has a long pedigree dating back to the 1830s. Shula Marks and Stanley Trapido argued that:

> In the 1870s at the beginning of the mineral revolution, South Africa was a geographical expression. Precapitalist and capitalist modes of production existed side by side, as did state forms of varying sizes with their own ruling groups and systems of exploitation. There were two British colonies, two ostensibly politically independent republics and numerous still autonomous African polities. All these were multi-ethnic and multilingual, although not all languages and ethnicities were equal. Colonists of British and European descent lived side by side in the colonies with large numbers of indigenous peoples, and in Natal with indentured labourers from the Indian subcontinent; African kingdoms were equally heterogeneous entities, composed of peoples of different origins (Marks and Trapido1987: 3).

What needs to be understood is how a geographical-figurative expression was translated into the idea of a nation. The translation took the form of a complex tapestry and catalogue of historical accidents, complex imaginations, evolving constructions, and contestations dating back to the age of cataclysmic migrations of Africans and Afrikaners historically referred to as the *Mfecane/ Difaqane* (time of troubles/crushing) and the 'Great Trek/Treks' respectively (Cobbing 1988; Hamilton 1995; Etherington 2001).

The complex imperial and colonial encounters involving the Afrikaners, the British and the wars of conquest and resistance of the late nineteenth and the early twentieth centuries also formed the broader discursive terrain within which the idea of South Africa developed as a contested concept with a racial tinge. The idea of South Africa also emerged between and betwixt clashes and syntheses between imperial and colonial imperatives, annexations, negotiations, reconciliations and unions that were invariably shaped by diverging and converging nationalisms of the English, Afrikaners and Africans.

At the centre of this idea of South Africa is the question of belonging, citizenship and access to strategic resources. This question is profoundly historical, political and cultural; hence the suitability of a historical approach that interrogates complex histories and unpacks ambiguous politics that coalesced towards the production and reproduction of the idea of South Africa as a conflict-laden arena of claims and counter-claims to membership of the imagined nation.

The idea of South Africa is a complex one with multiple genealogies, complex histories and different meanings, and any serious study of the making of the South African nation must engage with the complex genealogies of its constructions, ambiguous imaginations, changing receptions, consumptions, contestations, rejections, celebrations, condemnations and subversions. The idea of South Africa is both old and new as its constructions and imaginings pre-occupied imperialists, colonial-settlers, indigenous Africans, nationalists of British, Afrikaner and African stock as well as travellers and novelists of the nineteenth and twentieth centuries and the present-day leaders of South Africa.

Framing the debates on identity

Anderson (1983) popularized the idea of the social construction of nations, leading to the retreat of earlier theories of the nation such as perennialism or primordialism. In 1983 when Anderson's book first appeared, two historians Eric Hobsbawn and Terence Ranger reinforced the thesis of social construction of identities and invention of traditions. The current debate is no longer about whether nations and identities were constructed or not, it is about the various specific and contextual mechanisms used to construct identities and nations. Manuel Castells argued that what needs to be understood are some three-fold issues: from what were the identities constructed; by whon were they constructed, and what were they constructed for (Castells 1997: 6-7).

National identity formation in general emerged out of complex historical, political and social processes and events that sought to weave together, eliminate, blend or re-define a multiplicity of existing identities. Lewellen (2002: 90) argued that identity was a 'matter of imaginative and creative rediscovery in which contemporary interpretation and needs fill in the gaps, recreate the past and bridge the discontinuities with new mythologies'. In this sense, identity was never 'an accomplished end point, of a people's history, but a constant process of becoming' that was 'always temporarily positioned within a particular context that needs to be imaginatively interpreted'

(Lewellen 2002). In other words, an identity never existed as something out there waiting to be embraced and experienced. The importance of identities to human beings is emphasized by Craig Calhoun who argued that:

> We know of no people without names, no languages or cultures in which some manner of distinction between self and other, we and they, are not made [...] self-knowledge--always a construction no matter how much it feels like a discovery - is never altogether separable from claims to be known in specific ways by others (Calhoun 1994: 7).

Michel Foucault (1982: 212-221) argued that the processes through which reality was constructed and dissimulated were always acts of power and would always be resisted and contested. At the centre of identity construction is what is termed 'political frontiers', which Aletta J. Norval defined as follows:

> Political frontiers are those mechanisms through which social division is instituted, and 'insiders' distinguished from 'outsiders'; it defines opposition; it dissimulates social division; it makes it seem that the institution of social division is not itself a social fact (Norval 1996: 4-5).

In the South African case, the discursive formation of national identity was permeated by casting and recasting of political frontiers as attempts were consistently made to order the relations among the blacks, the Afrikaners, the English and other groups.

The political frontiers were mediated by race and ethnic vectors. It is not surprising, therefore, that colonial systems such as apartheid tried to maintain African fragmentations into various ethnic groups including putting some legislative speed traps on the process of coalescence of multiple ethnic African identities into a singular national identity. But such constructions of political frontiers provoked further imaginations of nation by the oppressed and excluded African people who agitated for inclusion in the nation.

It is impossible to understand the issues and problems of the making of the South African nation without clear historical knowledge of the catalogues of socio-political dislocations such as the 'Mfecane' (Bryant 1929; Lye and Murray 1980; Cobbing 1988; Hamilton 1995), the 'Great Trek' of Boer farmers of 1834-1836, the discovery of minerals of the 1860s and 1880s, the Anglo-Boer War/South African War of 1899-1902, Bambata Uprising of 1906, the Act of Union of 1910, the formation of the Native Congress in 1912; industrialization and proletarianization of the 1930s and 1940s, the Second World War of 1939-1945, institutionalization of apartheid in 1948, Defiance Campaigns and the Sharpeville Massacre of the 1960s, the rise of the Black

Consciousness Movement in the late 1960s and 1970s, the Soweto Uprising of 1976, the age of the United Democratic Front (UDF) of the 1980s, and many others. These events and processes constituted the broader discursive terrain within which seeds of identities germinated, coalesced and were contested and redefined.

Dubow (2007: 52) has lamented how existing master narratives about 'class', 'nation', 'race' and even 'the struggle' have avoided 'complex questions of subjectivity'. He added that despite the existence of 'outstanding work on the invention of tradition and the creation of spurious ethnic and tribal entities, it is remarkable that 'South Africa has so often been analysed as a unitary category; the presumption that all its people were and are South Africans has likewise been taken for granted' (Dubow 2007: 53). This confusion arises from the fact that the history of South African nation-building has been so little explored from a deep historical perspective that traces it back to the time when the term South Africa was a mere figurative expression.

Most of the recent literature such as Ivor Chipkin (2007) that focused on how an 'African people' as a collectivity organized in pursuit of a political agenda came into being tend to confine analysis of identities and the nation to the period of the African nationalist struggle and the post-apartheid period as though the idea of the nation started in the 1960s (Chipkin 2007). Chipkin's main concern was to correct a false idea common within existing narratives of resistance, oppression, exploitation and popular nationalist discourses whereby 'the people' were viewed as 'existing' prior to the period of the nationalist struggle (Chipkin 2007: 2).

The central thesis of Chipkin's study is that the African people that are today called South Africans emerged primarily in and through the process of nationalist resistance to colonialism. He made a clear distinction between 'the people as datum and the people as political subjects' (Chipkin 2007: 2). Chipkin made it clear that he was not interested in studying people as mere datum or as 'an empirical collectivity of individuals in a given geography', rather he was approaching the concept of 'the people' from a political angle as 'a collectivity organized in pursuit of a political end' (Chipkin 2007: 1-2).

To Chipkin, once the concept of the people was clarified as a political one, then it was possible to step up the argument to engage with the meaning of 'nation'. To him, a nation is 'not simply a cultural artefact' but a political phenomenon. His definition of a nation is: 'a political community whose form is given in relation to the pursuit of democracy and freedom' (Chipkin 2007: 2-3). he went further to say that:

> In this sense, the nation precedes the state, not because it has always already exis-
> ted, but because it emerges in and through the nationalist struggle for state power.
> The history of the postcolony is, in this sense, the history of 'the people' qua
> production (Chipkin 2007: 2).

While Chipkin's robust intellectual interventions on the subject of identity
and nation-building were useful in understanding the making of people and
nations in postcolonial Africa in general and post-apartheid South Africa in
particular, the key problem is that he confined his study to the period of the
African nationalist struggle. He missed the point that the African nationalist
struggle was just another layer and one version of nationalist imaginations
of the nation that emerged on top of earlier ones such as the 'Anglicization'
and 'Afrikanerization' processes that also contributed to the construction
of 'South Africanism' (Dubow 2006: v-vii). But in postcolonial Africa, the
thesis that 'the nation precedes the state' needs further interrogation because
African founding fathers have often managed to build states but failed to
build nations. This is a point well articulated by the Zimbabwean political
scientist, Eldred V. Masunungure, who argued that:

> Nation-building, like state-building, is a work of art and many African leaders
> have proven to be good state-building artists but poor nation-builders. In coun-
> tries with a kaleidoscope of cultural, ethnic, racial, religious and other salient so-
> cial identities, nation-building is a big challenge (Masunungure 2006: 3).

The point is that African nationalists inherited an already established colonial
state without a nation. Their task was mainly to 'de-racialize' and 'Africanize'
state structures. Nation-building is altogether a different structure and has
remained a daunting task. It has continued to be contentious work-in-
progress across the African continent. For South Africa, the challenge was
how to mould the various ethnic and racial groups into a stable nation of
diverse but equal citizens.

Dubow argued that 'South Africanism' as a form of imagination of a unitary
nation 'took many forms and resists easy definition,' adding that it developed as
a 'version of the patriotic or dominion nationalisms'. To him, South Africanism
began as 'the expression of a developing settler society, and as such marginalized
or denied the rights of indigenous African peoples' (Dubow 2006: vi).

What was paradoxical about this emerging 'South Africanism' within the confluence
of imperial and colonial ventures, was that while it excluded black races, it 'steadfastly
disavowed the politics of 'racialism' and 'its proponents professed their commitment
to ameliorating tensions between Afrikaners and English-speakers by stressing
common bonds of patriotism' (Dubow 2006: vi). This inclusionary-exclusionary

motif haunted the development of the idea of South Africa throughout various historical epochs and continues to reverberate even within the present 'rainbow nation'. Dubow (2006: v) further argued that investigations into the story of belonging should grapple with such pertinent questions as: 'How did understanding of the term 'South Africa' develop? What were considered to be its defining problems? Who laid claim to membership of the national community, and when?' Chipkin left these questions openended stating that: 'if South Africans were not a nation, they were, nonetheless, already some kind of people. The issue was therefore: Who was eligible for citizenship and who was not. At stake were the limits of the political community' (Chipkin 2007: 175).

It is important to investigate such processes as Anglicization that formed part of identity-forming mechanisms that put the English at the centre of the imagined nation and 'Afrikanerization' as a particular form of national identity construction that put the Afrikaner at the centre of the nation, while tolerating the English, but excluding Africans/blacks from the category of rights-bearing citizens. African nationalism was another layer of complex processes of imagination of the nation and construction of identity that sought to put the excluded Africans at the centre of the nation, while contesting the notions of racialized belonging that were exclusionary.

But African nationalist discourses of nation were not a homogenous body of thought but were always riddled by antinomies of various strands of thought such as radical 'Africanism' that was espoused by the Pan-Africanist Congress (PAC) and the African National Congress (ANC) that matured to articulate an inclusive nation founded on principles of non-racialism and liberal democracy (Ndlovu-Gatsheni 2007: 1-61; 2008: 53-85; 2009: 61-78).

The best way to gain a deeper understanding of the idea of South Africa is to read it carefully as a continuum that has been in the making since the late nineteenth century with various ideas of the nation germinating and cross-fertilizing each other, as well as contesting and blending with each other across various major historical epochs. The Foucualdian concept of genealogy as a tool for analysing the origins of social and political phenomena like nations and their embedment and implication in the complex political histories and social struggles taking place in 'unpromising places' is very useful (Foucault 1977: 42; Norval: 1996: 57). Aletta J. Norval captured the importance of genealogy as a tool of analysis in the following words:

> Genealogy is an irreverent, essentially political practice, disturbing what was previously considered immobile, fragmenting what was thought unified, showing the heterogeneity of what was imagined to be consistent with itself (Norval 1996: 57).

If one deploys Foucualdian genealogical analysis, it becomes clear that the triumphal and celebrated African nationalism that was dominated by the current ruling African National Congress (ANC), the PAC, Black Consciousness Movement (BCM), the South African Communist Party (SACP) and other smaller African political formations, were never 'original' political formations but were hybrid and successor formations and inheritors of earlier nascent 'inclusive' and 'progressive' traditions informed by Victorian Christianity, Trotskyism, Civil Rights Movements, Garveyism, imperial liberalism, anti-slavery humanitarianism and Western notions of modernity and well as resilient precolonial ideologies of freedom (Dubow 2006: 277).

It is clear that the Zulu warrior tradition and the figure of King Shaka influenced the politics of Inkatha Freedom Party (IFP) and that the 'Port Elizabeth-East London-Alice triangle' became the seedbed of nationalist ideas informed by the effects on the Xhosa of black-white confrontations of the colonial encounters that were followed by increasing Christianization and exposure to modern schooling. The early assimilation of liberal ideas by some Xhosa elites had a deep influence on subsequent African nationalism (Williams 1970: 383).

This reality of the ANC and other African political formations as successors and inheritors of those inchoate modernist, emancipatory, revolutionary, and progressive strands to become a unique grand synthesizers and mixers of various nationalisms led such scholars as Eric Hobsbawn to characterize the ANC in particular as the last great 'Euronationalist' movement (cited in Bhabha Comaroff 1994: 15-46). The literary scholar David Attwell articulated this question of a continuum in South Africa political history in a more dramatic way:

> South Africa became postcolonial in 1910 with the Act Union, which brought about a coalition of Boer and Briton in a white colonial state; a bleaker kind of postcoloniality emerged with the triumph of Afrikaner republicanism after the National Party's electoral victory in 1948; then, mercifully, in 1994, a constitutionally-defined, non-racial democracy was established, representing the point at which these various postcolonial histories have begun to coalesce, at least in the legal sense (Attwell 2005: 2).

Odendaal (1984: 287) also emphasized that the ANC is a successor to earlier traditions of resistance and an inheritor of the political mantle from previous African and non-African political formations and diverse ideological resources. He argued that the armed guerrilla struggle spearhead by the ANC and the PAC was legitimized as 'part of the struggle that started with eighteenth-and nineteenth-century frontier wars'.

Therefore, the development of both African and white political consciousness is studied from a genealogical perspective that takes into account nineteenth century intra- and inter-African and white rivalries and initiatives within which racialized imaginations of the nation emerged. This is a point reinforced by Odendaal (1984: 286) who argued that 'the line of continuity between tribal or primary resistance to white expansion, early constitutional protests politics and present day African nationalism' is 'clear and deserves more attention from scholars'.

The genealogies of the idea of South Africa

In the 1830s right up to the post-1902 period, there were no blacks and whites that existed as broadly defined racial identities. On the African side, such earlier identities as those of the Mbo, Thembe, Ndwandwe, Mthethwa, Ngwane and others had collapsed and were giving birth to new ones (Etherington 2001). What existed were numerous ethnic identities such as Zulu, Ndebele, Korana, Dutch, Griqua, Hurutshe, Hlubi, Xhosa, 'Hottentots', Afrikaner and Britons. These were at their formative and infancy stage. For instance, the nucleus of Afrikaner identity emerged in the interior in this form:

> A typical group consisted of a handful of families travelling together under the leadership of a senior male. These groups tended to be known by the name of their chiefs, i.e., the Cilliers Party, the Bronkhorsts Party, the Potgieter Party, etc., even though people with many other surnames were to be found among them (Etherington 2001: 244).

This means that what eventually became Afrikaners emerged as a historical coalescence of scattered families and smaller groups under some notable leaders, such as Hendrick Potgieter, Louis Trichardt, and Piet Uys. Such broader identities as native, Bantu, Coloured, and White did not exist. At times what eventually coalesced into African people were initially only known by the names of their leaders such as the Shangani of Soshangane. In this case, the leader's name became the name of his followers—it became a form of identity.

Like all identities, African identity developed in relation to white identity. White identity also developed in relation to black/African identity. In short, the 1830s were a period of identity formation in the midst of evolving colonial encounters, migrations and wars. Marks and Trapido (1987: 2) noted that new identities also emerged around 1910 when the state was being constructed as a single polity out of the British colonies, the conquered Afrikaner republics and African kingdoms. But the Act of Union of 1910 did not create a stable nation. As Marks and Trapido argued:

That this unification did not lead to a single pan-South Africa, pan-ethnic nationalism was the outcome of a history of regional divisions, the racism and social Darwinism of the late nineteenth century and the specific political-cum-class struggles which were being legitimated by the discourse of nationalism (Marks and Trapido 1987: 2).

In light of this, the argument that the 'development of humanity' as a 'series of interpretations' where the concept of genealogy 'is to record its history' becomes very important and revealing (Foucault 1977: 151-152). A genealogical analysis of the discursive formation of the South African nation makes visible the ambiguities, instabilities and fragmentary terrain within which it emerged.

Olive Cronwright Schreiner, whose words constitute the epigraph of this chapter, was an early creative and polemic writer who dreamt of a rainbow nation even prior to the Anglo-Boer/South Africa War of 1899-1902. She was described by her contemporaries as the spiritual progenitor of the South Africa nation (Rive 1976: vii-xxii). Schreiner died in 1920 having made clear her ideas of a united South Africa nation comprising of the Africans, Britons and Afrikaners. She posed the challenge of nation-building in this way: 'How, of our divided peoples, can a great healthy, harmonious and desirable nation be formed? This is the final problem of South Africa. If we cannot solve it, our fate is sealed' (Schreiner 1976: 62). Schreiner clearly identified the core problem of South Africa:

> If our view be right, the problem which South Africa has before it today is this: How from our political states and our discordant races, can a great, healthy, united, organized nation be formed? [...] Our race question is complicated by a question of colour, which presents itself to us in a form more virulent and intense than that in which it has met any modern people (Schreiner 1976: 62-64).

Sounding rather prophetic, Schreiner had this say about the future of South Africa:

> Our South African national structure in the future will not and cannot be identical with that of any other people, our national origin being so wholly unlike that of any other; our social polity must be developed by ourselves through the interaction of our parts with one another and in harmony with our complex needs. For good or evil, the South African nation will be an absolutely new thing under the sun, perhaps, owing to its mixture of races, possessing that strange vitality and originality which appears to rise so often from the mixture of human varieties: perhaps, in general human advance, ranking higher than other societies more simply constructed; perhaps lower—according as we shall shape it: but this,

certainly—will be a new social entity, with new problems, new gifts, new failings, new accomplishments (Schriener 1976: 370).

The genealogy of the idea of South Africa is traceable to the cataclysmic processes that engulfed the area which Norman Etherington termed the 'heartland'. This heartland referred to the interior of what finally became South Africa. It became a setting for 'great treks' of Africans, Griqua, Korana and Afrikaners in the period between 1815 and 1854 (Etherington 2001). The 'heartland' is a term used to distinguish the areas that were far from the coastal areas of Cape Town and Natal where white activities were concentrated during the period prior to 1834. The core area of the 'heartland' was the Caledon Valley that offered water and ideal places for settlement and security. Besides being a site of migrations and wars, it was also an arena of identity formation and imagining of new nations comprising people of different ethnic groups. It became the site of growth of Afrikaner identities that culminated in the birth of two Boer Republics.

Between 1815 and 1854, as noted by Etherington, the 'heartland' became a centre of contestation, war, migration, rise and fall of nations as well as emergence of new identities. In the first place, the 'heartland' witnessed some fragments of Nguni groups such as the Zulu, Ndwandwe, Qwabe, Dlamini, Ngwane, Mthewthwa, Hlubi and Mkhize, and Ndebele, trekking into the interior in smaller groups (Maggs 1976; Ayliff and Whiteside 1912). These fragments included the Zizi, the 'Transvaal Ndebele,' the Ndebele of Mzilikazi Khumalo, the Ngwane of Matiwane, the Tlokwa of MaNthatisi and Sekonyela and others (Rasmussen 1978; Hamilton 1995; Warmelo 1938). But the 'heartland' was not an empty space. It was inhabited by various Sotho-Tswana groups such as Hurutshe, Ngwaketse, Rolong, Kwena, Fokeng, Kgatla and many others (Ellenberger 1912).

The period also witnessed the entry into history of mixed race communities such as the Griqua and Korana under such leaders as Andries Waterboer, Adam Kok and others (Ross 1976). Added to this layer of identities were the Boer farmers that eventually established the Boer Republics of Transvaal and the Orange Free State. In the so-called 'British Zone', there existed not only the English Cape colonists but also Afrikaners and various Xhosa-speaking chiefdoms and remnants of the San and the Khoi Khoi. In the Durban areas there were British traders and others who eventually established the Natal Colony living alongside such communities as the Zulu and others (Etherington 2001).

But when did the name South Africa begin to be used as a form of identity and by whom? The term South Africa began to be used in the 1830s as a reference to the region extending northwards from the Cape to the Zambezi River. For instance, P. A. Molteno had this to say about what South Africa means:

> When we speak of South Africa, we speak of the country bounded by the sea on all sides except the north, where the boundaries may roughly be said to be the Cunene towards the west and the Zambezi towards the east (Molteno 1896: 39).

To Theal (1873), South Africa was a collective term for the Cape Colony, Natal, Orange Free State, South African Republic and all other territories south of the Zambezi. Moving away from understanding the idea of South Africa as a mere geographical expression, Dubow argued that the idea has always been 'an ideology of compromise' that 'developed out of a prior sense of colonial identity, namely, that which developed in the Cape from the early years of British occupation at the turn of the nineteenth century' (Dubow 2006: viii).

Dubow (2006: viii) traced the idea of South Africa from 'the institutions and associational life of Cape Town colonial culture, intellect, and politics'. What needs to be understood is the genealogy of South Africanism as a political aspiration, imagination of nation, a claim on citizenship rights as well as an initiative to promote indigenous/autochthonous forms of belonging and affiliation to a nation called South Africa. Early novelists like Anthony Trollope popularized the idea of South Africa as an identity of the people. In his popular novel entitled South Africa, Trollope wrote that:

> South Africa is a country of black men—and not of white men. It has been so; it is so, and it will continue to be so. In this respect it is altogether unlike Australia, unlike the Canadas, and unlike New Zealand (Trollope 1973: 454-455).

Trollope emphasized that unlike earlier British colonies of Australia, Canada and New Zealand where settlers were numerically superior to the indigenous people, in South Africa the number of indigenous black people far exceeded that of white settlers. While the English conceived of South Africa to be an expansion of the Cape Colony, a counter Afrikaner imagination of South Africa, as constituted by independent Boer republics, was also developing informed by emerging pan-Afrikaner identity (Lester 2001).

Anglicization as an identifiction process

It must be noted that by the late nineteenth century 'all the peoples of southern Africa existed to a greater or lesser extent under the hegemony of a mainly British merchant capitalism and imperialism (Marks and Trapido 1987: 4).

This omnipresence of British imperial power afforded any English-speaking settler some protection and power drawing from the ties with a powerful metropolis and its political, technological, economic and ideological resources (Marks and Trapido 1987: 4). It was during this period that the imperialist Cecil John Rhodes celebrated being born a British by becoming its dominant power and the 'mistress of oceanic trade', buttressing the arrogant British national ideology of 'splendid isolation'.

The British Queen and the British flag were symbols of national pride. Therefore, English imaginations of a South African identity were predicated on a developing British superiority over other races and ethnicities. The adherence and loyalty of English settlers to Britain made them pursue an ambiguous national agenda torn apart between a broader imperial mission and local colonial imperatives, unlike the Afrikaners that had a strong local agenda. Anglicization was also predicated on a contemptuous approach towards non-English people including Afrikaners who were considered an inferior race just like Africans. No wonder then that prior to 1902, a strong British jingoism locked horns with incipient Afrikaner republicanism leading to the Anglo-Boer war of 1899-1902. During this period Lord Milner was the face of British racial patriotism (Marks and Trapido 1987: 7).

Eventually, four contending conceptions of the South African nation emerged from the centre of imperial and colonial tensions. One was a liberal and civic trajectory that emphasized rational principles of economic and social progress founded on principles of constitutionalism as well as ethnic and racial tolerance informed by the Cape Colony experiences and liberal traditions. The second was the anti-liberal settler colonial version which was informed by upheavals of frontier life but still emphasizing freedom and autonomy as achievements of civilization and commitment to 'undying imperial loyalism' (Dubow 2006: 152). The Anglicization of South Africa aimed at incorporating the Afrikaners into the British colonial order with the Africans providing the needed cheap labour.

These two imaginations were part of the Anglicization process. The third strand emerged from the experiences of the Afrikaners and was informed by memories of the 'Great Trek' as a heroic struggle for independence and the experiences of Afrikaner republicanism as manifested in the existence of two Boer republics of Transvaal and Orange Free State. The fourth strand emerged from the experiences of African people who endured the pangs of being squeezed by both British and Afrikaners off their lands and being excluded from emerging white imaginations of the nation.

Dubow understood these related but differing imaginations as 'rival pan-South African nationalisms'. On the overall discursive terrain within which they emerged, Dubow had this to say:

> Yet, from a late nineteenth century perspective the colonial-imperial antinomy was all too apparent. Colonialism could well exist within a wider sense of imperial belonging, and it shared many common features with imperialism—most obviously a shared agreement that white political ascendancy should not be threatened. But those who considered themselves colonists took pride in their independence and achievements, and were resentful of unwanted external intervention. Jingo imperialists were scornful of pretensions to independence where these might challenge metropolitan interests, and were increasingly intolerant of local nationalisms (Dubow 2006: 153).

The template for Anglicization as a process of identity was the Cape Colony where the English language and other paraphernalia of British culture and ideology were in place. British colonial nationalism and British Crown imperialism tended to complement each other with some few areas of misunderstandings (Dubow 1997). The Cape Colony was a key launching pad for British imaginations of South Africa as an 'anglicized nation'. In the Anglicization mind-map, the South African nation was to be nothing other than a 'greater Cape Colony' together with its institutions replicated across South Africa. The British flag was to be the national symbol.

The realization of this 'grand national plan' was to take the form of bringing Natal and Cape Colony together. But in between the two British colonies lay two Boer republics and African kingdoms and chiefdoms. Two options were available: federation under British overlordship or conquest. The imperial imperative to conquer the interior unfolded in the form of conquest of the remaining independent African kingdoms alongside the conquest of independent Boer republics.

The confrontation between forces of Anglicization/imperialism and Afrikanerization/Boer republicanism resulted in the Anglo-Boer/South African War of 1899-1902 which became a decider of the future trajectory of imaginations and reconstructions of the idea of South Africa (Porter 1980). Dubow had this to say about the place of this war in the construction of South Africanism:

> A war that was at once fought over possession of the country's riches, by what were to become South Africans, in what was to become South Africa, has surely to be understood as war for South Africa, not only in the immediate sense of acquisition and control, but also in the forward-looking sense of making a new nation-state—in effect, a 'white man's country' (Dubow 2006: 158-159).

As Lord Milner said, the core thinking within Anglicization was to construct a white self-governing polity comprising both British and Afrikaners but subsisting under the British Union Jack as a national symbol (Dubow 2006: 159). Within this compromise between British imperialism and Afrikaner republicanism, Africans were to feature as labourers in the farms, mines and industries.

The problem with what was achieved by the Treaty of Vereeniging of May 1902 was a peace born out of conquest of the Boers and the exclusion of Africans from the nation. Both Afrikaners and Africans were resentful of British triumphalism. For the Africans, they expected the British to practise the liberalism they preached, including incorporating them into the nation as rights-bearing citizens. For the Afrikaners the war had affected their nascent republican nationalism where another imagination of a South African nation dominated by Afrikaners was emerging.

Anglicization did not succeeded in constructing a stable white South African nation. Afrikaners were mainly in agreement with the British on exclusion of blacks from citizenship but still resented being dominated politically and economically by a minority of British people. Boer republicanism was not totally defeated and Africans who had supported the British were betrayed. In the midst of these disappointments emerged new counter-imaginations of the nation. Let us begin with the continuing politics of Afrikaner republicanism and its imagination of the nation before looking at African imaginations.

Afrikaner republicanism and apartheid as versions of South Africanism

Just like the English, the Afrikaners were developing a particular vision of a South African nation informed partly by their tradition of ethnic republicanism engendered by the experiences of the 'Great Trek' and partly by challenges they met after the momentous events of the Anglo-Boer/South Africa (1899-1902 and the Act of Union of 1910. Norval argued that the specificity of Afrikaner nationalism and its re-emergence after the Act of Union of 1910 together with its radical ethnic republicanism was a response to a catalogue and series of 'painful and conflict-ridden experiences' (Norval 1996: 12). Post-1902 Anglicization policies of the British regime which were set to exclude Afrikaners from educational and administrative positions galvanized Afrikaner republican nationalism with the memories of the Great Trek providing the myth of foundation of Afrikaner nationhood.

Some of the upheavals that contributed to the development of particular Afrikaner identity together with a particular imagination of a South African nation included the much celebrated 'Great Trek,' the Battle of Vegkop which pitted the Boers against the Ndebele of Mzilikazi Khumalo in 1836, as well as the Blood River Battle involving Boers and the Zulu forces of Dingani in 1838. It also icluded the memories of independence under Boer republics that were destroyed by British imperialists through Anglo-Boer/South Africa War, the industrialization and urbanization of the 1930s and 1940s that found Afrikaners still confined to rural agricultural sectors of the economy and not prepared for fast urban life, and other events that had a dislocatory impact on the life of Afrikaners who had remained as a largely rural community compared to the British. How the Afrikaners interpreted these events informed their nationalism.

It must also be noted that Afrikaner identity itself had to be constructed and was just emerging by the time of the South African War. The Dutch Reformed Church was one of the building blocks in the construction of Afrikaner nationalism. Finding themselves in the interior of South Africa, surrounded by African communities and having to learn to adapt and distinguish themselves from other people, they nurtured a strong Calvinist faith and developed notions of the Biblical chosen nation. By the early twentieth century, Afrikaans was not yet an acceptable and respected language. (1987) has demonstrated empirically that Afrikaans was a twentieth century invention.

The language began as a language of the poor and as a mixture of Dutch, Khoisan, San and Malayo-Portuguese languages spoken by slaves in the seventeenth and eighteenth century Cape Colony (Hofmeyr 1987: 95-123). The development of Afrikaans as a language is one of the reflections of complex inter-racial and ethnic encounters of colonial modernity in a frontier region. But the upper and middle-classes continued to speak Dutch while looking down at Afrikaans as either 'Hottentot language' or 'kitchen language' which they found embarrassing (Hofmeyr 1987: 95-123). It had the status of a belittled vernacular language which eventually assumed a better status alongside the intensification of Afrikaner republican nationalism and its drive for 'nativization' of the Boers as South Africans.

At the centre of Afrikaner nationalism were perceptions and realities of the fragility of their nascent identity that they were developing and strengthening within a context of a hostile and ever shifting political and economic climate of the late nineteenth century and early twentieth century. The 'Apartheid' slogan emerged as a powerful but empty signifier promising the reconstruction of a lost unity (Norval 1996: 13). What the Afrikaners gained from Lord Milner's post-1902 reconstruction dispensation was agreement with the British to reject the principle of equality between whites and blacks.

This was concretized through the Report of the South African Native Affairs Commission (SANAC) chaired by Sir Godfrey Lagden which inaugurated the policy of segregation of whites and blacks (Odendaal 1984: 65). The SANAC was the first drive by a combination of the English and the Afrikaners to begin to deal with what became known as the 'native question'. The second concession to Afrikaners was the granting of 'responsible government' to the Boer republics in 1906 and 1907.

In 1908 the South Africa Party (SAP) dominated by members of the Afrikaner Bond assumed power at the Cape; this meant that in the four colonies (Cape, Natal, Transvaal and Orange Free State) the Afrikaners were becoming politically dominant to counter British imperial policies and designs. But they still had to cooperate with the economically powerful English elements that had the backing of the Crown. Their cooperation was demonstrated at the National Convention of 1908 that drafted the South African Act of Union that was released to the press on 9 February 1909 (Odendaal 1984:151). The Act of Union of 1910, while closing out Africans from the nation and denying them citizenship rights, did not succeed in eliminating intra-white tensions pitting the English against the Afrikaners.

The unfolding of South African capitalist industrial revolution backed by discovery of mineral wealth (diamonds and gold) was not favourable to Afrikaners who were agriculturalists. To scholars like Belinda Bozzoli, inspired by a materialist-Gramscian approach to the idea of South Africa, the early axis of intra-and inter-white conflicts in the late nineteenth and early twentieth century took the form of clashes between strong imperial 'mining and industrial' capital which was represented by the British and weak 'agricultural domestic capital' represented by Afrikaners (Bozzoli 1981: 29-38).

The emergence of a national bourgeoisie crystallized around the economically powerful British mine owners and industrialists who began to imagine the nation in capitalist terms. Strong economic interest-group associations, such as Transvaal Manufacturers' Association, the Colonial Industries Protectionist League and others projected a concept of a nation founded on a uniform goal of capitalist development. The emerging national bourgeoisie favoured a South African nation of English and Afrikaners and rejected intra-white racialism of the pre-1902 and pre-Act of Union periods. For instance 'manufacturing ideologists' as Bozzoli terms them had this to say:

> The Union of South Africa, being a nation in the making, cannot afford the luxury of perpetuating the race feud, with all its sordid insincerities, its internecine quar-

rels and its resulting blight [...] racial quarrels must be avoided like the plague if the Act of Union is to spell peace, progress and prosperity, and if the declarations of the Opposition leaders are sincere they will join hands with the Government in thwarting any attempt to revive the dying feud between Dutch and British members of the new South African brotherhood (Bozzoli 1981: 135).

The business elite even called for the formation of a new national party driven by national interests and representing a people under one flag. But Africans had to be excluded from this white nation. What was envisioned was a 'South African, white, version, of a bourgeois state' (Bozzoli 1978). But this imagination of a homogenous white South African nation masked important and deep-seated intra- and inter-white divisions mediated by ethnicity, class, ideological, and rural vs. urban cleavages. In short, the powerful English business class was trying to mobilize and incorporate a defeated Afrikaner community that was already 'subordinated' to imperial hegemony (Wolpe 1972; Martin 1974).

But imaginations of a white nation under British imperial tutelage did not succeed in containing Afrikaner republicanism due to a number of factors. In the first place, large-scale industrialization and urbanization created a group of poor Afrikaners that found themselves in the same strata with the despised and excluded Africans. Their plight was compounded by the failure of British liberal 'segregationism' (Norval 1996: 12). The result was a simultaneous proletarianization of majority of Africans and Afrikaners into poor labourers of the British.

The Afrikaners who expected a different life from that of Africans began to form interest-group associations on top of the old Afrikaner Bond and Federation of Afrikaans Cultural Association, and these included Economic Congress, National Youth League, Poor Welfare Council, and League for the Act of Rescue. Altogether these organizations began to push a common agenda of white Afrikaans-speaking people from economic, cultural and political fronts. The push for improvement of the plight of poor white Afrikaners became entangled with the question of black natives who were increasingly being proletarianized. Norval (1996: 19) argues that, 'Resolution of the Native question was thus central to the rectification of poor white problem, both socially and economically.'

To Afrikaner nationalists, urbanization led to 'denationalization' of their community and destruction of their hard-constructed identity. What they feared most was miscegenation as poor Afrikaner women intermingled with Africans in the urban centres. This problem was linked to the crisis of segregationism in the 1930s and 1940s. Increasingly, Afrikaners called for a more rigid political and social frontier dividing white and black races leading to the invention of natives as a homogenous identity. SANAC invented this category and stated that, 'Native shall be taken to include an aboriginal inhabitant of Africa, south of the Equator and to include half-castes and their descendants by Natives' (Ashforth 1990: 33).

Those categorized as natives were later confined to reserves and homelands (Bantustans) as a solution not only to the question of poor whites but also as a response to the rising tide of African nationalism and pan-Africanism seeking to unite black people as Africans and authentic national subjects of the South Africa nation. Norval, therefore, traces the birth of the National Party (NP) and its ideology of apartheid to the dislocation of identities provoked by vicissitudes of industrialization and urbanization together with such events as the Great Depression of the inter-war years. Apartheid was born from the way Afrikaners made sense of their situation within a society dominated by races and ethnicities (Norval 1996: 52-55).

In 1948, apartheid was institutionalized and it continued to live through 'negative operations' and drawing of frontiers as it tried to survive numerous dislocatory events and African resistance. Apartheid's four pillars were: increasing restriction of franchise for Africans while monopolizing and centralizing state power in the hands of Afrikaners as well as tightening repressive state apparatuses; spatial recasting of urban African townships while constructing homelands; enforcing regulation that ensured supply of cheap African labour to the mines, industries, farms and white domestic households; and direct state intervention in spheres of employment, education, health and other daily life human activities (Cohen 1986: 7-10).

Apartheid as social engineering also reorganized whites into separate schools and other social spaces for Afrikaners and English. To further entrench the Afrikaner *volk*, Coloureds who spoke Afrikaans were excluded and given their own space. In short, apartheid was launched into action as a solution to the relations of subordination between Afrikaners and the English, the fragmenting experience of urbanization that dislocated Afrikaner community into social classes, and the native question.

In general, during the time of decolonization and socialism, apartheid assumed a different import. Broader African nationalism was framed as an external imposition of communists that was not in synch with African traditions, culture and 'real nationalism' that espoused ethnic differentiation.

African nationalists were framed as rootless trouble-makers created by colonialism working under the influence of foreigners and preaching unrealistic imaginations of a unitary pan-African nation.

Proponents of apartheid ironically feared 'colour consciousness' developing among Africans and caricatured it as nothing but 'common hatred of whites' that was not sustainable and deep-rooted in a continent where people existed as different ethnic groups (Hugo 1988: 571). Apartheid ideologists were busy resisting decolonization and broader African nationalism through re-creating the African world in their own image of separate development. Apartheid was far from being an irrational ideology; it was a particular logic of identity construction through constant imposition of political frontiers. But apartheid had its inherent internal and external limits that were going to wear it down with time as it received blows from African resistance and rejection by the international community.

Its exclusion of blacks from citizenship and belonging constituted a strong internal limit. The international community could not tolerate it. Its multiple revisions and piecemeal reforms could not save it. Its three survival techniques were not sustainable: apartheid began with a strategy of separating what was intermingled by liberal segregationist policies; its second strategy was 'separate development' including creating Bantustans/homelands as independent republics for the Bantu; and then shifting to the rhetoric of 'multi-nationalism' whereby people were treated as 'equals' but enjoying separate lives and development (Vorster 1977). Increasing urban African population had no space within apartheid. Coloureds had no space too.

What had started as a 'conjunctural crisis' in the 1960s and 1970s has turned into an 'organic crisis' in the 1980s and 'full-scale crisis of apartheid hegemony' towards the 1990s (Norval 1996: 218-220). Apartheid precipitated the dislocation of identities and, in the process, enabled the emergence of a new search for new identity, new imagination of South Africa and formation of a new myth to 're-suture the dislocated structure of the old, dying imaginary' (Norval 1996: 275). African imaginations provided a new imagination of South Africa and the ANC's 1955 articulation of a non-racial society was to become a pragmatic solution to the racialized and ethnicized national question.

African nationalism and imagination of a non-racial 'rainbow' nation

By the 1880s, Africans did not exist as a collectivity pursuing common political objectives. Ethnic identities were dominant markers. The early educated elite that were a creation of mission and colonial schools had the mammoth task of creating an African identity. A political consciousness that could be called African took time to emerge from the fragmented ethnic identities rooted in precolonial history. Even the early educated elite were much more closely tied to their specific communities, home areas and towns (Odendaal 1984: xii). Furthermore, the early educated elite were not fully opposed to colonial modernity as they had imbibed Christian faith and Victorian ideas of liberalism and become committed to ideals of equality, non-racialism and enfranchisement of educated Africans.

African identity formation emerged concurrently with the intensification of scientific racism rooted in social Darwinist theories that were increasingly used by imperialists and colonialists as a powerful legitimating ideology of domination and segregation in early twentieth century South Africa (Marks and Trapido 1987: 6-7; Dubow 1987: 71-94). The rise of South Africanism as an imagination of a white nation unfolded concurrently with the rise of racism as a key variable in the development of the idea of South Africa. While the Afrikaners and the English were not united, they both had a common position regarding the exclusion of Africans from the nation except as sources of cheap labour. It is not true that there was 'a relative absence of virulent scientific racism in early twentieth-century South Africa' (Dubow 1987: 75). While racism was not forcefully articulated it was acted out by both the Afrikaners and the British since the time of colonial encounters and it was systematized into colonial policy from 1902.

As racism was entrenched into colonial policy, African people began to be given such homogenizing terms as 'natives' and 'Bantu' identities, thereby reconstructing of broad African identities. The British liberal incorporation of ideology, premised on the ultimate possibility of assimilating indigenous people whether white or black, worked briefly for those people who were part of the Cape Colony, namely, the Dutch, Coloureds and a few educated Africans. But the liberal thinking did not mean that the British did not view black people as constituting a vast pool of labour available for their exploitation (Marks and Trapido 1987: 5). The majority of early African educated elite benefitted from this short-lived liberal moment and they became the strongest supporters of Cape liberalism even after it was abandoned by its English formulators after 1902. What the black defenders of Cape liberalism did not realize was that it was shot through by an equally strong assumption of English supremacy, patronage and belief in the superiority of Western civilization.

After 1902, the liberal incorporativ ideology was abandoned and a new segregationist policy was constructed by Lord Milner. This is how Marks and

Trapido viewed and understood it and its rationale:

> The ideology of segregation did not only speak to the needs of the mining in-
> dustry. It addressed a number of different audiences. It served white farmers de-
> manding additional control over their tenants and labourers and white workers
> seeking protection from cheaper black labour. It was an attractive solution for
> the white ruling class in the face of the rapid urbanization of poor whites and
> poor blacks, with its increased possibilities of competition and conflict as well as
> miscegenation and a unified class struggle [...] That the segregationist solution
> emerged to solve the problems of industrialization was in a sense made possible
> ideologically through the development of the ideas of 'scientific racism,' social
> Darwinism and eugenics (Marks and Trapido 1987: 8).

This policy contributed to the making of broader African identities as excluded
people from the nation. Rhetoric of cultural differences, used to justify the
segregation of black people from white the people, was informed by commissioned
anthropological studies that fully operated as handmaidens of colonialism.
Afrikaners complained about the weaknesses of British segregationist policies as
having failed to prevent the danger of the white race being 'swamped' by blacks
and called for 'total segregation'. They also raised the dangers of 'black peril'
(miscegenation). Under total segregation Africans, now framed as natives, were
to be confined to the 'native reserves' as their 'homelands'. Under this policy
of total segregation even the 'Cape Native franchise' had to be abolished as
proposed under the Hertzog Bills of 1936. Norval noted that:

> The elaboration of a segregationist discourse on the Native question took place,
> *inter alia*, via a series of official inquiries. These inquiries, which forged new prac-
> tices of subjection, provide us with an important record of the construction of the
> Native problem. One of the most significant in this respect was the South African
> Native Affairs Commission (SANAC) (1903-5 [...] SANAC literally had to invent
> the category of 'the Native.' [...] This process of naming not only brought into
> being a new subjectivity, but also provided a highly contestable reconstruction of
> African history which redefined the nature of 'tribalism' (Norval 1996: 30-31).

The Native Economic Commission (NEC) of 1930-1932 framed 'Bantu
speaking people' as a proper noun for black people (Norval 1996: 31). The
important point here is that colonialists worked actively and deliberately to
create a political frontier between whites and blacks through discursive and
symbolic processes (a series of commissions of inquiry and a catalogue of
pieces of legislation) that produced native/Bantu identity as natural species
that deserved particular treatment and separate development, while justifying
their exclusion from the nation and citizenship rights.

Therefore African imaginations of a South African nation were born within the context of resisting imperial, colonial and apartheid imaginations that excluded Africans from the imagined nation. The first semi-political African political formation was the Native Educational Association (NEA) formed in 1882 as a vehicle to promote African interests in modern education, social morality and general welfare of the 'natives.' This was followed in September 1882 by the earliest political organization that captured African imagination of a nation known as *Imbumba Yaba Mnyama* formed in response to the growth of the Afrikaner Bond that was viewed as threat to African people's interests. *Imbumba's* key aim was to unite Africans to enable them fight for their 'national rights' (Odendaal 1984: 8). A construction of national African identity by Africans themselves was beginning. This construction of African identity had a clear political goal of fighting for national rights.

Odendaal's (1984) book *Vukani Bantu! The Beginnings of Black Protests Politics in South Africa to 1912* provides excellent details of the proto-African political formations that arose as a response to particular exclusionary manoeuvres of the colonial state from the 1880s up to 1912, the year of the formation of South African Native National Congress (SANNC) as a black national political movement. Odendaal's book also reveals how the print media played a central role in the formation of black political consciousness and imagination of a non-racial South Africa that accommodated them on an equal basis with whites. Independent newspapers with vernacular names such *as Ilanga lase Natal, Ipepa lo Hlanga, Isigidimi Sama Xhosa, Izwi Labantu, Inkanyiso lase Natal* and many others propagated African issues and opinions on key national policies that segregated them.

Beginning with the SANNC, the African political organizations simultaneously contested racial discrimination while working to create national unity among Africans. For instance, Pixley Ka Isaka Seme's speech at the formation of SANNC emphasized that the white people had formed the Union of South Africa that excluded black people and that this action called for an African counter-union 'for the purpose of creating national unity and defending our rights and privileges' (Odendaal 1984: 273).

The situation of racial exclusion, political effacement and denial of citizenship rights to Africans inevitably provoked different responses. The first strand is the liberal tradition rooted in nineteenth century Cape and Natal liberalism premised on the politics of inclusion of Africans into the body politic and white nation. Colonial and apartheid intransigence and violence proved this strategy to be futile in the 1960s. The second strand was a radical Africanist one that stressed a common African/black identity rooted in Ethiopianist and Garveyist ideas of 'Africa for Africans' (Hill and Pirio 1987: 209-253). It was represented by the PAC which imagined a black republic called Azania. The idea was deliverance of Africans from a white-dominated state instead of inclusion.

The founder president of the PAC Robert Sobukwe made it clear that the PAC did not claim Africa and South Africa for all people but for Africans and that their struggle was for complete overthrow of white domination (Ndlovu-Gatsheni 2009: 291; Ndlovu-Gatsheni 2008: 53-86). The third imagination of the nation is represented by the ANC. The ANC has always been an umbrella political formation that began as an advocate of a 'Native Union' that Pixley Isaka kaSeme called for in 1911. Seme was an advocate of African regeneration that looked towards activation and galvanization of the black race to take pride in themselves as a necessary condition for the birth of a proud African nation (Karis and Carter 1972).

In the 1940s, the ANC Youth League underwent a deep shift from mild liberalism to radical Africanism with Anton Lembede as the lead articulator. Lembede bluntly and openly asserted that 'Africa is a black man's country' (Lembede 1946: 317). But by 1955, the ANC still projected a liberal, non-racial imagination of multi-racial post-apartheid nation but without dropping the Garveyist slogan of 'I Afrika Mayi Buye' (Let Africa Be Restored To Us). The ANC claimed South Africa for all those who live in it as articulated in the Freedom Charter. The imagination of a South African nation as a multi-racial and democratic political formation was pragmatic for a society like South Africa whose history was dominated by complex historical interactions and coalescence of diverse people (Ndlovu-Gatsheni 2008; Chipkin 2007).

There were other imaginations of the nation that included Inkatha Freedom Party (IFP) that projected an ethno-cultural Zulu-focused nationalism that defended the idea of Zulu nation without necessarily ignoring broader nationalist politics. There is also the Black Consciousness Movement (BCM)'s imagination of a nation inhabited by thoroughly decolonized and proud Africans. Like the PAC, BCM also frequently used the name Azania as part of its rejection of white and colonial-constructed names. BCM's conception and definition of black people included Indians and Coloureds (Biko 1978: 103-106).

The African nationalist struggle crystallized around the idea of nation, the problem of race and that of class and ethnicity. The first issue was who was supposed to be the beneficiary of liberation in a context where the ANC defined belonging in terms of 'All' people living in South Africa. Radical

Africanist-oriented groups still insisted that black people were oppressed as a nation by whites; hence blacks were the subject of liberation from white oppression. Afro-Marxist groups increasingly defined the oppressed in class terms. The question of who were the oppressed people was not clearly defined by the Freedom Charter to the extent that at one time the people were invoked as 'national groups'; 'different races'; 'workers', and 'peasants' (Chipkin 2007: 72).

The South African Communist Party (SACP) became concerned about the identity of the revolutionary subject within the South African working class fraternity that was divided by race and professions. In 1962, the SACP coined two concepts of 'colonialism of a special type' to capture the complex situation of where the independent state of 1910 was created not as a victory over imperialism and colonialism but as a nominally independent nation created through compromise between imperialism and colonialism. Within this imperial-colonialist independent state, a white nation was given power to internally colonize, dominate and exploit black people (South African Communist Party 1962: 27). But the SACP, like the ANC, did not proceed to an outright definition of the black people as the subject of liberation but fell into the ANC trap of defining the oppressed as diverse classes and races.

It was also the SACP that came up with the concept of a National Democratic Revolution (NDR) where workers were identified as a revolutionary force. Within the NDR, 'workerism' and 'charterism' coexisted tendentiously mediated by tensions and blending between political interests of the people and those of workers. The NDR became an omnibus where the interests of all those opposed to apartheid across black, Coloured, Indian and white racial divisions as well as class cleavages were accommodated. The ANC became the bigger church leading this complex coalition of interests. The discourse of the NDR became more and more nationalist rather than revolutionary and worker-oriented. These developments within the liberation movements indicated how difficult it was to define in precise terms the subject of liberation and, by the same token, to pinpoint who was a South African beyond the rather elusive slogan that 'South Africa belongs to all who live in it, black and white.'

Wa Muiu (2008) examined the factors that influenced the Africans' conception of community, its specific characteristics, relations with other communities and how relations among groups within the community affected its development. She realized that African and Afrikaner imagined communities shared some similarities being separately influenced by religion and affected by class differences (wa Muiu 2008: 61). But the main difference was that the African imagined community was inclusive of all races unlike the exclusive community of white minority. This was so because, 'Apartheid represented a community that Africans wished to avoid at all costs' (Mueni wa Muiu 2008: 74). The ANC's multiracial debate developed as a reaction to apartheid and the PAC responded to apartheid by mobilizing its supporters as Africans -- a unitary identity that apartheid denigrated and preferred to see instead as different tribes with different political trajectories.

South Africa is a typical example where a movement of black people that started with a liberatory agenda was by the mid-1950s gravitating toward an emancipatory project having been hijacked by both white and black liberals. Even the socialism that was preached by the SACP was, to all intents and purposes, a form of 'Afro-liberal socialism'. The phase of negotiations involving liberation movements and the representatives of the apartheid state were an opportunity for both to further discipline and panel-beat the liberation movements away from radicalism into neoliberalism. The negotiation phase was a further moment to soften, if not corrupt, the ANC leadership to accept neo-apartheid and neocolonialism as liberation. Thus, in 1994, just like in 1910, South Africa gained democracy and the process of de-racialization of society began but without decolonization and liberation taking place.

This was made inevitable because the negotiations took place at a time of post-Cold War triumphalism of neoliberalism where any form of radicalism had to be beaten into supporting the global status quo that spoke the language of democracy and human rights. This argument is amplified by wa Muiu (2008: 149) who also concluded that the ANC got a neocolonial settlement that left it without control over South Africa's economy and security.

Conclusion

The emancipatory ideology of non-racialism triumphed over both radical Africanism proposing a black republic of Azania and white ultra-racism of apartheid. In 1994 a non-racial and democratic South Africa was born after a long and violent process that was characterized by incarceration and shooting of those who fought for a multi-racial and democratic post-apartheid nation. The metaphor of the rainbow was used to imagine an inclusive nation that was different from the apartheid nation that was underpinned by fragmenting of identities and selfish and instrumentalist notions of separate development of races. A pan-South African nationalism of a unique character ensued from 1994 onwards. This pan-South African nationalism promoted ideas of ethical and peaceful coexistence of people of diverse cultures and identities within a single nation. As articulated by Albie Sachs (1987), the current pan-South African nationalism existed in relation to apartheid which it sought to transcend.

This chapter has successfully deployed historical and genealogical analysis of the development, trials, tribulations and triumphs of the idea of South Africa and underscores how colonial modernity and its interaction with the African world created complex identities that Africans had to work hard to harmonize into stable nations. The race question was indeed a creation of Western and colonial modernity within the non-Western parts of the world. Such people as Afrikaners, English, Coloureds, Malayan, Indian, Chinese and other racial minorities were a creation of colonial modernity that threw then into foreign lands where they had to struggle to gain nativity through projection of particularistic and inflexible identities whose zenith was the apartheid system.

These groups had emerged at the tip of the African continent as a category of 'colonial-racial subjects of the empire' discussed in Chapter Five of this book. On the other hand, African ethnic identities were deliberately prevented from coalescing into nations by the policy of apartheid that further reinforced ethnic identities, which precolonial leaders like Moshoeshoe, Shaka, Mzilikazi and many others were constructing into broader identities like the Ndebele, Zulu and Suthu in the 1820s before the colonial moment ensued.

Over the years, African-oriented imaginations of nationhood had to develop as derivative and reactive phenomena that largely responded to questions of race and tribe which also directly impinged on politics of inclusion and exclusion. Since Africans experienced colonization, exploitation and domination as a racial group, their imagination of the nation emerged from the margins and the perspective of the subaltern, where they had to struggle to transcend racism and tribalism that was institutionalized by the colonial apartheid system which consistently created citizens and subjects as permanently divided political identities. Africans as a group that had experienced the harsh realities of racism and tribalism were careful during the struggles for decolonization to try and avoid the trap of reverse racism as a counter liberatory discourse. Africans carried the burden of fighting to build a new nation that was not permeated by racism and tribalism.

In short, the case study of South Africa indicated the difficulties of constructing stable national identity out of people of different racial and ethnic identities. It demonstrated the limits of the use of coercion to construct a national identity and the futility of trying to maintain a particular race as the authentic centre of the nation within a plural and multicultural society. For such societies to succeed required pragmatism founded on the principles of de-coloniality, tolerance and recognition of difference. But today, South Africa is still struggling to transcend the racial categories and identities constructed by apartheid. The post-apartheid government is seen as using race categories for affirmative action and such policies as Black Economic Empowerment (BEE) that continue to be contested as taking the form of reverse black racism within a democratic state. The ubiquity of race in post-apartheid South Africa is well captured by Pierre de Vos:

> In contemporary South Africa, the issue of race continues to permeate every aspect of public life. Citizens are regularly required to indicate their race when filling out government or other official forms; race often plays a role in decision on whether a job application or the application for admission to certain university programmes are successful; in political debates the race of various protagonists are often noted when evaluating the merits of their contributions; and when judges are appointed to positions on the High Court, Supreme Court of Appeal or Constitutional Court, the race of the appointees are duly noted or commented upon and taken into account when considering the suitability of the candidate for appointment to the bench. [...] We cannot escape our own race. Even when we claim that we have escaped the perceived shackles of race, we are merely confirming its presence by our stated yearning for its absence. This is the paradox: while South Africa has emerged from a period in its history in which the race of every individual played a decisive role in determining their life chances, allocating social status and economic benefits on the basis of race in terms of a rigid hierarchical system according to which very person was classified by the apartheid state as either white, Indian, coloured or black and allocated a social status and economic and political benefits in accordance with this race, in the post-apartheid era the potency of race as a factor in allocation of social status and economic benefit has not fundamentally been diminished in our daily lives—despite a professed commitment to non-racialism contained in the South African Constitution, the founding document of our democracy (de Vos 2010:2).

Erasmus (2010) described this ubiquity of race as the crisis of 'thinking with our eyes'. Ballim (2010:1) described race as a 'phantom tyrant whose language we have learnt and whose rule we quietly obey.' This ubiquity of race, seventeen years after the official end of apartheid, indicates the complexity of the social complexion of South Africa that cannot be easily solved by professed commitments to non-racialism. It also reveals the continued contestations over who is the authentic subject of the nation. The non-racial ideology as a public transcript is continuously threatened by the hidden script of 'Africanity' and

'Afrikanerity' and other particularistic identities that have a life of their own within the rainbow nation.

These particularistic identities are the ones that cause Afrikaners to sometimes raise old flags of the Boer republics during rugby matches as well as the apartheid ones during the funeral of such Afrikaner figures as Terre Blanche in 2010. It is also the search for Africanity as the centre of the South African nation that led the firebrand ANC Youth League President Julius Malema to continue singing the liberation song 'dubul' ibhunu' (shoot the Boer) seventeen years after the official end of apartheid. It was the same spirit that underpinned the formation and launch of the Native Club in 2006 as a forum for black intellectuals with a task to lead the public discourse on re-building South Africa as a black nation. The theme of the inaugural conference of the Native Club was a deeply revealing: Where are the natives? The question of nativity/indigeneity remains unsettled and highly contested in this multi-racial, multi-class, multi-cultural and multi-ethnic nation in the making.

7

Zimbabwe and the Crisis of *Chimurenga* Nationalism

A country that has become a pariah state needs to be talked about so that its situation is understood objectively and dispassionately.

Yash Tandon (2008: 47)

It is hard to think of a figure more reviled in the West than Robert Mugabe. Liberal and conservative commentators portray him as a brutal dictator, and blame him for Zimbabwe's descent into hyperinflation and poverty. The seizure of white-owned farms by his black supporters has been depicted as a form of thuggery, and as a cause of the country's declining production, as if these lands were doomed by black ownership. Sanctions have been imposed, and opposition funded with the explicit aim to unseating him.

Mahmood Mamdani (2008: 17)

Introduction

The term *Chimurenga* occupies a central place in the nationalist-oriented constructions of the Zimbabwe nation-state that came into being in 1980. It began to be widely used in the 1970s by the nationalists mainly in the Zimbabwe African National Union (ZANU) and its fighting wing known as the Zimbabwe African National Liberation Army (ZANLA) as a vernacular name for the armed liberation struggle against the settler colonial state. It is also used today by ZANU as an ideological thread capturing the undying spirit of African resistance to colonialism, running from primary resistance of the 1890s to the present attempts by the Harare nationalists to take the liberation and decolonization project to its logical conclusion of achieving economic empowerment of the black people through land redistribution and other initiatives aimed at indigenizing the economy. Of course, what has been hailed by ZANU-PF as the Third Chimurenga' has raised many debates, with some seeing it as controversy-ridden and African elite-dominated primitive accumulation drive under the cover of black economic empowerment, and others celebrating it as a genuine economic redistributive process that has seen land ownership imbalances and unequal access originating from settler colonialism being resolved (David Moore 2004; Raftopoulos and Phimister 2004; Moyo and Yeros 2007a, 2007b).

The current debates over the character of the Zimbabwe state, its ideological orientation and intentions makes the case study of Zimbabwe ideal to be interrogated in this book. Thus before one provides a detailed interrogation of the idea of Zimbabwe and the concomitant politics that has developed around it, including issues of identity, nation-building, violence and party politics, there is need to analyse the main contours of the intellectual debates that have been sparked off by the land reform programme and the crisis that has befallen the state since 2000. At one level, Zimbabwe provides a window into the operations of a schizophrenic neocolonial state whose politics exhibited a complex mixture of redemptive, grotesque and virulent nationalism mediated by a consistent anti-imperial and anti-colonialist rhetoric (Ndlovu-Gatsheni and Muzondidya 2011). At another level, it reveals the machinations of colonial matrix of power, the costs to be incurred by a small peripheral state if it tried to chart an autonomous path of development and defy commandments from the West, as well as the controversies that arise as an African state tries to resolve its intractable national question.

Is Zimbabwe a victim of new imperialism?

The case study of Zimbabwe manifests all the problems identified in the previous chapters related to the predicament of postcolonial states as they try to resolve the national question within a world governed by the invisible colonial matrix of power sustaining the racialized, hegemonic, patriarchal, capitalist and violent global order. While the Zimbabwean leadership has committed many blunders as it tried to survive in a world that does not accommodate African states that try to defy the neoliberal commandments, the experiences of Zimbabwe since 2000 indicates beyond doubt the ability of the Western nations' commitment to discipline and work towards dethroning those leaders that are considered to be deviating from the post-Cold War global normative framework of maintaining the status quo of neoliberalism and the Washington Consensus. As noted by Sam Moyo and Yeros (2007, 2009) hell was let loose on Zimbabwe the very time the government conceded to popular pressure from below and engaged in radical resolution of the national and agrarian questions that had been spoiled by settler colonialism.

Two broad, dominant and discernible schools of thought on the Zimbabwe question a reveal two ponts of enunciation of the Zimbabwe problem. The first one is the liberal reformist perspective informed by ideas of democracy, human rights and notions of civil society and concerned about the rising tempo of authoritarianism, militarism and violence that engulfed Zimbabwe at the beginning of 2000. This camp encompassed what is termed internationalist leftists and liberals. Within this camp the Zimbabwe question was framed as constituted by exhausted patriarchal, authoritarian and populist nationalism that had failed to undergo internal democratization in line with the post-Cold War global normative trends (Campbell 2003, Bond and Manyanya 2003, Ranger 2003, Raftopoulos 2006). The crisis deepened as the nationalist leadership found itself besieged by an array of 'unfinished business' (Hammar and Raftopoulos 2003). To this camp the land reform programme was nothing but a political gimmick that was seized by a desperate and bankrupt regime as a survival populist strategy that eventually destroyed a once vibrant agricultural sector which was a strong pillar of the national economy.

What is persuasive about the arguments of this camp is its moral outrage about a former liberation movement that has turned into a violent leviathan and is feasting on the citizens. Secondly, this camp is very alert to issues of cronyism and corruption that have accompanied the fast-track land reform programme. The camp squarely blames ZANU-PF and its leader Robert Mugabe for the Zimbabwean crisis as they mismanaged the economy and lacked good governance skills to keep the economy alive. But the camp is generally not very clear on the role of external factors, including sanctions, in contributing to the economic and political collapse of Zimbabwe into crisis. They say very little about ZANU-PF's efforts at restructuring a colonial state to serve African interests and even its commitment to redemptive nationalism informed by redistributive justice.

Facing this camp is another broad grouping of scholars comprising of nationalist left, regime intellectuals, outright nativists and populists, and even militarists with securocratic mentalities. The main contribution of the amorphous camps is that they have not missed any opportunity to point out the havoc being wrecked by the colonial matrix of power on Zimbabwe. The most sophisticated and scholarly articulation of the Zimbabwe question from a critical African and Global South perspective in represented by the classic work of Moyo andParis Yeros (2005, 2007, 2009) and Moyo (2011). What is refreshing about their arguments is that they take the issue of new imperialism very seriously and they also investigate two historical questions systematically (national and agrarian) as the core state businesses that needed to be resolved under whatever circumstances.

What Moyo and Yeros privilege in their analysis is not the state and ZANU-PF; instead, they investigate what they term a crisis of semi-proletarianism which enabled them to approach the national question 'from below' where the 'land occupation movement' originated (Moyo 2001, Yeros 2002). They also highlight that the state had to respond to agitation for land 'from below' and the ruling party risked losing rural and urban support simultaneously if it did not act positively on the land issue. Even more relevant for this book on the coloniality of power and the question of myths of decolonization and illusions of freedom is the continued engagement of Moyo and Yeros' with the question of imperialism as the broader discursive terrain within which the Zimbabwe question can be understood. There is no doubt that since the time of the liberation struggle, the future political trajectory of Zimbabwe mattered to imperial powers; hence their active participation at the Lancaster House Conference to soften the radical nationalists to accept a neocolonial arrangement in lieu of decolonization. Today the popularity of the opposition Movement for Democratic Change (MDC) across Europe and America indicates the continuing interests of imperial centres on Zimbabwe. The funding of ideologically-compliant political formations is a long-standing part of the global colonial matrix of power.

In a way, by 1997, Zimbabwe under ZANU-PF, broke ranks with the common African political habit of allying with external forces against the mounting demands of the local people. With the support of war veterans, the state began the difficult task of shedding off its neocolonial character which culminated in the radical land reform programme that provoked the anger of the West, leading to in sanctions being imposed on Zimbabwe. This alternative narrative of the Zimbabwean question, however, must not be taken to mean endorsement of ZANU-PF's authoritarianism, militarization of state institutions and politics, and violence. The message is that the Zimbabwean question is complex and cannot be explained from a one-dimensional approach. The complexity is compounded by the fact that there are numerous horizontal, vertical and lateral struggles emanating from the semi-proletarianized sector, the urban sector, ZANU-PF, the state, opposition and civil society about different as well as common issues. There is no clear monolithic ideological thrust open for a singular reading of the Zimbabwe question. Added to this is the question of complex identities which transcend race but spill over to generational questions as well.

At the same time, the recent work of Sam Moyo (2011) and Ian Scoones (2010), based on empirical research inside Zimbabwe has confirmed Mamdani's 2008 thesis that the fast-track land reform programme did not only result in crony capitalist primitive accumulation by the elite, but achieved a radical distribution of land to the landless people of Zimbabwe. This emerging body of research is an indictment of the earlier literature that emphasized chaos, violence and corruption as the hallmarks of the fast-track land reform programme. Such research also calls for re-evaluation of the intentions of ZANU-PF and its commitment to furthering the agenda of redistributive justice.

This chapter, therefore, provides a historical view of the development of the Zimbabwe question starting from the 1960s when the idea of a Zimbabwe nation-state liberated from colonial rule developed. The chapter begins with engagement with the ideology of *Chimurenga* as the political thread that runs through from the 1960s to the present, albeit being contested from inside and outside particularly about its emancipatory and liberatory potentials and commitments in a world where issues of democracy, human rights, human security and social peace have assumed a normative form. From here I delve into questions of both the nation and the state which are equally complex and open to intractable intellectual and academic interpretations.

The ideology of *Chimurenga*

Chimurenga's linguistic coinage is from the Shona language spoken by the majority of present-day Zimbabweans. Its historical roots are traceable to the 1896-1897 Ndebele-Shona uprisings, deriving from Murenga, a name of a spirit medium who was actively involved in the 1896-1897 war of resistance, providing the desperately needed ideological support to the African fighting forces. Murenga is said to have administered some traditional war medicine on the African fighting forces that would make them invulnerable and immune to white forces' bullets (Ranger 1967: 217-220).

In current nationalist discourse of the Zimbabwe African National Union-Patriotic Front (ZANU-PF), Zimbabwe is a product of *Chimurenga*. It was born as a result of two violent *Zvimurenga* (Shona plural for *Chimurenga*) of 1890s and 1970s. But Zimbabwe had to experience a Third *Chimurenga* at the beginning of 2000 that was dubbed *Impi YamaSimu* in Ndebele language and Hondo *Yeminda* in Shona language (meaning the war for land reclamation) (Mugabe 2001). In the dominant nationalist discourses of the nation, Zimbabwean history is nothing other than a catalogue of *Chimurengas* spearheaded by patriotic forces in search of independence and in defence of national sovereignty. This rendition of national history in terms of a series of 'nationalist revolutions', has been termed 'patriotic history' by some scholars (Ranger 2004; Tendi 2010).

By the 1970s, the concept of *Chimurenga* had found a dignified niche within African nationalist revolutionary politics as an anti-imperial and anti-colonial ideology. But worrisome are some of its recent uses within Zimbabwe to justify any form of nationalist violence even against citizens of the postcolonial state. In line with Chimurenga-oriented ideas of the nation, Zimbabwe is celebrated as a product of violent nationalist revolutions that has to be defended through the spilling of more of the blood of those considered to be opposed to ZANU-PF, which is taken as a symbol of Zimbabwe. The perpetrators of this crime use the Chimurenga language to justify the killing and torture of opposition political members and groups as well as other citizens who do not belong to ZANU-PF.

The ideologies of *Chimurenga* also incorporate a violent conception of political practice in which the periodic elections are taken as a war situation in which they must defeat their enemies. Thus, every time ZANU-PF has been cornered politically by the opposition forces, it has tendentiously reminded people that 'Zimbabwe *ndeyeropa*' (Zimbabwe came after a violent war of liberation) and that it would go back to the bush to fight another Chimurenga if defeated in an election.

The threats of fighting another *Chimurenga* were often issued to scare the people who still have fresh memories of the 15 year liberation war where they were caught in between violent Rhodesian forces and equally violent ZANLA and ZIPRA forces. In celebrating *Chimurenga* as a precursor of the nation of Zimbabwe, even the head of state, President Robert Mugabe, often brags about having degrees in violence and he punches the air at political rallies to emphasize the agenda of violence as a solution to the political question in Zimbabwe (Blair 2002; Chan 2003; Meredith 2002; Ndlovu-Gatsheni 2009).

The ideologies of *Chimurenga* were also being mobilized to fragment the people of Zimbabwe into patriots, war veterans, puppets, traitors, sellouts, born-frees and enemies of the nation. These political identities have resulted in a deep polarization of the nation. The space of patriots and veterans is reserved for those who participated in the liberation struggle (*the Second*

Chimurenga) in general and all members of ZANU-PF specifically. Members of the opposition Movement for Democratic Change (MDC) are categorized as traitors, sell outs and puppets that deserve to die if the Zimbabwean nation is to live. Instructively, White commercial farmers constitute the enemies of the nation (Ndlovu-Gatsheni 2008; Ndlovu-Gatsheni 2011). Such bifurcation of the nation forms a fertile ground for conflictual politics and violence that has sapped the strength of the nation and plunged it into a pariah stat.

At another level, the ideas of *Chimurenga* are also associated with onprogressive economic policies and partisan politics. For instance, the controversial fast-track land reform programme and the equally controversial economic indigenization legislation being pushed through by the Ministry of Youth and Empowerment were justified as part of the *Third Chimurenga* (Mugabe 2001). This once respected revolutionary ideology of liberation is now associated with political gimmicks and regime survival techniques of ZANU-PF. While some scholars like Mamdani (2008), Yeros (2002), Moyo and Paris (2007a; 2007b; 2009), and others, believe that the fast-track land reform was a revolution interrupted by forces of neocolonialism, there is an equally strong body of thought that views it as chaotic, partisan, ill-thought-out, ill-timed and, above all, part of selfish party-crony primitive accumulation that left the economy in tatters (Phimister and Raftopoulos 2004; Raftopoulos 2006).

Zimbabwe also projects complex politics of trying to sort out the intractable issues of incomplete decolonization and unresolved questions of social and economic justice within a constrained environment of a postcolonial neo-colonized world ensnared by global colonial matrices of power. It also demonstrates how liberatory rhetoric is used to justify the elite/native bourgeoisie's primitive capitalist accumulation as well as how the Western powers are able to discipline those African leaders considered to be deviating from the neoliberal template of economic and political policies.

Framing the debates and discourses on the nation

Zimbabwe is haunted by a repertoire of violence that has dominated pre-colonial, colonial and postcolonial epochs. This violence encompasses pre-colonial raids and conquests and imperial/colonial wars of domination of 1893-1894 and 1896-1897. The spectre of violence has continued into postcolonial Zimbabwe where it has been carried out under different code-names such as *Gukurahundi* (rains that wash away chaff) of the 1980s right into *Operation Murambatsvina* (clean-up of urban filth), post-29 March 2008 *Operation Mavhoterapapi* (who did you vote for), Operation *Chimumu* (silent night kidnappings) and the most recent *Operation Budiranai Pachena* (Let's tell each other the truth). David Coltart, a Zimbabwean lawyer and politician had this to say about violence in general:

> Zimbabwe is afflicted with a disease akin to alcoholism, namely endemic violence. For over 150 years, leaders of this beautiful country, bounded by the Zambezi and Limpopo Rivers, have used violence to achieve their political objectives. Violence was used by Lobengula to suppress the Shona. Violence was used to colonise and the threat of violence was used to maintain white minority rule. Violence was used to overthrow the white minority. And since independence, violence has been used to crush legitimate political opposition. The use of violence has been compounded by another phenomenon—namely a culture of impunity. Those responsible for use of violence have never been brought to book. Not only is there a long history of violence used successfully to achieve political objectives but also those who have committed horrendous crimes have prospered through their actions. As a result, the use of violence is now deeply embedded in our national psyche. Political violence is accepted as the norm. [But] political violence is not the norm in democratic societies. It may be the norm in tyrannical states. It may have been used in the formative stages of democracies. But it is now anathema in democracies. There is also no doubt that the use of violence inhibits economic development and creates a whole barrage of social problems, including domestic violence. The sustained and long-term use of violence in Zimbabwe lies at the very core of many of the problems our nation faces today. We are indeed afflicted by a very serious disease and need help (Coltart 2007: 48-54).

This violence is lodged deeply in the national psyche and it is the chief instrument of statecraft. The people who make up the citizenry of Zimbabwe have been invited into the nation on an invitation card written in blood. And instead of the leaders to seek the means of exorcizing this 'blood stained national invitation card' they celebrate blood-spilling in songs and speeches.

A number of academics have tried to explain both the spectre of violence and the other crises that bedevil Zimbabwe from different angles (see, for instance, (Raftopoulos and Mlambo 2009). Also Political scientists and activists from the civil society have focused their research on the murky present with a view to predicting the mysterious future (Masunungure 2009). In his comment on the present situation in Zimbabwe, Brian Raftopoulos said:

> Unfortunately, I think there are many activists in civil society whose sense of the past is compressed into the developments that have taken place in the last decade, namely the period that has been characterised as the 'Zimbabwean Crisis.' At one level this is understandable for activists who are faced with the enormous immediate challenges of an authoritarian state, and the debilitating effects of an economy that has been de-

constructed on a daily basis. The result however is that the activists often get trapped in the present, so to speak, where the need and opportunities to understand the past, do not seem immediately relevant. Moreover, when the discourse in which the problems of the crisis is constructed is limited to the areas of human rights and governance, important as these are, the longer term complexities of different historical legacies get occluded from the questions that are asked and the types of politics that are engaged in. [...] Additionally, this takes place in the face of a state whose political messaging is embedded in a broader, even if distorted, sense of the past (Kwabato 2009).

The tendency to use the present to explain the present even degenerated further into explaining processes and events through blaming certain political actors. This was most visible in international media where President Mugabe was framed as that individual who single-handedly brought about the liberation of Zimbabwe from colonialism only to preside over its destruction in the 2000s.

Even phenomena like race and ethnicity that need to be explained in their own right were deployed wrongly as causes of conflict and crisis. How can that which needs to be explained and which is part of the crisis serve as the language of intellectual analysis? Race and ethnicity are, indeed, imbricated and inextricably intertwined with politics, and what is needed is to explain why the situation is like that and what it is that is expressed through race and ethnicity. How did race and ethnicity emerge as markers of difference, and under what conditions, through whom, and to what end? A focus on race and ethnicity as the thing itself that causes crises and conflict tends to hide rather than reveal the underlying drivers of politics, causes of human action, and shapers of human relations.

Zimbabwe, like most postcolonial and post-apartheid societies suffers seriously from consequences of incomplete decolonization, incomplete nation-building and contested state-making. This politics is inextricably intertwined with the complex discourses of belonging, citizenship, resource ownership, meaning of freedom and sovereignty. Since 2000, these issues have become even more complex as they became imbricated in equally complex regime security and regime change politics, pitting ZANU-PF against MDC political formations.

Consequently, the politics of transition that the signing of the Global Political Agreement (GPA) inaugurated in September 2008 and the installation of the inclusive government in February 2009 has remained locked within the complex contestations over political power, strategic resources, state control, belonging and citizenship as well as mode of governance. Power politics were further articulated in the languages and idioms of partisanship, regionalism, race, ethnicity, class and nativity.

The Zimbabwean crisis is profoundly historical as well as political. It is linked to the legacies of colonialism as well as with the question of the making of Zimbabwe as a nationalist construction of the 1960s. What has come to be termed the 'Zimbabwean crisis' together with issues of ethnicity and race, are actually manifestations of the deep-seated challenges of nation-building within a state suffering from incomplete decolonization. This incompleteness of the nation, state and decolonization was described by Amanda Hammar, Brian Raftopoulos and Stig Jensen (2003) as 'Zimbabwe's unfinished business'. Raftopoulos further raised some of the key issues that are often ignored in scholarly interrogations of Zimbabwe's problems:

> The point is that [creating national identity] is a process of continuing contestation and struggles, with the dynamics of such struggles often led by, but not confined to, the dominant sections of particular societies. It is important that visions of national belonging continue to be open to debate and discussion, and that no party or group of people claim the sole right to set the parameters of such an ongoing process. For countries like Zimbabwe the experiences of colonial rule and imperial domination have been key vectors in determining the terms of debate around national identity. Moreover, the effectiveness with which Mugabe has deployed the anti-imperialist message demonstrates the continuing resonance of this trope in the historical imaginations and lived experiences of Africans. The continued inequalities in the relations between the West and Africa are a stubborn reminder of the conditions which generate such oppositions. What is important in this context is to fight the tendency of nationalist parties to monopolize the constructions of this past and to wield it to maintain an authoritarian hold on power (Kwabato 2009).

It is within this broader context that this chapter seeks to revisit the history of the imaginations and the making of the Zimbabwe nation-state project as the terrain within which one can find the roots of the present politics of race and ethnicity that continue to haunt the country in the twenty-first century. These questions of belonging, citizenship, modes of governance, power and ownership of resources have become sharpened in a country experiencing economic and political crisis and where politicians have resorted to the politics of denial, witch-hunting and formalizing crises as a culture. This is a point raised by Alois Mlambo, Maurice Vambe and Abebe Zegeye:

> The disquieting aspect is that there is now in Zimbabwe a culture of crisis; leaders taking crisis as normal, thriving from it, and holding the lives of the people to ransom. When the crisis has been formalized as a culture within state institutions, it distorts attempts at resolving tensions and conflicts that lead to crisis in the culture (Mlambo et al 2010: 89-91).

Zimbabwe is 'fractured along historical, spatial, political, racial, ethnic and personal lines' (Mlambo et al 2010: 89). It has continuously been haunted by the complex question of how to transform its various ethnicities into one nation and the former 'natives' and 'settlers' into a common citizenship mediated by equality and loyalty to the postcolonial state on the one hand, and how to mobilize different ethnicities into stable common nationhood on the other. The official policy of reconciliation of races and the rhetoric of unity of ethnicities of the 1980s have proven to be minimalist, inadequate and even problematic within societies characterized by unresolved colonially-induced economic inequalities and resilient ethnic tensions informed by a combination of precolonial, colonial and postcolonial experiences.

Zimbabwe has no strong primordial roots except that of naming derived from the prehistoric site of Great Zimbabwe located in Masvingo province. Some of those who read too much into this ritual of naming of postcolonial states and search for a foundation myth for Zimbabwe have tried to interpret Zimbabwe as a successor state--to the precolonial Munhumutapa state (Mudenge 1988). This raises the question of how some foundation myths do become sources of conflict, exclusion and alienation rather than facilite national cohesion and guarantee less problematic flow from the pre-colonial past into the present (Barthes 1972).

In a situation where the precolonial terrain was dotted with diverse socio-political formations ranging from independent chieftaincies, separate clans, kingdoms, states, and unstable confederacies, it becomes very difficult to find an acceptable myth of foundation for the postcolonial nation. For instance, picking the precolonial Munhumutapa state as the foundation of postcolonial Zimbabwe becomes problematic because this state was associated with only one ethnic group—the Karanga. Zimbabwe is a multi-ethnic society encompassing Karanga, Zezuru, Manyika, Shangani, Sotho, Tswana, Hlengwe, Tonga, Nambya, Venda, Nguni, Kololo, and other smaller groups. If Zimbabwe can be interpreted as a successor state, then it succeeded numerous and disparate precolonial social and political formations rather than one, including the colonially crafted Rhodesian state.

Further questions arise as to how adequate the liberation struggle is as the foundation myth of Zimbabwe if precolonial history cannot provide a credible and acceptable one. Does Zimbabwe need a single foundation myth? What about using various myths informed by various histories? Worse still, can the empty signifiers such as 'democracy' and 'human rights' offer Zimbabwe new myths of foundation not associated with race and ethnicity? There are no quick and ready answers to these historical and political questions, although this chapter tries to provide some of the useful pointers.

The other erroneous tendency has been to conflate diverse identities into Ndebele and Shona groups and, in the process, undermine the country's social pluralism. On top of this layer are racial groups of Coloureds, Indians, and Whites. The key political challenge is how to build a stable nation and forge common citizenship out of these diverse identities. The nationalism that emerged in the 1960s, together with the armed struggle of the 1970s, did not culminate in the emergence of a stable nation and state founded on an overall social, political, economic, psychological and ideological metamorphosis, whereby ex-colonizers and the former colonized were re-born as equal members of a single political community called Zimbabwe mediated by mutual consent. This is the bane of the Zimbabwe national project.

Social and political conflicts in Zimbabwe are partly rooted in and generated by a problematic formulation and articulation of national history and reluctance by professional historians to refute outright some 'erroneous' and 'false' views of history that have percolated into popular imagination. There are a number of popular but sometimes inaccurate accurate and incorrect accounts of national history that have been allowed to percolate into the minds of the people and in the process spoil human relations. These range from the popular view of Zimbabwe as characterized by a bimodal ethnicity of the Ndebele and Shona people who are naturally antagonistic because of ancient hatreds and historical grievances. To me, the correct characterization of Zimbabwe would be that of complex and plural society inhabited by various people, including racial minorities, all of whom speak over eighteen different languages. Contemporary ethnic tensions are often fuelled by recent histories rather than remote pasts.

The second fallacious and dangerous but popular view is that of conflating the Fifth Brigade (*Gukurahundi*) that committed atrocities in Matabeleland and the Midlands region in the 1980s, with the Shona people as a collectivity. The Fifth Brigade was a 'political army' fighting a 'political' if not purely partisan cause that was justified in ethnic terms (Nkomo 1984). A related erroneous view that is equally dangerous but popular is that Matabeleland and the Midlands region harboured politically motivated, structured and organized 'dissidents' fighting on behalf of the Ndebele people as a collectivity opposed to the Zimbabwe state in the 1980s.

If there were any 'dissidents,' they existed as a bizarre mixture and assortment of ordinary armed criminals, isolated bandits, terrified ex-ZIPRA escaping witch-hunts within the Zimbabwe National Army, a few ideologically persuaded elements not happy about the Lancaster House Agreement, mentally-deranged elements who missed the news of the ceasefire, pseudo and manufactured elements used by ZANU-PF to justify liquidation of PF-ZAPU, and Apartheid-sponsored Super-ZAPU elements (Ndlovu-Gatsheni 2009).

All these political issues were mainly logical residues of an armed liberation war rather than representatives of the aspirations of the people of Matabeleland and the Midlands region. It has recently come to light that what was considered as 'arms caches' discovered in PF-ZAPU properties around the cities of Bulawayo and Gweru, that contributed to the breakdown of the Government of National Unity concocted in 1980 were a farce and a mere *political pretext* to crush PF-ZAPU as an opposition movement. Frederick Charles Mutanda (war-name Chillis), a former senior ZIPRA officer in a foreword to the recent edition of Joshua Nkomo's autobiography *Nkomo: The Story of My Life*, wrote that 'Allegations that Dr Nkomo and PF ZAPU after losing elections were conspiring to overthrow the government in 1982, were false and mischievous statements.' Mutanda elaborated further on the issue:

> Elections results were announced on the 4th of March 1980 and the setting up of the Joint High Command started on the 6th of March under the command of Lieutenant-General Walls who had been appointed by Prime Minister Robert Mugabe. The Joint High Command appointed liaison officers to prepare for the integration of the three armed forces. Amongst the issues which were thrashed out at the beginning was the question of bringing all ZANLA and ZIPRA arms and equipment from Zambia and Mozambique. I was one of those who remained in Zambia and involved in preparing part of the ZIPRA list and movement of these ordnances. Before 18th April 1980 ZIPRA had presented its schedules of ordnances and as agreed, the Rhodesians gave our commanders their list. The ZIPRA list included battle tanks, Armoured Personnel Carriers, artillery and other fighting equipment. ZANLA did not present a single thing. The ZIPRA ordnance and armament matching the schedule eventually came into the country via Victoria Falls. No decision or instruction was made as to how and where the ZIPRA ordnance was to be stored. The administration of integrating the three armies, weapons and ordnances, including Assembly Points was the responsibility of the Joint High Command, thus removing political parties over military affairs. Arms which were then discovered at Ascot and Hampton Farms were not caches at all but had been procedurally declared and submitted to the Joint High Command (Mutanda 2010).

These revelations by those who actively participated in the struggle and in the transitional politics of 1980s were signs that, as historians, we need to rethink some of the issues taken as truth in Zimbabwe. What has escaped scholarly analysis is that these historically false views circulate as truth in popular imagination and are open to manipulation by politicians as well as deployment by ordinary people for favours and discrimination. Ranger (2004) described these deeply partisan histories as 'patriotic history'.

The real danger for nation-building is that false views have power to incite violence, confirming Mbembe's (2002: 239-273) notion of 'the power of the false'. Zimbabweans must be careful of 'the power of the false'. Powerful but false narratives of the historical development of Zimbabwe, from a colony to a sovereign state, from transitional state to crisis, permeate not only issues of power but also perceptions and conceptions of the social identity of the country. Those who raise these issues of identity have done so from a very emotional angle raising fears that open discussion of identity-related conflict is too risky for the nation. Even celebrated books like Becoming Zimbabwe that tracked the idea of national belonging and citizenship had no specific chapters on identity, as though this issue was not at the centre of creating a coherent nation (Raftopoulos and Mlambo 2009).

Tash Tandon correctly identified the general challenges that were confronted by postcolonial African states soon after attaining political independence:

> After independence, however, matters became complicated. People who fought and won independence, involving huge sacrifices...began to ask their political leaders and intellectuals some critical questions: Where do we go from here? What now? What do we do with this hard won independence? There also came to the surface even more difficult questions about self-identity that had been subdued during the struggle for independence: Who are we as a 'nation'? How do we forge nationhood out of disparate ethnic, racial, religious, linguistic, regional and sub-regional groupings? (Tandon 2005: 67)

For Zimbabwe, the veteran nationalist Joshua Nkomo lamented how immediately after attaining independence, Zimbabweans found themselves hostage to a violent African regime. This is how he put it:

> Today Zimbabwe is defenseless because the people live in fear, not of our enemies, but of their own government. What has happened to the brave and determined, confident and fearless people of Zimbabwe and their soldiers of liberation, who showed the world that no power on earth could prevent us from achieving our freedom? [...] Today our enemies laugh at us. What they see are a divided, confused, and frightened people, led by a divided, confused and frightened government. Government which has the love, respect and confidence of the people does not have to use the laws and weapons of colonial regimes to protect itself. The people themselves will protect their government if they have full trust

in it. Fear is a weapon of despair, used by those who fear the people. This is the time and opportunity to rebuild trust, find the solution to our problems and defend the country as a united people (Nkomo 1984: 5).

Zimbabwean nationalism was born with a very bad birthmark. The split of 1963 that gave birth to ZANU as a splinter movement from ZAPU was a concretization of the poor social basis of Zimbabwean nationalism that unfolded throughout the age of liberation as a site of ethnic and regional-inspired struggles that cost the lives of cadres like Herbert Chitepo and others. Poor nationalism gave birth to a predatory nationalist revolution that ate its own children and eventually led to a violent and intolerant postcolonial state that has consistently devoured its own citizens with utmost disdain (Ndlovu-Gatsheni 2009).

Some radical Zimbabwean scholars, particularly those informed by political economy such as Ibbo Mandaza (1986), noted that the liberation struggle enabled a problematic transition whose content and direction remained undefined beyond the rhetoric of socialism and reconciliation. Being independent was increasingly reduced to the assumption of state power by a black bourgeoisie that had spearheaded the liberation war. Until the late 1990s, the postcolonial state maintained a delicate balance of preserving and protecting white settler interests and serving the demands of the majority of African people, typical of all neocolonial entities.

In the words of Mandaza, the state assumed a 'schizophrenic' character whereby its pursuit of socio-economic transformation, developmental objectives and fulfilment of popular aspirations was happening concurrently with violent suppression of popular demands and longings (Mandaza 1986). Thus, once political independence was achieved; there was no systematic commitment to nation-building. Political elites spent energy on state consolidation that was itself a form of personal power consolidation by the triumphant leadership of ZANU-PF. Violence became the main method of hailing the people into the nation, beginning with the military conquest of Matabeleland and the Midlands regions that were considered to be wavering and not fully behind the Zimbabwe that was created in 1980 (Ndlovu-Gatsheni 2003: 17-38).

The policy of reconciliation aimed at hailing the white minority and the rhetoric of unity aimed at beckoning ethnicities into the nation did not succeed in creating a stable nation-state. Any nation-state project refers to that protean process of making the state-as-people (state-making) and the making of nation-as-people (nation-building). Ideally, therefore, a stable and durable political community is one whose citizens are actively engaged in deciding their common future together. Bound together by ties of national solidarity, they discover and implement principles of justice that all can share, and in doing so they respect the separate identities of minority groups within the community (Miller 2000). This has proved to be hard to achieve in a country that emerged from settler colonialism and that is inhabited by both former disfranchised 'natives' and ex-privileged settlers, separated not only by race but also by glaring material endowments.

Billig (1995) argued that the creation of the 'nation-as-people' has never been a harmonious process in which, for example, a traditional 'ethnie' grows from 'small shoot into the full flower of nationality, as if following a process of "natural" maturation.' The process typically is attended by conflict and violence. 'A particular form of identity has to be imposed. One way of thinking of the self, of community and, indeed of the world, has to replace other conceptions, other forms of life' (Billig 1995: 27). This process is even more complicated in ex-colonies where imperialism and colonialism added the politics of race on top of the equally complex layers of the 'tribe', ethnicity, religion and regionalism and other power struggles emanating from pre-colonial, colonial and postcolonial histories.

Raftopoulos and Mlambo (2009: xvii-xxvi) argue that the making of a national identity known as 'Zimbabwean' is still in a state of construction—a state of 'becoming national'. This is so because the nationalist struggle did not manage to create a nation in 1980. Pre-colonial leaders ranging from those of Great Zimbabwe, Munhumutapa, Rozvi and Ndebele political formations did not create one. The Rhodesian state created 'subjects' (black natives) and 'citizens' (white settlers) defined by race and concretized by spatial segregation.

Colonialism brought the issue of race into the centre of African national project as race had been the main criterion for inclusion and exclusion into colonial forms of citizenship. An imagined Zimbabwe nation was to emerge from the centre of settler colonialism within which race and ethnic identities were highly politicized divide and rule pillars. Inevitably, nationalist actors had to grapple with race and ethnic issues as they imagined a postcolonial nation and state founded on the principles of common citizenship and singular national identity.

Highlighting the centrality and imbrications of race and class within the African national project in general, Ekeh (1975: 102) argued that the African struggle for independence was nothing other than 'a struggle for power between the two bourgeois classes involved in the colonization of Africa', namely the entrenched white colonial bourgeoisie and the emerging black bourgeoisie. The African liberation struggle could not avoid assuming the form of a civil war between the black 'natives' and the white 'settlers', making the liberation war in Zimbabwe take the form of an identity-based-conflict in which the black 'natives' fought to defeat white 'settlers'.

Zimbabwean nationalists only succeeded in creating the 'nation-as-state' but failed dismally to create the 'nation-as-people' (Billig 1995; Ndlovu-Gatsheni 2009). The 'crisis' that engulfed the country at the beginning of 2000 has its deep roots in the legacies of settler colonialism and the miscarriage of African nationalism that enabled the emergence of a state without a stable nation. This reality had far-reaching implications for the evolving nation-state project.

Enfranchisement of the black majority was not accompanied by access to strategic national resources like land, mines and factories. No wonder then that control over and access to land continued to shape and influence postcolonial political contestations and imaginations of freedom (Rutherford 2007: 106). Rutherford noted that land in Zimbabwe became associated with the nation; the national liberation struggle was interpreted as a peasant struggle for land, and the political rhetoric of ZANU-PF as well as its policy prescriptions were subsequently formulated around agrarian issues (Rutherford 2001). The land and race questions formed the centrepiece of ZANU-PF's definition of belonging, citizenship, exclusion, and the whole history of the nation. President Robert Mugabe once articulated this very clearly in the following words:

> We knew and still know that land was the prime goal of King Lobengula as he fought British encroachment in 1893; we knew and still know that land was the principal grievance for our heroes of the First Chimurenga led by Nehanda and Kaguvi. We knew and still know it to be the fundamental premise of the Second Chimurenga and thus a principal definer of succeeding new Nation and State of Zimbabwe. Indeed we know it to be the core issue of the Third Chimurenga which you and me are fighting, and for which we continue to make such enormous sacrifices (Mugabe 2001: 92-3).

Even political contestation between ZANU-PF and the MDC did not escape imbrications of race. For example, Mugabe forcefully tried to delegitimize the MDC as nothing rather than a front for white colonial interests. This is how he framed the MDC:

> The MDC should never be judged or characterised by its black trade union face; by its youthful student face; by its salaried black suburban junior professionals; never by its rough and violent high-density lumpen elements. It is much deeper

than these human superficies; for it is immovably and implacably moored in the colonial yesteryear and embraces wittingly or unwittingly the repulsive ideology of return to white settler rule. MDC is as old and as strong as the forces that control it; that drives and direct; indeed that support, sponsor and spot it. It is a counter revolutionary Trojan horse contrived and nurtured by the very inimical forces that enslaved and oppressed our people yesterday (Mugabe 2001: 88).

This situation led Raftopoulos (2007: 181) to argue that one of the key features of the Zimbabwean crisis as it unfolded across the early 2000s was the emergence of a revived nationalism that was delivered in a particularly virulent form mediated by race as its main trope. To gain a full picture of the Zimbabwe problems, it is important to understand its social complexion.

Social identities

One of the most erroneous views on Zimbabwe is to frame its social composition in terms of Shona-Ndebele ethnic divisions that were said to be antagonistic due to historical reasons. This popular but false view ignored the ethnic and racial complexity of Zimbabwe. It also ignored the fact that ethnic polarities were informed mainly by recent rather than remote histories including elite manipulation of identity. Nation-building is adversely affected by emotional, subjective and powerful notions of identity, some of which were historically and philosophically 'false'.

For one to gain a clear understanding of the ethnic and racial complexion of Zimbabwe, there is need to reflect on the history of the 'peopling' of the lands bounded by the River Zambezi in the north and the River Limpopo in the south. Beach (1994: 78) argued that the vast region lying between the Zambezi and Limpopo rivers from as early as the tenth to the mid-nineteenth centuries was a theatre of immigration of different peoples that included the ancestors of the Shona, the Nguni, and other groups that have left an indelible ethnic complexion on modern Zimbabwe. As a result of precolonial historical processes of migration and settlement, Zimbabwe developed socially into a multi-ethnic society inhabited by the Shangani/Tsonga/Hlengwe in the south-eastern parts of the Zimbabwean plateau; the Venda in the south and border lands with South Africa; the Kololo, Tonga, Leya and Nambya in the north and borderland with Zambia; and the Kalanga, Sotho-Tswana, and Nguni in the south-west (McGregor 2009).

The numerically dominant groups collectively termed Shona were also dispersed spatially and linguistically into Karanga, inhabiting the southern parts of the plateau, including Masvingo province. The Zezuru and Korekore inhabit the northern and central parts of the plateau (Mashonaland West,

East and Central provinces), and the Manyika and Ndau in the east, covering the areas known as Manicaland and Chipinge, stretching to the border with Mozambique (Beach 1984; Ranger 1989). On the language ecology of the country Ndhlovu (2006: 305) says 'Zimbabwe is a multilingual country with eighteen African languages that include Shona, Ndebele, Kalanga, Nambya, Tonga, Sotho, Dombe, Xhosa, Tonga of Mudzi, Venda, Shangani, Tshwawo, Tswana, Barwe, Sena, Doma, Chikunda and Chewa' (Hachipola 1998). However, Shona and Ndebele have come to be the dominant national languages alongside English which serves as the official one.

What is known about identities prior to colonialism is that they were very fluid, permeated by complex processes of assimilation, incorporation, conquest of weaker groups by powerful ones, inter- and intra-marriages, alliances, fragmentation, and constant movements. Identities that crystallized from this complex milieu were social and moral in character rather than solid and political.

Identities founded on moral imperatives had more to do with culture and communal security, and social membership, as opposed to political identities that were mediated by competitive confrontation over material resources and over political power (Lonsdale 1992; 2004: 73-95). On the fluidity and flexibility of precolonial identities, Ranger argued: 'Before colonialism Africa was characterised by pluralism, flexibility, multiple identities; after it African identities of "tribe" gender and generation were all bounded by the rigidities on invented tradition' (Ranger 1993: 63).

It was colonialism that had the negative effect not of inventing identities from scratch, but re-inventing existing ones, rigidifying and politicizing them in a number of ways. This is a subject that attracted the attention of Mamdani (2006) who has demonstrated empirically and conceptually how colonialism constructed 'ethnic citizenship' in Africa. Mamdani noted that the advent of settler colonialism entailed differentiation of people within the boundaries of colonies according to race. This culminated in the development of the colonial state as a bifurcated phenomenon governing citizens and subjects differently. Citizens (white settlers) were governed through urban civil power, and this enabled them to enjoy all the fruits of civil and political freedoms and liberties. The subjects (natives/black Africans) were governed through 'decentralized despotism' permeated by tradition and customary order, overseen by a rural chiefly authority as the lowest ranking and salaried colonial official. Under this decentralized structure, Africans were fragmented into rigidified ethnic groups (Mamdani 1996: 18).

Under Rhodesian colonialism the population was categorized into Europeans, Asians, coloured, and native peoples. The natives were further categorized into: 'aboriginal natives' and 'colonial natives', the 'Mashona natives', and the 'Matabele natives' (Southern Rhodesia 1963). This was part of creating 'ethnic citizenship' that was regulated through a 'regime of ethnic rights' (Ndlovu-Gatsheni 2006: 1-18). Ethnic citizenship was enforced through the national identity card system that coded and classified Africans according to an assigned village and district of origin.

Every 'native district' in Rhodesia was represented by a specific numerical code and every adult 'native' was issued a national identity card known as *isithupha* in Ndebele and *chitupa* in Shona. This identity document provided details of one's chief, village of origin, and district of ancestral origin. Added to this, the colonial state went further to formulate an ethnicized wage differential systems within which 'native' workers were ethnically differentiated for specific jobs. This practice was rampant in the mines where Shangani were stereotyped as the 'best workers above and below ground', the Ndebele were said to be the best 'foremen' and the Manyika were said to be 'best house servants' (Ranger 1989).

Both historians and language specialists have revealed how missionaries and the colonial drive to standardize 'native' languages contributed heavily to the invention of ethnicity (Ranger 1985; 1989; Chimundu 1992: 103-129). Vernacular languages had to be codified and orthography established for missionary, educational, and administrative purposes. The Rhodesian government commissioned Clement M. Doke in 1929 to research the language varieties spoken by 'natives' for purposes of standardization into monolithic and homogenous linguistic categories. As put by Doke, his purpose was 'a settlement of the language problems involving the unification of the dialects into a literary form for educational purposes, and the standardization of a uniform orthography for the whole area'. He went further to brag that 'natives were placed at my disposal for investigations, and information was most readily supplied' (Doke 1931: iii).

Doke's work in the 'invention' of standard Shona culminated in the *Report on the Unification of Shona Dialects* of 1931 that created what is today called the Shona language, and indirectly contributed to the manufacturing of greater regional Shona identity that is today standing in polar opposition to the equally manufactured greater Ndebele regional identity (Doke 1931). Solomon Mombeshora well captured the overall contribution of colonialism to the identity problems in Zimbabwe by stating that 'the seeds of ethnic factor were derived from the precolonial past, [but] the colonial era provided fertile soil in which the ideology of tribalism germinated, blossomed and was further propagated' (Mombeshora 1990: 431).

The imagined common national identity could not be easily manufactured within a colonial environment in which ethnic identities were deliberately politicized. Colonialism never intended to create homogenous African nations based on common national identity because this was going to fuel African nationalism that would threaten colonialism as a system. Colonialism wanted to create colonial states as 'neo-Europes' that served metropolitan material needs while maintaining Africans fragmented into numerous tribes and unable to unite against colonial oppression and domination. Memories and histories of multiple layers of malignant and contested histories stretching from precolonial times right through to the present, did not make it easy to forge a monolithic Zimbabwean identity as required by nationalists.

On the precolonial situation, Gerald Mazarire argued that, 'the precolonial history of Zimbabwe is best appreciated from "breaking points" or those contexts of build up and fragmentation already written in the larger narratives of the "rise and fall" of states where new identities emerge and old ones are transformed, negotiated or accommodated' (Mazarire 2009: 2). This prescient analysis is very relevant for a new understanding of the issue of identities in postcolonial Zimbabwe. Where previous historians emphasized the existence of homogenizing precolonial 'empires' of Mutapa, Torwa, Rozvi and Ndebele, Mazarire points to the neglected heterogeneity (Mazarire 2009: 1-38).

In is clear from Mazarire's (2009: 1-8) analysis that Shona identity was a conflation of linguistic, cultural and political attributes of a people who did not even know themselves by that name until the 1930s. What is today homogenized as Shona is a conflation of people who were variously described as 'vaNyai', 'abeTshabi', 'Karanga', or 'Hole'. Jocelyn Alexander described the idea of a homogenized 'Shona' identity as 'an anachronistic label applied to a diverse range of groups with no single cultural or political identity' (Alexander 2006: 19).

One can add that in the south-west of the Zimbabwe plateau emerged another hegemonic identity known as Ndebele that conflated and homogenized such identities as Kalanga, Nyubi, Venda, Tonga, Tswana, Sotho, Birwa and Lozwi into a broad Ndebele identity (Ndlovu-Gatsheni 2009).Without this historical deconstruction of the processes of enlargement and homogenization of identities, a false view of a Zimbabwe divided into 'Shona' and 'Ndebele' identities will persist. Zimbabwe has already paid dearly for freezing people into this conflict and suspicion-ridden bimodal ethnicity as indicated by the low-intensity 'civil war' that engulfed Matabeleland and the Midlands regions in the 1980s (Catholic Commission for Justice and Peace and Legal Resources Foundation Report 1997; Lingren 2005).

Recent studies by Joann McGregor on Zambezi border areas inhabited by such groups as the Tonga, Nambya and other minority peoples, reveal complex ethnic politics revolving round politics of recognition and claim to local resources. McGregor wrote:

> These ethnic mobilizations in the Zambezi border were important for the emerging politics of landscape. As modernist cultural nationalist movements, they involved essentialised notions of culture that were territorialized and politicized. Their focus on specific evocative 'sites' within lost lands in which culture and the past were instilled made implicit or explicit claim to ownership and access, and demanded compensation and development (McGregor 2009).

Ethnic mobilizations have culminated in demands by Tonga and Nambya people for preferential employment at Hwange Coal Mines and recognition of their primal fishing rights on the Kariba Dam (McGregor 2009). Reko Patswe Mathe has unearthed similar ethnic nationalism developing among the Venda of Beitbridge border region informed by issues of recognition, belonging and language preservation (Mathe 2005).

Nationalist discourses of nation-building favoured unitary histories upon which to base the imagined postcolonial nation. In the process they ceaselessly constructed national nodal points on which to hinge and construct national identity. Some historians deliberately sought to construct a national rather than tribal history of Zimbabwe in which the Ndebele and the Shona united against colonialism in 1896 and 1897 (Ranger 1967). Roberts (2005) criticized the work of Terence Ranger for sustaining a linear unitary nationalist history running from 'Mukwati to Nkomo/Mugabe.' To him, Ranger produced a political history of Zimbabwe that fell into the old-fashioned Whiggish mould of Panglossian unilinear development (Roberts 2005).

But Roberts' criticism of Ranger does not take into account Ranger's latest intellectual interventions on Zimbabwean studies where he explored complexities and ambiguities of nationalism, including explaining how Joshua Nkomo (a leading Zimbabwean nationalist) became fascinated with identities to the extent of becoming 'a leading member of Kalanga Cultural Promotion Society and of the Matabeleland Home Society (MHS) as well as of Bantu Congress. His identity at home was Kalanga; in Bulawayo it was Ndebele; in Rhodesia as a whole it was nationalist' (Ranger 1999: 210-211). Ranger celebrated Nkomo's belief in possibilities and desirability of one person having multiple identities and 'possessing such a hierarchy of identities, each deep and valid and each enriching the other', concluding that: 'Nkomo was a great synthesizer' (Ranger 1999: 211).

Zimbabwean nationalism failed to continue the progressive process of 'synthesizing' different identities as a logical way to arrive at common identity. Added to this, some scholars like Masipula Sithole (1999) bought themselves into the bimodal ethnic categorization of Zimbabwe to the extent that Sithole even conflated 'Shangani' identity into 'Shona' identity. This is revealed in his analysis of ethnic grouping within nationalist movements and his listing of the Sitholes as 'Shona'. Progression of Zimbabwean nationalism has fossilized along these false Ndebele-Shona ethnic fault-lines with devastating implications for the postcolonial nation-building project.

A very xenophobic document entitled 'For Restricted Circulation: Progress Review on the 1979 Grand Plan' that defined the nationalist struggle as nothing but a Shona affair to establish Shona hegemony in Zimbabwe, circulated within the country in the 1990s. It partly read:

> The Ndebeles had no legal claim whatsoever upon Zimbabwean sovereignty just like their earlier cousins (followers of Soshangane) later led by Ndabaningi Sithole, that hobgoblin who tried to hijack the struggle. Sithole was foiled and summarily ejected from the party – an act he regretted till his grave ... ZANU's correction of Sithole's errors left the Shangaans a thoroughly confused group despite the modification of their identity to drift closer to Shona under the guise of a language called Ndau, generally accepted among the ignorant as a dialect of Shona. The truth remains – they are foreigners, unwilling to advance our cause as they huddle around and cling childishly to the 'Ndonga' (Progress Review on the 1979 Plan).

The authors of this document were never identified. Its origins were roughly linked to some Shona-speaking intellectuals based in the United Kingdom in the late 1970s who were deeply tribalist and xenophobic. It was aimed at the Ndebele whose presence in Zimbabwe was considered an irritation. ZANU-PF dismissed the document as a product of imperialist plans to divide the country, and it deeply infuriated those Ndebele-speaking people that had access to it. The document even celebrated the *Gukurahundi* conflict that left over 20,000 Ndebele civilians dead between 1980 and 1987. It created an impression of *Gukurahundi* as part of a ZANU-PF Grand Plan to eliminate the Ndebele.

Besides Sithole's (1999) *Struggles within the Struggle* that documented pulsations of ethnic identities within the rank and file of liberation movements, Zimbabwean historians have been reluctant to engage directly with issues of identities, leading James Muzondidya and Sabelo Ndlovu-Gatsheni to argue that:

> Until recently, Zimbabweans have been conspicuously silent about questions of ethnicity. As in the colonial period, especially during the days of the nationalist liberation struggle, all attempts to discuss ethnic identities, especially their manifestation in the political and economic spheres, were brushed aside. Yet, ethnicity has continued to shape and influence the economic, social and political life of Zimbabwe since the achievement of independence in 1980 (Muzondidya and Ndlovu-Gatsheni 2007: 276).

But in recent years, Enocent Msindo boldly engaged with the deconstruction and decoupling of Ndebele and Kalanga identities in the south-western part of the country, inaugurating a deconstruction of regional 'Ndebele' identity. Msindo argued that:

> The history of Matabeleland is one of a restless frontier where identities (ethnicity, regional and/or national) shifted and got different meanings in different historical contexts. It is not simply a *Ndebele* history, but a complicated history of many ethnic groups that have never attracted the scholarly attention of researchers who simply work under the illusion that Matabeleland is *Ndebele* land (Msindo 2004: 1).

While nationalism was meant to forge a common national identity as part of the imagination of the postcolonial nation, it quickly ran up against resilient local and regional identities that needed careful negotiation or marshalling into a common national identity. It became very hard for nationalism to ignore some identities with a precolonial origin. In the heydays of unitary mass nationalism (1957–62) the chairman of a cultural club that organized the Zimbabwe Festival of African Culture held in May 1963 stated that:

> We are descended from the great civilization of the Monomotapa Empire which even today enriches the archives of this land and literature of the Portuguese and Arab peoples. Let that be known by those who wish us ill or well. Let those who pour scorn and derision on this our modest beginning, know that we shall work untiringly to make Zimbabwe the heart of African culture (Turino 2000:181).

To some historians, postcolonial Zimbabwe is a successor state to precolonial Munhumutapa. This interpretation of the nation conflates being 'Karanga' with being 'Shona', and being 'Shona' with being an 'authentic' Zimbabwean. Stan Mudenge (1988) wrote that postcolonial Zimbabwe was 'not merely a geographical expression created by imperialism during the nineteenth century'. To him, it was 'a reality that has existed for centuries, with a language, a culture and a 'world view' of its own, representing the inner core of the Shona historical experience' (Mudenge 1988: 362-364). The danger of popularizing such a primordial origin of Zimbabwe tended to obliterate or suppress other histories.

On top of the sensitive issue of ethnicity is the issue of race that is equally important in the debate on forging national identity in the context of a neo-colonial environment. Mamdani explored the entanglement of race in struggles for national identity in postcolonial Africa in terms of the complex 'native–settler' question, arguing that:

> The settler–native question is a political question. It is also a historical question. Settlers and natives belong together. You cannot have one without the other, for it is the relationship between them that make one a settler and the other a native. To do away with one, you have to do away with the other (Mamdani 2001: 63-76).

The settler presence in Rhodesia made the crystallization of nationalism and the concomitant issue of identity to be permeated by race. The daunting tasks to African nationalists as nation-builders in ex-settler colonies like South Africa and Zimbabwe is how to create a stable, common and single citizenship for settlers and natives. This task involves more than the de-racializing of institutions and removal of racial pieces of legislation from the statute books.

To build a nation out of settlers and natives requires 'an overall metamorphosis' within which 'erstwhile colonizers and colonized are politically reborn as equal members of a single political community' (Mamdani 2001: 65). For both Zimbabwe as in South Africa, the African nationalists have attempted to use the policy of reconciliation as a methodology of bringing the former 'native' and the former 'settler' into common citizenship. This has proven to be an inadequate formula. What is lacking is the building of a new political order that is not tainted by colonial and apartheid legacies that is based on consent rather than conquest, capable of creating equal and consenting citizens.

Nation formation

In the 1960s, African nationalism sought to create and mobilize what Manuel Castells termed 'resistance identity' to create a postcolonial Zimbabwean nation. Castells used the term 'resistance identity' to refer to 'those actors that are in positions/conditions devalued and/or stigmatized by the logic of domination' (Castells 1997: 8-9). With specific focus on Zimbabwe, Msindo argued that the founding fathers of nationalist parties used nationalism loosely, without clearly defining the nation, adding that:

They were not clear who the future national citizens were to be, and to them, it does seem nationalism was a desire for freedom, justice and self-governance. The project required an imagined collective Zimbabwean community of *abantwana benhlabathi* (children of the soil/land), transcending ethnicities. Interestingly, this definition was flouted by the very people who coined it, making it difficult to assert that there was any founded collective ideology of 'the nation' as we know it intellectually (Msindo 2004: 21).

Msindo posed crucial questions about nationalism's mission in Zimbabwe prior to independence:

> Was nationalism just about anti-colonialism or simply the desire for Independence? In which case did it become a struggle for power? Was it mere xenophobia, justifying an anti-white stance? … Alternatively, was it about defining a nation in which questions such as 'Who are we?' And 'Who should be part of the nation?' became issues in those years? (Msindo 2004: 21).

To respond to these questions one needs to track how the nationalist parties and the nationalist actors defined and articulated the pertinent issues of nation, national identity, and citizenship. The first mass modern nationalist movement was the liberal-oriented Southern Rhodesia African National Congress (SRANC) formed in 1957. Its ideological position was framed within very moderate and conservative liberal imagination of liberation and definition of citizenship. The issue of national belonging was not given a careful thought beyond the rhetoric of a multiracial society of equal citizens. SRANC's statement of principles had this to say on national identities:

> Its aim is the NATIONAL UNITY of all inhabitants of the country in true partnership regardless of race, colour and creed. It stands for a completely integrated society, equality of opportunity in every sphere and the social, economic and political advancement of all. It regards these objectives as the essential foundation of that partnership between people of all races without which there can be no peaceful progress in this country (SRANC 1957).

The Congress affirmed complete loyalty to the British Crown as the symbol of national unity and maintained that it was not a racial movement. Its pronouncements opposed both tribalism and racialism to the extent of welcoming as members persons of any race who were sympathetic with its aims and objectives of the SRANC. It also recognized the rights of all who were citizens of the country, whether African, European, Coloured or Asian, to retain and enjoy permanently the fullest citizenship. It believed that the imagined democratic society could only advance through non-racial thinking and acting, and that an integrated society provided the only alternative to tribalism and racialism (SRANC 1957).

The SRANC emphasized that it was opposed to tribalism alongside racism in its imagination of an integrated nation founded on 'true partnership regardless of race, colour and creed'. There was fear by early nationalists that to cause panic on the white settler community was going to make them dig in and resist African nationalism as an anti-white phenomenon. Opposition to racism informed SRANC's policy on citizenship as it stated:

> Congress believes that full citizenship must be extended to all those of any race or colour who are lawful and permanent inhabitants of the country, and have demonstrated this through their satisfactory residence and integration in the life of the community over the course of five years' residence in the country (SARANC 1957: 10).

But despite its moderate agenda, the SRANC met with increased colonial repression that culminated in the declaration of a state of emergency, the banning of the party, and detention and restriction of its leadership in 1959. The SRANC was succeeded by the NDP that was formed on 1 January 1960 and launched in the suburb of Highfields in Salisbury (Harare). The NDP defined itself as 'a political party initiated and led by Africans'. Among its aims was pursuing 'the struggle for, and attainment of freedom for African people of Southern Rhodesia', and 'establishing and granting one man one vote for all inhabitants of Southern Rhodesia' (Samkange 1960: 21).

The NDP committed itself to 'working in conjunction with other freedom organizations in Africa for the establishment and maintenance of democracy in Africa and the achievement of Pan-Africanism' (Samkange 1960: 21). While the SRANC was preoccupied with anti-racism, the NDP emphasized 'one man one vote' as the solution to what became known as the 'Rhodesian Problem' (Weinrich 1975). Unlike the SRANC, that was mainly an urban political formation, the NDP made deep inroads into rural areas and its rallies were massive.

The ethnic composition of the NDP leadership was dominated by nationalists of Kalanga ethnic extraction. These were Joshua Nkomo (President), George Silundika (Financial Secretary), and Jason Ziyaphapha Moyo (Secretary General). Msindo noted that these were powerful posts in the seven-man Executive Committee of the NDP. The Kalanga ethnic group is said to have celebrated the dominance of people from their tribe in the leadership of NDP (Msindo 2004: 233).

Ethnic divisions emerged strongly within the NDP that touched on the suitability of the name Zimbabwe for the imagined postcolonial nation. Some people from Matebeleland, whose imagination of political independence was influenced by memories of the powerful precolonial Ndebele state, were opposed to the naming of the imagined nation as 'Zimbabwe'. To them the name 'Zimbabwe' conjured up the promotion of Shona history and memory. Both Ndebele and Kalanga nationalist activists pushed for the name 'Matopos'. Mbobo, the Secretary General of the Matebele Home Society (MHS), pushed the idea of 'Matopos' as the name for the country in these words:

> [...] both historically and traditionally (Matopos) was of greater significance and spiritual importance [that] attempts to belittle it would be resisted by all in Matabeleland. Those leaders ... were best advised to stop thinking in tribal terms and we in Matabeleland are going to resist any imposed leadership (*Bantu Mirror*, 23 September 1960).

Msindo correctly noted that such regional concerns and tensions indicated the fragility of the emerging territorial nationalism. A split within the NDP occurred that had partly to do with issues of regional identities. The split saw a group of Karanga nationalists breaking from the NDP to form the Zimbabwe National Party (ZNP), the first political party to use the name 'Zimbabwe' for the country. Michael Mawema, a Karanga from Fort Victoria (Masvingo) where the Zimbabwe Ruins are located, is credited with coming up with the name 'Zimbabwe' for the imagined postcolonial nation. Msindo (2004) argued that Nkomo managed to contain a severe split in the NDP by outmanoeuvring the Karanga clique that had formed the ZNP by quickly bringing more Shona leaders into the upper echelons of the NDP.

But NDP was banned on 9 December 1961 and it was succeeded by Zimbabwe African People's Union (ZAPU) within six days. ZAPU had a more tumultuous political existence before it was banned on 20 September 1962. It was the first mass nationalist party to use the name 'Zimbabwe' to signify its acceptance of the imagination of the postcolonial nation as 'Zimbabwe'. ZAPU was a more radical political formation that inaugurated a period of sabotage to cause panic on the white settler population as part pressure to grant independence to Africans. ZAPU intensified theagitation one man one vote as the foundation of democratic governance in the country, and relentlessly demanded majority rule.

Nyangoni (1977: 50) argued that the major significance of ZAPU was that it was the first African political organization to apply the concepts of imperialism and pan-Africanism to Zimbabwe liberation. ZAPU was also the first African political formation to entertain the idea of a bloody nationalist revolution as a way of achieving independence. But this radical political discourse invited the wrath of the colonial forces that increased its arrest of the nationalist leaders.

In the midst of laying the foundation for confrontational politics ZAPU suffered a devastating internal split in 1963 that badly affected efforts to create a national identity called 'Zimbabwean'. The split led to the formation of a Shona-dominated Zimbabwe African National Union (ZANU). With the split, the fossilization of nationalism took a bimodal form of ZAPU and ZANU mediated by the spectre of Shona and Ndebele antagonistic ethnicities. Nationalism as a unifying force had miscarried and 'black-on-black violence' was let loose.

ZANU soon branded itself as a new political formation that favoured 'confrontational politics' compared to ZAPU. ZANU's approach to the issue of belonging was not radical though and did not differ from that of ZAPU. It defined itself just like ZAPU as 'a non-racial union of all the peoples of Zimbabwe who share a common destiny and a common fate believing in the African character of Zimbabwe and democratic rule by the majority regardless of race, colour, creed or tribe' (ZANU 1963).

ZANU's policy on citizenship simply stated that: 'All people born in Zimbabwe or who have been citizens of Zimbabwe shall be citizens of the republic. Foreigners may qualify for citizenship under conditions prescribed in accordance with the Law of the Republic' (ZANU 1963). At the ZANU Inaugural Congress held in Gwelo (Gweru) from 12 to 13 May 1964, its founder president, Reverend Ndabaningi Sithole, asserted that: 'ZANU which was formed on the 8th of August 1963, stands for democracy, socialism, nationalism, one man one vote, freedom, Pan-Africanism, non-racism and republicanism' (Sithole 1964).

Both ZAPU and ZANU premised their politics on the language of majority rule and one man one vote as the key nationalist trope. Joshua Nkomo, the leader of ZAPU argued that: 'Being, as I am, an ardent exponent of majority rule, as the only and natural solution to the political, social and economic problems that beset the country, let me give a picture of the majority rule that we are struggling for' (Nkomo 1964). He did in the following words:

> There is talk by some people that 'majority rule' means rule by Africans only; that Africanisation will deprive Europeans of their jobs and that there will be a general lowering of standards. To us majority rule means the extension of political rights to all people so that they are able to elect a Government of their own choice, irrespective of race, colour or creed of the individual forming such a government. All that matters is that a Government must consist of the majority party elected by the majority of the country's voters. 'Africanisation' means the opening of all those jobs and extension of the ceiling which had been closed to Africans, without necessarily

eliminating those who at present hold such jobs, unless they chose to do so on their own accord, or are proved to be disloyal to the administration (Nkomo 1964).

Nationality and citizenship have always and constantly been defined in terms of Africans versus whites, as though Africans were already a collectivity pursuing a single and common political goal. The unity of Africans was taken as given even in the face of the split of 1963 that was followed by a clear 'black-on-black' violence. But in the 1970s when political parties continued to fragment along many fault lines of Ndebele vs. Kalanga, Kalanga vs. Shona, Karanga vs. Manyika, and Karanga vs. Zezuru, the rhetoric of unity came into political discourses of the nationalist parties, particularly from such newcomers to the political scene as Bishop Abel Muzorewa, and new political formations like the Front for the Liberation of Zimbabwe (FROLIZI).

At the formation of FROLIZI, one of its leaders Nathan Shamuyarira emphasized its commitment 'to the unity of all Africans within and across borders', adding that unity was the overriding concern that led to the formation of FROLIZI (Shamuyarira 1971).

However, those closer to politics of the the the struggle saw FROLIZI as nothing but a tribal political formation and blamed Shamuyarira for championing tribal Zezuru clique politics (Bhebe 2004). FROLIZI was derided as the 'Front for the Liaison of Zezuru Intellectuals' (Ndlovu-Gatsheni 2009). On the other hand, ZAPU and ZANU fought over 'authenticity' and which party was more committed to the liberation of the country than the other while suffering under proscription.

Another new political formation called the African National Council (ANC), which was launched on 10 March 1972, also emphasized the centrality of unity. The ANC was founded within a conjectural context of resisting the Peace Commission at a time when ZAPU and ZANU were proscribed. So to ZAPU and ZANU leaders, the majority of whom were in detention, the ANC was a stop-gap measure to continue nationalist politics and close the political vacuum created by Ian Smith's post-UDI politics of intensified repression. The ANC was also formed within a context in which the disunity between ZAPU and ZANU had caused terrible violence in Salisbury (Harare) and Bulawayo (Muzorewa 1972). Indeed, efforts to forge unity among major nationalist political formations remained elusive throughout the time of the liberation struggle and even beyond, up until 22 December 1987 when Patriotic Front-Zimbabwe African People's Union (PF-ZAPU) was finally swallowed by Zimbabwe African National Union-Patriotic Front (ZANU-PF).

Zimbabwean nationalism was, therefore, highly contested from within and from without. Tribalism and regionalism affected ZAPU and ZANU as well as other smaller political formations. The interlocutors of nationalism, while agreeing on the need for a decolonized nation as the central moral and normative frame of reference, still held on to a variety of beliefs and divergent methods of realizing this dream of forging nationhood and were active in tribal, ethnic and regional squabbles.

Leading nationalist leaders fought to blur the nationalist visions of some of their ranks and project others as sell outs, counter-revolutionaries and puppets as the struggles for power intensified within the liberation movements of different ideological persuasions. Suffice it to say the Zimbabwean nationalists were affected by ethnic divisions, ideological difference, as well as by tactics and strategies for achieving political independence. Some preferred a negotiated settlement even in the face of settler colonial intransigence, others preferred a combination of coercion and diplomacy, yet others thought violence was the only solution to the colonial problem. Zimbabwe was eventually born out of a combination of violence and diplomacy.

Birth of neocolonial Zimbabwe

Zimbabwe joined the community of African nations as the fiftieth independent African state on 18 April 1980. At birth, the young state was forced to dream in both socialist and liberal terms. Its political ideology was captive to these antagonistic worldviews. In addition, the transfer of political power from the white settler political elite to the black elite took the form of negotiated settlement at Lancaster House in Britain under direction of Britain and America. One of the objectives of these Western patrons was to ensure that the radical Marxist ideology the liberation forces had imbibed and by which they advocated the smashing up of the colonially constructed state and building of a new socialist republic did not materialize. At the end of decolonization, Zimbabwe was born as a successor to the Rhodesia colonial state rather than as a new alternative to it.

The Lancaster House Conference of 1979 was a neocolonial trap. The settlement was directly responsible for compromising a 'revolutionary' transition, under which racially biased inequalities in land and asset distribution could have been resolved. A 'revolutionary' transition was also made remote by the dominance of the African bourgeois elite like Joshua Nkomo, Robert Mugabe and many others who had not completely 'committed class suicide' to fully embrace the radical demands of the peasants, workers and the fighting forces of ZIPRA and ZANLA who needed radical changes. The bourgeois elite throughout Africa were mainly concerned with taking over as new leaders where the white colonial bourgeoisie had left; radical transformation was not built into their plan.

The failure of the Zimbabwean transition to assumed 'revolutionary' character has been described as a 'revolution that lost its way' (Astrow 1983). The Zimbabwean transition to independence took a form of 'half-way house' between 'revolutionary' and 'settlement' patterns. Despite the limitations imposed by the Lancaster House Agreement and the Lancaster House Constitution, ZANU-PF that had emerged triumphant in the elections of 1980 committed itself to fulfil some of the key tasks of the liberation project. The national liberation project remained vaguely defined and ambiguously articulated across both ZAPU and ZANU nationalist political formations compared, for instance, to the South African's African National Congress (ANC) wich had the 1955 Freedom Charter as its ideological guide that spelt out what type of nation they imagined and wanted.

The ZANU-PF government set for itself an ambitious postcolonial agenda of ending poverty and underdevelopment among Africans; bridging the disparities between the formerly colonized and the former colonizers in terms of wealth, income and opportunities and de-racializing the patterns of ownership of productive property; ensuring economic growth that benefitted every Zimbabwean; entrenching democracy by ensuring the greater involvement of the masses of the people in the system of governance that was denied under settler colonialism; and securing Zimbabwe's rightful place in Southern Africa, Africa and the rest of the world (Ndlovu-Gatsheni 2009; Mbeki 2001).

But from the 1980s, ethnicity reared its ugly head and plunged Matabeleland and the Midlands regions dominated by Ndebele-speaking people into violence -- this time orchestrated by the ZANU-PF dominated state. This violence led to the collapse of the coalition government in 1982 as PF-ZAPU became framed as a dissident party that deserved to be destroyed. Zimbabwe soon assumed the character of an ethnocracy with the Shona-speaking people becoming the authentic subjects of the nation, while the Ndebele were subjected to state-sanctioned ethnic-cleansing (Ndlovu-Gatsheni 2003; Ndlovu-Gatsheni 2009).

The violence that engulfed the south-western part of the country in the 1980s dented ZANU-PF and Mugabe's positive contribution in reversing some colonial policies in the areas of health and education particularly. But ZANU-PF demonstrated reluctance in entrenching democratic and human rights culture from the beginning. Democracy and human rights remained part of their rhetoric and propaganda. ZANU-PF's political practice did not emphasize democracy and human rights as its cardinal policy. What the ZANU-PF government concentrated on was consolidation of regime security at the expense of a clear nation-building agenda beyond the policy of reconciliation.

The celebrated redistributive project of the 1980s that saw Zimbabwe opening educational opportunities for black people, raising the standard of living of rural people, while making health care accessible to the majority of people was predicated on sharing what was available without clear plans of reproducing what was being consumed and distributed (Davies 2004; Ndlovu-Gatsheni 2006). Zimbabwe was also benefitting from the goodwill of the international community that was generous with financial support in spite of ZANU-PF's deplorable human rights record that left 20,000 Ndebele-speaking people dead and its reluctance to embrace liberal forms of governance and strict corporate management that worked against corruption. Throughout the 1980s, ZANU-PF and Mugabe consistently talked left and walked right while consolidating their internal authoritarian system of governance that tolerated violence. Every election since 1980 was dominated by violence that exposed ZANU-PF as an authoritarian political formation not committed to fair political competition.

Early economic policies were geared towards large expenditure on education, health and welfare; significant expenditures on rural development; and subsidization of essential commodities such as food and fuel. This was followed by subsidization of the state corporations to keep the prices of the goods and services they supplied down. The third pillar was training and deployment of black Zimbabweans in senior positions in all areas of the public sector. The fourth was an upward adjustment of wages and salaries in the public sector to bridge the gap between black and white earnings; and a limited programme to encourage the emergence of a black rural and urban petit bourgeoisie (Libby 1984).

Among the key economic flaws was the failure to harmonize the private and public sectors' efforts to address poverty and underdevelopment. The private sector remained a sacred cow and a domain of the few economically powerful, white bourgeoisie, playing a minimal role in the government's effort to bridge the material disparities between the black and white communities (Mbeki 2001). This was partly due to ZANU-PF's surprising religious adherence to the Lancaster House Agreement's 'sunset clauses' on the economic arena, while violating its human rights and democratic clauses willy-nilly (Mandaza 1986).

What was immediately poignant was that the 'economy and the national budget could not carry the costs imposed on it by the requirement to respond to two of the tasks [ending poverty and underdevelopment] of the Second

Phase of the National Democratic Revolution, of meeting the needs of the people' (Mbeki 2001). The only way out was to increase borrowing and to turn to international financial organizations such as the International Monetary Fund (IMF) for assistance, resulting in the accumulation of debt by the young postcolonial state of Zimbabwe. While all this was happening, the ZANU-PF government 'maintained a complex system of government controls over the economy, which increased the cost of doing business in Zimbabwe and acted as a disincentive for investors who had the choice to invest in less regulated markets' (Mbeki 2001).

In the economic arena, the postcolonial state failed from the beginning as ZANU-PF adopted a subjective and populist approach to the accomplishment of the tasks of the liberatory project in the field of the economy. In pursuing these tasks, it did not take into account the objective reality of fiscal and economic constraints. By as early 1984, the state was already running out of resources and began to appeal to the IMF for financial help. Thus a subjective approach to the economy, which was solely driven by the populist desire to serve the interests of ZANU-PF supporters, imposed new and heavy burdens on the national economy.

This situation was compounded by the failure of ZANU-PF to prevent the rise of cronyism, clientelism, neo-patrimonialism and corruption, which saw those close to the ruling party dividing up the national cake among themselves at the expense of the masses. George B. N. Ayittey (2005) argued that 'Africa's postcolonial development effort may be described as one giant false start', where African leaders (with few exceptions) adopted the wrong political systems such as sultanism or one-party states; the wrong economic system (statism); the wrong ideology (socialism); and took the wrong path (industrialization via import substitution). He added that most leaders were functionally illiterate and given to schizophrenic posturing and sloganeering. The leadership lacked basic understanding of the development process (Ayittey 2005: 92-95).

By the end of the 1980s, the distributive agenda of the 1980s collapsed as the resources had been drained beyond repair. Adoption of Economic Structural Adjustment Programme (ESAP) was a desperate measure and did not manage to rehabilitate the economy that was now experiencing destructive patronage, corruption and clientelism (Mlambo 1997, Ndlovu-Gatsheni 2006). When ESAP was eventually officially abandoned in 1997, Zimbabwe was governed through crisis management and some destructive economic decisions were being taken, including giving lump sums of unbudgeted money to war veterans and intervening militarily in the DRC (Ndlovu 2006; Ndlovu-Gatsheni 2009).

By the beginning of 2000, Zimbabwe had lost social peace within and political peace without. The nationalist project entered its most populist, militaristic and reckless trajectory mediated by what Horace Campbell (2003) termed executive lawlessness. A number of indicators demonstrated this degeneration. First was the consolidation of an 'imperial presidency' together with the concomitant spreading of the personality cult of President Mugabe as the embodiment of the nation-state. Second was the increasing deployment of violence and coercion as a governance strategy through military operations that began with Operation Gukurahundi in the 1980s, Operation Murambatsvina in 2005 and many others that followed. Third was the increasing and profound closure of the democratic space through tightening screws of repression and oppression.

Fourth was the appearance of the war veterans and the nationalist leaders as the 'first citizens' of the nation to whichom all other people were expected to pay homage as liberators, the alpha and omega of Zimbabwe. This happened alongside the militarization of state institutions and further increase in executive lawlessness. All this combined to make democracy an orphan in Zimbabwe. In attempting to make sense of all these negative political developments, Ranger (2003) mounted one of the most robust critiques of the character of Zimbabwean nationalism, revealing that the nationalist liberation wars had proven to be a dangerous terrain of authoritarianism, personality cults, 'commandism' and violence where 'disagreement could mean death'.

But how and why did the ZANU-PF government fall into this mess? A number of explanations can be given. The first is that ZANU-PF emerged within a terrain marked by violence from both the intransigent colonial settler state and from the ZAPU it had split from in 1963. The intransigence and bellicosity of the Rhodesian settler state also forced both ZAPU and ZANU into militancy and to embrace violence as a legitimate tool of liberation.

On this development, John Makumbe argued that 'supposedly democratic political parties, formed for the twin purposes of putting an end to colonialism and creating a democratic dispensation in Zimbabwe, were forced to become militant and militaristic liberation movements' (Makumbe 2003:24). Both ZAPU and ZANU received military support and training from the former Soviet Union, Eastern Europe, Cuba, and China, on top of the support from fellows Africans on the continent. Thus the Socialist bloc had a lasting impact on the liberation movements to the extent that: 'The political organization of ZANU [...] assumed the eastern bloc format, complete with a central committee and politburo' (Makumbe 2003: 24).

The conduct of the armed struggle against a belligerent settler colonial state implied a number of developments that left a lasting impression on ZANU-PF and the state it created in 1980. The first was militarization of the liberation movement, together with the development of commandist and regimental attributes. The second was the prominence of the party leader within the movement that gradually developed into the postcolonial cult of personality. The third was that the militarist approach tended to brook no dissent. The fourth was the building of a nationalist-military alliance that has remained up to today, in which top commanders of the army are loyal ZANU-PF members (Ndlovu-Gatsheni 2006).

Makumbe (2003: 34) argued that these developments implied that ZANU 'would become vulnerable to tendencies of authoritarianism and personalized rule'. Under the influence of Eastern bloc countries that had one-party political systems, ZANU's pronouncements and propaganda throughout the liberation period into the 1980s and beginning of 1990s, emphasized their need to create a one-party socialist state in Zimbabwe (Mandaza and Sachikonye 1991; Reed 1993). Even today, the way ZANU-PF conducts itself politically is as though Zimbabwe is under a one party-state political system. Makumbe further argued that ZANU-PF's adherence to socialist party organizational structures and systems of operational management had resulted in its failure to transform itself into a democratic political party, concluding that:

> The genesis of a political party seems to have a bearing on that party's future develo-
> pment. The Zimbabwe case seems to illustrate that liberation movements struggle to
> transform themselves into democratic political parties when their countries become
> liberated or independent. Indeed, whenever they are threatened with loss of political
> power, former liberation movements tend to resuscitate their original achievements
> as liberators as a license to continued tenure of office. They also harness their wartime
> tactics of instilling fear in the electorate to win elections (Makumbe 2003: 35).

ZANU-PF became concerned with regime security above all other considerations. It took a number of strategies to safeguard its regime security. The first was intolerance of opposition that manifested itself in the violent elimination of PF-ZAPU as the first postcolonial credible opposition in Zimbabwe. The second was the increasing call for a one-party state, and the justification for these calls on a number of grounds.

The justifications included the question of economic development that was said to need monolithic unity; African tradition that was said to have no space for opposition parties; and the idea that a multi-party system was not just a luxury in Africa but that it promoted instability, regionalism and tribalism that stood opposed to the nation-building agenda. This was indicated in Mugabe's speeches that included envisioning 'one state with one society, one nation, one party, one leader' (*Moto Magazine*, 1 August 1982). Mugabe emphasized that as an indication of the unity of the people in Zimbabwe, 'They should be one party, with one government and one Prime Minister' (*The Chronicle*, 25 January 1982). This rhetoric of unity was used to destroy any site of pluralism within society (Sylvester 1986: 246).

As the national cake continued to shrink in the 1990s, the ZANU-PF government responded with increasing closure of democratic space coupled with use of violence against those considered opponents. There were also noticeable changes to ZANU-PF's conception of nationalism, democracy, and economic development. Dorman (2001: 50) claimed that 'the joint nation and party-building [...] was defined in terms of three interlocking concepts: reconciliation and unity; development; and nationalist rhetoric and symbolism'. She added that 'the regime's new legislative and security powers based upon the oppressive laws of the Rhodesian state, allowed it to regulate widely providing a political-military framework through which to dominate and demobilize society' (Dorman 2001: 51).

Norbert Tengende (1994) reinforced Dorman's analysis, arguing that the ZANU-PF nation-building project was nothing but an instrument of domination and control marked by the marginalization of popular participation (Tengende 1994: 153; Sachikonye 1996: 142). The tree of democracy was easily uprooted and substituted by the tree of presidentialism in the late 1980s. This was symbolically represented by what Dorman termed 'the omni-present "official portrait" of the president' that even substituted nationalism (Dorman 2001: 57). With the establishment of the 'imperial executive presidency' in 1987 there followed the inauguration of the Robert Mugabe 'father of the nation motif', backed by liberation war credentials and nationalist iconography that is proving very hard to transcend democratically.

Disillusionment with ZANU-PF authoritarianism resulted in the formation of the Movement for Democratic Change (MDC) in September 1999. The MDC soon gained national support across racial, ethnic, gender, class, and religious divides through its promised commitment to restore democracy, human rights, constitutionalism, rule of law, and economic growth. These were issues that ZANU-PF had downplayed in their political agenda (Sithole 1997: 127-141; Sithole 2001). In the place of democracy and human rights ZANU-PF emphasized social and economic justice issues that were soon undermined by ZANU-PF elite accumulation of land ahead of peasants and workers, together with state-sanctioned violence against peasants and workers.

Over the years, membership of ZANU-PF and support for Mugabe personally had become conditions for access to positions of employment, resources, and authority. This happened alongside the loss of support among sections of the population who did not benefit from its political patronage. Worse still, as this process evolved, the structures of the party showed signs of atrophy, and the organization began to deviate from its role as representatives of the popular will. The party was now being perceived as the state, abusing public resources and dispensing public resources to clients and cronies in a brazenly partisan and very destructive primitive accumulation manner (Mbeki 2001).

By 2000 popular democracy had found its way into intensive care; and other agents as the war veterans, youth militias, and the military came to be the basis of ZANU-PF and Mugabe's power. While ZANU-PF thought it would continue to have strong control the war veterans, another development occurred, with a negative impact on the structures of the party: According to Mbeki (2001):

> [T]he 'war veteran' structures are not subject to the processes of control and accountability binding the normal structures of the party of revolution. Accordingly, the 'war veterans' have achieved a level of autonomy that further weakens the capacity of the party of revolution to influence and lead the masses of the people. Because they are not bound by the practices of normal party of revolution, the 'war veterans' resort to ways and means predicated on the use of force against the people, rather than the education and persuasion of these masses to support the revolutionary cause. For these reasons, they also attract into their ranks the lumpen proletariat in particular. … *Inevitably, therefore, to the extent that it sustains these parallel structures, the party of the revolution becomes an opponent of the democratic institutions of governance and democratic processes that it has itself established and encouraged and for whose establishment it fought most heroically, with many of its militants laying down their lives* [my emphasis].

Having burst into Zimbabwe's body politic as storm-troopers of ZANU-PF, the war veterans in collusion with youth militias and 'militarized' members of the national army, constituted themselves into an extra-party and built parallel political structures that were inimical to democracy, constitutionalism, and the rule of law. They were seen to constitute a huge stumbling block to democracy and transitional justice in Zimbabwe. In short, those who fought for democracy had turned around to become serious obstacles to the democratic project in Zimbabwe.

On the foreign policy arena, Zimbabwe degenerated into pursuit of abrasive foreign policy towards the West at a wrong time when the country had no capacity to contain the disciplinary responses of the West and its impact on the domestic sphere. Since the collapse of the Soviet Union and implosion of the socialist republics of eastern and central Europe, the developed capitalist world assumed a hegemonic position in global economic and political affairs.

What Zimbabwe considered to be its allies in the war against the West such as China and others in the East were themselves opening up to significant inflow of private capital from the developed capitalist world, while Zimbabwe went in the opposite direction by 'Looking East[ward]'. ZANU-PF and Mugabe miscalculated strategically and tactically as 'it is clear that, at this historical moment, it is impossible to mobilize the disciplined socialist and anti-imperialist forces that it might have been possible to mobilize two decades ago, to act as a counterweight to the developed capitalist countries' (Mbeki 2001: 24).

The fact that the country would end up in isolation, confronted by an array of international forces that could not be defeated outright eluded the ZANU-PF leadership. Zimbabwe also needed to work harder to avoid sinking into an ever-deepening social and economic malaise that would result in the reversal of many of the gains of the 1980s. As ZANU-PF's popularity was sinking lower and lower, Mugabe developed an Afro-radical discourse that assumed a deeply racialized character.

Fighting racial domination in a neocolonial state

In December 1997, President Robert Mugabe declared that:

> We are now talking of conquest of conquest, the prevailing sovereignty of the people of Zimbabwe over settler minority rule and all it stood for including the possession of our land [...] Power to the people must now be followed by land to the people (*The Herald*, 6 December 1997).

In December 2000, President Mugabe told the ZANU-PF Congress that:

> This country is our country and this land is our land...They think because they are white they have a divine right to our resources. Not here. The white man is not indigenous to Africa. Africa is for Africans. Zimbabwe is for Zimbabweans (cited in Norman 2008: 110).

These two statements and others marked official repudiation of the previous national policy of reconciliation that formed Mugabe's approach towards race relations in the 1980s. What has not been adequately explained is why racism became official policy of ZANU-PF in the late 1990s. Or rather, what factors made race attractive to politicians? How did ordinary people respond to the race discourse of the 1990s and 2000s? Don Robotham provided part of the answer to these questions:

> When these hundreds of years of common history include merciless cruelties, denigrations, and exploitation by the same oppressor, a particularly fierce nationalism is often the result. This collective sentiment simmers over centuries and then may burst forth with fanatical ferocity. While at the abstract level one can extract the universal human from the particular experience of local groups, all people make history in the concrete. It is this actually concrete common historical experience that generates distinctive identities and necessarily finds expression in national movements dedicated to that specific cause (Robotham 2005: 567).

What is not clearly unexplained is why and when does African nationalism degenerate into racism and under what conditions beyond Frantz Fanon's explanations? To respond to this question, it is necessary to focus on the material and historical conditions that fuel this behaviour. In Zimbabwe, race became a major concern even for moderate politicians like Joshua Nkomo because of its historical linkages with colonial dispossession politics. The Lancaster House Conference and the subsequent decolonization formula postponed the race issue. It also ignored the ethnic issue. No wonder then that ethnicity plunged the country into violent crisis barely two years into independence and race plunged the country into violence in the 1990s. What are the rational reasons for all this type of politics?

It was almost inevitable that the issue of race would continue to haunt Zimbabwe beyond the policy of reconciliation. This was partly because the policy of reconciliation failed to percolate into changing actual race relations on the ground and partly because unequal material realities still remained largely shaped by race. James Muzondidya argues it this way:

> Far from being exhausted, the political rhetoric on race, black economic empowerment and radical, exclusive black nationalism, despite all the ambiguities and contradictions, continued to resonate with many Zimbabweans in both rural and urban areas who recognized the unfair balance of ownership of land and other important economic resources between blacks and whites (Muzondidya 2010: 13).

What is clear is that the Lancaster House Agreement was just an armistice for ten years rather than a resolution of the race problem. The manifestations of this race problem in a postcolonial Zimbabwe took various forms. The first indicator was the continued dominance of white minorities in the ownership of strategic resources like land, mines and industries. In the 1980s, an estimated three per cent of the population consisting mainly of white farmers and a very small black bourgeoisie owned the bulk of strategic national resources and controlled two-thirds of gross national income.

A 1989 report of on black advancement in the private sector revealed the following racial distribution at management level: *senior management*: 62.5 per cent white, 37.5 per cent black; *middle management*: 35. 5 per cent white, 64,5 per cent black; *junior management*: 22 per cent white, 78 per cent black (Raftopoulos 1996:6). The Financial Gazette of 8 January 1998 indicated that by 1993, there was only 2 per cent of black participation in all sectors of the economy.

The second indicator of the continuation of the race problem was the disengagement of whites from national politics once the Conservative Alliance collapsed and the white reserved seats were scrapped from the voters' roll in 1987. Politically speaking whites withdrew into their farms, secluded suburbs and business premises only to re-surface in 2000 when their privileged economic life was threatened by the fast-track land reform programme. This is a point emphasized by Muzondidya:

> Until the removal of the 20 reserved seats in 1987, politically active whites conti-
> nued to see themselves as existing outside the new nation state and overwhelmin-
> gly continued to support the conservative Rhodesia Front...After the demise of
> the Rhodesia Front and the enactment of the constitutional amendment which
> abolished the separate voter's roll, most whites withdrew from national electoral
> politics while others continued to hold on to their political imagination of Rho-
> desia (Muzondidya 2010: 24, see also Godwin and Hancock 1993).

The white community seemed to adhere to what Peter Godwin and Ian Hancock described as the spirit of 'Rhodesians Never Die' which prevented them from embracing the policy of reconciliation fully, socially, politically, psychologically and economically (Godwin and Hancock 1993; Kinloch 1997: 820-838).

The third indicator of the continuation of the race problem was the white maintenance of a colonial settler culture revealed through coercive control over black labour and their manipulative approach to the maintenance of their economic interests as well as social seclusion from the black population. Throughout the 1980s and 1990s the white community tied to maintain what Dan Kennedy termed 'islands of white' within Zimbabwe (Kennedy 1987).

Lack of racial social integration also continued to conjure up a society of two separate races, one white and the other black. The social apartheid was manifest in attempts by the white community to ring-fence itself round away from blacks through withdrawal to expensive and 'gated communities' guarded by dogs and black guards; and building of independent schools whose fees structures excluded the majority of black children from middle and low-income families (Muzondidya 2010: 25; Kilgore 2009). The isolation and lack of racial contact extended to the sporting field where such sport as rugby and cricket were dominated by whites (Muzondidya 2009: 167-200).

The net effect of all this was catastrophic for the white community. As Selby (2006: 242) noted, the visible white community's affluence and continued isolation provoked anti-white sentiment among blacks and exposed whites as targets. Many whites failed to cross over from racism to new coexistence with blacks. This continued existence of racism made it very easy for political gladiators in ZANU-PF to mobilize people on a racial basis when their political fortunes were diminishing in the late 1990s and early 2000s.

Racial politics of redress resonated among the emerging black middle classes who were thirsty for fast incorporation among the bourgeoisie. As Maphosa (1998) said, many aspiring black businessmen and women were desperate to enter into those sectors of economy the like land ownership, mining and manufacturing that were monopolized by whites. Such groupings as Indigenous Business Development Centre (IBDC) and Affirmative Action Group (AAG) began to blame race for their failure to make a bold entry into the private sector and thus embraced ZANU-PF politics of racial redress as a vehicle to advance their business interests.

Similarly, the former freedom fighters who had languished in poverty since demobilization enthusiastically embraced ZANU-PF politics of redress as advancement of the liberation project (Ndlovu Gatsheni 2006: 23). On this reality of resonance of race within society, Muzondidya argued that:

> [...] the continued existence of deep racial inequalities and racial prejudice in Zimbabwe, two decades after the end of colonial rule, enabled the incumbent ZANU-PF to mobilize the political idiom of race to defend its control of the state by blaming all its weaknesses and failure to deliver on social and political demands on white control over the land and economy (Muzondidya 2010: 26).

The latest manifestations of racial politics since the coming to power of inclusive government in February 2009 include the continued invasion of remaining white farms and the refusal by President Mugabe to swear-in Roy Bennett as Deputy Minister of Agriculture as he was appointed by MDC-T to that portfolio. Bennett, a former Rhodesian soldier and commercial farmer is the Treasurer-General of MDC-T.

But since Bennett's return from self-imposed exile in South Africa, he has been undergoing prosecution for an alleged terrorist plot. Even after the courts have found him innocent Mugabe has not sworn him in as Deputy Minister.

One of the explanations for the refusal is that Bennett was a member of the Rhodesian security forces that murdered a lot of innocent black people in defence of the white settler colony of Rhodesia in the 1970s. His commercial farm was taken away from him by the ZANU-PF government under its fast-track land reform programme. It is these realities on the ground that led Muzondidya to conclude that:

> Opportunistically mobilizing on the rhetoric of race and land, ZANU-PF was able to articulate the Zimbabwe crisis as a racial issue whose solution could only be found in addressing issues of racial domination and inequalities. While oppression and coercion were important aspects of ZANU-PF rule in the late 1990s onward, the rhetoric on race and land was its political draw-card. [...] mobilizing on the basis of race, an increasingly repressive and waning ZANU-PF was not only able to rally a significant proportion of the masses in Zimbabwe behind it but also to build its political legitimacy inside the country and abroad. [...] the insensitivity to, and inability to deal with, issues of race and racial domination within both domestic and international opposition movements helped not only to internationalize the Zimbabwe crisis but also to prolong its resolution as it came to polarize regional and international opinion. [...] The mobilization on the basis of race indeed concealed the multiplicity of causes of the crisis and ZANU-PF leaders' individual responsibility for the crisis. However, the visibility of racial differences in poverty and wealth among blacks and whites enabled race to assume a broad appeal as a political mobilizing idiom. The above observations regrettably are some of the disconcerting but greatest lessons of the Zimbabwe crisis which have been shunned or silenced by most intellectual and academic debates on the crisis (Muzondidya 2010: 27).

Muzondidya's analysis of the importance of race dovetails into the arguments of Mamdani (2008), and Yeros and Moyo (2007) who also strove to indicate that something needed to be done to resolve material inequalities rooted in settler colonialism. For instance, Mamdani noted that: 'The inadequacy of the Lancaster House provisions for the decolonization of land ensured that it remained the focus of politics in Zimbabwe' (Mamdani 2008: 2). Also Yeros and Moyo (2009: 1-10) argue that the question of resolution of material inequalities is as important as the question of democracy and human rights and that there can be no deeper democracy and comprehensive human rights without economic and social justice. It is within this context that race, has continued to haunt Zimbabwe. But besides race, is the problem of ethnicity that continues to complicate politics in the country and compromise efforts towards forging common citizenship and heal the nation.

Ethnocracy and the nation

Norma Kriger (2003: 75) argued that ZANU-PF sought to create a 'party-state' and a 'party nation.' By this she meant that the processes of state-making and nation-building were deliberately channelled to crystallize around ZANU-PF and ZANLA liberation histories, symbols and regalia. The history of ZANU-PF was turned into national history. Party symbols became national symbols and national symbols like Great Zimbabwe became party symbols as well.

This building of a 'party-state' and a 'party-nation' happened in tandem with deepening politics of modelling the state and nation into an ethnocracy. Ethnocracy arises where the distinction between nation and ethnicity is eliminated. The result is a form of 'cultural despotism' exercised by the privileged ethnic groups. In an ethnocracy, the state undergoes deep ethnicization and 'nationality itself is often defined in terms of the majority ethnicity' (Peterse 1997: 373).

Edgar Tekere, a veteran nationalist, former ZANU-PF secretary general and former leader of the Zimbabwe Unity Movement (ZUM) decried the building up of ethnocracy in Zimbabwe. To him, this took the form of asking members of ZANU-PF to stand for elections in the provinces and cities where they originated from. Tekere was deployed to stand for Mutare urban because he was Manyika and Mutare is the capital of Manicaland (Tekere 2005).

There are increasing voices emanating from minority groups about turning Zimbabwe into an ethnocracy. In a recent opinion piece entitled *Zimbabwe: The Case of Two States*, George Mkhwanazi described Matabeleland as suffering from 'colonial subjugation' by Zimbabwe. This how he puts it:

> Zimbabwe, as a new colonial power over Mthwakazi, has abused the numerical advantage of Shona people to effectively exclude Mthwakazi nationals from any meaningful participation in the country's political and economic affairs. [...] There is something unmistakably colonial in Zimbabwe's attitude to its Mthwakazi subjects. Colonialists impose their values, language, culture and filth on the colonized and Zimbabwe did just that. [...] The Shona term for ethnic and racial domination of minorities is *Chimurenga* (Mkwanazi 2010).

But since 22 December 1987, the government of Zimbabwe tried to use the signing of the Unity Accord between ZANU-PF and PF-ZAPU to contain Ndebele feeling of marginalization and exclusion from power through elevation of a few political actors from the region to cabinet positions and reserving one of the vice-president posts to a person from former PF-ZAPU. This arrangement came after almost a decade of state-orchestrated violence that devastated Matabeleland and the Midlands regions (Catholic Commission for Justice and Peace Report 1997).

Recent studies on language and ethnicity have revealed that ethnocracy does not only reveal itself in language policies, government recruitment and composition of armed forces, but also in naming of basic commodities such as meal-meal (*Ngwerewere*), meat (*Chidzwa*), chicken pieces (*Machikishori*) and soup (*Usavi*), thick meal-meal porridge (*Sadza*) and many others (Ndhlovu 2009). All these vernacular names are drawn from the language of the dominant 'ethnie'. On the issue of language use in building ethnocracies, Richard Fardon and Graham Furniss posited that:

> Nothing so readily places a voice on the national sound stage as its language of address. That language may already connote a particular group or else an alliance of forces may coalesce to identify it as proprietary badge. To broadcast in one language is to fail to broadcast in another and that is always taken as a message (Fardon and Furniss 2000:3).

There is indeed widespread complaint among minority language speakers about the space and airtime given to Shona and Ndebele vis-a-vis other languages like Kalanga, Nambya, Tonga, Venda and many others (McGregor 2009). The Zimbabwean political elite have focused their nation-building approach into managing rather than trying to eliminate ethnicity in society. They have realized the futility of trying to coerce people into changing their identities.

Perhaps the attempts to force the Ndebele not only to abandon PF-ZAPU and join ZANU-PF but also to speak Shona were a good lesson. The results included further deepening of resentment to ZANU-PF and consistent rejection of ZANU-PF long after PF-ZAPU was swallowed by ZANU-PF. The leading scholar on management rather than elimination of ethnicity was the renowned political scientist Masipula Sithole who argued that:

> As long as politics is about power, advantage and disadvantage, ethnicity will be one of the resources political gladiators utilize to gain it. The task is to moderate and manage the use of this resource by consciously accommodating it in the structures of power. Until we accept and firmly grasp this idea, democratic stability, and thus economic development will remain elusive (Sithole 1995: 122).

But one of key weaknesses on existing literature on ethnicity in Zimbabwe is to confine the debate on ethnicity to the Ndebele-Shona binaries. This approach is premised on a false idea of Zimbabwe as a 'bimodal country' suffering only from ethnic polarization between the majority Shona-oriented group and the minority Ndebele-oriented ones (Masunungure 2006: 5). Ethnic issues in Zimbabwe are more complex than this.

As earlier noted, during the liberation struggle, ZAPU experienced a form of ethnicity that involved Kalanga, Ndebele and Shona identities whereas ZANU suffered from intra-Shona ethnic cleavages involving the Karanga against the Manyika, and Zezuru against the Karanga. The triumph of ZANU-PF in the 1980 elections temporarily united Shona-oriented groups through ruling group identity whereas the *Gukurahundi* violence of the 1980s united the Ndebele-oriented groups through fostering a victimhood identity (Ndlovu-Gatsheni 2008: 27-55).

The 1990s witnessed the unravelling of Shona-group consensus and the revival of intra-Shona competition for power within ZANU-PF. There was increasing realization that Zimbabwe was ruled by what Maloreng (2005: 77-88) termed a 'Zezuru tribal clique' with President Mugabe at the apex. Zimbabwe's 'Zezuru Sum Game' played itself through deliberate allocation of government and party positions to the Zezuru ethno-linguistic group as a security measure for President Mugabe's continued tenure of office.

The top security positions in the Central Intelligence Organization (CIO), army and police are all headed by people hailing from the Zezuru branch of Shona-oriented groups (Ndlovu-Gatsheni 2006: 49-80). This continued domination of the 'Zezuru clan' in politics provoked the emergence of regional-ethnic factions within ZANU-PF -- the most well-known being the Mnangagwa and Mujuru factions competing to succeed President Mugabe. These realities led Muzondidya and Ndlovu-Gatsheni to argue that:

> Ethnic polarization has not just developed between the Shona and the Ndebele, but also among various Shona groups—the Karanga, the Manyika, the Zezuru, the Korekore and the Ndau, which have accused and counter-accused each other of ethnic favouritism. Minority groups like the Shangani, Kalanga, Tonga and Venda, located in the marginal borders with little economic development and less physical and social infrastructure, have felt marginalized from both the economy and society and have complained of political and cultural domination by both Shonas and Ndebeles (Muzondidya and Ndlovu-Gatsheni 2007: 289).

The recent history of Zimbabwe has witnessed such cases as that of Shona-Venda tensions in Beitbridge that came to a boiling point in 2002 when a group of 'war veterans' dismissed the head of primary school in the district, allegedly because she was employing mainly Shona teachers, and not Vendas. Mathe has noted the high levels of politicized language issues at the border town of Beitbridge reinforcing identity group boundaries between the local Venda-speaking groups and the Shona (Mathe 2005). There is the case of Shangani-speaking communities' agitation against the employment of *vanyai*—a derogatory term used locally to describe the Karanga as foreigners (Muzondidya and Ndlovu-Gatsheni 2007: 290).

The recent fast-track land reform has also sparked ethnic tensions, and examples include the angry reactions of the Shangani of Chiredzi against resettlement of Karanga-speaking groups in what they considered their land; the Korekore being agitated against resettlement of Karangas in Muzarabani, an area they consider their ancestral lands, and the 2003 case of the refusal of Ibbo Mandaza to occupy his newly acquired farm in Bubi district of Matabeleland North province (Muzondidya and Ndlovu-Gatsheni 2007: 290-291). These realities led to Muzondidya and Ndlovu-Gatsheni's arguement that:

> In spite of all official pretences to the contrary, Zimbabwe has increasingly become ethnically polarized. As in the 1970s, ethnic and regional tensions have been quite dominant in the power contestations within both the ruling ZANU-Pf and the opposition Movement for Democratic Change. Zezuru, Manyika, Karanga and Ndebele ethno-regional identities have become the main basis through which power has been contested. The dominant factions in the ongoing struggle for succession of the leadership of ZANU-PF and the country, for instance, have all mobilized on regional and ethnic basis (Muzondidya and Ndlovu-Gatsheni 2007: 292).

A discussion document prepared by the Zimbabwe Institute (2006) indicated complex ethnic politics at play within ZANU-PF with leading proponents of Mugabe's continued stay in office being such people as Nathan Shamuyarira, Webster Shamu, Ignatius Chombo and Nicholas Goche hailing from Mashonaland West. Those in the Mujuru faction largely come from Chikomba and Chivhu districts.

There are many factors that explain the birth of ethnocracy in Zimbabwe. These range from colonialism's divide and rule practices of governance to African nationalism as a terrain of re-tribalization of politics. The ZANU-PF leadership adopted authoritarian and ethnically-biased postcolonial nation-building strategies which justified violent conquest of Matabeleland and the Midlands regions in the 1980s. The violence of the 1980s and other factors such as deployment of Shona speaking people to occupy strategics position in Matebeleland created realities and perceptions of economic marginalization.

This perception is further confirmed by asymmetrical power configurations that banish some groups to the peripheries of the corridors of power and exportation and deployment of human resources into cities and regions where they are considered aliens. The memories of violence and injury that have not been accounted for, officially recognized or settled properly to the satisfaction of victims also exacerbate ethnic consciousness in Zimbabwe. The current contestations over state power coupled with realities of unfair distribution of national resources across regions and ethnicities is a cause for ethnic concern. Finally, the long tenure of public office and incumbency by people from one identifiable ethnic group and from one region also increases ethnic anxieties.

For Matabeleland, a group known as *uMhlahlo we Sizwe sika Mthwakazi* listed the following issues as the key drivers of ethnicity in that region: marginalization of the elected MPs from the region; institution of reign of terror in the region; perpetration of ethnic cleansing against the people of the region; translocation of economic resources of the region to Mashonaland; reserving of key jobs for the Shona in the region; depriving people of the region of opportunities; and retarding the cultural identity of the Ndebele. These grievances have coalesced to produce various political formations--some oriented towards the democratization agenda as a solution; some pushing for federalism as solution; or revival of inclusive ZAPU nationalism; and others taking a radical irredentist slant such as the recently launched Matebeleland Liberation Front (MLF).

The violence of the 1980s that left an estimated 20,000 people dead and many others missing in Matabeleland and the Midlands regions has remained a catalyst to emotional ethnicity mediated by anger, resentment and even entertainment of irredentist politics. As a motivation for his *Gukurahundi National Memorial Bill*, Jonathan Moyo (2006: 12) argued that:

> It remains indubitable that the wounds associated with the dark Gukurahundi period are still open and the scars still visible to the detriment of national cohesion and national unity. The open wounds and visible scars have diminished the prospects of enabling Zimbabweans to act with a common purpose and with shared aspirations on the basis of common heritage regardless of ethnic origin.

Moyo's analysis is amplified by Lindgren (2005: 158) who argued that the atrocities committed by the Fifth Brigade in the 1980s heightened the victims' awareness of being Ndebele and hatred for Shona-oriented groups. But feelings of marginalization and exclusion from power are experienced by other communities outside Matabeleland too. The Ndau of the Eastern border clung to ZANU-Ndonga until the death of its leader Rev. Ndabaningi Sithole. The Eastern border areas are dominated by a mixture of Shangani and Manyika peoples.

What is even intriguing is that ZANU-PF has become a theatre of ethnic politics as regional leaders from Masvingo, Manicaland, Matabeleland and other areas try to come into the centre of politics like the Zezuru. The apogee of this jostling for power was the Tsholotsho declaration of 18 November

2004 that sought to institutionalize ethnicity at the top level of ZANU-PF power hierarchy. As Jonathan Moyo said, the Tsholotsho Declaration was meant to creatively manage ethnicity's free will within top power politics of Zimbabwe.

The Tsholotsho Declaration sought to re-configure politics with ZANU-PF so that they reflected and balanced ethnic considerations. The first suggestion was that the top four leadership positions in ZANU-PF (president and first secretary; two vice-presidents and second secretaries; and national chairman) that make up the presidium, should reflect the country's four major ethnic groupings (Karanga, Manyika, Zezuru and Ndebele) in order to promote and maintain representative national cohesion, national belonging and identity. The second proposition was that the top position of president and first secretary of the party should not be monopolized by one sub-tribe (or clan) but should reasonably rotate among the four major ethnic groups.

The third proposition was that the filling of these top four positions should not be by imposition by party hierarchy but through democratic elections done by secret ballot. The final one was that the filling of the top four leadership positions and the democratic elections should be defined and guided by and done in accordance with the constitution of the party to promote the rule of law within the party as a foundation for maintaining the rule of law in the country (Moyo 2005).

Moyo revealed that the Tsholotsho Declaration was a 'culmination of a protracted internal ZANU-PF process of debate, discussion and consultation that started soon after the June 2000 parliamentary elections in which the opposition shocked the ruling party into serious self-doubt by getting 57 out of 120 seats' (Moyo 2005). In short, the Tsholotsho Declaration sought to mainstream ethnicity as a determinant factor in Zimbabwean politics. A particular model of ethnocracy was envisioned within ZANU-PF that had direct impact on broader structures of governance in Zimbabwe.

Ethnicity also plays itself within opposition circles. While the split within the MDC of 2005 was articulated in constitutional terms provoked by debates over the party's participation in senatorial elections, there were also ethnic undertones as Welshman Ncube who led the split was soon framed as a Ndebele politician who was trying to challenge Morgan Tsvangirai, a Shona politician. Ncube quickly contained the spreading of ideas that his faction was a Ndebele faction by inviting Arthur Mutambara to lead it.

Ncube's faction also retained a number of Shona members in its ranks. Tsvangirai too had to move fast to contain ethnic politics by elevating Thokozani

Khupe and Lovemore Moyo to the position of Deputy President and National Chairman of MDC respectively. Tsvangirai feared losing the Matabeleland and the Midlands constituencies to either Ncube's faction or to ZANU-PF. In short, differences over strategy and disrespect for internal constitutional orders, complaints over rising authoritarianism of Tsvangirai as well as critiques over use of violence within the party soon assumed ethnic lines. But what was MDC's approach towards issues of race and ethnicity in general?

MDC imagination of a new Zimbabwe nation

Soon after its formation, the MDC began to formulate an alternative vision of the nation founded on the imperatives of good governance, democracy, and human rights on the one hand and pan-ethnic and racial solidarity on the other. The MDC also sought to set itself apart from ZANU-PF by embracing embers of a post-nationalist politics founded on social movements rather than the tradition of nationalist liberation which has been used to install personality cults, authoritarianism, cronyism, and violence. In June 2000, Tsvangirai confidently located his party's project within a post-nationalist terrain, openly declaring that:

> In many ways, we are moving from the nationalist paradigm to politics grounded in civic society and social movements. It's like the role and influences that in South Africa, the labour movement and civil society organizations had over the African National Congress in the early 1990s. MDC politics are not nationalist inspired, because they focus more on empowerment and participation of the people. ZANU-PF's nationalist thinking has always been top-down, centralized, always trapped in a time warp. Nationalism was an end in itself instead of a means to an end. One of ZANU-PF's constant claims is that everyone in Zimbabwe owes the nationalist movement our freedom. It has therefore also become a nationalism based on patronage and cronyism (Southern Africa Report 2000).

Tsvangirai and his MDC sought to imagine and construct a new national project that was imbued with the spirit of inclusion of all races, all ethnicities, as well as driven and propelled by the overarching desire to democratize the state. This new national project was inspired by the unfolding of new struggles that advocated new politics grounded in 'basic-needs' and 'people-centred' development paradigms. It seems that the MDC was further encouraged by the global mood of possibilities that culminated in Francis Fukuyama (1993) declaring: 'The End of History and the Last Man'.

Michael Hardt and Antonio Negri (2000: 305) also celebrated this age of political possibilities claiming that 'the concept of national sovereignty is losing its effectiveness, so too is the so-called autonomy of the political'. In the region, the rise of the Movement for Multiparty Democracy (MMD) in Zambia under a trade unionist, Frederick Chiluba, and its successful challenge of the nationalist-founded United National Independence Party (UNIP) under the veteran nationalist leader Kenneth Kaunda, may have given hope to the MDC in its struggle against ZANU-PF.

The era was also dominated by numerous vocal grassroots social movements that were celebrated by John S. Saul 'as a significant signpost on the road to a post-neoliberal and post-nationalist politics ... and as an impressive rallying point for those forces from below that might yet get things back on track in their country' (Saul 2002: 13). These celebrations of politics grounded in social movements tended to ignore the continued resonance of nationalist sentiment in a post-Cold War Africa, with some social movements inspired by nationalism and advocating increased state intervention and more neo-Keynesian economic policies, rather than anti-state slogans and rhetoric.

The key intellectual challenge is whether these indications of exhaustion of nationalism really opened possibilities for post-nationalist politics? Scholars like Mkandawire (2005: 1-28) noted that nationalism defied its death and it displayed a remarkable enduring resonance. Krista Johnson (2005) added that post-nationalism emerged as an ill-defined phenomenon that was used 'to characterize multiple and disparate political projects'. At one level, post-nationalism was used to connote a critique of post-independence state nationalism.

At another level the idea of post-nationalism was deployed as a concept to explain a burgeoning socialist and anti-imperialist movement or sentiment. To the liberal scholars, post-nationalism connoted a liberal democratic political project that placed emphasis on individual rights and multi-party politics. Radical Africanist and pan-Africanist scholars were generally wary of so-called post-nationalist political projects that were detached from the pan-African ideal and free of its moral imperatives. They viewed post-nationalism as promoting a more exclusionary and adversarial image of the nation (Johnson 2005).

The advocates of the post-nationalist alternative in Zimbabwe tended to ignore the ability of nationalism to renew its agendas and projects. Throughout the 2000s, ZANU-PF mobilized enormous energy to revive nationalism as the authentic and progressive pan-African phenomenon. Within this revival, President Mugabe tried hard to portray himself as dedicated to the continuation of the historic mission of taking decolonization to its logical end of economic decolonization.

But Mkandawire (2002) argued that nationalism had always been double-sided, with virtues and darker aspects. Among its virtues were fostering a sense of community, patriotism, and a sense of shared historical past. Its dark sides included promotion of strong communal feeling that could easily be turned into xenophobia, and emphasis on monolithic unity that could degenerate into undemocratic pressures for conformity and blind loyalty. In Zimbabwe, ZANU-PF tried hard to reclaim the virtues of nationalism to counter a possible post-nationalist takeover.

The MDC projected a leaning towards a social democratic transformation agenda crafted within the neoliberal paradigm at one level. They emphasized that a post-nationalist dispensation was claiming Zimbabwe for democracy, human rights, economic prosperity, constitutionalism, and rule of law. But at its formation it also tried to appropriate the liberation struggle as having been propelled by the working class.

Gibson Sibanda, the founder deputy president of the MDC, argued that the political struggle in Zimbabwe was historically led by the working class and was fought for dignity and sovereignty of the people. He noted that in the *First Chimurenga*, workers fought against exploitation in the mines, farms, and industry, and peasants against the expropriation of their land. To him, the nationalist movement that led the *Second Chimurenga* was born from, and built on, struggles of the working people. What then happened was that the current nationalist elite in ZANU-PF hijacked this struggle for its own ends, betraying the people's hopes and aspirations (MDC Election Manifesto 2000).

The MDC did not seek to disparage the nationalist liberation tradition as a foundation myth of the postcolonial nation of Zimbabwe. Rather it sought to liberate the tradition from being monopolized by one political party as though it was not a national heritage of all Zimbabweans. To the MDC, the liberation struggle was made possible by the people of Zimbabwe not by a few nationalist elites who continued to claim that they 'died' for all the people.

In a way, the post-nationalist discourse was not a negation of the liberation tradition but a rescue of the national project from abuse and betrayal of the people. In a 2003 document on the core values, goals, and policy principles, the MDC recognized 'the struggle of the Zimbabwean people throughout our history for economic, social and political justice' and acknowledged 'the continuing liberation struggle for social, economic and political rights and freedoms' (MDC 2003: 5).

Its 2008 policy documents projected the MDC as pursuing 'social liberation policies aimed at completing the unfinished business of the national liberation struggle and shall strive for the democratic structural economic liberation, rehabilitation and transformation of Zimbabwe' (MDC Manifesto 2008). Tsvangirai himself emphasized that the struggle in Zimbabwe had always been one for dignity and freedom, and that the workers and peasants were always in the forefront of the first and second liberation struggles that brought the country to independence and gave sovereignty to its people. What the MDC was fighting against was the evident fact that the ruling nationalist elite in ZANU-PF were exploiting this long history of struggle for its own ends (MDC 2000).

The MDC's 2005 manifesto for the parliamentary election portrayed the party as a non-racial and a 'truly national party that recognizes no ethnic, tribal, religious or racial boundaries. We offer the people a new Zimbabwe, a new beginning' (MDC Manifesto 2005). As part of their agenda of delivering this 'new Zimbabwe and a 'new beginning', their goal was:

> A sovereign, democratic, prosperous and self-sufficient nation led by a compassionate government that respects the rule of law and the rights of all its people, pursuing their welfare and interests in an honest, transparent and equitable manner (MDC 2007).

The MDC's relentless emphasis on issues of democracy and human rights has forced ZANU-PF to fight to claim the democratic question as well. Recent speeches by both ZANU-PF and MDC following the elections of 29 March 2008 indicate how the issue of democracy and human rights has come to be the core of party politics in Zimbabwe. This politics is intertwined with the issue of land, food, and jobs, with ZANU-PF emphasizing land, and MDC jobs and food.

Thus, following the victory of his party in the parliamentary elections of 2008, Tsvangirai issued a press statement in which he reiterated that in a 'New Zimbabwe' there would be restoration and not retribution; equality and not discrimination; love, not war; and tolerance, not hate. He portrayed the votes cast on Saturday 29 March 2008 as 'a vote for jobs; it was a vote for food, for dignity, for respect, for decency and equality, for tolerance, for love, and for trust' (Tsvangirai 2008). The March 2008 elections and the controversies surrounding them resulted in further internationalization of the Zimbabwe situation and the birth of a very problematic discourse of transition.

Conclusions

Zimbabwe is currently being governed by a shaky inclusive government that was born out of the Global Political Agreement (GPA) of September 2008. The objective of the GPA was to facilitate a transition from crisis to normalcy and from violence and authoritarianism to democracy. But one of the key problems in any transition is denial by political actors of any wrong doing. As long as the previous regime does not see anything wrong with what it was doing before signing any peace agreement then no transition can take place. President Mugabe once stated that those calling for change in Zimbabwe must repent before he can work with them in government. This was a clear sign that the incumbent regime decided to see something wrong with those calling for change and was hailing them to come back to the fold provided they have seen that they were pursuing a wrong agenda.

Up until the time of the signing of the GPA in September 2008, the radical nationalist position of ZANU-PF had not been fully delegitimized and rendered totally immoral by the opposition locally, regionally, continentally and even in the non-Western world. ZANU-PF still maintained high moral ground on such issues as redistribution of land and defence of sovereignty. The MDC position on democracy and human rights was dented from the beginning because of its close association with the local white farmers as well as Western and American hegemonic agenda that is interpreted by ZANU-PF and Mugabe as pursuing neoliberal imperialism with a re-colonizing agenda.

Thus, while ZANU-PF had to answer for violence, MDC had to cleanse itself from being considered a front for Western and American interests. The transition had to take place within this situation where no political party has clear high moral and political ground. This complicated the prospects for transition roud Zimbabwe. The current political stalemate in the negotiations is revolving not only on individuals like Gideon Gono, Johannes Tomana and Roy Bennett, but also on the issue of sanctions, which ZANU-PF is using to continue framing MDC-T as a dangerous force to national sovereignty.

A large constituency of war veterans, youth militias, sections of academia and all those who benefited from ZANU-PF patronage and its distribution of land and other resources expect MDC-T to make a transition from being a front for foreign interests into a genuinely national political formation. While others mainly operating within the civil society, in the Diaspora and urban areas expect ZANU-PF to change from being a militarized and violent political party into a modern political formation that embraces democracy and human rights. MDC-M is standing in the middle, emphasizing that both MDC-T and ZANU-PF must come and embrace core national interests.

What has been happening is that both ZANU-PF and MDC-T have been trying to fault each other, hence the intractable and unending negotiations over what has come to be termed 'outstanding issues'. What is really outstanding is a clear direction of 'transition from what to what'. In the absence of clear ideological direction and national vision, then issues like race, ethnicity, personalities and generational differences occupy the centrestage of politics and masquerade as outstanding issues. What is happening in Harare was well captured by Pondai Bamu in these words:

> [...] ZANU-PF seeks to incorporate the MDC into government rather than a transition to democracy since ZANU-PF argues that democracy already exists. The MDC, at least the Tsvangirai faction, seeks to take the reins of power rather than be incorporated into a coalition government, since it believes it won the March 2008 election (Bamu 2009).

One of the key problems of the GPA was how to synthesize the radical nationalist position of ZANU-PF premised on uncompromising socialist-oriented redistributive project with the equally radical neoliberal position of MDC-T premised on democratization and human rights discourse. Was this not like trying to mix water and oil in one bottle called inclusive government? Throughout the negotiations and even beyond the dream of a new national project underpinned by a democratization discourse represented by the MDC locked horns with a nationalist discourse represented by ZANU-PF that emphasized continuing opposition to colonialism and espoused politics of black entitlement to strategic resources of the country based on notions of nativity and indigeneity.

The GPA, as the foundation script for the new inclusive government in Harare, could not escape a measure of vagueness on some crucial issues that have haunted the nation-state project since its conception in the 1960s because it emerged as a form of crisis management. In the first place, it remained vague on the crucial issue of transitional justice as a foundational form for national healing, national reconciliation and national unity.

While the MDC tried to push for a mechanism to make those who violated human rights accountable for their misdeeds, ZANU-PF buried its head on letting 'bygones be bygones' for the sake of national stability. The approach to transitional justice founded on the lie of forgetting the past has haunted the Zimbabwe nation-state project since 1980. In the second place, the GPA failed to be explicit on the issue of security sector reform despite overwhelming evidence of securitization of the state and the abuse of security organs of the state in the resolution of political power games (Rupiah 2005: 117-118).

The current stage of the unfolding of the nation-state project can therefore be best described as gridlocked within a situation where the old represented by ZANU-PF are taking time to die or exit the political stage and the new ones represented by MDC-T and MDC-M are slow to be born. In the interval (interregnum) monsters represented by the 'secrocrats/military junta' in alliance with ZANU-PF hardliners are trying to ruin everything. Past practices of undemocratic governance and brutality are currently contesting and putting all sorts of speed traps on the road towards democratization. The continuation of racialized politics is symbolically represented by some spates of new violent farm invasions and legal battles involving Roy Bennett. It is within this context that the inclusive government has been trying to unroll national healing, reconciliation and national integration.

The flag ship of the inclusive government in terms of nation-building is the *Organ on National Healing, Reconciliation and Integration*, a very poor political relations exercise without strong legal statutory backing. In the first place white citizens seem not to be included in this process of healing, reconciliation and integration. This is reflected in ZANU-PF's continued discourse of framing the remaining whites as enemies of the nation. The second indicator are the trials and tribulations of Bennett which symbolizes continuity of persecution of whites including open refusal by President Mugabe to allow some of them to play a role in national politics. The third is the continued sporadic invasions of remaining white farms by sponsored ZANU-PF supporters.

Worse still, indications are that ZANU-PF and MDC political formations have remained poles apart. They continue to behave like dogs whose tails have been tied together. Reconciliation must start at the top level of government for it to percolate into the grassroots. Deng (2008: 44) argued that mediators and facilitators of conflicts in Africa in general tend to concentrate on those issues that are more amenable to negotiation such as political representation and power-sharing and ignore the equally important but intractable issues of wealth-sharing and questions of identity. He further to said that, 'Identity issues are often left unaddressed in peace agreements because, while deeply felt, they are highly intractable. But it is ultimately what is not said that divides' (Deng 2008: 44). According to him, identity in African countries must be understood contextually and historically with special reference to the precolonial, colonial, and independent periods. A combination of these historical interludes 'shaped the sharing of power, wealth, social services, and development opportunities' (Deng 2008: 39).

It is important to add that what is generally ignored in African Studies is that nationalism in Africa was by and large ethnicity writ large that crystallized around the histories of dominant 'ethnie'. No wonder then that the postcolonial state in Africa, as a product of both colonialism and nationalism 'has not become a reassuring presence but remains a formidable threat to everyone except the few who control it' (Ake 1994: 31).

The current challenge to the inclusive government in Harare is how to reconcile fragmented identities; some ethnic and others racial, generational, class-based, regional, political and partisan. Looked at from another angle, what has come to be termed the Zimbabwe crisis can be better understood as a general crisis of the postcolony without necessarily ignoring its contextual origins and features that are equally important.

It is a crisis generated by too many 'unfinished businesses', postponed struggles and frustrated expectations. It reflects many things: incomplete nation-building; uncertainty of a young and captured state always worried about its completeness and security; contestations over the meaning of liberation; crisis of long presidential incumbency by one individual from a particular ethnic group; and interferences of external powers giving those in power all sorts of scapegoats to justify their undemocratic measures as part of defending national sovereignty.

It also reveals the symptoms of crumbling hegemonic histories that trammelled over and deliberately ignored balancing historical pluralities and diversities impinging on postcolonial nation-building and state-making. The nationalist lie of a monolithic nation with strong primordial roots is undergoing a very hard test. The leadership of the country is called upon to demonstrate its qualities of nation-building and state-making that take into account pluralities and diversities.

The key challenge is how to reconstruct the state and nation into an ethical community where wealth is fairly distributed, power is exercised in a responsible and caring manner, and society is united behind a common national vision. The current drive for national healing, happening concurrently with the constitutional process, reveals a society crying out for closure on past abuses but is lacking a committed, visionary and selfless leadership to guide society into new humanity. What is displayed by the inclusive government is a crisis of leadership that has allowed race and ethnicity to occupy the space of ideology and concerns about individuals to constitute national issues—the so-called outstanding issues in the language of the disputants within government.

For the Zimbabwe nation to be reborn and the state to be re-made, there is need for serious consideration of how peripheral societies can forge future-oriented politics within a postcolonial neo-colonized world where Western interference is rife. This future-oriented politics must be founded on an ethical and humanistic spirit that transcends race and ethnicity as framers of national agenda. What is also needed is a transcendence of the current crisis of political language and crisis of imagination that leads to what Frantz Fanon termed 'repetition without change'. The hard question is: is the crisis of 'repetition without change' not part of cul-de-sac created by neo-colonialism?

What is needed is a new language of articulating the multitude of longings, demands, dreams and popular expectations without degenerating to race, ethnicity, victimhood or blaming particular individuals. What is lacking in Zimbabwe now is a correct reading and naming of the signs of the time. The signs of the time indicate that both nationalism and neoliberalism are failing to stand up confidently to the demands, longings and expectations of the people. The first step is to break out of the tensions between belonging and apartness at both leadership and societal level. A clear criterion of belonging and citizenship is needed. This cannot happen where there is a clear epistemological rupture in the official discourse at leadership level indicated by opposition between the presidency and the premiership.

Conclusion

8

The Murky Present and the Mysterious Future

We have been thrown into a time in which everything is provisional. New technologies alter our lives daily. The traditions of the past cannot be retrieved. At the same time we have little idea of what the future will bring. We are forced to live as if we were free.

(John Gray 2004: 110)

Introduction

What runs through this concluding chapter is the complex theme of phenomenology of human uncertainty. The question of human uncertainty in this present century is obvious even to historians who are generally comfortable with engagement of human pasts rather than the murky present and the mysterious future. Becker (1994: xii-xiv) explained 'phenomenology of uncertainty' as being characterised by appearances of convergence and intersection of epochs resulting in instabilities and doubts about the adequacies of the existing normative order of life, lack of confidence in existing worldviews, fragmentation of identities, rupturing of known values of sociality and civility, and visible signs of emptiness of notions of the nation-state. This uncertainty engenders a new search for certainty and alternative forms of organization of human life beyond Westphalian ideas that put the nation-state at the centre of human life.

Wole Soyinka in his 2004 BBC Radio 4 Reith Lectures, spoke on one aspect of human uncertainty which he called the 'climate of fear'. His words:

A few decades ago the existence of collective fear had an immediate identifiable face—the nuclear bomb. While that source is not totally absent today, one can claim that we have moved beyond the fear of the bomb. A nuclear menace is also implicated in the current climate of fear, but the atom bomb is only another weapon in its arsenal [...] What terrifies the world, however, is no longer the possibility of over-muscled states unleashing on the world the ultimate scenario—the *Mutual Assured Destruction* (MAD) that once, paradoxically, also served as its own mutually restraining mechanism. Today the fear is one of furtive, invisible power, the power of the quasi-state, that entity that lays no claim to any physical boundaries, flies no national flag, is unlisted in any international associations, and is in every bit as mad as the MAD gospel of annihilation that was so calmly enunciated by superpowers (Soyinka 2004: 8-9).

Soyinka was meditating on global terrorism as a source of global uncertainty and insecurity which was personified by Osama Bin Laden who was killed by the United States military forces in Pakistan on the Easter eve of 2011. The human race is also facing the threat of HIV&AIDS which continues to ravage in Africa partly because antiretroviral treatment is scarce and unaffordable for the poor communities affected. The uncertainty that has engulfed the world has shaken the foundations of the strong post-Cold War neoliberal humanism that was even eclipsing well-known religious eschatologies of the twentieth century, be they of Islamic or Christian motif. What is at stake and in crisis is the ides of progress. Progress is that strong human belief in people's agency to free themselves from any kind of external limits and constraints to their lives.

Uncertainty has also manifested itself in discourses of development studies. The intellectual uncertainty and the crisis of belief in progress were traced to the 1990s. It was openly encapsulated in various versions of postmodern thinking and the rise of the notions of the risk society. The idea of a risk society was introduced by the German sociologist Ulrich Beck in 1986, capturing a developing feeling that it was useless to look into the future and to plan ahead because of unpredictable uncertainties (Beck 1994). This thinking came on the heels of development pessimism of the 1980s informed by the notions of the unbridgeable gap between the poor and rich countries that continued to widen since 1945. Wolfgang Sachs (1992:1) threw in the towel on development and proposed that: 'It is time to dismantle this mental structure.'

Uncertainty about development was felt more strongly in the 'postcolonial neocolonized world' that is discussed in this book where serious economic development has been elusive since the 1970s. The miscarriage of the decolonization project that became manifest in the late 1960s and early 1970s opened the doors for uncertainty to reign within Africa. But the uncertainty has always coexisted with both pessimism and optimism. Nevertheless, scholars like Lopes (2010) have remained very optimistic of the economic future of Africa. Lopes argued that the African postcolonial nation-states were the youngest in the world and have strong potential to achieve economic development and claim the 21st century.

Among the positive signs of Africa's economic potential, Lopes (2010) cited the example of South Africa that is debt-free, a rare occurrence in Africa. Secondly, he cited the case of emerging powers such as Brazil, India and China that are increasingly investing on the African continent, with China becoming the biggest investor. Thirdly, he cited the growth of South-South relations that is poised to eclipse the previous exploitative South-North relations dominated by donor-recipient engagement that failed to contribute to African economic development.

To Lopes, therefore, (2010) the developing countries of the South have learnt a good lesson of working together with strategic groups from the South such as BRIC (Brazil, India and China) and G22 that enabled them space within global governance to articulate common interests. These robust and articulate groups of the developing countries have successfully turned Dowa Roundtables and World Trade Organization (WTO) summits into sites of struggle. They have claimed a voice and space in global politics and economy and Africa is benefitting from this opened policy space. Lopes talked about the emergence of what he termed 'the South Agency' capable of opening the policy space for developing countries within the top global tables where economic and political decisions are made, such as the IMF and World Bank.

Lopes (2010) also argued that what was written on the global screen was increasing African renewal that was often overshadowed by concentration on such cases as the political theatrics of leaders like President Robert Mugabe of Zimbabwe which were then overblown to show that Africa was doomed. To him, the positive trends in Africa far outweighed the negative in the economic spheres of life. There has been a noticeable de-escalation of civil wars that have compromised the continent's economic potential and initiatives (Lopes 2010). Lopes noted that Africa survived the global financial crisis very well because their banks were not fully integrated into the global Western ones. Indeed, instead of going into crisis like other countries, Africa maintained steady economic growth during the crisis of 2008 to 2009. The optimism of Lopes was shared by John Weeks (2010) who cited the case of the Freetown Declaration drawn by African Finance Ministers in August

2009 where they declared their freedom from IMF and World Bank tutelage and committed themselves to taking control of the economic destiny of the African continent.

This optimism must also be careful not to minimize the structural straitjacket of colonial matrix of power that continues to maintain the hierarchical hegemonies of domination between the South and the North. Africa cannot maintain a good policy space at the global economic and political high table as long as the realities of neocolonialism are not completely broken and swept away in every area of life, such as culture, epistemology, discourse, language and images. What can be said with confidence is that Africa has a long battle to fight before it can claim the 21st century as its own.

At the political level, Africa currently manifests a deep ideological crisis emanating from the retreat of revolutionary imagination, exhaustion of utopian registers of freedom, and inherent limitations of neo-liberal emancipatory pretensions. While the end of the Cold War launched a new world dominated by neoliberal democracy and global capitalism, this Fukuyamite 'end of history' euphoria was short-lived and was soon replaced by a cloud of uncertainties engendered by the crisis of millennial capitalist humanism.

Since Fukuyama pronounced his 'end of history thesis', revolutionary radicalism of any kind, became considered as profoundly anti-systemic if not terror-inducing. Once depicted in this negative manner the concept of revolution became criminalized and open to systematic disciplining to serve the status quo. It was within this context that African imaginations of freedom became prisoner of the naïve neoliberalism mediated by notions of globalization, free reign of the market, and romantic celebrations of de-territorialization, cosmopolitanism, multiculturalism, and multipartyism.

Human uncertainties were generated by human anxieties to grasp the elusive Lacanian 'Real'. According to the French psychoanalyst Jacques Lacan the 'Real' denoted the heaven-paradise-like 'non-space' within which human identity, aspirations, dreams, visions and imaginations resided in their ideal form (Lacan 1977). What is intriguing about the 'Real' is that it has resisted comprehension and symbolization and continues to exist as that which human beings aspire to comprehend. It resides beyond human knowledge and escapes human linguistic representation; as such any attempt to describe and define the 'Real' is destined to culminate in dead-ends.

But this 'Real' existed in opposition to what Lacan (1977) termed 'reality', which was the creation or result of certain historically and sociologically specific set of discursive practices and power mechanisms (Zizek 2001: 66). The 'Real' becomes that external boundary (that present which is absent) to borrow Ernesto Laclau's terminology, existing beyond human lived experiences. Zizek (2001: 166) sees the 'Real' as an 'illusion' which persistently exist against the pressure of reality. This Lacanian and Zizekian analysis of 'reality' and the 'Real' helps our in understanding of how human beings cope with realities during inhospitable, traumatic and uncertain moments in history through production of utopian registers such as nationalism, democracy, liberalism, human rights, socialism, capitalism, civil society and public sphere, etc., as they strive to narrow the gap between reality and the 'Real'. What human beings do tirelessly and ceaselessly is to try and know and capture the 'Real' through symbolization, representation, naming and other forms of political and social engineering (Stavrakakis 1999:74). This is part of how human beings fight to transcend the phenomenology of uncertainty. Jean Hillier had this to say:

> It is this 'play' which leads to the emergence of politics between different symbolic viewpoints of what the 'world' should look like and to the political institution of a new fantasy (decision/accepted view, etc.) in place of a dislocated one (Hillier 2003: 46).

The English philosopher John Gray (1994) argued that one of the key characteristics of human beings is their rejection of humanity's contingency. This they do through religious and philosophical mediations. The other common human characteristic is a belief of being a special species that are able to master its own destiny unlike cows, dogs and cats. According to Gray (2004: 4), human belief in progress is nothing but faith and superstition.

For Africans and non-Africans across the world, coping with phenomenology of uncertainty, has seen increasing deployment of utopian register of democracy which has assumed an umbrella meaning and form covering various human longings and demands articulated in languages of freedom, reform, equality, fraternity, good governance, ethical coexistence, material welfare, social justice, liberation, recognition of difference, good corporate management, emancipation, social peace, human security and even progressive nationalism.

Human rights, human dignity and people's entitlements were all implied in democracy. In post-Cold War Africa where the state in such places as Zimbabwe, Sudan, Liberia, Somalia, Chad, Northern Uganda, and the eastern part of the Democratic Republic of Congo (DRC) is failing to cater for its citizens' human security, material welfare and social peace, utopian registers of civil society and public sphere have come to provide hope for the weak and vulnerable, whereas the powerful but illegitimate and unwanted 'big men' continue to pursue politics of the warlord and violence (Reno 1999).

The vulnerable segments of the population, including the elderly, women, disabled and , were longing for the return of social civility, social peace and human security in those societies torn asunder by war and violence. But the African 'big men' comprising of people like Jonas Savimbi of Angola who fought a long war for power until his assassination in 2002, Robert Mugabe of Zimbabwe who has clung to power by all means for over thirty years; Charles Taylor of Liberia who led one of the most brutal campaigns that cost thousands of lives; and Joseph Kony of Uganda whose Lord's Resistance Army (LRA) is not godly at all, among many others; who control means and instruments of violence, continue to pursue power and wealth through employment of some of the most predatory, brutal and violent means that make life for ordinary citizens very uncertain. Outside Africa there were also numerous war mongers like the former president of the USA, George Bush, and the late Saddam Hussein of Iraq. Where the weak and the vulnerable talk of and aspire for democratic governance and human rights conscious societies, the powerful talk of nationalism and patriotism. This situation is currently obtaining in Zimbabwe where:

> Patriotic history asserts the centrality of Zimbabwe's radical revolutionary tradition and it is premised on four themes: land, race, a dichotomy between 'sell-outs' and 'patriots'; and the rejection of western interference based on what are perceived as 'Western ideals' such as human rights (Tendi 2010: 1).

In the midst of this uncertainty some thinkers like the veteran journalist John Pilger have become very critical of liberal democracy as a utopic register of liberation as well as of some of the ways the discourse of democracy has been deployed by the powerful states to exacerbate human uncertainty in places like Iraq and Afghanistan. According to him:

> 'Democracy' is now the free market--a concept bereft of freedom. 'Reform' is now the denial of reform. 'Economics' is the relegation of most human endeavour to material value, a bottom line. Alternative models that relate to the needs of the majority of humanity end up in the memory hole. And 'governance' – so fashionable these days, means an economic approval in Washington, Brussels and Davos. 'Foreign policy' is service to dominant power. Conquest is 'humanitarian intervention.' Invasion is 'nation-building' (Pilger 2008:1).

All these changing meanings and instrumental uses of the once celebrated concepts create uncertainties. These signs of global uncertainty were what provoked Zizek to write a book entitled *In Defense of Lost Causes* where he spoke directly to this apocalyptic imagery of the world (Zizek 2008). John L. Comaroff and Jean Comaroff described our current epoch as dominated by 'millennial capitalism' (Comaroffs 2000: 291-343), and Zizek posed the problem of phenomenology of uncertainty in this way:

> [...] Which Cause should speak? Things look bad for Great Causes of today, in a 'postmodern' era when, although the ideological scene is fragmented into a panoply of positions which struggle for hegemony, there is underlying consensus: the era of big explanations is over, we need 'weak thought,' opposed to all foundationalism, a thought attentive to the rhizomatic texture of reality; in politics too, we should no longer aim at all-explaining systems and global emancipatory projects; the violent imposition of grand solutions should leave room for forms of specific resistance and intervention (Zizek 2008: 1).

Zizek is a believer in socialist 'strong thought', 'large-scale explanations' and is confident about the possibilities of a better post-capitalist world. He does not believe that human emancipation is a lost cause and that universal values were outdated relics of an earlier age. But he is very critical of any emancipatory potential and humanistic pretentions of industrial capitalism as well as post-industrial capitalism. To Zizek (2009a), the time for capitalist-liberal and moralistic pretensions and rhetoric of salvation and emancipation is over.

In Zizekian thought two recent events, namely, the attacks of 9/11 on America and the global credit crunch of 2008/2009 pushed the last nail onto the coffin of capitalist-liberalism and delivered a double-death: 'as a political doctrine and as economic theory' (Zizek 2009a). Zizek's imagination of the future is driven by what he terms 'a Leap of Faith, faith in lost Causes' (Zizek 2008: 1-2). His key thesis is that 'true ideas are eternal, they are indestructible, they always return every time they are proclaimed dead' (Zizek 2008: 4). Zizek is also very critical of the present-day millennial capitalist strategy of trying to conceal its exploitative features through a process of 'culturalization' of politics. He fought against this tendency in the following words:

> Why are so many problems today perceived as problems of intolerance, rather than as problems of inequality, exploitation or injustice? Why is the proposed remedy tolerance, rather than emancipation, political struggle, even armed struggle? The immediate answer lies in the liberal multiculturalist's basic ideological operation: the 'culturalisation of politics.' Political differences—differences conditioned by political inequality or economic exploitation—are naturalised and neutralised into 'cultural' differences, that is into different 'ways of life' which are given, something that cannot be overcome. They can only be 'tolerated.' [...] the cause of this culturalisation is the retreat, the failure of direct political solutions such as the Welfare State or various socialist projects. Tolerance is their post-political ersatz (Zizek 2009b: 19).

Zizek is not alone in trying to explain the phenomenology of uncertainty marked by questioning of existing capitalist-informed ethics of human coexistence. The Comaroffs were equally concerned about rethinking the shifting 'provenance of the nation-state and its fetishes, the rise of new forms of enchantment, and explosion of neo-liberal discourses of civil society' (Comaroffs 2000: 293). They have engaged with what they term 'our present predicament'. They endeavoured to make sense of why the politics of consumerism, human rights, and entitlement were coinciding with new patterns of violence, exclusion, and why there was this puzzling and bizarre coupling of 'legalistic with the libertarian; constitutionality with deregulation; hyper rationalization with the exuberant spread of innovative occult practices and money magic, pyramid schemes and prosperity gospels; the enchantments, that is, of a decidedly neoliberal economy whose ever more inscrutable speculations seem to call up fresh spectres in their wake' (Comaroffs 2000: 292).

However, there is need to carefully sieve through what Western-oriented scholars were advocating as the solution to the uncertainty in Africa. Some reflection on Zizek's ideas will reveal some uncomfortable Eurocentrism offered as a solution to global problems. When read closely, the Lacanian Marxist thought is offering regressive ideologies as beacons of innovation and hope for global salvation. Maldonado-Torres (2003) has successfully analysed Zizek's thinking and has reveal what they really represent in the current age of global ideological crisis.

Zizek's agenda is to rescue Marxism through an appeal to orthodoxy, i.e., re-rooting communist hope in Western Christianity after the collapse the Soviet Union (Maldonado 2003). Zizek is providing the world with a materialist reading of Christianity as part of a worthy but lost cause of human emancipation. Maldonado-Torres (2003, 2004) is very critical of Zizek's open Eurocentrism where he defends Christianity and lambasts non-Western religions and spiritualities that also promise salvation to its adherents. Zizek, in his seemingly radical postulations has failed to 'hide the amount of epistemic racism' rooted in Enlightenment (Maldonado-Torres 2003). His radical criticism of Western modernity fails because it is part of attempting to save the same modernity. One can read Zizek's defence of Christianity and attempts to rescue Marxism which is part of ideologies of Eurocentrism in *The Fragile Absolute* (2000) and *Puppet and the Dwarf* (2003).

In the midst of this human uncertainty, where do African imaginations of freedom and liberation lie and which form and direction are they taking? To respond to this question there is further need to critically engage the utopcan registers of nationalism that continue to inspire dreams of homogenous entities called nation-states as well notions of sovereignty and public sphere and civil society as sites of imagination of particular forms of freedom enjoyed by citizens without the interference of the state and the 'big men'. The complexities of the situation which Africans found themselves in vis-a-vis colonial modernity and their conditioned response to it is well articulated by David Attwell. According to him:

> There is no escape clause from the encounter with modernity, unless one is to accept isolation or eccentricity. In practice, however, people facing this situation make a continual effort to translate modernity's promises into their own situations and histories, indeed to de-Europeanise them wherever possible (Attwell 2005: 4).

African nationalism still occupies a special place in African histories of freedom and deserves attention as a future-oriented ideology. But scholars like Mbembe (2002a, 2002b) and Appiah (1992) have criticized present-day Afro-radical nationalism as nothing but 'shibboleths of discredited geographies and histories' that served to ignite primordial pathologies, ancient hatreds, nativism and Afro-phobias including xenophobia. But some critics and rejectionists of the 'posts' (postcolonial, postmodernist and post-structuralist) such as Zeleza (2003: vi; 2006: 89-129) and Mkandawire (2005) view this assault on nationalism as 'fashionable nonsense'.

Zeleza and Mkandawire are still confident of the redemptive force of nationalism. Zeleza argues that those who dismiss nationalism do not make any attempt to:

> [...] distinguish the problematic and projects of nationalism, between the repressive nationalism of imperialism and the progressive nationalism of anticolonial resistance, between the nationalism that have led to control, conquest and genocide and those that have sought decolonisation and emancipation for oppressed nations and communities, between struggles for domination and struggles for liberation, between the reactionary, reformist, or revolutionary goals of different nationalisms (Zeleza 2003: vi).

Mkandawire (2005) reinforced Zeleza's argument by saying despite its internal inconsistencies and contestations, African nationalism still sought to achieve decolonization, nation-building (the making of African people as a collectivity in pursuit of a political end and making nation-as-state, i.e., the making of sovereign African states); ceaseless search for tolerant, stable, inclusive, legitimate and popular modes of rule (democratization); achievement of economic growth and improvement of material welfare of the people (economic and social development) as well as the construction and consolidation of political power (hegemony) (Calhoun 1997; Calhoun 2007).

But African nationalism remains as a problematic utopian register of liberation, freedom and democracy, particularly if one closely analyses its social base and understands its contingent and derivative character. Mamdani revealed the inherent weakness of African nationalism, when he said:

> I argue that the social base of nationalism was the native who had crossed the boundary between the rural which incorporated the subject ethnically and the urban that excluded the subject racially. Though beyond the lash of customary law, this native was denied access to civic rights on racial grounds. It is this native—Nkrumah's veranda boys, Cabral's boatmen, and Frelimo's cadres—who formed the social basis of nationalism. For a mass-based militant nationalism to be created, though, it was necessary for the boundary between the customary and the civic to be breached. Having crossed that boundary from the rural to the urban, it was once again necessary for cadres of militant nationalism to return to the countryside to link up with peasant struggles against Native Authorities. Nationalism was successful in gaining a mass base only where it succeeded in breaching the double divide that power tried to impose on society: the urban-rural, and the inter-ethnic (Mamdani 2000: 45).

Jean-Paul Sartre was referring to a similar problem of the social base of African nationalism when he said:

> The European elite undertook to manufacture native elite. They picked out promising adolescents; they branded them, as with red-hot iron, with the principles of Western culture; they stuffed their mouth full with high-sounding phrases, grand gluttonous words that stuck to teeth. After a short stay in the mother country they were sent home whitewashed. These walking lies had nothing left to say to their brother (Sartre in Fanon 1967: 7).

This was true of such founding fathers of African nation-states as Jomo Kenyatta of Kenya, Leopold Sedar Senghor of Senegal, Kwame Nkrumah of Ghana, and Kamuzu Banda of Malawi. Zeleza (2002) noted that these educated Africans dreamt in both African and European languages. They suffered from a terrible crisis: they had been taught to hate Africa that produced them and to like Europe that rejected them.

It is these 'walking lies' that became leading nationalists and founding fathers of African nation-states. No wonder that African nationalism became constrained in its ability to deliver and reproduce African colonial subjects as autonomous citizens from the beginning. Such important task of nationalism as achieving national self-determination for the former colonies, remaking colonies into sovereign nation-states, initiating economic development beneficial to former colonized Africans, and installation of democracy, human dignity and human rights that were denied under colonialism became vaguely articulated through and through (Mamdani 1996; Zeleza 2003).

What is beyond doubt is that African nationalism had a redemptive mission and progressive trajectory albeit a very complicated, compromised, half-baked and problematic one. Nationalism, however, cannot be totally dismissed as nothing but 'shibboleths of discredited geographies and histories' and a purveyor of 'primordial pathologies' (Zeleza 2003). The fact that its redemptive and liberatory aspects remained submerged within the complex colonial matrices of power and that it has not fully succeeded in bringing about full decolonization of Africa does not justify wholesale repudiation and total dismissal. As Moyo and Yeros (2007) have argued, African nationalism still retains some revolutionary and progressive attributes despite its usual often fall into crises of authoritarianism and violence. Moyo and Yeros provide the detailed case study of Zimbabwean nationalism that was able to deliver land to the landless people within a restrictive post-Cold War neo-liberal environment. Moyo and Yeros proceed to credit Zimbabwe for standing courageously and single-handedly for the African cause:

> Zimbabwe effectively defaulted on foreign debt and has imposed heavy controls on its capital account and banks; Zimbabwe has been a leading player in the global alliances that stalled WTO negotiations in Seattle, spoke truth to power at Doha, and rejected opportunistic reform of the United Nations; and Zimbabwe has single-handedly undermined NEPAD and repeatedly confronted South African sub-imperialism and US imperialism, including in the Democratic Republic of Congo (DRC), at great cost to itself (Moyo and Yeros 2007b: 178).

But it is that 'great cost to itself' that made some scholars doubt the revolutionary and redemptive power of nationalist inspired state activism as a salvation for Africa (Ndlovu-Gatsheni and Muzondidya 2011). Unless African nationalism managed to completely rise above the core contradictions bequeathed it by colonialism, which includes repressive, authoritarian and intolerant tendencies, it will continue to be repudiated by some of its former supporters and formulators. The current state of African nationalism is that however hard it tris to dissociate its ideologies and practices from colonial epistemology, 'The authoritarianism of the colonial era [continues to] reproduce itself within the nationalist movements' (Mair and Sithole 2002: 23). Even the current African public sphere depicts its interpellation by the colonial public sphere which existed as a sacred site reserved for colonial white settler bourgeois group that drove colonial public discourse and 'thought' and 'spoke' on behalf of disenfranchized and subalternized African colonial 'subjects' in very paternalistic and condescending terms. This time the paternalist and maternalistic colonial role is being played by the local and international NGOs together with international funding bodies like the Westminster Foundation, DFID and others.

One of the main realities of African life under colonialism was thorough and systematic de-oracization of Africans. Austin Bukenya defined 'productive oracy' as entailing 'self-definition, self-assertion, negotiation of relationships, claiming of rights, and indictment of their violation' (Bukenya 2001: 32; Zirimu & Bukenya 1977). De-oracization of Africans was a logical part of colonialism's denial of Africans access to the colonial public sphere that was protected by strong halls of race and racialized conceptions of citizenship (Ndlovu-Gatsheni 2001: 53-83; Ndlovu-Gatsheni 2006: 1-18). Since colonial conquest, definition of African destiny fell into the hands of colonial masters and the public discourse was shaped and determined by colonial imperatives rather than African concerns and interests.

Inevitably, African nationalism fought partly for Africans to gain access into the racially fenced-in colonial public sphere to benefit from imagination and creation of new social sites and spaces within which Africans as citizens could get together to freely deliberate on matters of common concern and to take control of their destiny. But once direct colonialism was rolled back, the postcolonial African state continuously manifested a terrible proclivity towards destroying the emerging vibrant public sphere that Africans fought for. The African ruling elite, just like the white colonial rulers, have often demonstrated a consistent desire to close the emerging public sphere rather than to widen it and support its flourishing.

Does this character of the postcolonial state have anything to do with its complicated social base? Of course the postcolonial state is deeply interpellated by the authoritarian character of its predecessor—the colonial state. Kuan-Hsing Chen argued that 'the contemporary moment of the (ex-) colonies is still one of a process of decolonization, and in at least three connected but convolute forms: nationalism, nativism, and civilizationalism' (Chen 1998:1). Africans are captive to the invisible snares of the colonial matrix of power that continue to constrain possibilities of democracy and economic development.

The public sphere in Africa continues to exhibit the indelible imprint of colonialism and deep traces of western values that are now re-packaged as global values. The public sphere is infused with intellectual formulations coming from the (ex-) imperial centres rather than African values, concerns and interests. It is within this context that Africans fall back on nativism as they continue to resist the forcible confinement of their history, values and identities to the barbarian margins of the world (Ndlovu-Gatsheni, 2008, 2009).

What ends up being depicted as nativism begins as redemptive nationalism focused on enabling Africans to try and take control of the public sphere so as to publicly articulate their common concerns. Nativism also begins as a form of reverse discourse and an attempt to challenge Western hegemony. The key challenge remains how to articulate African problems in an authentic African voice without falling into nativism. How to talk and think about democracy without mimicking Western liberal democracy. How to talk about African public sphere without repeating the notions of the public sphere articulated and drawn by Jurgen Habermas.

Habermas defined public sphere as a 'sphere where private people come together as public and discuss matters of common concern' and this site is 'governed neither by the intimacy of the family, the authority of the state, nor the exchange of the market, but by the 'public reason of private citizens' (Habermas 1989: 27). Habermas understood the importance of this sphere in the context of the classical liberal emancipatory transition from feudalism to capitalism in Europe together with the concomitant emergence of the bourgeois as a revolutionary class critical of monarchical rule based on heredity and religion.

In broad terms, Habermas was concerned with the early development of liberal democracy that was linked to the rise of bourgeois class in Europe and the discourses of enlightenment that underpinned modernity (Peters 1993: 542). But Africa which experienced the darker side of modernity that even prevented the formation and emergence of a black bourgeois class cannot follow the same path that Habermas is mapping as its public sphere.

A coalescence of 'negatives' of modernity culminated in the birth of what Mahmood Mamdani described as bifurcated colonial states that segregated its population along racial lines into 'citizens' and 'subjects' (Mamdani 1996). This colonial set-up of the state had far- reaching consequences not only for the nature of African response to colonialism but also on the development and reconfiguration of the African public sphere and the overall structure of postcolonial political communities. Craig Calhoun defined the public sphere as 'an arena simultaneously of solidarity and choice' and 'a crucial site for the production and transformation of politically salient identities and solidarities—including the basic category and practical manifestation of 'the people' that is essential to democracy' (Calhoun 2002: 165).

Key debates on the public sphere were characterized and influenced by the post-modernist liberal thought whose starting point of narration of the African story is Western modernity and its emancipatory agenda that uncritically accepted neoliberal democracy as a global movement 'into which African experiments are expected to fit' without a contest (Osaghae 2005: 1). The key problem in this discourse, as noted by Calhoun, is not only that of overemphasizing 'thin identities' as adequate underpinnings for democracy but also that of blind acceptance of 'economistic, modernising imaginaries without giving adequate attention to the formation of solidarity and the conditions that enable collective choices about the nature of society' (Calhoun 2002: 148). This post-modernist neoliberal paradigm is sweeping if not fundamentalist in what it claims and annihilatory in what it rejects, which includes Afro-radicalism that contests global colonial hegemony.

This paradigm is being contested by decolonial-liberationist approach whose starting point of narration of the African story is contestation of coloniality in its various disguises. This decolonial-liberationist paradigm is still struggling to set itself free from politics of neurosis of victimhood to enable Africans to re-launch themselves on a radical struggle to create a post-imperial and postcolonial future that the post-1945 decolonization project failed to achieve. The African desire to transcend the 'colonial-straitjacket' enveloping the African continent has seen scholars like Ekpo (2010), calling for what he terms 'post-Africanism' in the face of the poverty of such philosophies of liberation as Negritude. Ekpo motivated for post-Africanism in these words:

> One such candidate for a redemptive post-Negritude renewal of Africa's modernity is what has come to be known as Post-Africanism. [Post-Africanism] is a post-ideological umbrella for a diversity of intellectual strategies seeking to inscribe newer, more creative moves beyond the age-old fixations, obsessions and petrifactions of thinking that had crystallised in and around the racial-cultural worries not only of Negritude generation but also the so-called postcolonial zeitgeist. The idea came from the painful realisation that the cultural-nationalist ethos, reflexes and vocabulary that came to structure African philosophical, political and development thinking had not only dragged Africa and the African mindset into crippling Afrocentric trap, but also muddled most of Africa's modernisation projects. Post-Africanism was proposed as an attempt first to deconstruct the disaster-prone emotionalism, hubris and paranoias indwelling to most ideologies of Africanism whether in art, politics or development discourse and, second, to seek newer, fresher conditions for a more performative African intellectual engagement with Africa, modernity and the West (Ekpo 2010:181-182).

Finding itself antagonizing under the heavy weight of triumphant neo-liberalism and globalization, the decolonial-liberationist perspective continued to try and confront neocolonialism and proposed strategies of decolonizing the mind of the colonized through laying bare the hidden structures of imperial domination. This has taken the form of political economy approaches some of whose advocates even deny the importance of such discourses as human rights and democracy. The case in point is Issa G. Shivji who had this to say about the human rights discourse:

> Human rights discourse has succeeded in marginalising concrete analysis of our society. Human rights ideology is the ideology of the status quo, not change. Documentation of human rights abuses, although important, in its own right, by itself does not help us in understanding the social and political relations in our society. It is not surprising that given the absence of a political economy context and theoretical framework, much of our writings on human rights, rule of law, constitution etc., uncritically reiterates or assume neo-liberal precepts. Human rights is not a theoretical tool of understanding social and political relations. At best [it] can be only a means of exposing a form of oppression and, therefore, perhaps, an ideology of resistance (Shivji 2003: 115).

Ekpo is not opposed to those like Shivji who are still committed to the struggle against colonial modernity. Instead, he encouraged what he calls 'postcolonial subjects' to concentrate in learning, copying and even stealing 'the ruses and skills of imperialist domination for the purpose of hastening economic growth and socio-political modernization in the postcolonies' (Ekpo 2010: 182). But he seems to minimize if not ignore the power of the colonial matrix of power discussed in this book that does not allow for authentic, bold, free, liberated, empowered and confident 'postcolonial subjects' to emerge. On the other hand, Shivji is also not totally opposed to discourses of human rights and democracy. He has consistently argued in support of new liberatory struggles that creatively combine material, national, democratic and social justice questions into a single new democratic consensus that is simultaneously ranged against global colonial hegemony and local/domestic authoritarianism and oppression (Shivji 2000; Shivji 2003; Mafeje 1995). For Ekpo though:

> Post-Africanism's second African Enlightenment concerns a massive disburdening of mind and vision, so that Africa can embark again on its journey of modernisation, this time deliberately travelling light (Ekpo 2010: 183).

What is difficult is that the immanent logic of colonialism is still a reality that cannot be simply wished away easily. African liberation discourse is deeply shaped by colonialism that is well analysed by such scholars as

Mannoni (1950); Fanon (1952:1963); Memmi (1957); Mamdani (1996) and Mbembe (2001). These scholars have revealed how psychology and praxis of colonization had devastating impact on the evolution of African political consciousness including imaginations of liberation.

Kuan-Hsing Chen has concluded that 'colonialism is not yet a legacy, as mainstream postcolonial studies would have it, but still a lively operator in any geocolonial site' (Chen 1998: 34). Besides interpellation of its nemesis (which is African nationalism), colonialism also influenced the nature of the African public sphere in many ways as it shaped and constrained African imagination of liberation and ways of knowing. The hated nativism emerged from this milieu of the psychology of colonialism as a reverse-discourse seeking to subvert and undermine colonial ideologies through mobilization of decentred African identity and culture. Writing on the utopian register of liberation, Benita Parry said:

> When we consider the narrative of decolonisation, we encounter rhetorics in which 'nativism' in one form or another is evident. Instead of disciplining these, theoretical whip in hand, as a catalogue of epistemological errors, of essentialist mystifications, as a masculinist appropriation of dissent, as more than an anti-racist racism etc., I want to consider what is to be gained by an unsententious interrogation of such articulations which, if often driven by negative passion, cannot be reduced to mere inveighing against iniquities or repetition of the canonical terms of imperialism's work (Parry 2004: 40).

The development of African political ideologies and imaginations of freedom have been consistently constrained and shaped into particular directions by the hidden mechanics of the hegemonic modern/colonial capitalist/ patriarchal world system. The crisis of African liberation discourse has partly to do with what Quijano termed repression of alternative modes of knowing, of producing knowledge and of producing perspectives—a consequence of colonization of the imagination of the dominated (Quijano 2007: 168-178).

This reality also explains the existence of a very complex public sphere that is highly contested and dominated by overlapping civic, deviant, primordial and indigenous public associations made up of a bizarre assortment of labour, professional, intellectual, student, farmers, women, and ethnic groups, articulating overlapping forms of politics, including those inspired by nativism (Ekeh 1992: 83-104; Ekeh 1975: 91-112; Osaghae 2006: 233-245). As Eghosa Osaghae argued, the ambiguities and contradictions reflected in the African public sphere are in turn reflective of the deeper fractured social foundations of African politics marked by serious disjuncture between state and society giving birth to equally fractured and highly contested citizenship prone to retribalization (Osaghae 2006: 233-245).

It is against this background that African experience and imagination of freedom is subject to two meta-narratives with one of them informed by Western epistemology and the other by resistance to coloniality. It is important to briefly explore the key tenets of the postmodern neo-liberal and decolonization-liberation paradigms as two sides of the same coin. The African national project that encompasses strategies of achieving nation-building, state-consolidation, economic development and poverty reduction, and introduction of popular forms of governance, is hostage to these two ways of making sense of the African world in particular and the human globe in general.

Epistemologies of freedom

Walter D. Mignolo emphasized that ways of analysis and speaking are always influenced by analysts' particular location in the power structures and that ways of knowing and perceiving the world were always situated (Mignolo 2000). For Africa, two dominant epistemic loci of enunciation of histories, discourses and developments are easily discernable though they were not mutually exclusive.

The first is that which sought to tell the story of Africa from the perspective of Western modernity and the interpretation of African history in analogous fashion. The second is that which begins the story of Africa from the perspective of coloniality and is linked to subaltern epistemic perspectives that are critical of Western philosophy's claims to a single version of truthful universal knowledge (Mignolo 2000: 721-748). The first is broadly a narrative of the story of modernist emancipatory project whose starting point is Enlightenment discourses that were opposed to feudal monarchs with their hereditary notions of power, the conservative churches with their privileging of beliefs over knowledge and superstition based on blind religiosity underpinned fear and ignorance.

The postmodern neo-liberal discourse is permeated through and through by bourgeois Enlightenment intellectual thought, intellectual arrogance including celebration of violent conquest of Africa in such colonial euphemisms as 'pacification', 'civilizing mission', 'white man's burden' and 'modernization' (Crong 1984; Rostow 1960; Roper 1965; Ndlovu-Gatsheni 2001; Ndlovu-Gatsheni 2006). This paradigm has assumed universalism and pretends not only to be universalistic but also to be a neutral and objective point of view.

While the second paradigm tells the complex and unfinished story of liberation from colonialism, neocolonialism, neo-liberal imperialism and hegemonic globalization, the first tells the human story from the perspective of Western modernity which 'lays claim to the homogeneity of the planet from above—economically, politically and culturally' (Mignolo 2000: 721). It is backed up by what Wallerstein (1991: 1) termed the 'nineteenth century social science paradigms' that were consumed holus bolus in the African academy and have terribly constrained the development of autonomous and original African intellectual thinking and imagination of the world. Wallerstein noted that:

> It is quite normal for scholars and scientists to rethink issues. When important new evidence undermines old theories and predictions do not hold, we are pressed to rethink our premises. In that sense, much of nineteenth-century social science, in the form of specific hypotheses, is constantly being rethought. But, in addition to rethinking, which is 'normal,' I believe we need to 'unthink' nineteenth-century social science, because many of its presumptions—which, in my view, are misleading and constrictive—still have far too strong a hold on our mentalities. These presumptions, once considered liberating of the spirit, serve today as the central intellectual barrier to useful analysis of the social world (Wallerstein 1991: 1).

African intellectual and liberation initiatives have found it very difficult to 'unthink' the epistemologies created by enlightenment intellectuals and to 'reproduce itself outside these relations' (Quijano 2007: 169). The end product has been 'scholarship by analogy' that has pervaded some of the influential intellectual works in and on Africa (Mamdani 1996; Zeleza 1997). Osaghae defined the neo-liberal narrative of the African experience as taking a globalist and comparative format in which it evaluated the African world on the basis of the extent to which African states have conformed with the precepts of liberalism, including liberal democracy, as determined by the post-Cold War global hegemonies. Within this discourse capitalism and liberalism were projected as trajectories that all societies have to pass through (Osaghae 2005: 14).

Osaghae contrasted this trajectory with the decolonial-liberationist narrative of the African experience that is more discerning and more sympathetic of the peculiar challenges facing the state in Africa. Within this discourse, democratization and development were approached as instruments of liberation from political domination and economic underdevelopment. Even the accent on human rights was understood and seen not as a matter of democratic finesse, but as a weapon of weak and oppressed groups struggling for liberation and empowerment (Osaghae 2005: 14-15).

But this decolonial-liberationist approach was under the constant policing eye of the postmodernist neo-liberal approach. If it was not dismissed outrighly, it was disciplined. If it was not disciplined, its agenda was stolen, diluted and destroyed. But it has refused easy burial. Its resurrections have taken various forms such as insurrectionist nationalism, Afro-radicalism, cultural nationalism and nativism. All these resurrections were taking place within a terrain in which neoliberal dispensation had assumed hegemonic proportions. This neoliberal paradigm has since the end of the Cold War attained global outreach and continued to evaluate African experiences, successes and achievements in terms of how far they have 'conformed with the precepts of liberalism, including liberal democracy, as determined by the post-Cold War global hegemonists' (Osaghae 2005: 14).

Neoliberal evaluative criteria of African progress was informed by the extent to which market reforms have been embraced; the extent to which African political systems have been opened up to pluralist and multi-party politics; the extent to which good governance, measured by constitutionalism, civil control of the military, popular participation, respect for human rights and rule of law, as well as transparency and accountability, has been entrenched; and the extent to which free and fair elections as well as orderly change of government were possible (Osaghae 2005: 14). What must be made clear is that the decolonization-liberatory approach is not opposed to democracy; rather it is consistently trying to appropriate democracy and human rights tenets as weapons of the oppressed and the weak in its endeavour to push forward the frontiers of decolonization into new horizons of economic empowerment, social justice and autonomous control of African destiny.

However, the postcolonial state has continued to serve the interests of global capital rather than the interest of the people of Africa because of the snares of the colonial matrices of power. The African state is yet to serve the interests of the popular masses rather than global capitalism (Nyong'o 1987:25). This is no easy task to achieve because of the disciplining power of global capital and the policing eye of powerful multilateral institutions such as the World Bank, the International Monetary Fund and the World Trade Organization all informed by the interests of the rich nations of the North.

One of the difficult questions that continue to pulsate within the decolonization-liberatory narratives is how to restructure the postcolonial African state in line with the popular African demands? Ake (2000: 167) provides two options for the transformation of the African state:

> One direction is for the state to become a community that is embedded in a mo-
> dern republic. This will require among other things a highly accelerated capitalist
> development, which does not appear to be on the cards for much of Africa. This
> will entail the breakdown of African countries into something like ethnic polities,
> a process which could be extremely violent and traumatic. One possible compro-
> mise could be a confederal, federal or consocietal arrangement. But there are no
> easy solutions to this formidable problem, which is hardly recognised much less
> addressed (Ake 2000: 167).

Ake argued that a transformation of the state only is not enough. It needs
to go hand-in-glove with societal transformation to rectify the situation
of bifurcation of society into 'the country of the elite, usually less than 10
percent of the population' that is 'organically linked and oriented to the
highly industrialized societies' on the one hand, and the country of the
poor symbolized by the rural dweller engrossed in mere survival (Ake 2000:
167-168). He suggests that postcolonial Africa must adopt 'structural
democratization' as opposed to 'processional' democratization. Structural
democracy involves restructuring of the state and transformation of the
society simultaneously (Ake 2000: 186).

But those scholars wedded into the postmodern neoliberal thinking,
see the salvation of Africa as lying with the civil society as the fertile terrain
embodying the popular interests of the people. What is often not opened to
critical analysis is the question of representation and the values driving civil
society in Africa. Osaghae (2005) is very critical of the legitimacy of civil
society as the embodiment of popular mass interests. To him civil society was a
middle-class/elite project that did not approximate the broad range of popular
forces. Second, the emergent civil society (as opposed to embedded one) was
largely a creation of global capitalism that has continued to finance it in its
concubinage with non-governmental organizations (NGOs). Third, NGOs
were nothing but important agents of globalization and Western hegemony
in Africa. Finally, 'civil society today does not have the national appeal and
conviction that distinguished the anti-colonial alliances of the old' (Osaghae
2005: 17). As such, civil society is not a legitimate embodiment of popular
forces capable of delivering a people-sensitive state in postcolonial Africa.

Osaghae's critique of the civil society agrees with that of Moyo and Yeros
(2007: 177) who deployed a class analysis and exposed the following weaknesses
if not dangers of Zimbabwean civil society. Its membership is largely urban in
a largely agrarian country; its leadership is largely middle-class professionals;
its autonomy is heavily mortgaged and dependent on donors and its ideology
is petty-bourgeois, bourgeois and even neocolonial (Moyo and Yeros 2007:

177-178). In the face of all these intellectual and political contestations over the state and civil society, where does African redemption lie? This is a difficult question to answer

Murky present and the mysterious future

Peter Ekeh's 1975 seminal article on 'colonialism and the two publics' became the first serious academic engagement with the issue of African public sphere, defining it as differentiated into primordial and the civic public. Ekeh located the bifurcated character of African public sphere at the centre of colonial modernity:

> If we are to capture the spirit of African politics we must seek what is unique in them. I am persuaded that the colonial experience provides that uniqueness. Our post-colonial present has been fashioned by our colonial past. It is that colonial past that has defined for us the spheres of morality that have come to dominate our politics (Ekeh 1975: 111).

In 1992, Ekeh expanded his 'two publics' thesis as he engaged with the character of civil society in postcolonial Africa. He identified four-fold core types of civil society organizations, namely: *civic public organizations* (labour, professional and student associations, mass media); *deviant civic organizations* (secret societies, fundamentalist religious movements); *primordial public associations* (ethnic and communal associations); and *indigenous development associations* (farmers' and traditional women's associations) (Ekeh 1992: 187-212).

What is clear from Ekeh's four-fold categorization of civics was that it reflected unique historical foundation of African experiences particularly the experiences as shaped by colonialism and nationalism. It revealed how African civics were mediated by professional, religious, ethnic, indigeneity, and gender imperatives fashioned by colonial modernity.

Mamdani seems to reinforce Ekeh's basic argument about how the legacy of colonialism bequeathed a particular kind of civil society on postcolonial societies. He analysed the exclusionary character of colonial civil society founded on racial hierarchy of natives and settlers. In this colonial set-up, the excluded natives remained squashed into primordial sphere marked by rigidified and compartmentalized ethnic categorizations.

African nationalism and the anti-colonial struggles were therefore partly aimed at de-racialization and Africanization of existing white-dominated civil society as well as opening of sites for public deliberation by Africans beyond the policing eye of the colonial state. Mamdani (1996: 21) was correct in arguing that at the end of colonialism, the initiatives to de-racialize civil society happened simultaneously with its increasing tribalization. This was inevitable for a people emerging from a bifurcated colonial discursive set-up where race and ethnicity were the key vectors in the social organization colonial population.

At the end of colonial rule, civil society developed a complex relationship with the postcolonial state as the state became the most ubiquitous phenomenon regulating people's lives. Consequently, to the triumphant postcolonial nationalists in charge of the state the objectives of new struggles that were located in the civil society were not understandable. Was it to substitute the state or just to make it more open to pluralism and diversity? To African nationalist leaders, particularly those who participated in protracted armed liberation struggles in countries like Mozambique, Angola, Namibia, South Africa, Algeria, Guinea-Bissau and Zimbabwe, the decolonization project resulted in the emergence of African states serving the interests of the ex-colonized peoples. They consistently pushed forward the idea of a 'people's state' that needed to be supported by everyone rather than opposed as it carried forward the historical mission of economic liberation.

Within this thinking that was often informed by Marxist-Leninist-Maoist avant-garde notions of the state and party, there was no room for civil society and public sphere existing separate from the state. But to those scholars informed by liberal notions of organization of political and social life like Michael Walzer (1991: 293-304), civil society was important as it was constituted by associational networks within which civility was constructed that enabled democratic politics to take place.

In liberal thinking, civil society existed mainly to make the state more accountable in its governance practices. But, to the nationalist elite running the postcolonial state, they needed no other form of association than their political parties to make them accountable as they brought both democracy and freedom to the ex-colonized peoples. To them, the postcolonial state was inherently pro-people as it was fought for and knew what the people wanted. Guarding the postcolonial state's sovereignty became the most prized value. Zimbabwe provides us with a typical example of a 'nationalist state' that does not tolerate existence of civil society and public sphere unmonitored by the state and the ruling party. President Mugabe does not mince words on who brought democracy to Zimbabwe:

> We, not the British, established democracy based on one person one vote, democracy which rejected racial or gender discrimination and upheld human rights and religious freedom... In short, the advent of an independent Zimbabwe restored dignity to our people (*The Herald*, 19 April 2008).

In this context where the state and its leadership proclaim a high moral ground, civil society was often branded as a threat to state sovereignty and civil society organizations that deal with issues of democracy and human rights were delegitimized as fronts for external enemies of the state (Tendi 2010). Civil society is not free from complex workings and dynamics of power pitting advocates of nationalism against those for democratization on the one hand, and on the other, the South-North power division. The question of power is well treated by radical scholars like Rita Abrahamsen (2000) who identified how power imbalances between the rich North and the poor South tainted discourses of democracy, development and good governance as mere pillars of global governmentality, open to use as justifications to discipline deviant states of the South.

The challenging question in African studies in general is what exits for ordinary people who do not benefit from juridical freedom and who are at the receiving end of postcolonial states that have metamorphosed into 'privatized', 'patrimonial', 'rentier', 'kleptocratic', and 'gate-keeper' states? (Chabal and Daloz 1999; Cooper 2002; Nugent 2004) Are notions of civil society and public sphere as those empty signifiers and utopian registers that were conjured up and deployed by ordinary citizens to envision a life beyond the statist spheres where there is no human care the solution?

Grappling with the global meaning of civil society, the Comaroffs (2000: 330) argued that the notion emerged as a 'Big Idea of the Millennial Moment' and 'as an all-purpose panacea for postmodern, post-political, post-native, even 'post-human' condition.' They further argued that civil society 'is known primarily by its absence, its elusiveness, its incompleteness, from the traces left by struggles conducted in its name' (Comaroffs 2000: 330). Indeed, when subjected to closer analysis, the notions of civil society and public sphere were better understood as utopian registers capturing human aspirations for popular freedom unencumbered by state's interferences.

The notion of civil society and public sphere are today serving as the remarkable potent battle cry across the world for freedom. At the centre of these imaginations and aspirations are utopian registers of democracy, moral community, justice, and populism politics that were mobilized and deployed to breathe life back into societies of uncertainty that have been 'declared dead almost twenty years ago by the powerful magi of the Second Coming' (Comaroffs 2000: 331).

John Ralston Saul in his book *The Collapse of Globalism and the Reinvention of the World* (2009:15) wrote about the crisis of globalism whose core beliefs were that the power of the nation-state was waning; states as we knew them were dying; in the future, power would lie with global markets; economics rather than armies and politics, would shape human events; global markets freed of narrow national interests would establish international economic balances; and that there would be a 'shrivelling-away of irresponsible nationalism, racism and political violence'. At the global level, it is these values of globalism and others that fell into crisis and were increasingly questioned at the beginning of the new millennium.

Across the world, it is clear that human beings do not tire of trying to make sense of their murky present with a view to prescribing the mysterious future if the current beliefs proved inadequate. Nationalism continues to pre-occupy human minds particularly those still confident about the future of the nation-state, territoriality and sovereignty within a fast globalizing world. The nation-state has not withered away as globalists predicted. Alongside nationalism is civil society and public sphere that exist as empty signifiers with a potential to fire human imagination into another life of civility, sociality and peace within and beyond the precincts of the postcolonial state that has tended to use its juridical freedom to deny popular democracy within its boundaries.

The bigger struggle today is that of trying to revive revolutionary and liberatory politics and to originate a new language that resonated with the present generation and capture the future so as to restore lost human certainty. All this is taking place at a time dominated by what the radical thinker Chantal Mouffe described as the 'democratic paradox' characterized by the intermingling of popular democratic aspirations with questions and struggles of definition of the people as well as re-constitution of human identities (Mouffe 2000: 56).

What the notion of 'democratic paradox' reveals are the inherent limitations of neo-liberal democracy as an utopian register capable of firing human imagination beyond the current dead-ends. African nationalism has metamorphosed into such phobias as nativism and xenophobia that devoured those Africans deemed to be the toxic other, to use a Zizekian terminology. Such other utopian registers as civil society and the treasured notions of public sphere where rational thinking is said to reign, remain part of 'aspirational politics' emerging within the context of phenomenology of uncertainty.

The current global and local challenges are very complex and some scholars like Samuel Huntington had turned xenophobic as revealed in his book *Who are We? The Challenge to America's National Identity* (2004) where he identified those people he considered non-Americans, particularly the growing Hispanic presence in the US, as constituting a threat to American national identity. Such publications indicated ideological confusion of the first order where culturalism was turned into a tool of analysis to the extent of singling out multiple languages and cultures as constituting cultural terrorism. It is paradoxical that a country like America which is basically a nation of immigrants and settlers can turn around and worry about immigration and multiculturalism in the 21st century. We are back to the medieval fear of barbarians at the gate! This argument is reinforced by Francoise Verges who argued that:

> Xenophobia is back in Europe. The foreigner is once again the target of attacks, the explanation for everything that goes wrong: loss of jobs, insecurity, criminality. He embodies the fear of being overwhelmed in one's own country, of losing 'national' values, 'national' identity, of no longer feeling 'at home' (Verges 2011).

Conclusion: Is another world therefore possible?

Western humanism informed by coloniality is in crisis. The people from the South have continuously contested Western domination. The credit crunch has indicated serious cracks within the seemingly strong edifice of capitalism. Western hegemony that was hidden under notions of 'Whiteman's Burden,' civilizing mission, developmentalism and liberal democracy has been unmasked and declared as coloniality that is supposed to die for a new humanism to be born. John Ralston Saul (2009: 281) concluded that:

> The economic collapse of 2008 represents the failure of Globalism. It is a mistake to treat this crisis as something provoked by a financial crisis. A burst boil is a symptom, not a cause: lance it fast and move on in search of the real problems.

He went further to emphasize that:

> Everyone can now see that the Globalist approaches of the last three decades were old fashioned. And most of us can see how the ground has shifted. The key to dealing with this crisis is not to rebuild the old structures based on the old assumptions. We have an opportunity to build a more sophisticated sort of wealth based upon a balancing of social, environmental and market needs. This could easily be the project of a century (Saul 2009: 296).

But from the African side, it is clear that another world cannot be possible as long as the continent and its people are not fully decolonized and the snares of the postcolonial neocolonized world are not broken. This will require an epistemic rebellion that enables the formerly colonized people to gain self-confidence, enabling them to re-imagine another world free from Western tutelage and African dictators that enjoy Western protection. A new imagination that liberates both the colonizer and the colonized simultaneously is needed. This will mean levelling of the racial hierarchies created by colonial modernity as well as fundamentalism created by various nationalisms. Perspectives from the South must be given more space as they promise another world free from Western hegemonic thought that was constructed on oppressive and exploitative values of slavery, imperialism and colonialism.

The recent revolutionary and popular events that began in Tunisia forcing dictator Zine El Abidine Ben Ali to flee the country on 14 January 2011 and which spread to Egypt forcing Hosni Mubarak to step down from power after thirty years as president raises some hope about the power of the ordinary people to shape their destiny through freeing themselves from autocracies (Arieff 2011: 1-23). The Maghreb region had survived the democratic changes of the 1990s with autocratic governments maintaining their grip on power. But what began in Tunisia is shaking not only the Maghreb region but also the Middle East and the rest of Africa. The popular uprisings that have sent fears down the spines of dictatorial leaders across the world provides some hope that ordinary people are still prepared to claim and shape the destinies of their nations. But let me end this book with the searching questions of Santos (2007: 49) as an indication of the future research and direction of intellectual in the Global South:

> How can we identify the perspective of the oppressed in real-world interventions or in any resistance to them? How can we translate this perspective into knowledge practices? In search for alternatives to domination and oppression, how can we distinguish between alternatives to the system of oppression and domination and alternatives within the system or, more specifically, how do we distinguish between alternatives to capitalism and alternatives within capitalism? In sum, how can we fight against abyssal lines using conceptual and political instruments that don't reproduce them? And finally, a question of special interest to educators: what would be the impact of a post-abyssal conception of knowledge (as an ecology of knowledges) upon our educational institutions and research centres?

The struggle must continue. Aluta continua—this time taking the form of a committed epistemological resistance against epistemic violence that had prevented alternative imaginations of the world and freedom from the knowledges and cosmologies of the Global South!

Bibliography

Adejumobi, S. and Olukoshi, A., 2008, 'Introduction: Transition, Continuity, and Change', in S. Adejumobi and A. Olukoshi, eds, *The African Union and New Strategies for Development in Africa*, New York: Cambria Press: 3-19.

Adibe, J., 2009, 'Introduction: Africa without Africans', in J. Adibe, ed., *Who is an African? Identity, Citizenship and the Making of the Africa-Nation*, London: Adonis & Abbey Publishers Ltd: 16-25.

African Union Commission, 2004, 2004 to 2007 *Strategic Framework of the African Union Commission*, (2 May).

Agbese, P. O. and Kieh, G. K, jr., eds, 2007, *Reconstituting the State in Africa*, New York: Palgrave Macmillan.

Ahluwalia, P., 2001, *Politics and Post-Colonial Theory: African Inflections*, London & New York: Routledge.

Ahluwalia, P., 2003, 'The Struggle for African Identity: Thabo Mbeki's African Renaissance', in A. Zegeye and R. L. Harris, eds, Media, *Identity and the Public Sphere in Post-Apartheid South Africa*, Leiden and Boston: Brill: 27-39.

Ahmad, Aijaz , 1992, *In Theory: Classes, Nations, Literatures*, London: Verso.

Ake, C., 1993, 'Academic Freedom and Material Base', in M. Diouf and M. Mamdani, eds, *Academic Freedom in Africa*, Dakar: CODESRIA: 17-25.

Ake, C. 1994, *Democratization of Disempowerment in Africa*, Lagos: Malthouse.

Ake, C., 2000, *The Feasibility of Democracy in Africa*,Dakar: CODESRIA.

Ake, C., 1979, *Social Science as Imperialism: The Theory of Political Development*, Ibadan: Ibadan University Press.

Alexander, J., 2006, *The Unsettled Land: State-Making and the Politics of Land in Zimbabwe*, 1893– 2003, London: James Currey.

Amin, S., 2009, *Eurocentrism: Second Edition*, New York: Monthly Review Press.

Amin, S., 2006, *Beyond US Hegemony?: Assessing the Prospects for a Multipolar World*, London and New York: Zed Books.

Amin, S., 2000a, 'The Political Economy of the Twentieth Century', in *Monthly Review*, 52 (2) (June): 1-28.

Amin, S., 2000b, 'Economic Globalisation and Political Universalism: Conflicting Issues?' in *Journal of World-Systems Research*, 3 Fall/Winter: 582-622.

Amin, S., 1991, 'The Ancient World System versus Modern Capitalist World System', *in Review*, XIV (3): 349-385.

Amin, S., 1990, *Delinking: Towards a Polycentric World*, London and New York: Zed Books.

Amin, S., 1974, *Accumulation on a World Scale: A critique of the Theory of Underdevelopment*, New York: Monthly Review Press.

Amin, S., 1997, *Capitalism in the Age of Globalization*, London: Zed.

Amin, S., 1989, *Eurocentrism*, London: Zed Books.

Amin, S., 1989, *Spectres of Capitalism: A Critique of Current Intellectual Fashions*, New York: Monthly Review.

ANC, 1972, *African National Council: Aims and Objectives*, Salisbury, 10 March.

Anderson, B., 1983, *Imagined Communities: Reflections on the Origin and Spread of Nationalism*, London: Verso.

Anderson, R. 2005, 'Redressing Colonial Genocide under International Law: The Hereros' Cause of Action Against Germany', in *California Law Review*, 93 (4), (July): 1155-1189.

Appiah, K. A., 1993, *In My Father's House: Africa in the Philosophy of Culture*, Oxford: Oxford University Press.

Appiah, K. A., 2006, *Cosmopolitanism: Ethics in a World of Strangers*, New York: Norton and Co..

Armah, A. K., 1971, *The Beautiful Ones Are Not Yet Born*, London: Heinemann.

Armah, A. K., 2010, 'Remembering the Dismembered Continent: On the 125th Anniversary of the Berlin Conference of 1884-85 that Fragmented Africa', in http://www.thefreelibrary.com/Remembering+the+dismembered+continent%B+on+t.. (accessed 10/09/2010).

Arieff, A., 2011, 'Political Transition in Tunisia', in *Congressional Research Service Report for Congress*, February: 1-23.

Arowosegbe, J. O., 2008, *Decolonising the Social Sciences in the Global South: Claude Ake and the Praxis of Knowledge Production in Africa*, Leiden: ASC Working Paper 79.

Asante, M. K., 1988, *Afrocentricity*, Trenton, N.J: Africa World Press.

Asante, M. K., 1987, *The Afrocentric Idea*, Philadelphia: Temple University Press.

Ashcroft, B., 1997, 'Globalism, Post-colonialism and African Studies', in P. Ahluwalia and P. Nursery-Bary, eds, *Postcolonialism: Culture and Identity in Africa*, New York: Nova Science Publishers.

Ashforth, A., 1990, *The Politics of Official Discourse in Twentieth Century South Africa*, Oxford: Clarendon Press.

Astrow, A., 1983, *Zimbabwe: A Revolution That Lost Its Way?* London: Zed Books.

Attwell, D., 2005, *Rewriting Modernity: Studies in Black South African Literary History*, Scottsville: University of KwaZulu-Natal Press.

Author unknown, 1979, 'For Restricted Circulation: Progress Review on the 1979 Grand Plan'.

Austen, D. and Luckham, R., eds, *Politicians and Soldiers in Ghana*, 1966-1972, London: Frank Cass, 1975.

Ayittey, G. B. N., 2005, *Africa Unchained: The Blueprint for Africa's Future*, New York: Palgrave Macmillan.

Ayittey, G. B. N., 1991, *Indigenous African Institutions*, Ardsley-on-Hudson, NY: Transnational Publishers.

Ayliff. J. and Whiteside, J., 1912, *History of the Abambo, Generally Known as Fingos*, South Africa: Butterworth.

Azarya, V. and Chazan, N., 1998, 'Disengagement from the State in Africa: Reflections on the Experience of Ghana and Guinea', in P. Lewis, ed., *Africa: Dilemmas of Development and Change*, Boulder: Westview Press: 109-120.

Ballim, Y., 2010, 'On the Persistent Tyranny of Race in South Africa: A Perspective on Student Access to University', (Unpublished Paper Presented at the Revisiting Apartheid Race Categories: A Colloquium, University of the Witwatersrand, 13-15 October): 1-19.

Bamu, P., 2009, 'Transitional Justice without Transition in Zimbabwe?' in *Pambazuka News*, Issue 421 (26 February).

Banegas, R., 2006, 'Cote D'Ivoire: Patriotism, Ethno nationalism and Other African Modes of Self- Writing', in *African Affairs*, 1: 1-18.

Bantu Mirror, 6 May 1961.

Barthes, R., 1972, *Mythologies*, London: Farrar, Straus and Giroux.

Bayart, J-F., 2000, 'Africa in the World: A History of Extraversion', in *African Affairs*, 99 : 217- 249.

Beach, D. N., 1984, *Zimbabwe Before 1900*, Gweru: Mambo Press.

Beach, D. N., 1994, *The Shona and Their Neighbours*, (Oxford: Blackwell.

Beck, U., et al.,1994, *Reflexive Modernization: Politics, Tradition and Aesthetics in the Modern Social Order*, Cambridge: Polity Press.

Bhabha, H. and Comaroff, J., 1994, 'Speaking of Postcoloniality, in the Continuous Present: A Conversation', in D. T. Golberg and A. Quayson, eds, *Relocating Postcolonialism*, Oxford: Blackwell: 15-46.

Bhabha, H., 1994, *The Location of Culture*, London and New York: Routledge.

Bhebe, N., 2004, *Simon Vengayi Muzenda: The Struggle for and Liberation of Zimbabwe*, Gweru: Mambo Press.

Biko, S. I *Write What I Want: A Selection of His Writings*, (Harmondsworth: Penguin 1978).

Billig, M., 1995, *Banal Nationalism*, London: Sage Publications.

Blair, D., 2002, *Degrees in Violence: Robert Mugabe and the Struggle for Power in Zimbabwe*, London: Continuum,.

Blair, T., 2007, 'A Battle for Global Values', in *Foreign Affairs* (Jan/Feb): 3-4.

Blaut, J. M., 1993, *The Colonizer's Model of the World: Geographical and Eurocentric History*, New York: The Guilford Press.

Blyden, E. W., 1967, *Christianity, Islam and the Negro Race* (1887 Reprint), Edinburgh: Edinburgh University Press.

Bozzoli, B., 1978, 'Capital and State in South Africa', *in Review of African Political Economy*, 11 (January-April).

Bozzoli, B., 1981, *The Political Nature of a Ruling Class: Capital and Ideology in South Africa 1890-1933*, London & Boston: Routledge & Kegan Paul.

Bridgman, J. M., 1981, *The Revolt of the Hereros*, Berkeley/London: University of California Press.

Brumer, J., 1971, *For the President's Eyes Only*, Johannesburg: Hugh Keartland.

Bryant, A. T. 1929, *Olden Times in Zululand and Natal*, London: Longman.

Bundy, C., 2007, 'New Nation, New History? Constructing the Past in Post-Apartheid South Africa', in E. Stolten, ed., *History Making and Present Day Politics: The Meaning of Collective Memory in South Africa*, Uppsala: Nordic Africa Institute: 73-97.

Cabral, A. 1969 *Revolution in Guinea: An African People's Struggle*, New York: Monthly Review Press.

Calhoun, C., ed., 1994, *Social Theory and the Politics of Identity*, Oxford: Blackwell.

Calpin, G. H., 1941, *There are No South Africans*, London: Thomas Nelson and Sons Ltd.

Cardoso, F. H. and Faletto, E., 1979, *Dependency and Development in Latin America*, Berkeley: University of California Press.

Castells, M., 1997, *The Information Age: Economy, Society and Culture Volume II: The Power of Identity*, Oxford: Blackwell Publishers.

Catholic Commission for Justice and Peace (CCJP) and Legal Resources Foundation (LRF), 1997, *Breaking the Silence, Building True Peace: Report on the Disturbances in Matabeleland and the Midlands*, 1980–1989, Harare: CCJP and LRF.

Chabal, P. and Daloz, J. P., 1999, *Africa Works: Disorder as Political Instrument*, London: James Currey

Chakrabarty, D., 2000, *Provincialising Europe: Postcolonial and Historical Difference*, Princeton: Princeton University Press.

Chakrabarty, D., 1992, 'Postcoloniality and the Artifice of History: Who Speaks for 'Indian' Pasts?' *in Representations*, 37.

Chan, S., 2003, Robert Mugabe: *A Life of Power and Violence*, London: IB Tauris.

Chen, K. H., 1998, 'Introduction: The Decolonization Question', in K. H. Chen, ed., *Trajectories: Inter-Asia Cultural Studies, London: Routledge*: 3- 28.

Cheru, F., 2002, *African Renaissance: Roadmaps to the Challenge of Globalization*, London & New York: Zed Books.

Chimhundu, H., 1992, 'Early Missionaries and the Ethnographic Factor during the "Invention of Tribalism" in Zimbabwe', *Journal of African History*, 33 (1) (1): 78– 109.

Chinweizu, 1987, *Decolonizing the African Mind*, Lagos: Pero Press.

Chinweizu, 1975, *The West and the Rest of Us: White Predators, Black Slaves and the African Elite*, New York: Vintage Books.

Chipkin, I., 2007, *Do South Africans Exist? Nationalism, Democracy and the Identity of 'the People'*, Johannesburg: Wits University Press.

Chronicle, 25 January 1982.

Clapham, C., 1996, *Africa and the International System: The Politics of State Survival*, Cambridge: Cambridge University Press.

Cobbing, J., 1988, 'The Mfecane as Alibi: Thoughts on Dithakong and Mbolompo', in *Journal of African History*, 29: 487-519.

Cohen, R., 1986, *Endgame in South Africa? The Changing Structures and Ideology of Apartheid*, London: James Currey.

Collier, P. & Hoeffler, A., 2001, *Greed and Grievance in Civil War* Washington: The World Bank.

Coltart, D., 2007, 'Why I Cannot Join Tsvangirai's Faction', in *New Africa: Zimbabwe Special Issue* (Summer): 48-54.

Comaroff, J. and Comaroff, J. L., eds, 2006, *Law and Disorder in the Postcolony*, Chicago and London: University of Chicago Press.

Comaroff, J., 1996, 'Occult Economies and the Violence of Abstraction: Notes from the South Africa Postcolony,' in *American Ethnologist*, 26: 279-301.

Comaroff, J. and Comaroff, J. L., 2000, 'Millennial Capitalism: First Thoughts on a Second Coming', in *Public Culture*, 12 (2): 310-312.

Comaroff, J. L. and Comaroff, J., 2009, *Ethnicity, Inc.* Chicago: University of Chicago Press.

Comaroff, J. L. and Comaroff, J., 1997, *Of Revelation and Revolution: The Dialectics of Modernity on a South African Frontier: Volume Two*, Chicago and London: The University of Chicago Press.

Cooper, F., 2002, *Africa since 1940: The Past of the Present*, Cambridge: Cambridge University Press.

Cornwall, A., 2007, 'Buzzwords and Fuzzwords: Deconstructing Development Discourse', in *Development in Practice*, 17 (4/5) (August): 471-497.

Cornwall, A., 2010, 'Introductory Overview-Buzzwords and Fuzzwords: Deconstructing Development Discourse', in A. Cornwall and D. Eade, eds, *Deconstructing Development Discourse: Buzzwords and Fuzzwords*, London: Practical Action Publishing: 1-18.

Davies, R., 2004, 'Memories of Underdevelopment: A Personal Interpretation of Zimbabwe's Economic Decline', in B. Raftopoulos and T. Savage, eds, *Zimbabwe: Injustice and Political Reconciliation*, Cape Town: Institute for Justice and Reconciliation: 20-39.

Davis, R. W., 2002, 'Series Foreword', in R. H. Taylor, ed., *The Idea of Freedom in Asia and Africa*, Stanford: Stanford University Press: i-xii.

Dedering, T., 1993, 'The German-Herero War of 1904: Revisionism of Genocide or Imaginary Historiography?' in *Journal of Southern African Studies*, 19 (1): 80-88.

Deng, D. M., 2008, *Identity, Diversity and Constitutionalism in Africa*, (Washington, DC: United States Institute of Peace Press.

De Vos, P., 2010, 'Looking Backward, Looking Forward: Race, Corrective Measures and the South African Constitutional Court,' Unpublished Paper Presented at the Revisiting Apartheid Race Categories: A Colloquium, University of the Witwatersrand, October.

Diamond, L., 1998, 'Africa: The Second Wind of Change', in P. Lewis, ed., *Africa: Dilemmas of Development and Change*, Boulder: Westview Press: 263-271.

Diawara, M., 1990, 'Reading Africa through Foucault: V. Y. Mudimbe's Reaffirmation of the Subject', in *October*, 55, (Winter): 65-96.

Diop, C. A., 1974, *The African Origin of Civilisation: Myth or Reality*, Chicago: L Hill.

Dirk, A., 2000, *Postmodernity's Histories: The Past as Legacy and Project*, New York: Rowman and Littlefield Publishers.

Doke, C. M., 1931, *Report on the Unification of the Shona Dialects*, Hartford: Stephen Austin and Sons.

Doke, C. M., 1931, A *Comparative Study in Shona Phonetics*, Johannesburg: University of Witwatersrand Press.

Dorman, S. R., 2001, 'Inclusion and Exclusion: NGOs and Politics in Zimbabwe', Unpublished DPhil dissertation, University of Oxford.

Dorman, S., Hammett, D., and Nugent, P., 2007, 'Introduction: Citizenship and Its Casualties in Africa', in S. Dorman, D. Hammett, and P. Nugent, eds, *Making Nations, Creating Strangers: States and Citizenship in Africa*, Leiden and Boston: Brill: 3-26.

Dubow, S., 2006, *A Commonwealth of Knowledge: Science, Sensibility, and White South Africa 1820-2000*, Oxford: Oxford University Press.

Dubow, S., 1997, 'Colonial Nationalism, the Milner Kindergarten and the Rise of South Africanism', 1902-10, in *History Workshop Journal*, 43.

Dubow, S., 1987, 'Race, Civilization and Culture: The Elaboration of Segregationist Discourse in the Inter-War Years', in S. Marks and S. Trapido, eds, *The Politics of*

Race, Class and Nationalism in Twentieth-Century Africa, London and New York: Longman: 71-94.

Dubow, S., 2007, 'Thoughts on South Africa: Some Preliminary Ideas', in H. Erik Stolten (ed.). *History Making and Present Day Politics: The Meaning of Collective Memory in South Africa*, Uppsala: Nordic Africa Institute: 51-72.

Dunn, K. C., 2009, '"Sons of the Soil" and Contemporary State Making: Autochthony, Uncertainty and Political Violence in Africa,' in *Third World Quarterly*, 30 (1): 114-125.

Dussel, E., 1995, 'Eurocentrism and Modernity :Introduction to the Frankfurt Lectures', in J. Beverley, J. Oviedo and M. Aronna (eds.). *The Postmodernism Debate in Latin America*, (Durham: Duke University Press,: 65-77.

Dussel, E., 2000, 'Europe, Modernity and Eurocentrism', in *Nepantla: Views from South*, 1 (3): 465-478.

Drechsler, H., 1980, *'Lets Us Die Fighting': The Struggle of the Herero and Nama Against German Imperialism* (1884-1915), London: Zed Books.

Ekeh, P. P., 1975, 'Colonialism and the Two Publics in Africa: A Theoretical Statement', in *Comparative Studies in Society and History*, 17 (1): 88-106.

Ellenberger, D. F., 1912, *History of the Basuto, Ancient and Modern*, London: Shutter.

Emerson, B., 1979, *Leopold II of the Belgians: King of Colonialism*, New York: St. Martin's Press.

Eno, M. A. and Eno, O. A., 2009, 'Surveying through the Narratives of Africanity', in J. Adibe, ed., *Who is an African? Identity, Citizenship and the Making of the Africa-Nation*, London: Adonis & Abbey Publishers Ltd: 61-78.

Erasmus, Z., 2010, 'The Audacity to Think Differently: Questioning Apartheid Race Categories', Unpublished Paper Presented at Revisiting Apartheid Race Categories: A Colloquium, University of the Witwatesrand, 13-15 October.

Escobar, A., 2007, 'Worlds and Knowledges Otherwise: The Latin American Modernity/Coloniality Research Program,' in *Cultural Studies*, 21 (2/3) (March/May): 197-210.

Etherington, N., 2001, *The Great Treks: The Transformation of Southern Africa, 1815-1854*, London: Pearson Education.

Ewans, M., 2002, *European Atrocity, African Catastrophe: Leopold II, the Congo Free State and its Aftermath*, London: Routledge.

Falola, T., 2006, 'Writing and Teaching National History in Africa in the Era of Global History', in P. T. Zeleza, ed., *The Study of Africa: Volume 1: Disciplinary and Interdisciplinary Encounters*, Dakar: CODESRIA Books: 165-189.

Falola, T. 2001, *Nationalism and African Intellectuals*, Rochester: The University of Rochester Press.

Fanon, F., 1968a, *The Wretched of the Earth*, New York: Grove Press.

Fanon, F., 1968b, *Black Skins, White Masks*, New York: Groves Press .

Fardon, R. and Furniss, G., 2000, African Broadcast Cultures, in R. Fardon and G. Furniss, eds, *African Broadcast Cultures: Radio in Transition*, London: James Currey : 1-23.

Financial Gazette, 22 November 2008.

Financial Gazette, 28 January 1998.

Fine, B., 2006, 'Debating the "New" Imperialism', in *Historical Materialism*, 14 (4): 133-156.

Foltz, W. J., 2002. 'African States and the Search for Freedom', in R. H. Taylor, ed., *The Idea of Freedom in Asia and Africa*, Stanford: Stanford University Press: 39-51.

Foucault, M., 1980, *Power/Knowledge: Selected Interviews and Other Writings, 1972-1977*, New York: Pantheon.

Foucault, M., 1977, 'Nietzsche, Genealogy, History', in D. F. Bouchard, ed., *Language, Counter- Memory, Practice: Selected Essays and Interviews*, New York: Ithaca: 135-182.

Foucault, M., 1982, 'The Subject and Power', in H. L. Dreyfus and P. Rabinow, eds, *Michel Foucault: Beyond Structuralism and Hermeneutics*, Brighton: 212-221.

Foucault, M., 1972, *The Order of Things: An Archaeology of the Human Sciences*, London: Routledge.

Frank, A. G., 1976, *Capitalism and Underdevelopment in Latin America*, New York: Monthly Review Press.

Freidman, S., 2009, 'Belonging of another Type: Whiteness and African Identity', in J. Adibe, ed., *Who is an African? Identity, Citizenship and the Making of the Africa-Nation,* London: Adonis and Abbey Publishers Ltd: 79-83.

Front for the Liberation of Zimbabwe (FROLIZI), 1971, FROLIZI Draft Constitution, Lusaka: FROLIZI.

Fukuyama, F., 1993, *The End of History and the Last Man,* New York: Harper Collins Publishers.

Geschiere, P., 2009, *The Perils of Belonging: Autochthony, Citizenship and Exclusion in Africa and Europe*, Chicago: University of Chicago Press.

Gewald, J. B., 1999, *Herero Heroes: A Socio-Political History of the Herero of Namibia 1890-1923*, Oxford: James Currey.

Godwin P. and Hancock, I., *Rhodesians Never Die: The Impact of War and Political Change on White Rhodesia, c.1970-1980*, Oxford: Oxford University Press, 1993.

Gordon, M., 1964, *Assimilation in American Life*, New York: Oxford University Press.

Gramsci, A., 1971, *Selections from Prison Notebooks*, London: Lawrence and Wishart.

Gray, C. C., 2001, *Afrocentric Thought and Praxis*, Trenton, NJ: Africa World Press.

Gray, J., 2003, *Straw Dogs: Thoughts on Humans and Other Animals*, London: Grant Books.

Grosfoguel, R., 2007, 'The Epistemic Decolonial Turn: Beyond Political-Economy Paradigms', in *Cultural Studies*, 21, (2/3) (March/May): 203-246.

Grosfoguel, R., 2008, 'Latinas and the Decolonization of the US Empire in the 21st Century', in *Social Science Information: Special Issue on Migrants and Clandestinity*, 47 (4): 605-622.

Grosfoguel, R., 2004, 'Race and Ethnicity or Racialised Ethnicities: Identities within Global Coloniality', in *Ethnicities*, 4 (3): 315-336.

Grosfoguel, R., 2000, 'Developmentalism, Modernity, and Dependency Theory in Latin America', in *Nepantla: Views from South*, 1 (2): 347-374.

Guevara, C., 1965, 'Speech by Che Guevara to the Second Economic Seminar on Afro-Asia Solidarity, Algiers, Algeria, 24 February, 1965', in http://www.marxists/org/archive/guevara/1965/02/24.html (accessed 1/1/ 2011).

Hachipola, S. J., 1998, *A Survey of the Minority Languages of Zimbabwe*, Harare: University of Zimbabwe Publications.

Hamilton, C., ed., 1995, *The Mfecane: Reconstructive Debates in Southern African History*, Johannesburg: Wits Press.

Hammar, A. and Raftopoulos, B., 2003, 'Introduction: Zimbabwe's Unfinished Business: Rethinking Land, State and Nation', in Hammar, Raftopoulos, and Jensen eds., *Zimbabwe's Unfinished Business: Rethinking Land, State and Nation in the Context of Crisis*, Harare: Weaver Press: 1–47.

Hammar, A., and Raftopoulos, B., and Jensen, S., eds, 2003, *Zimbabwe's Unfinished Business: Rethinking Land, State and Nation in the Context of Crisis*, Harare: Weaver Press.

Hardt, M. and Negri, A., 2000, *Empire*, Boston: Harvard University Press.

Harvey, D., 2007, 'In What Ways Is 'The New Imperialism' Really New?' in *Historical Materialism*, 15: 57-70.

Harvey, D., 2003, *The New Imperialism*, Oxford: Oxford University Press.

Hegel, G. W. H., 1975, *Lectures on the Philosophy of the World*, trans. H. B. Nisbet and D. Forbes, Cambridge: Cambridge University Press.

Hensbroek, P. B. van., 1999, *Political Discourse in African Thought, 1860 to the Present*, Westport: Praeger.

Hill, R. A. and Pirio, G., 1987, '"Africa for the Africans": The Garvey Movement in South Africa, 1920-1940', in S. Marks and S. Trapido, eds, *The Politics of Race, Class and Nationalism in Twentieth Century South Africa*, London and New York: Longman: 209-253.

Hobsbawn, E. and Ranger, T. O., 1983, *The Invention of Tradition*, Cambridge: Cambridge University Press.

Hochschild, A., 1998, *King Leopold's Ghost: A Story of Greed, Terror, and Heroism in Colonial Africa*, Boston: Houghton Mifflin.

Hofmeyr, I., 1987, 'Building a Nation from Words: Afrikaans Language, Literature and Ethnic Identity, 1902-1924,' in S. Marks and S. Trapido, eds, *The Politics of Race, Class and Nationalism in Twentieth Century South Africa*, London and New York: Longman, 95-123.

Hugo, P., 1988, 'Towards Darkness and Death: Racial Demonology in South Africa', in *Journal of Modern African Studies*, 26 (4): 545-580.

Hume, M., 2010, 'Battle Between Optimism and Pessimism', Paper presented at the Battle of Ideas Seminar, London, December.

Huntington, S. P., 2004, *Who are We?: The Challenges to America's National Identity*, New York: Simon & Schuster.

Huntington, S. P., 1991, *The Third Wave: Democratization in the Late Twentieth Century*, Norman, OK.

Hyden, G., 1980, *Beyond Ujamaa in Tanzania*, Berkeley: University of California Press.

Irene, A., 1991 'The African Scholar: Is Black Africa Entering the Dark Ages of Scholarship', in *Transition*, 51: 28-58.

Jackson, R. H., 1990, *Quasi-States: Sovereignty, International Relations and the Third World*, Cambridge: Cambridge University Press.

Jeater, D., 2007, *Law, Language and Science: The Invention of the 'Native Mind' in Southern Rhodesia*, 1890-1930, Portsmouth, NH: Heinemann,.

Johnson, K., 2005, 'Whither Nationalism? Are We Entering an Era of Post-Nationalist Politics in Southern Africa?' *Transformation*, 58: 1-21.

July, R. W, 1968, *The Origins of Modern African Thought: Its Development in West Africa during the Nineteenth and Twentieth Centuries*, London: Faber and Faber.

Kabwato, Z., 2010, 'Interview with Prof. Brian Raftopoulos: In Search of the Meaning of Zimbabwe', in *Zimbabwe in Pictures* http://www.zimbabweinpictures.com(Accessed 29/6/2010).

Karis, T. and Carter, G. M., eds, 1972, *From Protest to Challenge: A Documentary History of African Politics in South Africa, Volume 2*, Stanford: Stanford University Press.

Karlstrom, M., 2003, 'On the Aesthetics and Dialogics of Power in the Postcolony', in *Africa*, 73 (1): 57-76.

Kennedy, D., 1987, *Islands of White: Settler Society and Culture in Kenya and Southern Rhodesia, 1890-1939*, Durham: Duke University Press.

Khadiagala, G. M., 2010, 'Two Moments in African Thought: Ideas in Africa's International Relations', in *South African Journal of International Affairs*, 17 (3) (December): 375-386.

Kieh, G. K. ed., 2007, *Beyond State Failure and Collapse: Making the State Relevant in Africa*, Lanham, MD: Lexington Books.

Kilgore, J., 2009, *We are All Zimbabweans Now*, Cape Town: Umuzi.

Kinloch, G. C., 1997, 'Racial Attitudes in the Post-Colonial Situation: The Case of Zimbabwe', in *Journal of Black Studies*, 27: 820-838.

Kriger, N. J., 2003, *Guerrilla Veterans in Post-War Zimbabwe: Symbolic and Violent Politics*, 1980-1987, Cambridge: Cambridge University Press.

Laakso, L. and Olukoshi, A. O., 1996, 'The Crisis of the Post-Colonial Nation-State Project in Africa', in A. O. Olukoshi and L. Laakso, eds, *Challenges to the Nation-State in Africa*, Uppsala: Nordic Africa Institute: 7-39.

Laclau, E., 1996, *Emancipation(s)*, London and New York: Verso.

Laclau, E., 2005, *On Populist Reason*, London and New York: Verso.

Lembede, A. M., 'Policy of the Congress Youth League', in T. Karis and G. M. Carter, eds, *From Protest to Challenge: Volume 2*, Stanford: Stanford University Press, 1973: 313-317.

Lester, A., 2001, *Imperial Networks: Creating Identities in Nineteenth-Century South Africa and Britain*, London: Routledge.

Lewellen, T. C., 2002, *The Anthropology of Globalization: Cultural Anthropology Enters the 21ˢᵗ Century*, Connecticut: Bergin and Garvey.

Lewis, M. W. and Wigen, K. W.,1997, *The Myth of Continents: A Critique of Metageography*, Berkeley: University of California Press,.

Leys, C., 'Underdevelopment and Dependency: Critical Notes', in C. Leys, ed., *The Rise and Fall of Development Theory*, Oxford: James Currey.

Libby, R. T., 1984, 'Development Strategies and Political Division within the Zimbabwean State', in M. Schwartzberg, ed., *The Political Economy of Zimbabwe*, New York: Praeger.

Lindgren, B., 2005, 'The Politics of Identity and the Remembrance of Violence: Ethnicity and Gender at the Installation of a Female Chief in Zimbabwe', in V. Broch-Due, ed., *Violence and Belonging: The Quest for Identity in Post-Colonial Africa*, London and New York: Routledge.

Lonsdale, J., 2004, 'Moral and Political Argument in Kenya', in B. Bernam, D. Eyoh, and W. Kymlika, eds, *Ethnicity and Democracy in Africa*, Oxford: James Currey: 73–95.

Lonsdale, J., 1992, 'The Moral Economy of Mau Mau', in B. Berman and J. Lonsdale, eds, *Unhappy Valley: Conflict in Kenya and Africa*, London: James Currey.

Lopes, C., 2010, 'Keynote Address, International Conference: Fifty Years of African Independence – Continuities and Discontinuities', University of Mainz, Germany, 8-10 April.

Lumumba-Kasongo, T, 1994, *Political Re-Mapping of Africa: Transnational Ideology and Re-Definition of Africa in World Politics*, Lanhan & New York: University Press of America.

Lye, W. F. and Murray, C., 1980, *Transformations on the Highveld: The Tswana and Southern Sotho*, Cape Town: David Philip.

Massiah, G., 2011, 'Lessons from the Uprisings in the Maghreb', in *Pambazuka News*, 513, 26 May: 1-2.

Mafeje, A., 2000, 'Africanity: A Combative Ontology', in *CODESRIA Bulletin*, 1: 66-67.

Maggs, T. M., 1976, *Iron Age Communities of the Southern Highveld*, Pietermaritzburg.

Makumbe, J, 2003, 'ZANU-PF: A Party in Transition', in R. Cronwell, ed., *Zimbabwe's Turmoil: Problems and Prospects*, Pretoria: Institute for Security Studies: 24-38.

Maldonado-Torres, N., 2007, 'On the Coloniality of Being: Contributions to the Development of a Concept', in *Cultural Studies*, 21 (2/3) (March/May): 240-270.

Maldonado-Torres, N., 2006, 'Post-Continental Philosophy: Its Definition, Contours, and Fundamental Sources', in *Worlds and Knowledge Otherwise*, (Fall): 1-29.

Maldonado-Torres, N., 2004, 'The Typology of Being and the Geopolitics of Knowledge: Modernity, Empire, Coloniality', in *City*, 8 (1): 1-33.

Maldonado-Torres, N., 2003, 'The Regressive Kernel of Orthodoxy: A Review of Slavoj Zizek, The Puppet and the Dwarf', in *Radical Philosophy Review*, 6 (1): 325-361.

Maldonado-Torres, N., n.d., 'Religion, Conquest, and Race in the Foundation of Modern/Colonial World', Unpublished Draft Paper, p. 3-4.

Maloreng, C., 2005, 'Zimbabwe's Zezuru Sum Game: The Basis for the Security Dilemma in which the Political Elite finds itself', in *African Security Review*, 14 (3): 77-88.

Mamdani, M., 2011, 'The Importance of Research in a University', in *Pambazuka News*, 526, (21 April .

Mamdani, M., 2011, 'The Invention of the Indigene', in *London Review of Books*, 33 (2), 20 January.

Mamdani, M., 1996, *Citizen and Subject: Contemporary Africa and the Legacy of Late Colonialism*, Princeton, NJ: Princeton University Press.

Mamdani, M., 1998, 'When Does a Settler Become a Native? Reflections on the Roots of Citizenship in Equatorial and South Africa', Text of Inaugural Lecture delivered as A. C. Jordan Professor of African Studies, University of Cape Town, Wednesday, 13 May.

Mamdani, M., 2001, 'When Does a Settler Become a Native? Citizenship and Identity in a Settler Society', *Pretext: Literacy and Cultural Studies*, 10 (1) (July): 63–73.

Mamdani, M., 2001, '*When Victims Become Killers: Colonialism, Nativism, and the Genocide in Rwanda,* Oxford: James Currey.

Mamdani, M., 2008, 'Lessons of Zimbabwe', in *London Review of Books*, 30 (23) (December): 1-18.

Mamdani, M., 2009, *Saviours and Survivors: Darfur, Politics and the War on Terror*, New York: Pantheon Books.

Mandaza, I., ed., 1986, *Zimbabwe: The Political Economy of Transition, 1980-86*, Dakar: CODESRIA.

Mandaza, I., 1999, 'Reconciliation and Social Justice in Southern Africa: The Zimbabwe Experience', in M. W. Malegapuru, ed., *African Renaissance: The New Struggle*, Cape Town: Mafube Publishing Ltd.

Mandaza, I., 1998, 'Southern Africa: The Political Economy of Transition: A Research Agenda', in I. Mandaza, ed., *Governance and Human Development in Southern Africa: Selected Essays*, Harare: SAPES Books.

Mandaza, I. and Sachikonye, L., eds., 1991, *The One Party State and Democracy: The Zimbabwe Debate,* Harare: SAPES Books.

Maphosa, F., 1998, 'Towards a Sociology of Zimbabwean Indigenous Entrepreneurship', in *Zambezia*, 25, (2): 176-178.

Marchesin, P., 1995, 'Mitterrand l'Africain', in *Politique Africaine*, 58: 5-24.

Marks, S. and Trapido, S., 1987, 'The Politics of Race, Class and Nationalism', in S. Marks and S. Trapido, eds., *The Politics of Race, Class and Nationalism in Twentieth-Century South Africa*, London and New York: 1-70.

Marshal-Fratani, R., 2007, 'The War of "Who is Who": Autochthony, Nationalism and Citizenship in the Ivorian Crisis', in S. Dorman, D. Hammett and P. Nugent, eds, *Making Nations, Creating Strangers: States of Citizenship in Africa*. Leiden and Boston: Brill: 29-67.

Martin, D. and Johnson, P., 1981, *The Struggle for Zimbabwe: The Chimurenga War*, Harare: Zimbabwe Publishing House.

Martin, M., 1974, 'South: Capital Accumulation and Violence', in *Economy and Society*, 3 (3).Masunungure, E. V., ed., 2009, *Defying the Winds of Change: Zimbabwe's 2008 Elections,* Harare: Weaver Press.

Masunungure, E. V., 2006, 'Nation-Building, State-Building and Power Configuration in Zimbabwe', in *Conflict Trends Magazine*, 1: 3-8.

Mathe, R., 2005, *Making Ends Meet at the Margins: Grappling with Economic Crisis and Belonging in Beitbridge, Zimbabwe*, Dakar: CODESRIA.

Mathews, K.,2008, 'Renaissance of Pan-Africanism: The AU and the New Pan-Africanists', in J. Akokpari, A. Ngida-Muvumba and T. Murithi, eds., *The African Union and Its Institutions*, Johannesburg: Jacana Media: 25-39.

Matsinhe, D. M., 2011, 'Africa's Fear of Itself: The Ideology of *Makwerekwere* in South Africa', in *Third World Quarterly*, 32 (2): 295-313.

Mazarire, G. C., 2009, 'Reflections on Pre-Colonial Zimbabwe, c. 850-1880s', in B. Raftopoulos and A. Mlambo, eds, *Becoming Zimbabwe: A History from the Pre-Colonial Period to 2008*, Harare and Johannesburg: Weaver Press and Jacana: 1-38.

Mazrui, A., 1988, 'Growing Up in a Shrinking World: A Private Vantage Point', in J. Kruzel and J. Rosenau, eds, *Journeys through World Politics: Autobiographical Reflections of Thirty-Four Academic Travellers*, Lexington MA and Toronto: Lexington Books: 469-87.

Mazrui, A., 1967, *On Heroes and Uhuru Worship: Essays on Independent Africa*, London: Longman.

Mazrui, A. A., 2010, 'Preface: Black Berlin and the Curse of Fragmentation: From Bismarck to Barack', in A. Adebajo, *The Curse of Berlin: Africa After the Cold War*, London: Hurst & Company,: ix-xxviii.

Mazrui, A. A., 1986, *The Africans: A Triple Heritage*, London: Little Brown & Co.

Mazrui, A. A., 2009, 'Preface: Comparative Africanity: Blood, Soil and Ancestry', in J. Adibe, ed., *Who is an African?: Identity, Citizenship and the Making of the Africa-Nation,* London: Adonis & Abbey Publishers Ltd,: xi-xv.

Mbeki T., 2001, 'Discussion Document: The Mbeki-Mugabe Papers: What Mbeki Told Mugabe', August.

Mbeki, T., 1999, 'Speech of the President of South Africa at the Launch of the African Renaissance', Pretoria: South Africa, 11 October

Mbeki, T., 2010, 'The Role of Africa's Student Leaders in Developing the African Continent: Carthage Must Be Rebuilt', Address by Thabo Mbeki at the African Student Leaders Summit Meeting, University of Cape Town, 6 September.

Mbeki, T., 1996, 'Speech delivered on the occasion of the adoption of Constitutional Assembly of the Republic of South Africa Constitutional Bill', Cape Town, South Africa.

Mbembe, A., 2001, *On the Postcolony*, Berkeley: University of California Press.

Mbembe, A., 1992, 'Provisional Notes on the Postcolony', in *Africa*, 62 (1): 3-37.

Mbembe, A., 2002a, 'African Modes Self-Writing', in *Public Culture,* 14 (1): 239-273.

Mbembe, A., 2002b, 'On the Power of the False', in *Public Culture*, 14 (1): 239-273.

Mbembe, A., 2006, 'On the Postcolony: A Brief Response to Critics', in *African Identities*, 4 (2) : 143-178.

Mbembe, A., 'What is Postcolonial Thinking? An Interview with Achille Mbembe', in *Eurozine,* www.eurozine.com

McGregor, J., 2009, *Crossing the Zambezi: The Politics of Landscape on a Central African Frontier*, Harare and Oxford, James Currey and Weaver Press.

MDC, 2007, 'A New Zimbabwe, A New Beginning', Harare: Harvest House.

MDC, 2003, 'From Crisis to Democratic Human-Centred Development: Values, Goals and Polices of the Movement for Democratic Change', Harare: Harvest House.

MDC, 2000, *MDC Election Manifesto.* Harare: Harvest House.

MDC, 2005, *MDC Manifesto.* Harare: Harvest House.

MDC, 2008, *MDC Manifesto* Harare: Harvest House.

Meredith, M., 2002, *Mugabe: Power and Plunder in Zimbabwe*, Oxford: Public Affairs Ltd.

Mignolo, W. D., 2007, 'Delinking: The Rhetoric of Modernity, the Logic of Coloniality and the Grammar of De-Coloniality', in *Cultural Studies*, 21 (2/3), (March/May): 449-514.

Mignolo, W. D., 2007, 'Introduction: Coloniality of Power and De-Colonial Thinking', in *Cultural Studies*, 21, (2/3), (March/May): 155-167.

Mignolo, W. D., 1995, *The Darker Side of the Renaissance: Literacy, Territoriality, and Colonization*, Ann Arbor: University of Michigan Press.

Mignolo, W., 2000, *Local Histories/Global Designs: Essays on the Coloniality of Power, Subaltern Knowledges and Border Thinking*, Princeton: Princeton University Press.

Miller, D., 2000, *Citizenship and National Identity*, Cambridge: Polity Press.

Mkandawire, T., 2001, 'Thinking About the Developmental State in Africa', in *Cambridge Journal of Economics*, 25 (3): 289-314.

Mkandawire, T., 1995, 'Three Generations of African Scholars: A Note', in *CODESSRIA Bulletin*, 2.

Mkandawire, T., 1997, 'Globalisation and Africa's Unfinished Agenda', in *Macalester International*, 7 (1): 71-107.

Mkandawire, T., 2003, 'Institutions and Development in Africa', Unpublished Paper Submitted to Cambridge Conference 'Economics for the Future', 17-19 September.

Mkandawire, T., 2003, 'African Intellectuals and Nationalism', in T. Mkandawire, ed., *African Intellectuals: Rethinking Politics, Language, Gender and Development*, London: Zed Books: 1-26.

Mkandawire, T., 2002, 'From Liberation Movements to Governments: On Political Culture in Southern Africa', *African Sociological Review*, 6 (1): 12–13.

Mkhwanazi, G., 2010, 'Zimbabwe: The Case of Two States', in New Zimbabwe. Com http:/www.newzimbabwe.com/news/printVersion.aspx?newsID=2571 (accessed 7 June 2010).

Mlambo, A. S., 2006, 'Western Social Sciences and Africa: The Domination and Marginalisation of a Continent', in *African Sociological Review*, 10 (9): 161-179.

Mlambo, A., Vambe, M. T., and Zegeye, A., 2010, 'The Culture of Crisis and Crisis of Culture in Zimbabwe', in *African Identities*, 8 (2): 89-111.

Mlambo, A. S., 2009, Becoming Zimbabwe: A History from the Pre-Colonial Period to 2008, Harare and Johannesburg: Weaver Press and Jacana: 167-200.

Molteno, P. A., 1896, *A Federal South Africa*, London: Juta.

Mombeshora, S.,1990, 'The Salience of Ethnicity in Political Development: The Case of Zimbabwe', in *International Sociology*, 5 (4) : 401- 431.

Moore, D., 1991, 'The Ideological Formation of the Zimbabwean Ruling Class', in *Journal of Southern African Studies*, 17 (3), (September): 472-495.

Moore, D., 2004, 'Marxism and Marxist Intellectuals in Schizophrenic Zimbabwe: How Many Rights for Zimbabwe's Left? A Comment', in *Historical Materialism*, 12 (4): 405-425.

Moore, D. 2001, 'From King Leopold to King Kabila in the Congo: The Continuities and Contradictions of the Long Road from Warlordism to Democracy in the Heart of Africa', in *Review of African Political Economy*, 28 (87), (March): 130-135.

Moore, D., 1995, 'Democracy, Violence and Identity in the Zimbabwean War of Liberation: Reflections from the Realms of Dissent', in *Canadian Journal of African Studies*, 29 (3), (December).

Moore, D., 1995, 'The Zimbabwe People's Army: Strategic Innovation or Moore of the Same?' in N. Bhebe and T. Ranger, eds, *Soldiers in Zimbabwe's Liberation War*, London: James Currey, 1995: 73-103.

Moore-Gilbert, B.,1997, *Postcolonial Theory: Contexts, Practices, Politics*, London: Verso .

Moto Magazine, 1 (4) (August 1982).

Moyo, J., 2007, 'Tsholotsho Saga: The Untold Story', in newzimbabwe.com http://www. newzimbabwe.com/pages/sky95.14039.htmail (accessed 3 May).

Moyo, J., 2006, *Gukurahundi Memorial Bill*.

Moyo, S. and Yeros, P., 2007a, 'The Radicalized State: Zimbabwe's Interrupted Revolution', in *Review of African Political Economy*, 111: 103-121.

Moyo, S., 'Three Decades of Agrarian Reform in Zimbabwe: Changing Agrarian Relations', in *Journal of Peasant Studies (forthcoming)*.

Moyo, S. and Yeros, P., 2007b, 'Intervention: The Zimbabwe Question and the Two Lefts', in *Historical Materialism,* 15 : 171-2004.

Moyo, S. and Yeros, P., 2009, 'Zimbabwe Ten Years On: Results and Prospects', in *Pambazuka News*, 419, (January): 1-10.

Msindo, E., 2004, 'Ethnicity in Matabeleland', Zimbabwe: A Study of Kalanga–Ndebele Relations, 1860s–1980s', Unpublished PhD thesis, University of Cambridge, August).

Mudenge, S. I. G., 1988, *A Political History of Munhumutapa, 1400-1902*, Harare: Zimbabwe Publishing House.

Mudimbe, V. Y., 1988, *The Invention of Africa: Gnosis, Philosophy, and the Order of Knowledge*, London: James Currey.

Mudimbe, V. Y., 1994, *The Idea of Africa*, Bloomington: Indiana University Press.

Mueni wa Muiu and Martin, G., 2009, *A New Paradigm of the African State: Fundi wa Africa*, New York: Palgrave Macmillan.

Mueni wa Muiu, 2008, *The Pitfalls of Liberal Democracy and Late Nationalism in South Africa*, New York: Palgrave Macmillan.

Mugabe, R. G., 2001, *Inside the Third Chimurenga*, Harare: Department of Information and Publicity.

Murithi, T.,2005, *The African Union: Pan-Africanism, Peace-Building and Development*, Hampshire: Ashgate.

Mutanda, F. C., 2010, 'Foreword', in J. Nkomo, *Nkomo: The Story of My Life* (Reprint), London: Methuen.

Muzondidya, J. and Ndlovu-Gatsheni, S. J., 2007, 'Echoing Silences: Ethnicity in Postcolonial Zimbabwe, 1980–2007', in *African Journal on Conflict Resolution*, 7 (2): 275-297.

Muzondidya, J., 2010, 'The Zimbabwe Crisis and the Unresolved Conundrum of Race in the Post-Colonial Period', in *Journal of Developing Societies*, 26 (2): 5-38.

Muzondidya, J., 2009, 'From Buoyancy to Crisis, 1980-1997', in Raftopoulos

Muzorewa, A. T., 1972, 'African National Council: Aims and Objectives', (Salisbury, 10 March.

Muzvidziwa, V. N., 2005, 'Globalisation and Higher Education in Africa: The Case of the African University', in *UNISWA Research Journal*, 19 (December): 67-98.

Nabudere, D. W., 2011, *Afrikology, Philosophy and Wholeness: An Epistemology*, Pretoria: Africa Institute of South Africa, 2011.

Ndhlovu, F., 2009, *The Politics of Language and Nation-Building in Zimbabwe,* Oxford: Peter Lang AG.

Ndhlovu, F., 2006, 'Gramsci, Doke and the Marginalization of the Ndebele Language in Zimbabwe', in *Journal of Multilingual and Multicultural Development*, 27 (4): 288-305.

Ndlovu-Gatsheni and Muzondidya, J., 2011, 'Introduction: Redemptive or Grotesque
    Nationalism in the Postcolony?' in S. J. Ndlovu-Gatsheni and J. Muzondidya (eds.).
    Redemptive or Grotesque Nationalism? Rethinking Contemporary Politics in Zimbabwe,
    (Oxford and Bern: Peter Lang AG: 1-33.
Ndlovu-Gatsheni, S. J., 2008, 'Black Republicanism, Nativism and Populist Politics in
    South Africa', in *Transformation: Critical Perspectives on Southern Africa*, 68: 53-86.
Ndlovu-Gatsheni, S. J., 2003, 'The Post-Colonial State and Matabeleland: Regional
    Perceptions of Civil-Military Relations, 1980-2002', in R. Williams, G. Cawthra & D.
    Abrahams, eds, *Ourselves to Know: Civil-Military Relations and Defence Transformation
    in Southern Africa*, Pretoria: Institute of Security Studies: 17-38.
Ndlovu-Gatsheni, S. J. and Willems, W., 'Making Sense of Cultural Nationalism and the
    Politics of Commemoration under the *Third Chimurenga* in Zimbabwe', in *Journal of
    Southern African Studies* 35(4), (2009): 943-965.
Ndlovu-Gatsheni, S. J. and Willems, W., 2010, 'Reinvoking the Past in the Present:
    Changing Identities and Appropriations of Joshua Nkomo in Postcolonial Zimbabwe',
    in *African Identities*, 8 (3): 191-208.
Ndlovu-Gatsheni, S. J., 2006a, 'How Europe Ruled Africa: Matabeleland Region of
    Zimbabwe', in *International Journal of Humanistic Studies*, 5: 1–18.
Ndlovu-Gatsheni, S. J., 2006b, 'Nationalist-Military Alliance and the Fate of Democracy
    in Zimbabwe', in *African Journal on Conflict Resolution*, 6 (1): 49-80.
Ndlovu-Gatsheni, S. J., 2006c, 'The Nativist Revolution and Development Conundrums
    in Zimbabwe', in *ACCORD Occasional Paper Series*, 1 (4): 1-40.
Ndlovu-Gatsheni, S. J., 2007, 'Re-Thinking the Colonial Encounter in Zimbabwe in the Early
    Twentieth Century', in *Journal of Southern African Studies*, 33 (1) (March): 173-191.
Ndlovu-Gatsheni, S. J., 2008a, 'For the Nation to Live, the Tribe Must Die': The
    Politics of Ndebele Identity and Belonging in Zimbabwe', in B. Zewde ed., *Society,
    State and Identity in African History*, Addis Ababa: Association of African Historians
    and Forum for Social Studies: 167-199.
Ndlovu-Gatsheni, S. J., 2008b, 'Nation-Building in Zimbabwe and the Challenges of
    Ndebele Particularism', in *African Journal on Conflict Resolution*, 8 (3): 27-55.
Ndlovu-Gatsheni, S. J., 2008c, 'Patriots, Puppets, Dissidents and the Politics of Inclusion
    and Exclusion in Contemporary Zimbabwe', in *Eastern Africa Social Science Research
    Review*, XXIV (1) (January): 81–108.
Ndlovu-Gatsheni, S. J., 2008d, 'Reaping the Bitter Fruits of Stalinist Tendencies in
    Zimbabwe', *African Concerned Scholars Bulletin: Special Issue on the 2008 Zimbabwe
    Elections*, No. 79, (Spring : 21–31.
Ndlovu-Gatsheni, S. J., 2009a, *Do 'Zimbabweans' Exist? Trajectories of Nationalism,
    National Identity Formation and Crisis in a Postcolonial State*, Oxford and Bern: Peter
    Lang AG.

Ndlovu-Gatsheni, S. J., 2009b, 'Making Sense of Mugabeism in Local and Global Politics: 'So Blair Keep Your England and Let Me Keep My Zimbabwe", in *Third World Quarterly*, 30 (6): 1139-1158.

Ndlovu-Gatsheni, S. J., 2009c, 'Africa for Africans or Africa for 'Natives' Only? 'New Nationalism and Nativism in Zimbabwe and South Africa", in *Africa Spectrum*, 1: 61-78.

Ndlovu-Gatsheni, S. J., 2009d, 'From Pixley Ka Isaka Seme to Jacob Zuma: The Long Walk to Freedom and the Future of the National Democratic Revolution in South Africa', in T. Kamusella and K. Jaskulowski, eds, *Nationalism Across the Globe 1: Nationalisms Today*, Oxford & Bern: Peter Lang AG: 285-314.

Ndlovu-Gatsheni, S. J., 2007a, 'Giving Africa Voice within Global Governance: Oral History, Human Rights and the United Nations (UN) Human Rights Council', in V. B. Malleswari, ed., *Human Rights: International Perspectives*, India: The ICFAI University Press.

Ndlovu-Gatsheni, S. J., 2007b, *Restless Natives and Panicking Settlers: Tracking the Historical Roots of Post-Apartheid Citizenship Problems in South Africa*, Leiden: Africa Studies Centre Working Paper 72: 1-66.

Ndlovu-Gatsheni, S. J., 2009e, *The Ndebele Nation: Reflections on Hegemony, Memory and Historiography*, Amsterdam and Pretoria: Rozenberg Publishers and UNISA Press.

Neocosmos, M., 2008a, 'Africa and Migration in a Globalised World: Understanding Migrancy through the Lenses of Political Subjectivities', Inaugural Lecture delivered at Monash South Africa, Johannesburg, South Africa.

Neocosmos, M., 2008b, 'The Politics of Fear and the Fear of Politics: Reflections on Xenophobic Violence in South Africa', in *Journal of Asian and African Studies*, 43 (6): 58-594.

Ngugi wa Thiong'o, 2005, 'Europhone or African Memory: The Challenges of the Pan-African Intellectuals in the Era of Globalization', in Thandika Mkandawire, ed., *African Intellectuals: Rethinking Politics, Language, Gender, and Development*, London: Zed Books.

Ngugi wa Thiong'o, 1986, *Decolonising the Mind: The Politics of Language in African Literature*, London: James Currey.

Ngugi wa Thiong'o, 2009, *Re-Membering Africa*, Nairobi: East African Education Publishers Ltd.

Nkomo, J., 1964, 'The Case for Majority Rule in Rhodesia', Gonakudzingwa Camp.

Nkomo, J. 1984. *Nkomo: The Story of My Life*, London: Methuen.

Nkrumah, K., 1962, *I Speak of Freedom: A Statement of African Ideology*, New York, Heinemann.

Nkrumah, K., 1965, *Neo-Colonialism: The Last Stage of Imperialism*, London: Nelson.

Nietzsche, F., 1990, *Beyond Good and Evil*, New York: Penguin.

Norman, A., 2008, *Mugabe: Teacher, Revolutionary, Tyrant*, Gloucestershire: History Press.

Norval, A. J., 1996, *Deconstructing Apartheid Discourse*, London & New York: Verso.

Nuttall, S., 2009, *Entanglement: Literary and Cultural Reflections on Post-Apartheid*, Johannesburg: Wits Press, 2009.

Nyamnjoh, F. B., 2001, 'Concluding Reflections on Beyond Identities: Rethinking Power in Africa', in H. Melber, ed., 2001, *Identity and Beyond: Rethinking Africanity: Discussion Paper 12*, Uppsala: Nordic Africa Institute: 15-35.

Nyangoni, W. W., 1977, *African Nationalism in Zimbabwe (Rhodesia)*, Washington DC: University Press of America.

Nzongola-Ntalaja, 2002, *The Congo from Leopold to Kabila: A People's History*, London: Zed Books.

Nzongola-Ntalaja, 1987, *Revolution and Counter-Revolution in Africa: Essays in Contemporary Politics*, London and New Jersey: Zed Books.

Obi, C., 2001, 'Beyond 'Isms' and 'Posts': Imagining Epistemology in Africa in the Age of Globalisation', in *Journal of Cultural Studies*, 3 (1).

Odendaal, A., 1984, *Vukani Bantu! The Beginning of Black Protest Politics in South Africa to 1912*, Cape Town & Johannesburg: David Philip.

Osaghae, E., 2010, 'Citizenship and Reconstruction of Belonging in Africa', Oral Presentation, Department of Political Studies, University of the Witwatersrand, 11 August.

Osaghae, E. E., 2006, 'Colonialism and Civil Society in Africa: The Perspective of Ekeh's Two Publics', *Voluntas*, 17: 205-235.

Olson, T., 2008, *Leopold II: Butcher of the Congo: A Wicked History*, New York: Franklin Watts.

Ottaway, M., 1998, *Between Democracy and Personal Rule: New African Leaders and Reconstruction of the African State*, Washington, D.C.: Brooking Institute.

Pakenham, T., 1991, *The Scramble for Africa, 1876-1912*, New York: Random House.

Parry, B., 1995, 'Problems in Current Theories of Colonial Discourse', in B. Ashcroft, G. Griffiths and H. Tiffin ed., *The Postcolonial Studies Reader*, London: Routledge

Parry, B., 2004, *Postcolonial Studies: A Materialist Critique*, London and New York: Routledge.

Phimister, I. and Raftopoulos, B., 2004, 'Mugabe, Mbeki and the Politics of Anti-Imperialism', in *Review of African Political Economy*, 101: 285-415.

Pieterse, J. N., 1997, 'Deconstructing/Reconstructing Ethnicity', in *Nations and Nationalism*, 3 (3) : 365-385.

Porter, A. N., 1980, *The Origins of the South Africa War*, Manchester: Manchester University Press.

Prah, K. K., 2009, 'A Pan-Africanist Reflection: Point and Counterpoint', Unpublished Paper, Centre for Advanced Studies of African Society (CASAS), University of Cape Town.

Prah, K. K., 2009, 'Who is an African?' in J. Adibe ed., *Who is an African? Identity, Citizenship and the Making of the Africa-Nation*, London: Adonis & Abbey

Publishers Ltd: 57-60.

Pratt, M. L., 1992, *Imperial Eyes: Travel Writing and Transculturalism*, London and New York: Routledge.

Prunier, G., 2008, 'Kenya: Roots of Crisis', in *OpenDemocracy*, 7 January 2008 in http://www.opendemocracy.net/article/democracy-power/kenya_roots_crisis (accessed 8 August 2010).

Quijano, A., 2007, 'Coloniality and Modernity/Rationality', in *Cultural Studies*, 21 (2/3) (March/May) : 168-178.

Quijano, A., 2000a, 'The Coloniality of Power and Social Classification', in *Journal of World-Systems Research*, 6 (2), (Summer/Fall 2000a): 342-386.

Quijano, A., 2000b, 'Coloniality of Power, Eurocentrism and Latin America', in *Nepantla: Views from South*, 1 (3): 533-579.

Raftopoulos, B., 2007, 'Nation, Race and History in Zimbabwean Politics', in S. Dorman, D. Hammett and P. Nugent, eds, *Making Nations, Creating Strangers: States and Citizenship in Africa*, Leiden & Boston: Brill, 2007: 176-191.

Raftopoulos, B. and Mlambo, A., eds, 2009, *Becoming Zimbabwe: A History from the Pre-Colonial Period to 2008*, Harare and Johannesburg: Weaver Press and Jacana.

Raftopoulos, B., 1995, *Zimbabwe: Race and Nationalism in a Post-Colonial State*, Harare: SAPES.

Raftopoulos, B., 2001, 'The Labour Movement and the Emergence of Opposition Politics in Zimbabwe', in B. Raftopoulos and L. Sachikonye, eds, *Striking Back: The Labour Movement and the Post-Colonial State in Zimbabwe, 1980-2000*, Harare: Weaver Press: 1-24.

Raftopoulos, B., 2004, 'Unreconciled Differences: The Limits of Reconciliation Politics in Zimbabwe', in B. Raftopoulos and T. Savage, eds, *Zimbabwe: Injustice and Political Reconciliation*, Cape Town: Institute for Justice and Reconciliation, 2004: 1-19.

Raftopoulos, B., 2006, 'The Zimbabwe Crisis and the Challenges of the Left', in *Journal of Southern African Studies*, 32 (2), (June): 203-219.

Raftopoulos, B. and Phimister, I., 2004, 'Zimbabwe Now: The Political Economy of Crisis and Coercion', in *Historical Materialism*, 12 (4): 355-382.

Ranger, T. O., 1997, 'Leaving Africa: Making and Writing History of Zimbabwe', Harare, Zimbabwe: Valedictory Lecture, Monomotapa, Monomotapa Crown Plaza, 19 June.

Ranger, T., 1985, *The Creation of Tribalism in Zimbabwe*, Gweru: Mambo Press.

Ranger, T., 1967, *Revolt in Southern Rhodesia: A Study in African Resistance*, London: Heinemann.

Ranger, T., 1999, *Voices from the Rocks: Nature, Culture and History of the Matopos Hills of Zimbabw e*, Harare: Baobab.

Ranger, T., 2004, 'Nationalist Historiography, Patriotic History and the History of the

Nation: The Struggle Over the Past in Zimbabwe', in *Journal of Southern African Studies* 30 (2), (June): 215-234.

Ranger, T., 2008, 'Elections and Identities in Kenya and Zimbabwe', Opening Address of the Britain- Zimbabwe Research Society (BZS) Annual Conference, St. Anthony's College, University of Oxford.

Ranger, T. and Vaughan, O., eds, 1993, *Legitimacy and the State in Twentieth Century Africa*, London: Macmillan.

Ranger, T. O., 1989, 'Missionaries, Migrants and the Manyika: The Invention of Ethnicity in Zimbabwe', in Leroy Vail, ed., *The Creation of Tribalism in Southern Africa*, London: James Currey.

Rasmussen, R. K., 1978, *Migrant Kingdom: Mzilikazi's Ndebele in South Africa*, Cape Town: Rex Collings.

Reed, W. C., 1993, 'International Politics and National Liberation: ZANU and the Politics of Contested Sovereignty in Zimbabwe', in *African Studies Review,* 36 (2) (September): 31–59.

Religious Tolerance Organization, 2011, '*Mass Crimes Against Humanity: The Congo Free State Genocide Circa 1895-1912* at http://www.religioustolerance.org/genocong.html accessed 18 January 2011.

Rive, R., [1923] 1976, 'Foreword to the Reprint Edition', in O. Schreiner, *Thoughts on South Africa: Africana Reprint Library Volume Ten*, Johannesburg: Africana Book Society: vii-xxii.

Roberts, R. S., 2005, 'Traditional Paramountcy and Modern Politics in Matabeleland: The End of the Lobengula Royal Family – and of Ndebele Particularism?' in *Heritage of Zimbabwe*, 24: 1-34.

Robin, S., 1996, 'Heroes, Heretics and Historians of the Zimbabwe Revolution: A Review Article of Norma Kriger's 'Peasant Voices' (1992)', in *Zambezia*, XXIII (i): 31-74.

Robinson, P., 1994, 'The National Conference Phenomenon in Francophone Africa', in *Comparative Studies in Society and History*, 36: 575-610.

Robotham, D., 2005, 'Cosmopolitanism and Planetary Humanism: The Strategic Universalism of Paul Gilroy', in *The South Atlantic Quarterly*, 104 (3): 543-570.

Rodney, W., 1973, *How Europe Underdeveloped Africa*, Da-ers-salam: Bogle L'Ovwerture and Tanzania Publishing House.

Ross, R. 1999, *A Concise History of South Africa*, Cambridge: Cambridge University Press.

Ross, R., 1976, *Adam Kok's Griquas: A Study in the Development of Stratification in History*, Cambridge: Cambridge University Press.

Rostow, W. W., 1960, *The Stages of Economic Growth: A Non-Communist Manifesto*, Cambridge: Cambridge University Press.

Rupiya, M., 2005, 'Zimbabwe: Governance through Military Operations', in *African Security Review* 14 (3): 117-118.

Rutherford, B., 2001, *Working on the Margins: Black Workers, White Farmers in Postcolonial Zimbabwe*, London & Harare: Zed Books & Weaver Press.

Rutherford, B., 2007, 'Shifting Grounds in Zimbabwe: Citizenship and Farm Workers in the New Politics of Land', in S. Dorman, D. Hammett and P. Nugent, eds, *Making Nations, Creating Strangers: State and Citizenship in Africa*, Leiden & Boson: Brill: 105-126.

Sachikonye, L., 1996, 'The National-State and Conflict in Zimbabwe', in L. Laakso and A. Olokoshi, eds, *Challenges to the Nation-State in Africa*, Uppsala: Nordic Africa Institute: 138-152.

Sachs, A., 1987, 'The Constitutional Position of White South Africans in A Democratic South Africa', in *Social Justice*, 18 (1-2): 12-43.

Sachs, W., ed., 1992, *The Development Dictionary: A Guide to Knowledge as Power*, London: Zed Books.

Samkange, S., 1969, 'Statement of Appeal by Interim President Michael Mawema', Salisbury.

Santos, B. S., 2007, 'Beyond Abyssal Thinking: From Global Lines to Ecologies of Knowledges', in *Review*, XXX (1): 45-89.

Santos, B. S., 2009, 'A Non-Occidentalist West? Learned Ignorance and Ecology of Knowledge', in *Theory, Culture and Society*, 26 (7/8): 103-125.

Saul, J. S., 2008, *Decolonization and Empire: Contesting the Rhetoric and Reality of Resurbordination in Southern Africa and Beyond*, Wales and Johannesburg: Merlin Press and Wits University Press.

Saul, S. J., 2002, 'Starting from Scratch?: A Reply to Jeremy Cronin', in *Monthly Review*, 54 (7): 1-23.

Saul, J. R., 2009, *The Collapse of Globalism and the Reinvention of the World*, London: Atlantic Books.

Schreiner, O. C., 1976, *Thoughts on South Africa: Africana Reprint Library Volume Ten* Johannesburg: Africana Book Society.

Scoones, I., Marongwe, N., Mavedzenge, B., Murimbarimba, F., Mahenehene, J., and Sekume, C., 2010, *Zimbabwe's Land Reform: Myths and Realities*, Oxford: James Currey.

Selby, A., 2006, 'Commercial Farmers and the State: Interest Group Politics and Land Reform in Zimbabwe', Unpublished DPhil Dissertation, Oxford University.

Sen, A., 2000, *Development as Freedom*, New York: Anchor Books.

Shamuyarira, N., 1971, 'Explanation of why FROLIZI was formed', Lusaka.

Shivji, I. G. 2003, 'The Rise, the Fall, and the Insurrection of Nationalism in Africa', Paper presented as Keynote Address to CODESRIA East African Regional Conference, Addis Ababa, Ethiopia, 29-31 October.

Shivji, I. G., 2009, *Where is Uhuru? Reflections on the Struggle for Democracy in Africa*, Oxford: Fahamu Books, 2009.

Sibanda, E., 2005, *The Zimbabwe African People's Union, 1961–87: A Political History of Insurgency in Southern Rhodesia*, Trenton: Africa World Press.

Sisulu, E., Moyo, B., and Tshuma, N., 2007, 'The Zimbabwean Community in South Africa', in *The State of the NAtion, 2007*, Pretoria, HSRC Press.

Buhlungu, J. Daniel, R. Southall and J. Lutchman, eds, 2007, *State of the Nation: South Africa 2007*, Pretoria: HSRC Press: 552-573.

Sithole, M., 1995, 'Ethnicity and Democratization in Zimbabwe: From Confrontation to Accommodation', in H. Glickman, ed., *Ethnic Conflict and Democratization in Africa*, Atlanta: The African Studies Association: 113-135.

Sithole, M., 1997, 'Zimbabwe's Eroding Authoritarianism', *Journal of Democracy*, 8 (1), : 127–141.

Sithole, M, 1999, *Zimbabwe: Struggles within the Struggle: Second Edition*, Harare: Rujeko Publishers.

Sithole, M., 2001, 'Fighting Authoritarianism in Zimbabwe', *Journal of Democracy*, 12 (1), : 56-79.

Sithole, N., 1964, 'Presidential Address to the Inaugural Congress of Zimbabwe African National Union', Gwelo, Gwelo, 12–13 May.

Sithole, N., 1959, *African Nationalism*, London: Oxford University Press.

South African Communist Party (SACP), 1962, *The Road to South African Freedom: Programme of the South African Communist Party*, London: Inkululeko Press. *Southern Africa Report*, 2000, 15 (3) (June).

Southern Rhodesia African National Congress, 1957, 'Statement of Principles, Policy and Programme', Salisbury.

Southern Rhodesia, 1963, *Statute of Law of Southern Rhodesia: Volume 7*, Salisbury: Government Printer.

Soyinka, W., 2004, *Climate of Fear*, London: Profile Books.

Spivak, G. C., 1990, 'The Political Economy of Women As Seen by a Literary Critic', in E. Weed , ed., *Coming to Terms*, London: Routledge.

Spivak, G. C., 1991, 'Theory in the Margin: Coetzee's *Foe* Reading Defoe's *Crusoe/Roxana*', in J. Arac and B. Johnson, eds, *Consequences of Theory*, Baltimore: The John Hopkins University Press: 154-180.

Spivak, G. C., 1990, *The Post-Colonial Critic: Interviews, Strategies, Dialogues*, London: Routledge.

Spivak, G. C., 1988, *In other Worlds: Essays in Cultural Politics*, New York: Routledge.

Stoneman, C., 1998, 'The Economy: Recognizing the Reality', in C. Stoneman, ed., *Zimbabwe's Prospects: Issues of Race, Class, State and Capital in Southern Africa*, London: Macmillan.

Sylvester, C., 1986, 'Zimbabwe's 1985 Elections: A Search for National Mythology', *Journal of Modern African Studies*, 24 (1): 234-289.

Tandon, Y., 2008, *Ending Aid Dependence*, Oxford, Fahamu Books

Taylor, R. H., 2002, 'Introduction', in R. H. Taylor, ed., *The Idea of Freedom in Asia and Africa*, Stanford: Stanford University Press: 1- 8.

Tekere, E., 2007, *Edgar 2-Boy Tekere: A Life in Struggle,* Harare: SAPES Books.

Tendi, B. M., 2010, *Making History in Mugabe's Zimbabwe: Politics, Intellectuals and the Media*, Oxford: Peter Lang AG.

Tengende, N., 1994, 'Workers, Students and the Struggles for Democracy: State–Civil Society Relations in Zimbabwe', Unpublished PhD thesis, Roskilde University.

The Bantu Mirror, 20 August 1960.

The *Chronicle,* 25 January 1982.

The Herald, 6 December 1997.

The Herald, 6 December 1997.

Theal, G. M., 1873, *A Compendium of South African History: The Cape Colony, Natal, Orange Free State, South African Republic and All Territories of the Zambezi*, Lovedale.

Theron, M. and Swart, G., 2009, 'South Africa and the New Africa: Chasing African Rainbows', in J. London: Adonis & Abbey Publishers Ltd: 153-177. Adibe, ed., *Who is an Africa? Identity, Citizenship and the Making of the Africa-Nation,*

Thuynsma, P. N., 1998, 'On the Trial of Christopher Okigbo', in Omari H. Kokole, ed., *The Global African: A Portrait of Ali A Mazrui*, Trenton, NJ: Africa World Press.

Tibaijuka, A., 2005, *Report of the Fact Finding Mission to Zimbabwe to Assess the Scope and Impact of Operation Murambatsvina by the UN Special Envoy on Human Settlements Issues in Zimbabwe,* New York: United Nations.

Trollope, A., 1973, *South Africa: A Reprint of the 1878 Edition, with an Introduction and Notes* by J. H. Davidson, Cape Town.

Tsvangirai, M., 2008, 'Press Conference Statement', 1 April.

Turino, T., 2000, *Nationalists, Cosmopolitans and Popular Music in Zimbabwe*, Chicago: Chicago University Press.

Vambe, V., ed., 2008, *The Hidden Dimensions of Operation Murambatsvina in Zimbabwe,* Harare: Weaver Press.

Verges, F., 2011, 'Xenophobia and the Civilising Mission', in *OpenDemocracy*, 13 May.

Vilakazi, H., 1999, 'The Problem of African Universities', in M. W. Makgoba, ed., *African Renaissance: The New Struggle*, Cape Town: Mafube Publishing Ltd, 1999).

Vilakazi, H. W., 2001, 'African Intellectuals and the African Crisis', in *Africa Insight*, 31 (3): 3-18.

Vorster, B. J., 1977, 'Extract from a Speech Made at Koffiefontein on 11 August 1967', in O. Geyser, ed., *B. J. Vorster: Selected Speeches*, Cape Town.

Wallerstein, I., 1991, 'Introduction: Why Unthink?' in I. Wallerstein, ed., *Unthinking Social Science: The Limits of Nineteenth-Century Paradigms*, Cambridge: Polity Press: 1-20.

Warmelo, N. J. V., ed., 1938, *History of Matiwane and the Amangwane Tribe, as Told By Msebenzi to his Kinsman Albert Hlongwane*, Pretoria.

Weeks, J., 2010, 'Roundtable 3: Can Africa Still Claim the 21st Century?' Presentation delivered at the International Conference: Fifty Years of African Independence-Continuities and Discontinuities, University of Maiz, 8-10 April.

Weinrich, A. K. H., 1973, *Black and White Elites in Rural Rhodesia,* Manchester: Manchester University Press.

West, M. O., 2002, *The Rise of an African Middle Class: Colonial Zimbabwe 1898–1965* Bloomington: Indiana University Press.

White, L., 2003, *The Assassination of Herbert Chitepo: Text and Politics in Zimbabwe,* Bloomington and Indianapolis: Indiana University Press.

Whiteman, K., 1997, 'Obituary: The Man Who Ran Francafrica -- French Politician Jaques Foccart's Role in France's Colonization of Africa under the Leadership of Charles de Gaulle', in *The National Interest,* (Fall).

Williams, D., 1970, 'African Nationalism in South Africa: Origins and Problems', in *Journal of African History,* II (3): 371-383.

Windrich, E., 1975, *The Rhodesian Problem: A Documentary Record 1923–1973,* London and Boston: Routledge and Kegan Paul.

Wiredu, K., 1980, *Philosophy and an African Culture,* Cambridge: Cambridge University Press.

Wolpe, H., 1972, 'Capitalism and Cheap Labour Power in South Africa: From Segregation to Apartheid', in *Economy and Society,* 1 (4).

Worby, E., 1998, 'Tyranny, Parody, and Ethnic Polarity: Ritual Engagements with the State in Northwestern Zimbabwe', in *Journal of Southern African Studies,* 24: 337-354.

World Bank, 1995, *A Continent in Transition: Sub-Saharan Africa in the Mid-1990s,* Washington: World Bank.

Wood, E. M., 2003, *Empire of Capital,* London: Verso.

Yeros, P., 2002, 'Zimbabwe and the Dilemmas of the Left', in *Historical Materialism,* 10 (2): 3-15.

Young, C., 2002, 'Itineraries of Ideas of Freedom in Africa: Precolonial to Postcolonial', in R. H. Taylor, ed., *The Idea of Freedom in Asia and Africa,* Stanford: Stanford University Press : 9-39.

Young, C., 1992, *The African Colonial State in Comparative Perspective,* New Haven, CT: Yale University Press.

ZANU, 1963, 'Policy Statement', Salisbury, 21 August.

Zeleza, P. T., 2003, *Rethinking Africa's Globalisation: Volume 1: The Intellectual Challenges,* Trenton, NJ: Africa World Press.

Zeleza, P. T., 2007, 'African Studies in the Postcolony', Keynote address, Opening of the Centre for African Studies, University of Free State, 5 November

Zeleza, P. T., 2006, 'The Troubled Encounter Between Postcolonialism and African History', in *Journal of Canadian Association,* 17 (2): 89-129.

Zeleza, P. T., 2008, 'Introduction: The Causes & Costs of War in Africa: From Liberation Struggles to the "War on Terror"', in A. Nhema & P. T. Zeleza, eds., *The Roots of African Conflicts: The Causes & Costs,* Oxford: James Currey:1-35.

Zeleza, P. T., 2010, 'Imagining and Inventing the Postcolonial State in Africa', in *Contours: A Journal of African Diaspora* in http://www.press.uillinois.edu/journal/contours/1.1/zeleza.html (accessed 12 January 2010).

Zeleza, P. T., 2006a, 'The Inventions of African Identities and Languages: The Discursive and Developmental Implications', in O. F. Arasanyin and M. A. Pemberton, eds, *Selected Proceedings of the 3th Annual Conference on African Linguistics: Shifting the Centre of Africanism in Languages and Economic Globalization*, Somerville, MA: Cascadilla Proceedings Project: 15-26.

Zeleza, P. T., 2007, *Manufacturing African Studies and Crises*, Dakar: CODESRIA Books, 2007.

Zimbabwe African National Union, 1963, *Policy Statement*, Salisbury, 21 August .

Zimbabwe Institute, 2006, 'The Dynamics of ZANU-PF Politics in the Post-Tsholotsho Phase', Unpublished Discussion Paper, June.

Zizek, S., 1999, *The Ticklish Subject: The Absent Centre of Political Ontology*, London: New York: Verso.

Zizek, S., 2009a, *Violence: Six Sideways Reflections*, London: Profile Books.

Zizek, S., 2009b, *First as Tragedy, Then as Farce*, London and New York: Verso.

Zizek, S., 2008, *In Defence of Lost Causes*, London and New York: Verso.

Zizek, S., 2003, *The Puppet and the Dwarf: The Perverse Core of Christianity*, Cambridge MA: The MIT Press.

Zizek, S., 2000, The *Fragile Absolute or Why is the Christian Legacy worth Fighting For?* London: Verso.

www.ingramcontent.com/pod-product-compliance
Lightning Source LLC
Chambersburg PA
CBHW032116020426
42334CB00016B/979